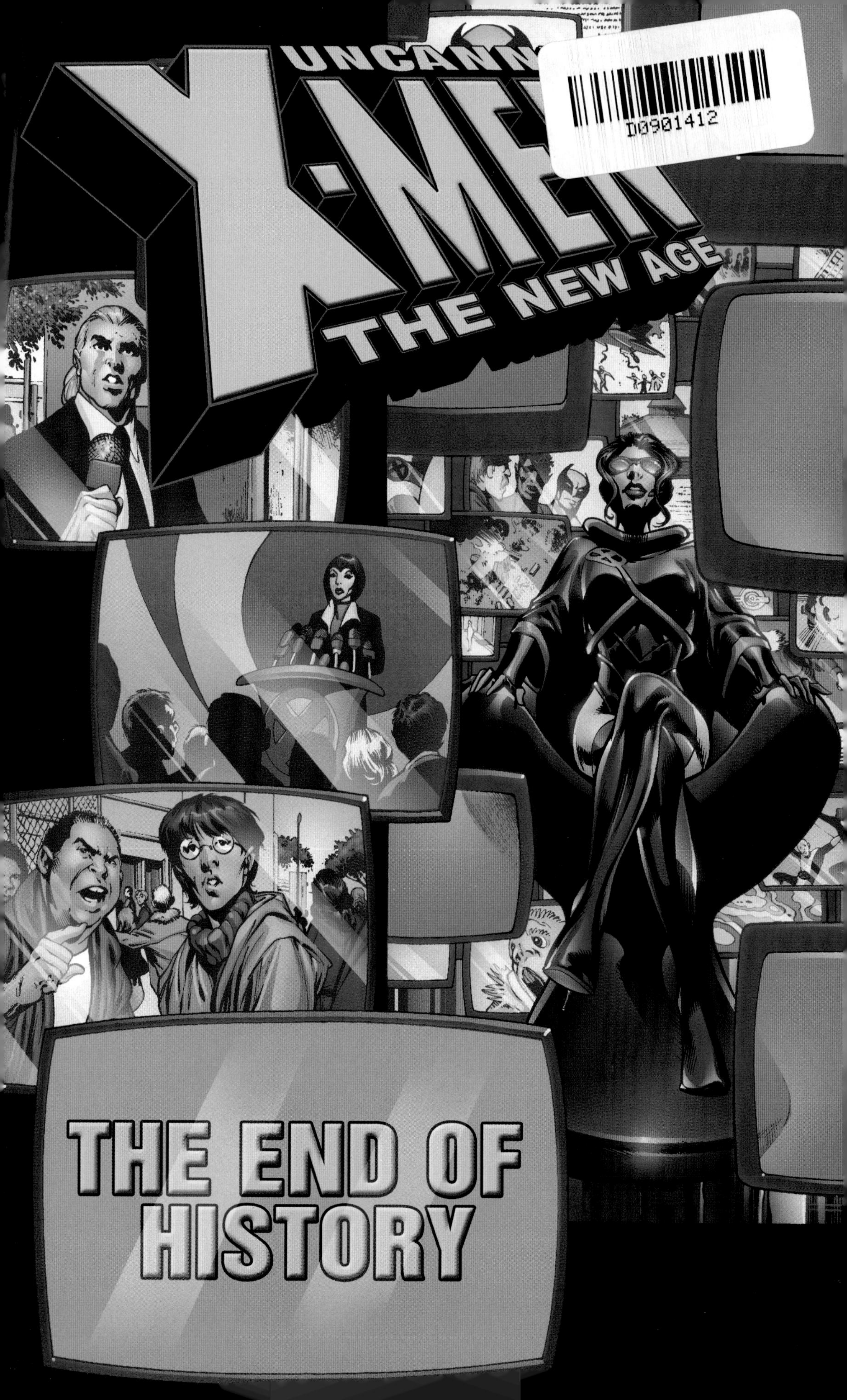

UNCANN
X-ME
THE NEW AGE
THE END OF HISTORY

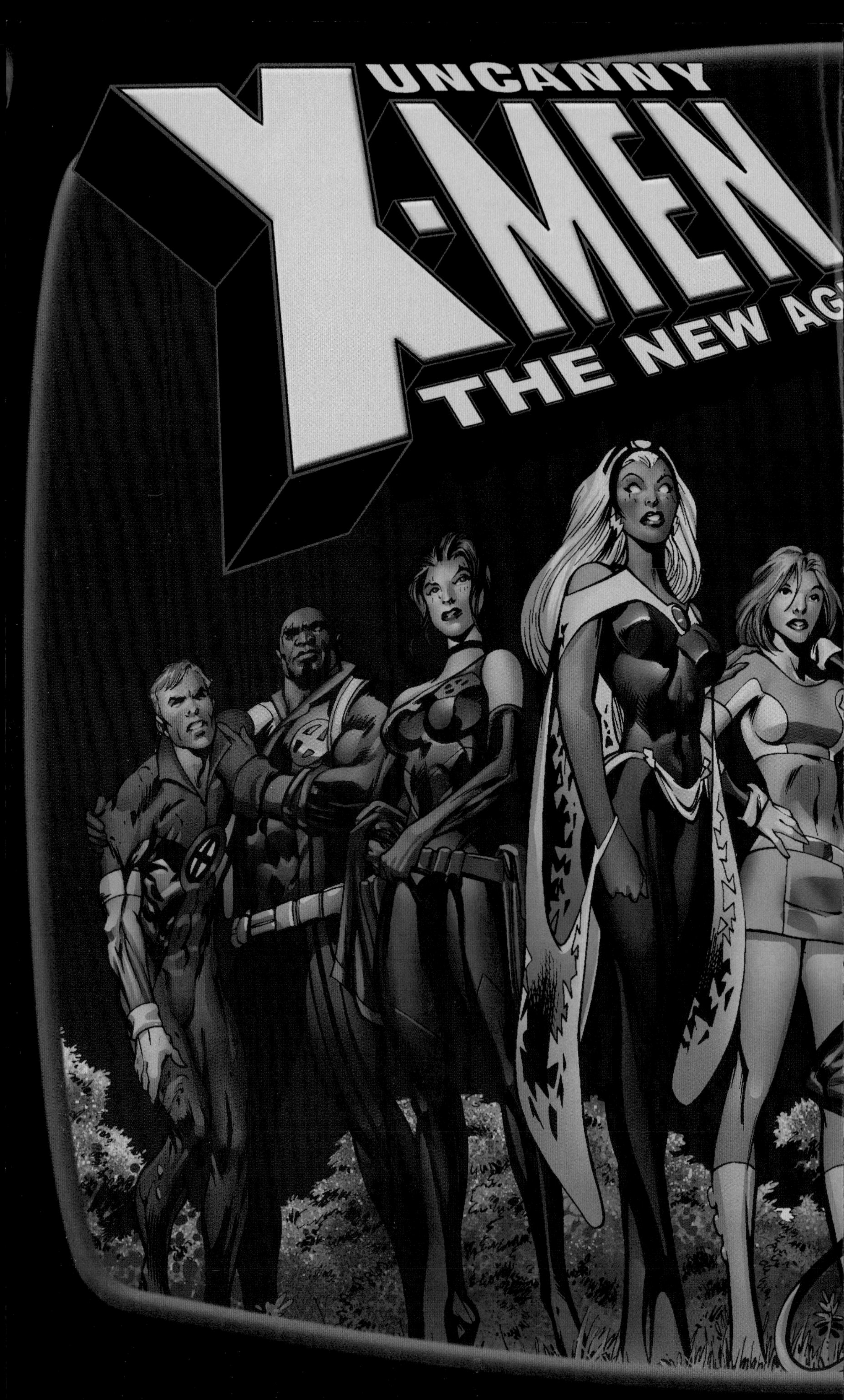
UNCANNY
X-MEN
THE NEW

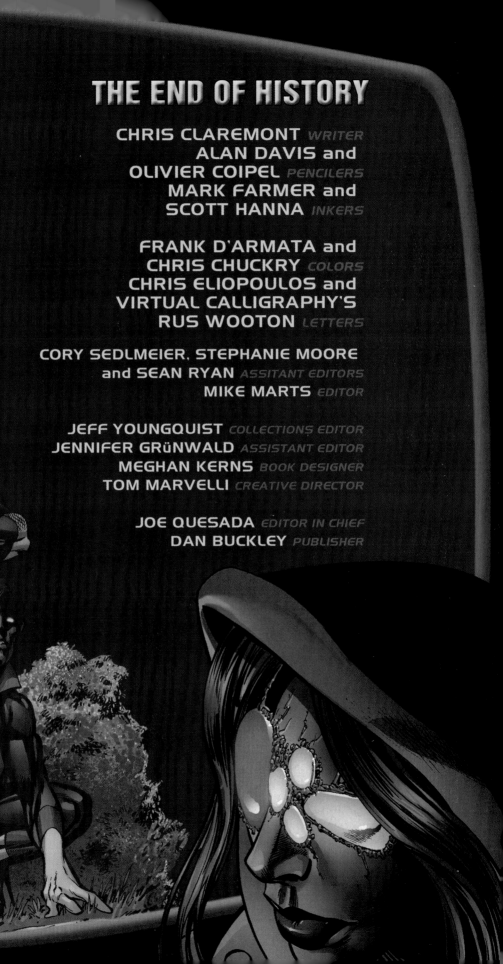

THE END OF HISTORY

CHRIS CLAREMONT *WRITER*
ALAN DAVIS and
OLIVIER COIPEL *PENCILERS*
MARK FARMER and
SCOTT HANNA *INKERS*

FRANK D'ARMATA and
CHRIS CHUCKRY *COLORS*
CHRIS ELIOPOULOS and
VIRTUAL CALLIGRAPHY'S
RUS WOOTON *LETTERS*

CORY SEDLMEIER, STEPHANIE MOORE
and SEAN RYAN *ASSITANT EDITORS*
MIKE MARTS *EDITOR*

JEFF YOUNGQUIST *COLLECTIONS EDITOR*
JENNIFER GRüNWALD *ASSISTANT EDITOR*
MEGHAN KERNS *BOOK DESIGNER*
TOM MARVELLI *CREATIVE DIRECTOR*

JOE QUESADA *EDITOR IN CHIEF*
DAN BUCKLEY *PUBLISHER*

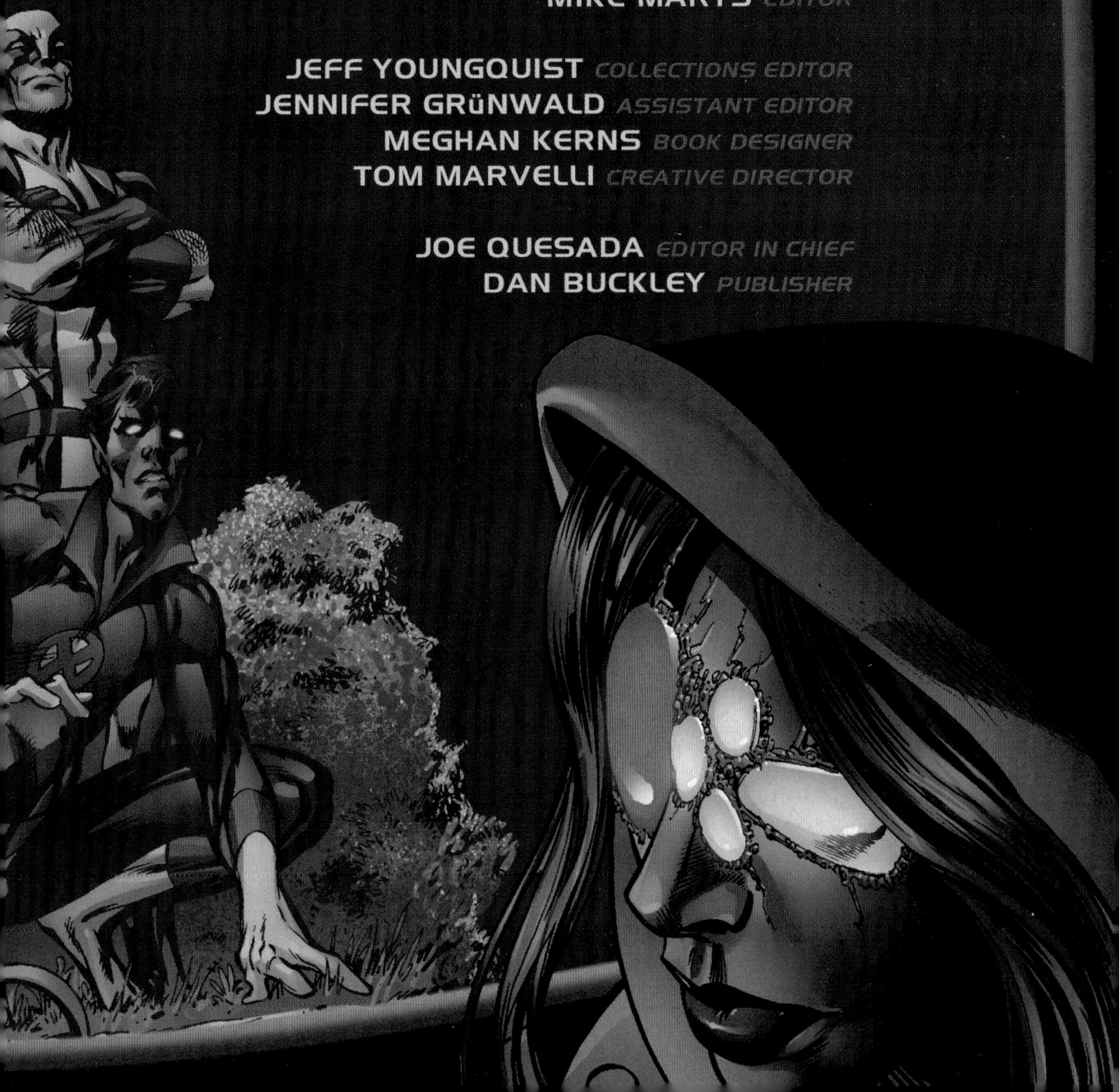

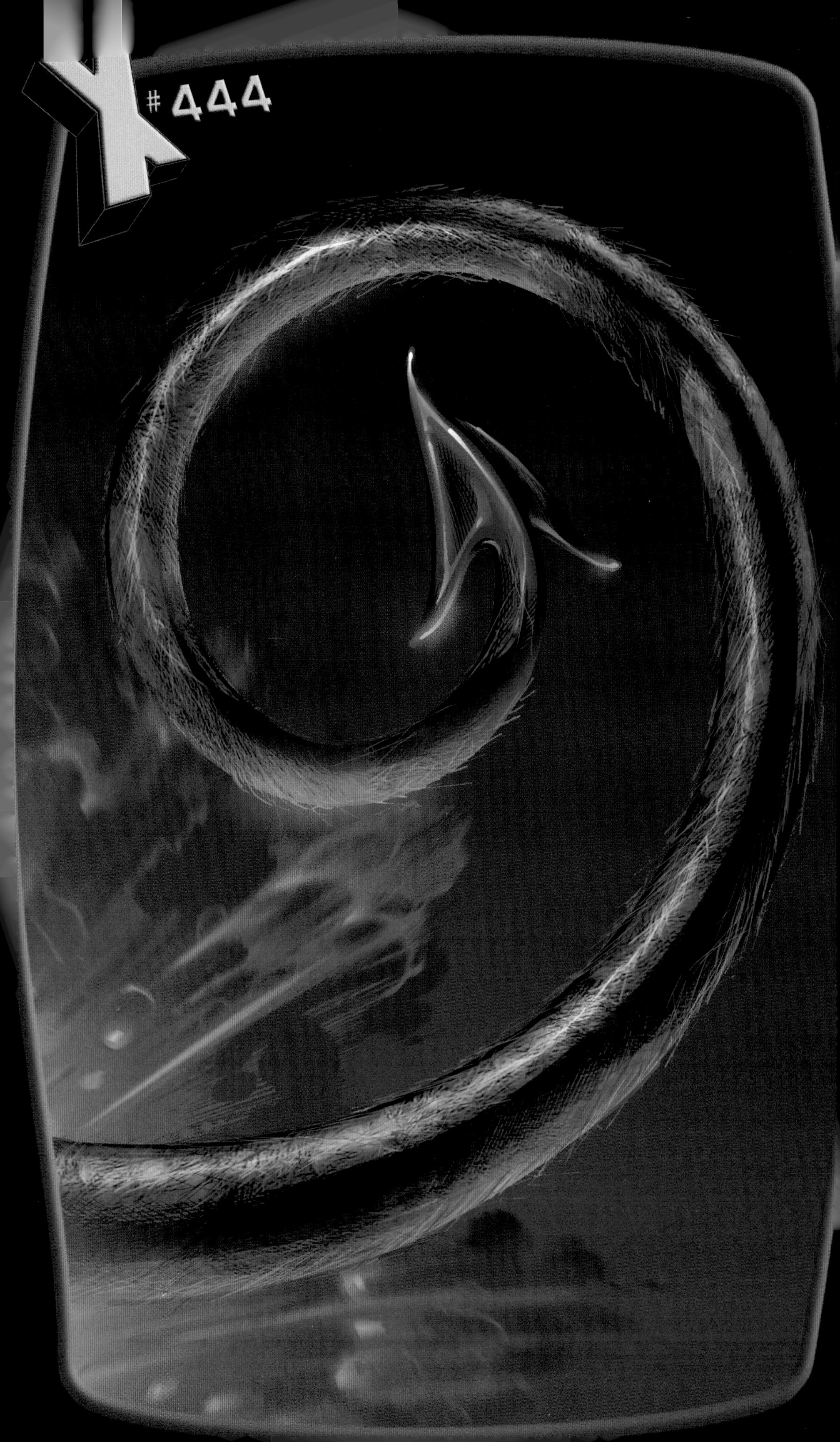

X
#444

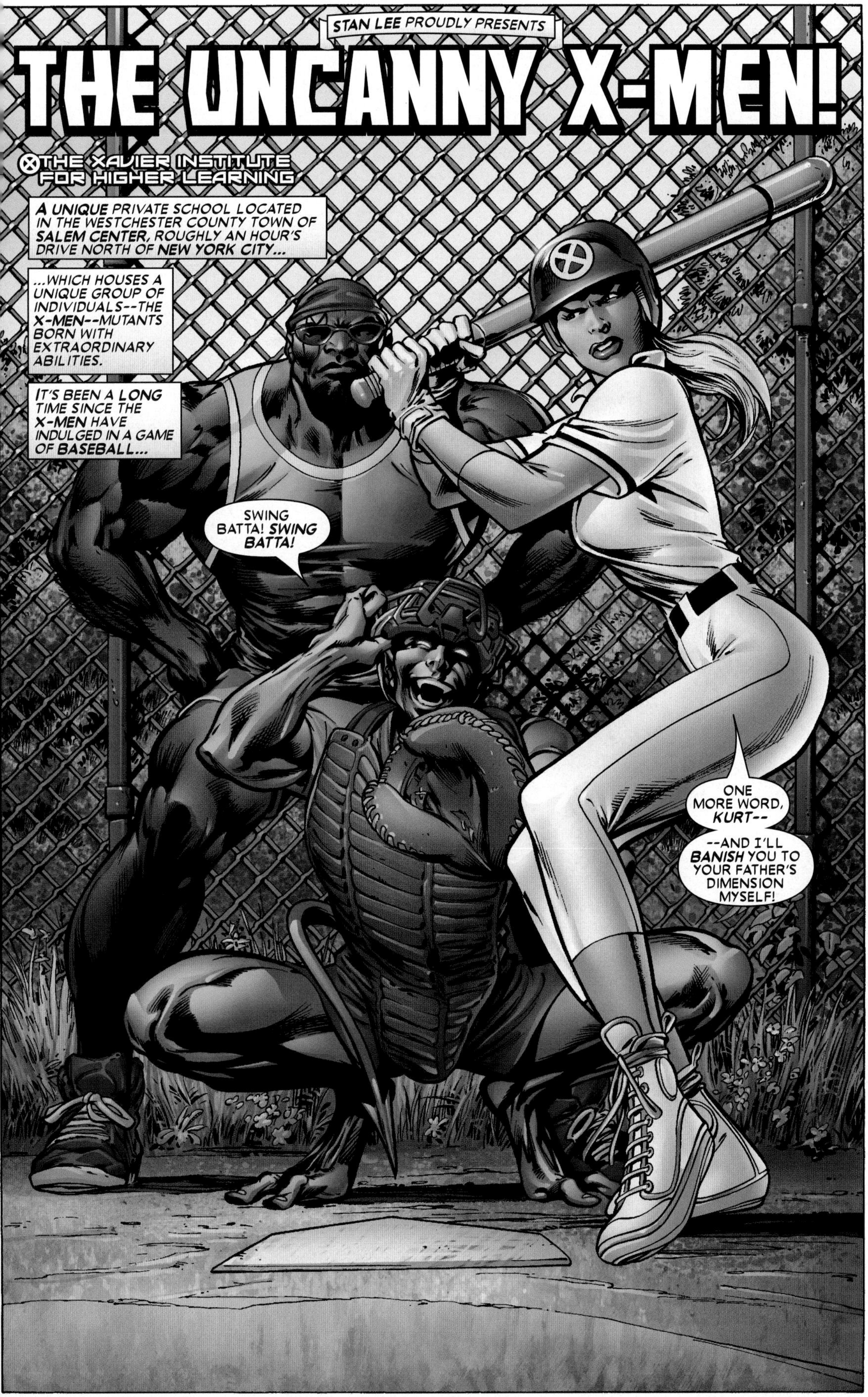
STAN LEE PROUDLY PRESENTS
THE UNCANNY X-MEN!
THE XAVIER INSTITUTE FOR HIGHER LEARNING
A UNIQUE PRIVATE SCHOOL LOCATED IN THE WESTCHESTER COUNTY TOWN OF SALEM CENTER, ROUGHLY AN HOUR'S DRIVE NORTH OF NEW YORK CITY...
...WHICH HOUSES A UNIQUE GROUP OF INDIVIDUALS--THE X-MEN--MUTANTS BORN WITH EXTRAORDINARY ABILITIES.
IT'S BEEN A LONG TIME SINCE THE X-MEN HAVE INDULGED IN A GAME OF BASEBALL...
SWING BATTA! SWING BATTA!
ONE MORE WORD, KURT--
--AND I'LL BANISH YOU TO YOUR FATHER'S DIMENSION MYSELF!

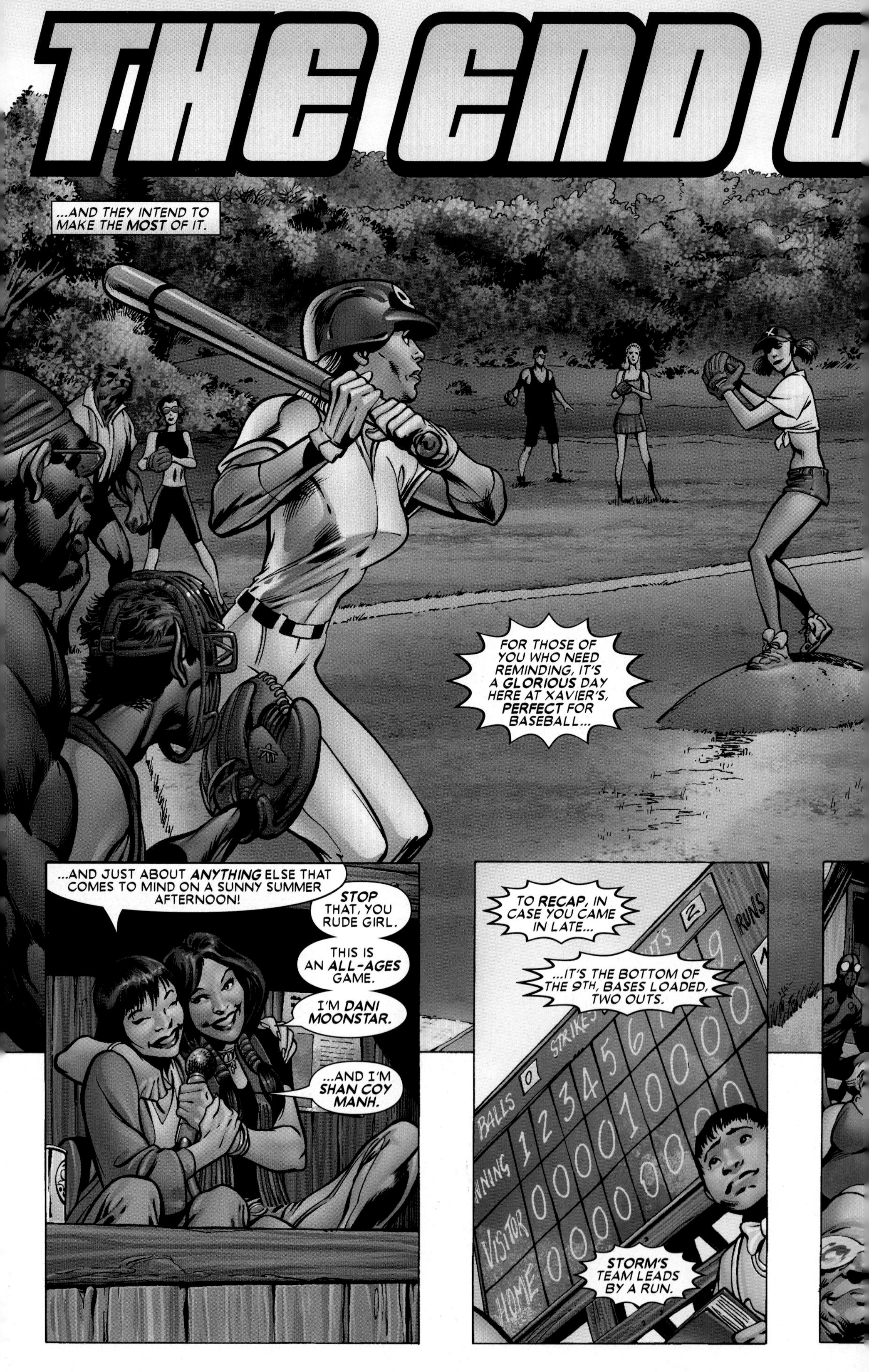
THE END
...AND THEY INTEND TO MAKE THE MOST OF IT.
FOR THOSE OF YOU WHO NEED REMINDING, IT'S A GLORIOUS DAY HERE AT XAVIER'S, PERFECT FOR BASEBALL...
...AND JUST ABOUT ANYTHING ELSE THAT COMES TO MIND ON A SUNNY SUMMER AFTERNOON!
STOP THAT, YOU RUDE GIRL.
THIS IS AN ALL-AGES GAME.
I'M DANI MOONSTAR.
...AND I'M SHAN COY MANH.
TO RECAP, IN CASE YOU CAME IN LATE...
...IT'S THE BOTTOM OF THE 9TH, BASES LOADED, TWO OUTS.
STORM'S TEAM LEADS BY A RUN.
BALLS
STRIKES
RUNS
VISITOR
HOME

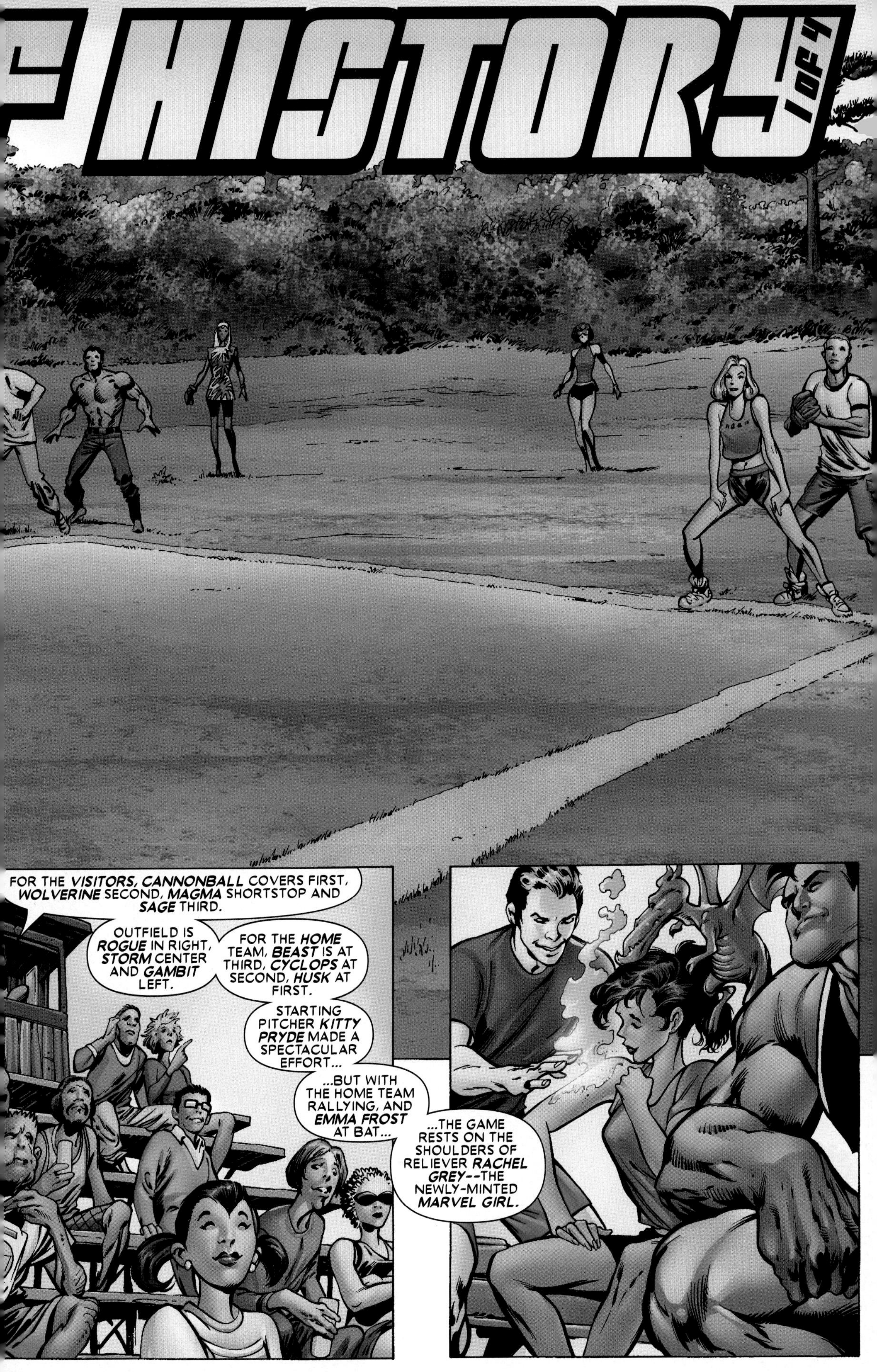
HISTORY
1 OF 4
FOR THE VISITORS, CANNONBALL COVERS FIRST, WOLVERINE SECOND, MAGMA SHORTSTOP AND SAGE THIRD.
OUTFIELD IS ROGUE IN RIGHT, STORM CENTER AND GAMBIT LEFT.
FOR THE HOME TEAM, BEAST IS AT THIRD, CYCLOPS AT SECOND, HUSK AT FIRST.
STARTING PITCHER KITTY PRYDE MADE A SPECTACULAR EFFORT...
...BUT WITH THE HOME TEAM RALLYING, AND EMMA FROST AT BAT...
...THE GAME RESTS ON THE SHOULDERS OF RELIEVER RACHEL GREY--THE NEWLY-MINTED MARVEL GIRL.

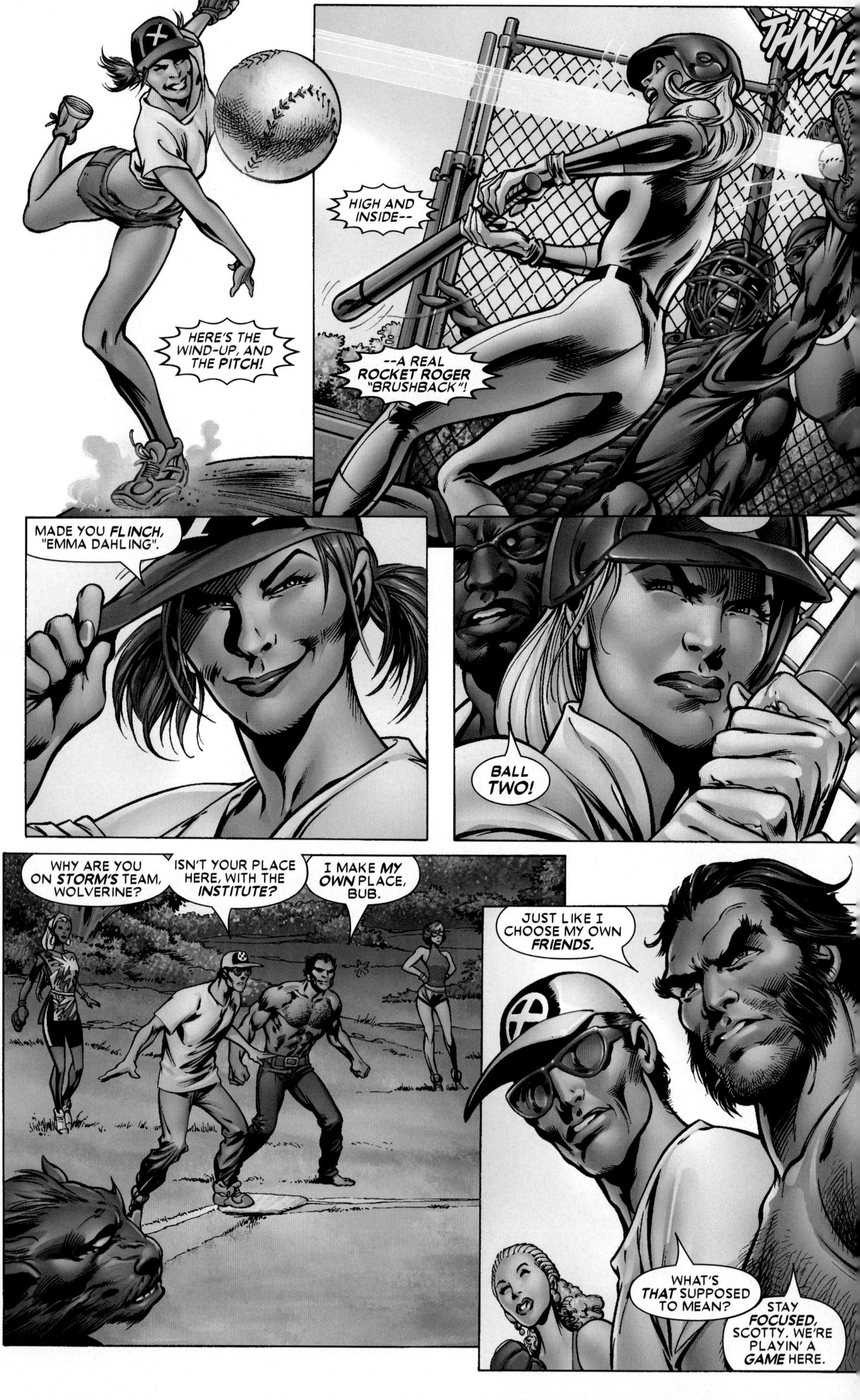
HERE'S THE WIND-UP, AND THE PITCH!
THWAP
HIGH AND INSIDE--
--A REAL ROCKET ROGER "BRUSHBACK"!
MADE YOU FLINCH, "EMMA DAHLING".
BALL TWO!
WHY ARE YOU ON STORM'S TEAM, WOLVERINE?
ISN'T YOUR PLACE HERE, WITH THE INSTITUTE?
I MAKE MY OWN PLACE, BUB.
JUST LIKE I CHOOSE MY OWN FRIENDS.
WHAT'S THAT SUPPOSED TO MEAN?
STAY FOCUSED, SCOTTY. WE'RE PLAYIN' A GAME HERE.

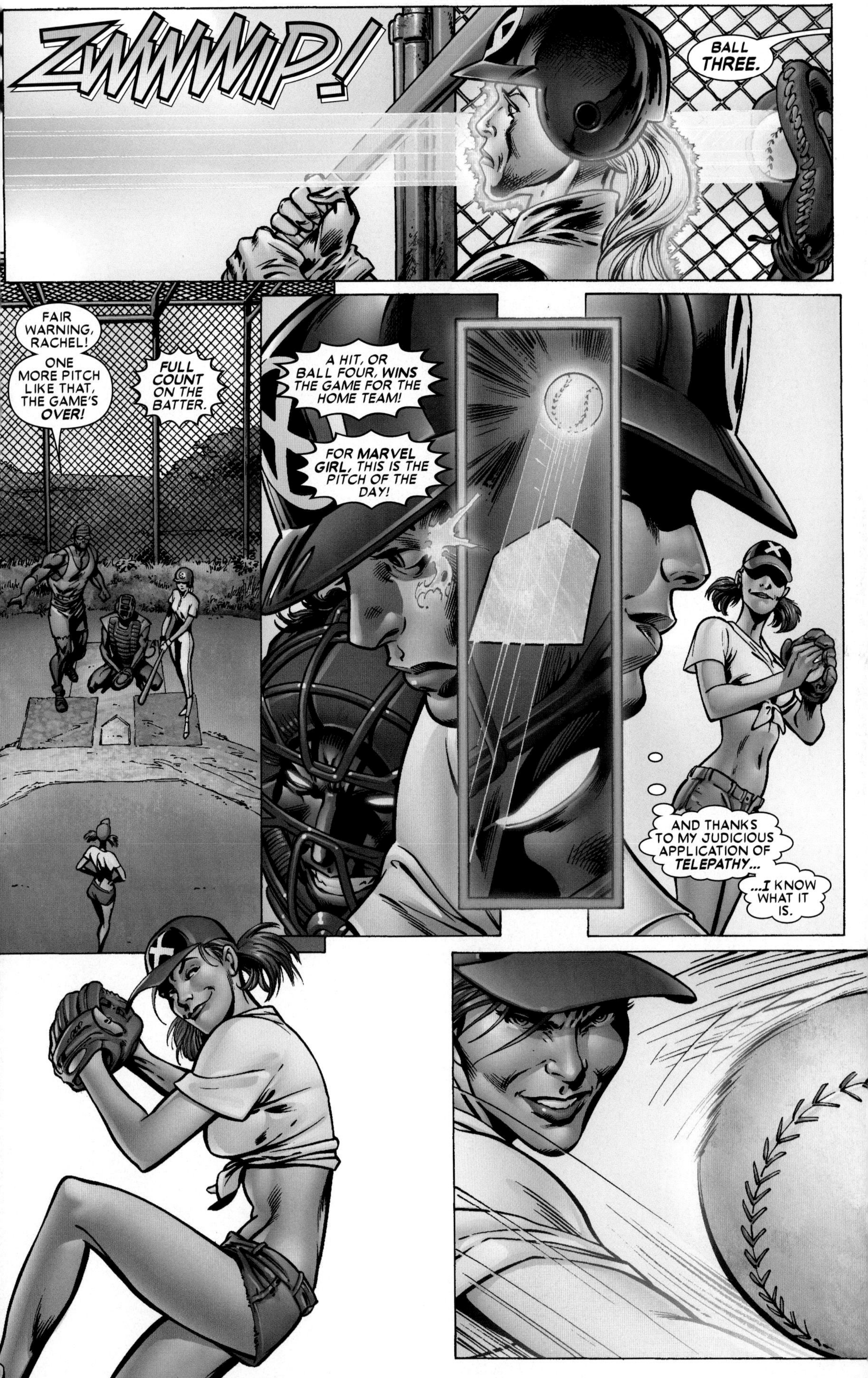
ZWWWMP!
BALL THREE.
FAIR WARNING, RACHEL!
ONE MORE PITCH LIKE THAT, THE GAME'S OVER!
FULL COUNT ON THE BATTER.
A HIT, OR BALL FOUR, WINS THE GAME FOR THE HOME TEAM!
FOR MARVEL GIRL, THIS IS THE PITCH OF THE DAY!
AND THANKS TO MY JUDICIOUS APPLICATION OF TELEPATHY...
...I KNOW WHAT IT IS.

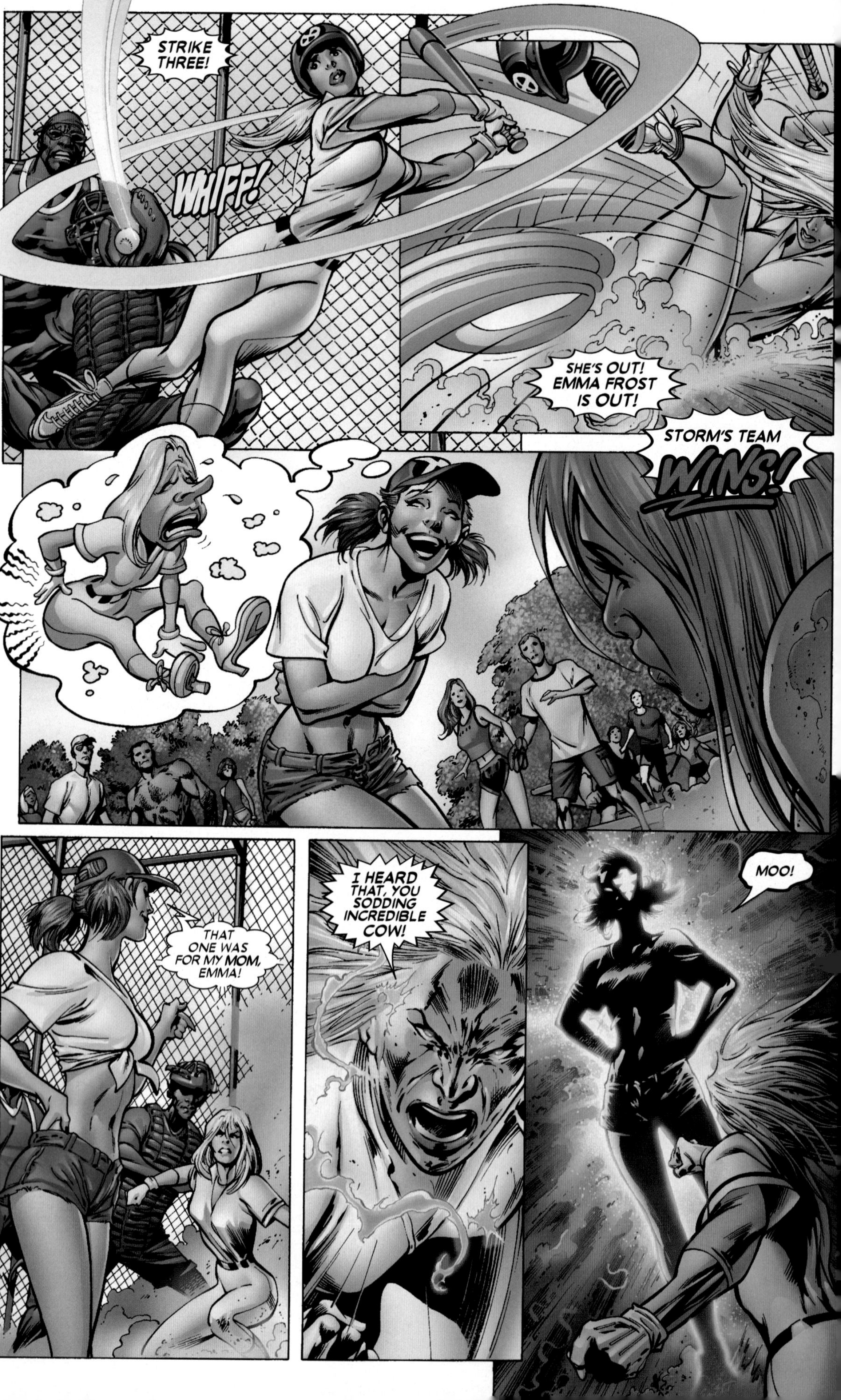
STRIKE THREE!
WHIFF!
SHE'S OUT! EMMA FROST IS OUT!
STORM'S TEAM WINS!
THAT ONE WAS FOR MY MOM, EMMA!
I HEARD THAT, YOU SODDING INCREDIBLE COW!
MOO!

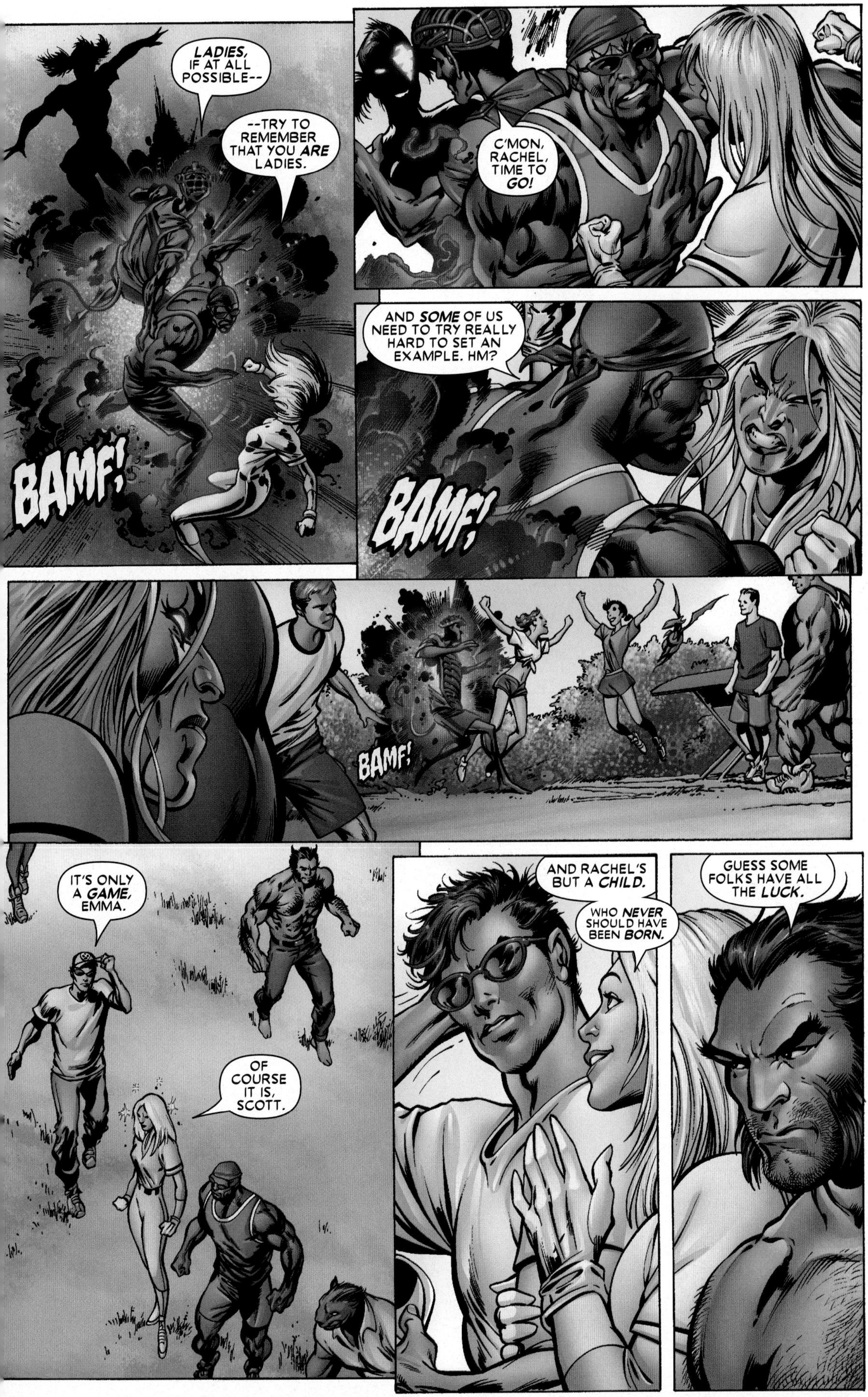

LADIES, IF AT ALL POSSIBLE--
--TRY TO REMEMBER THAT YOU ARE LADIES.
BAMF!
C'MON, RACHEL, TIME TO GO!
AND SOME OF US NEED TO TRY REALLY HARD TO SET AN EXAMPLE. HM?
BAMF!
BAMF!
IT'S ONLY A GAME, EMMA.
OF COURSE IT IS, SCOTT.
AND RACHEL'S BUT A CHILD.
WHO NEVER SHOULD HAVE BEEN BORN.
GUESS SOME FOLKS HAVE ALL THE LUCK.

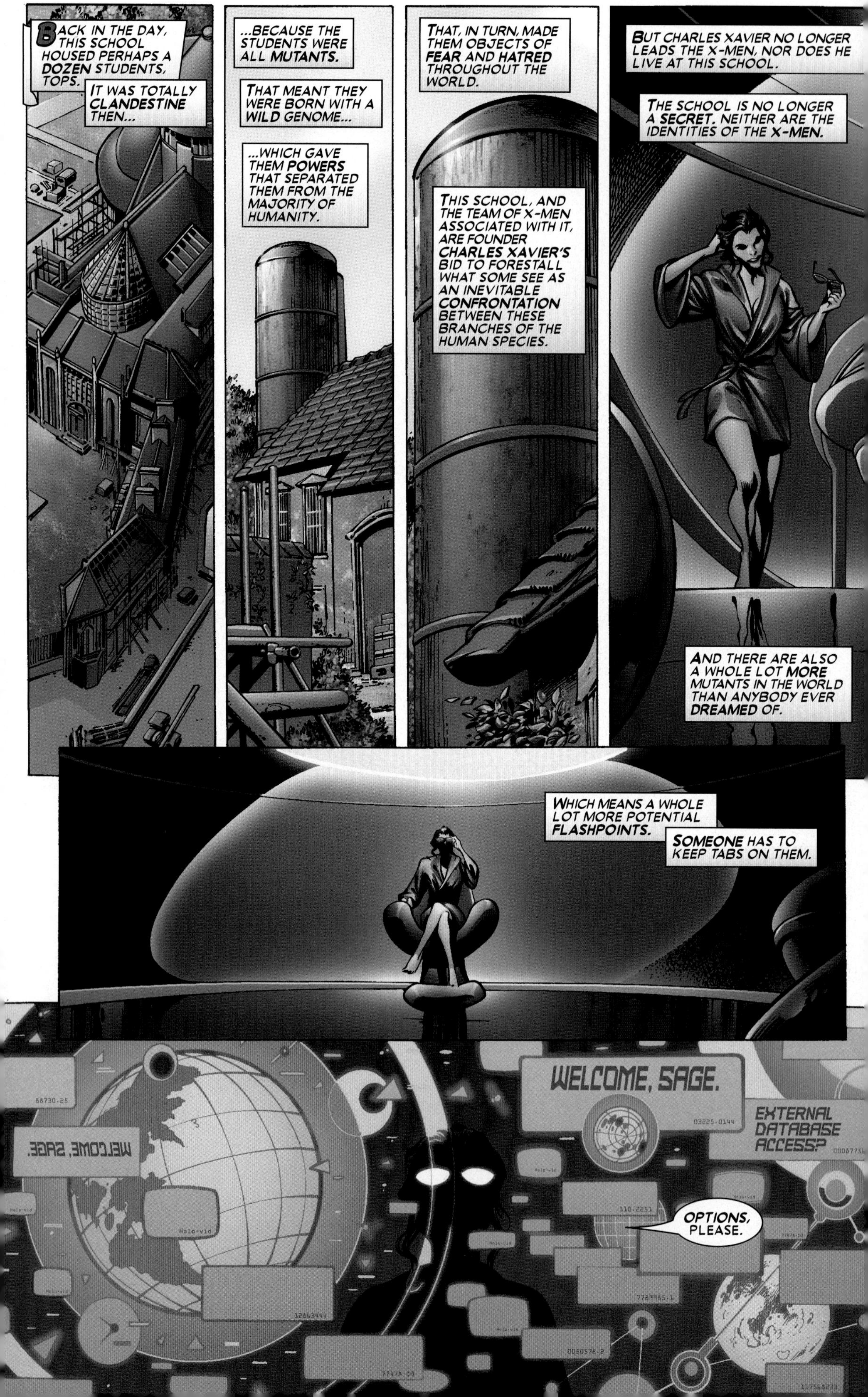
BACK IN THE DAY, THIS SCHOOL HOUSED PERHAPS A DOZEN STUDENTS, TOPS.
IT WAS TOTALLY CLANDESTINE THEN...
...BECAUSE THE STUDENTS WERE ALL MUTANTS.
THAT MEANT THEY WERE BORN WITH A WILD GENOME...
...WHICH GAVE THEM POWERS THAT SEPARATED THEM FROM THE MAJORITY OF HUMANITY.
THAT, IN TURN, MADE THEM OBJECTS OF FEAR AND HATRED THROUGHOUT THE WORLD.
THIS SCHOOL, AND THE TEAM OF X-MEN ASSOCIATED WITH IT, ARE FOUNDER CHARLES XAVIER'S BID TO FORESTALL WHAT SOME SEE AS AN INEVITABLE CONFRONTATION BETWEEN THESE BRANCHES OF THE HUMAN SPECIES.
BUT CHARLES XAVIER NO LONGER LEADS THE X-MEN, NOR DOES HE LIVE AT THIS SCHOOL.
THE SCHOOL IS NO LONGER A SECRET. NEITHER ARE THE IDENTITIES OF THE X-MEN.
AND THERE ARE ALSO A WHOLE LOT MORE MUTANTS IN THE WORLD THAN ANYBODY EVER DREAMED OF.
WHICH MEANS A WHOLE LOT MORE POTENTIAL FLASHPOINTS.
SOMEONE HAS TO KEEP TABS ON THEM.
WELCOME, SAGE.
EXTERNAL DATABASE ACCESS?
OPTIONS, PLEASE.

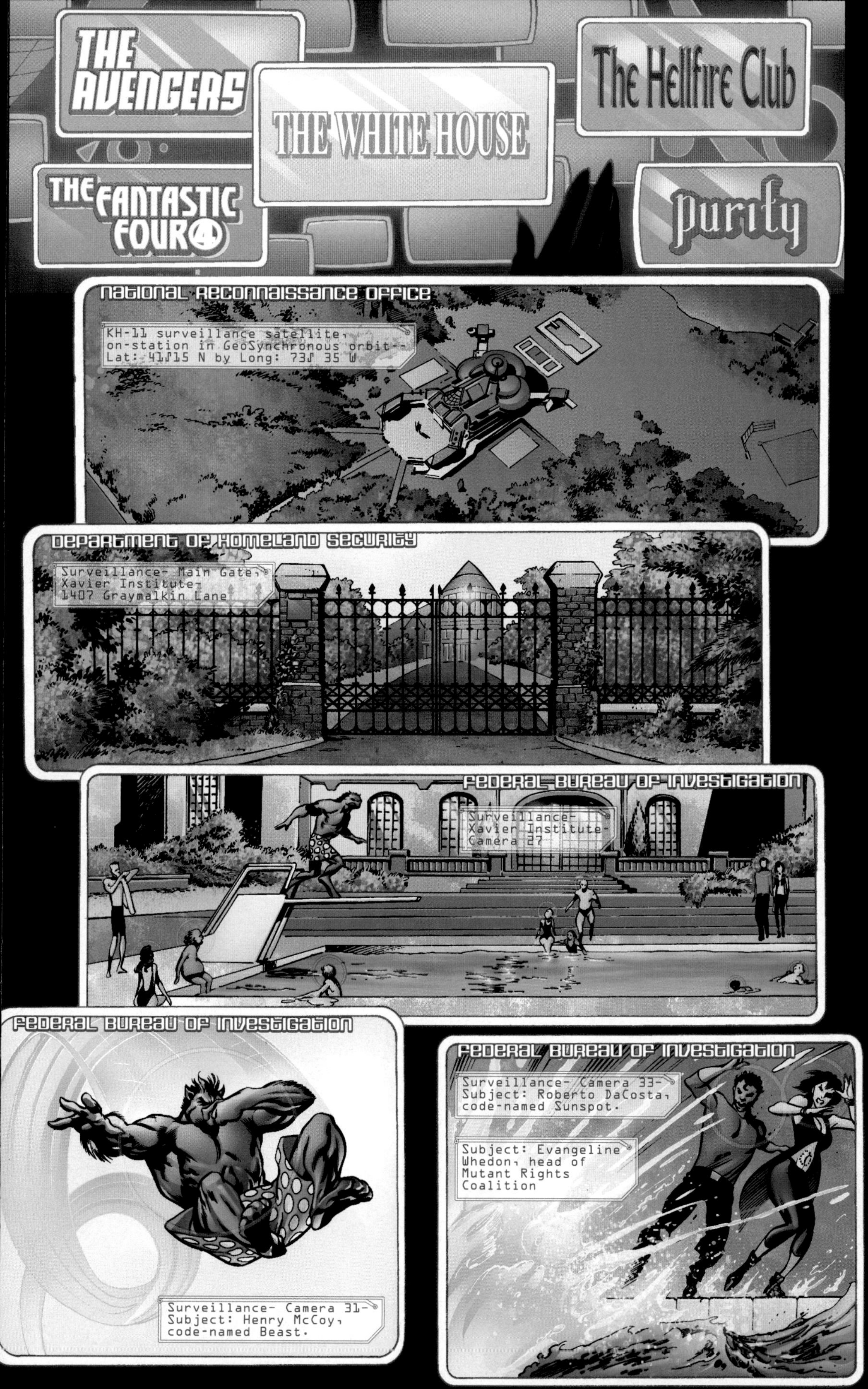

THE AVENGERS
THE WHITE HOUSE
The Hellfire Club
THE FANTASTIC FOUR
Purity
NATIONAL RECONNAISSANCE OFFICE
KH-11 surveillance satellite, on-station in GeoSynchronous orbit-- Lat: 41J15 N by Long: 73J 35 W
DEPARTMENT OF HOMELAND SECURITY
Surveillance- Main Gate, Xavier Institute- 1407 Graymalkin Lane
FEDERAL BUREAU OF INVESTIGATION
Surveillance- Xavier Institute- Camera 27
FEDERAL BUREAU OF INVESTIGATION
Surveillance- Camera 31- Subject: Henry McCoy, code-named Beast.
FEDERAL BUREAU OF INVESTIGATION
Surveillance- Camera 33- Subject: Roberto DaCosta, code-named Sunspot.
Subject: Evangeline Whedon, head of Mutant Rights Coalition

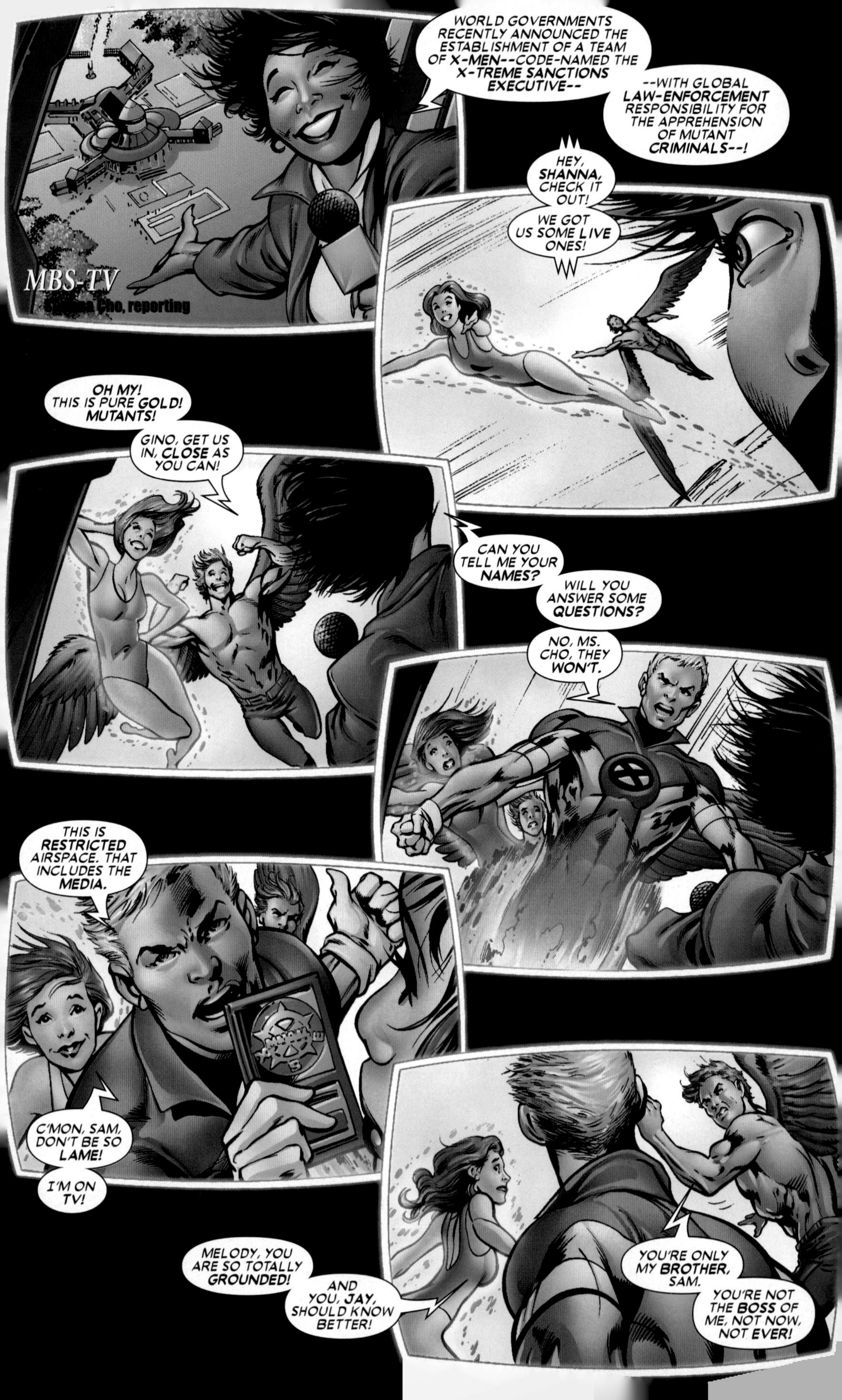
WORLD GOVERNMENTS RECENTLY ANNOUNCED THE ESTABLISHMENT OF A TEAM OF X-MEN--CODE-NAMED THE X-TREME SANCTIONS EXECUTIVE--
--WITH GLOBAL LAW-ENFORCEMENT RESPONSIBILITY FOR THE APPREHENSION OF MUTANT CRIMINALS--!
MBS-TV
Cho, reporting
HEY, SHANNA, CHECK IT OUT!
WE GOT US SOME LIVE ONES!
OH MY! THIS IS PURE GOLD! MUTANTS!
GINO, GET US IN, CLOSE AS YOU CAN!
CAN YOU TELL ME YOUR NAMES?
WILL YOU ANSWER SOME QUESTIONS?
NO, MS. CHO, THEY WON'T.
THIS IS RESTRICTED AIRSPACE. THAT INCLUDES THE MEDIA.
C'MON, SAM, DON'T BE SO LAME!
I'M ON TV!
MELODY, YOU ARE SO TOTALLY GROUNDED!
AND YOU, JAY, SHOULD KNOW BETTER!
YOU'RE ONLY MY BROTHER, SAM.
YOU'RE NOT THE BOSS OF ME, NOT NOW, NOT EVER!

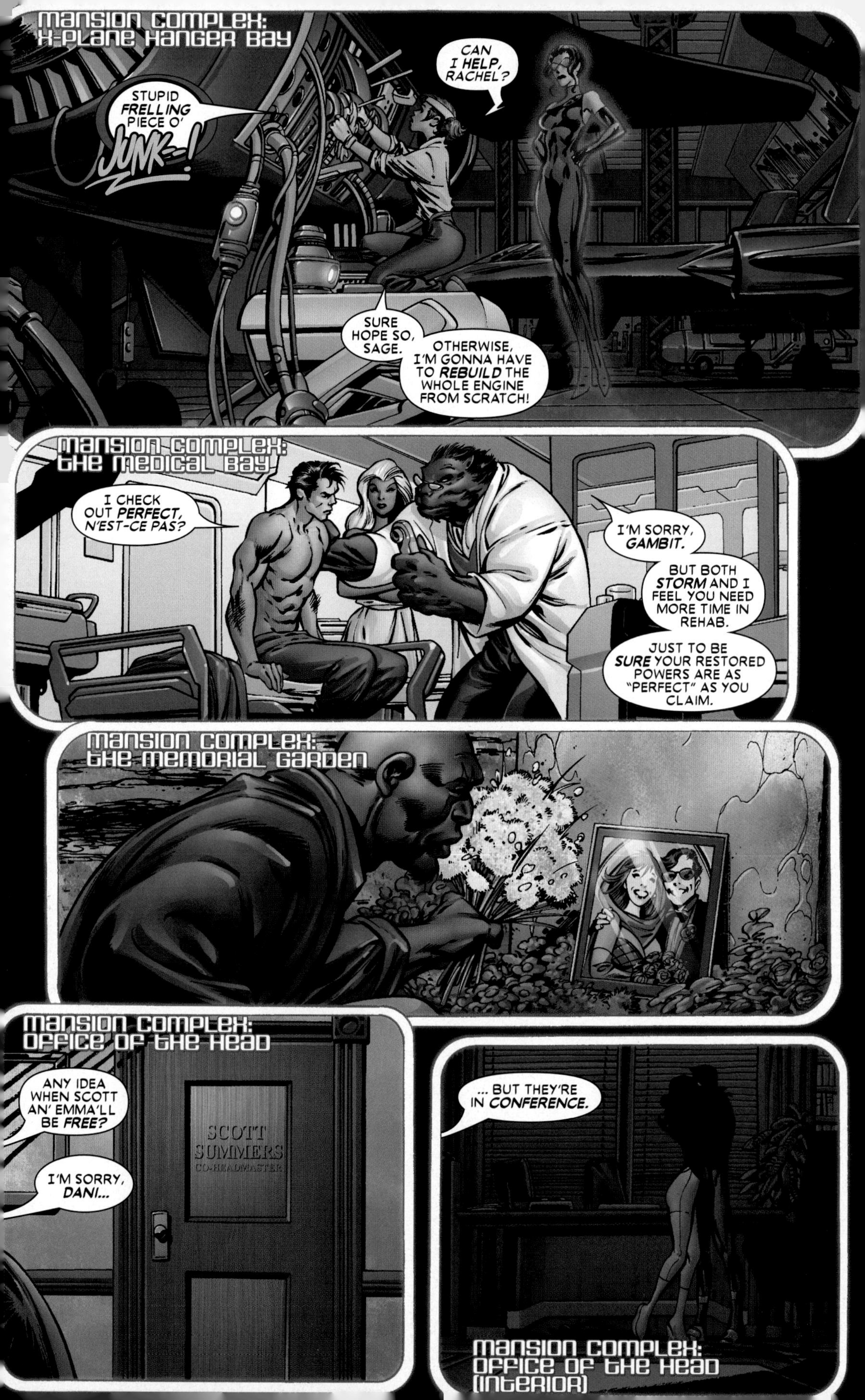

MANSION COMPLEX:
X-PLANE HANGER BAY
STUPID FRELLING PIECE O' JUNK--!
CAN I HELP, RACHEL?
SURE HOPE SO, SAGE.
OTHERWISE, I'M GONNA HAVE TO REBUILD THE WHOLE ENGINE FROM SCRATCH!
MANSION COMPLEX:
THE MEDICAL BAY
I CHECK OUT PERFECT, N'EST-CE PAS?
I'M SORRY, GAMBIT.
BUT BOTH STORM AND I FEEL YOU NEED MORE TIME IN REHAB.
JUST TO BE SURE YOUR RESTORED POWERS ARE AS "PERFECT" AS YOU CLAIM.
MANSION COMPLEX:
THE MEMORIAL GARDEN
MANSION COMPLEX:
OFFICE OF THE HEAD
ANY IDEA WHEN SCOTT AN' EMMA'LL BE FREE?
SCOTT SUMMERS
CO-HEADMASTER
I'M SORRY, DANI...
... BUT THEY'RE IN CONFERENCE.
MANSION COMPLEX:
OFFICE OF THE HEAD
(INTERIOR)

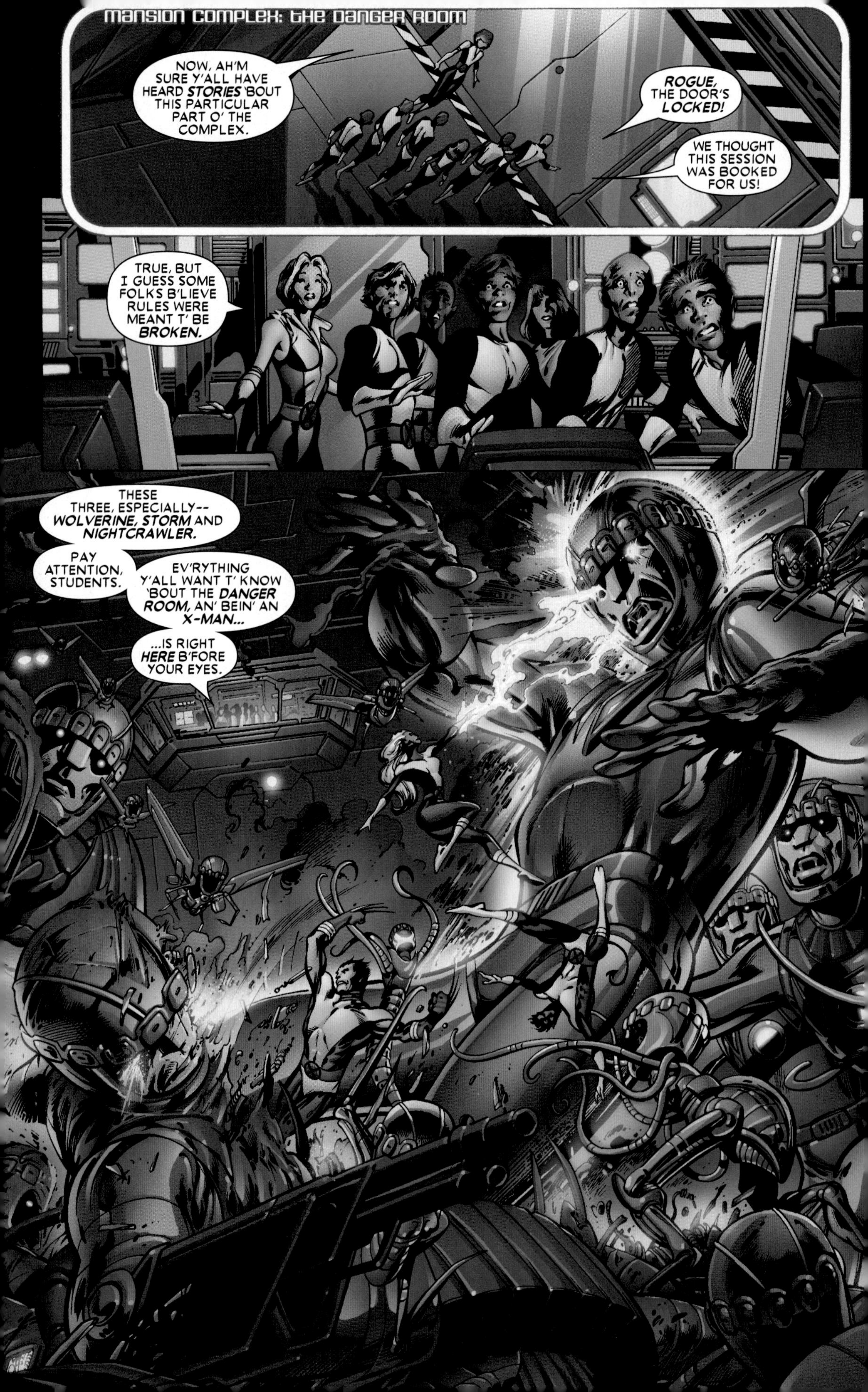
MANSION COMPLEX: THE DANGER ROOM
NOW, AH'M SURE Y'ALL HAVE HEARD STORIES 'BOUT THIS PARTICULAR PART O' THE COMPLEX.
ROGUE, THE DOOR'S LOCKED!
WE THOUGHT THIS SESSION WAS BOOKED FOR US!
TRUE, BUT I GUESS SOME FOLKS B'LIEVE RULES WERE MEANT T' BE BROKEN.
THESE THREE, ESPECIALLY-- WOLVERINE, STORM AND NIGHTCRAWLER.
PAY ATTENTION, STUDENTS.
EV'RYTHING Y'ALL WANT T' KNOW 'BOUT THE DANGER ROOM, AN' BEIN' AN X-MAN...
...IS RIGHT HERE B'FORE YOUR EYES.

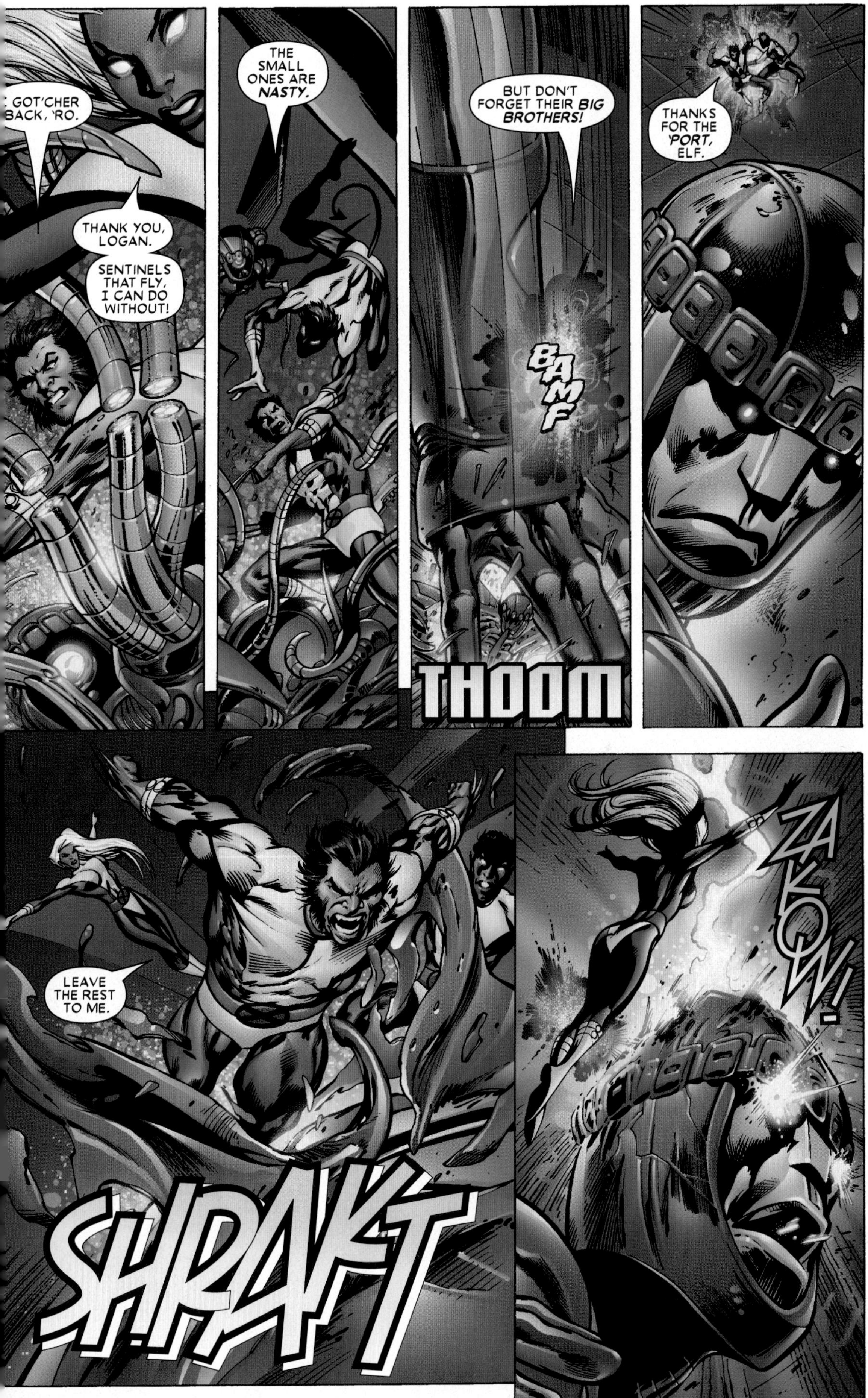

GOT'CHER BACK, 'RO.
THANK YOU, LOGAN.
SENTINELS THAT FLY, I CAN DO WITHOUT!
THE SMALL ONES ARE *NASTY.*
BUT DON'T FORGET THEIR *BIG BROTHERS!*
BAMF
THOOM
THANKS FOR THE *'PORT,* ELF.
LEAVE THE REST TO ME.
SHRAKT
ZAKOW!

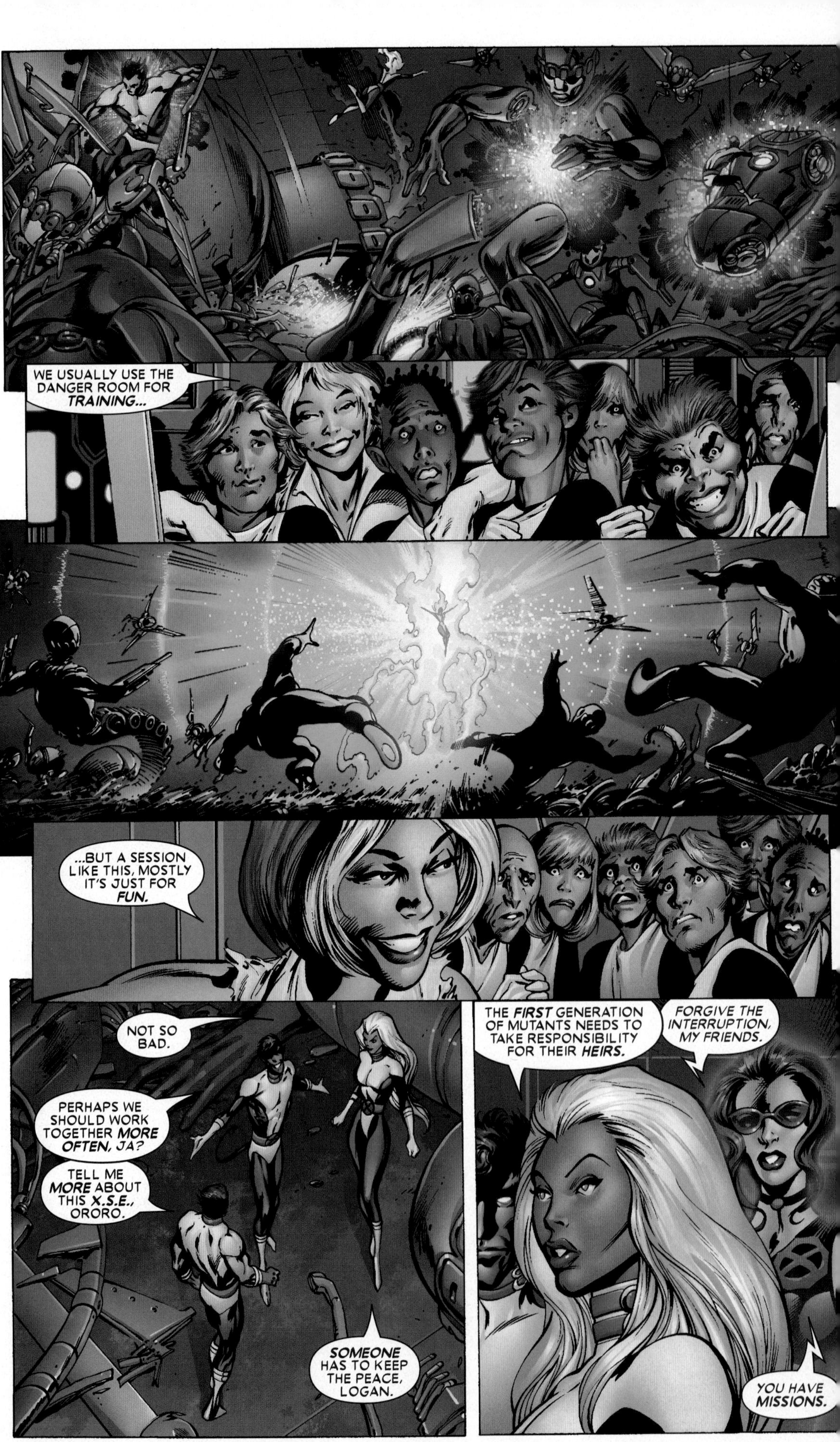
WE USUALLY USE THE DANGER ROOM FOR TRAINING...
...BUT A SESSION LIKE THIS, MOSTLY IT'S JUST FOR FUN.
NOT SO BAD.
PERHAPS WE SHOULD WORK TOGETHER MORE OFTEN, JA?
TELL ME MORE ABOUT THIS X.S.E., ORORO.
SOMEONE HAS TO KEEP THE PEACE, LOGAN.
THE FIRST GENERATION OF MUTANTS NEEDS TO TAKE RESPONSIBILITY FOR THEIR HEIRS.
FORGIVE THE INTERRUPTION, MY FRIENDS.
YOU HAVE MISSIONS.

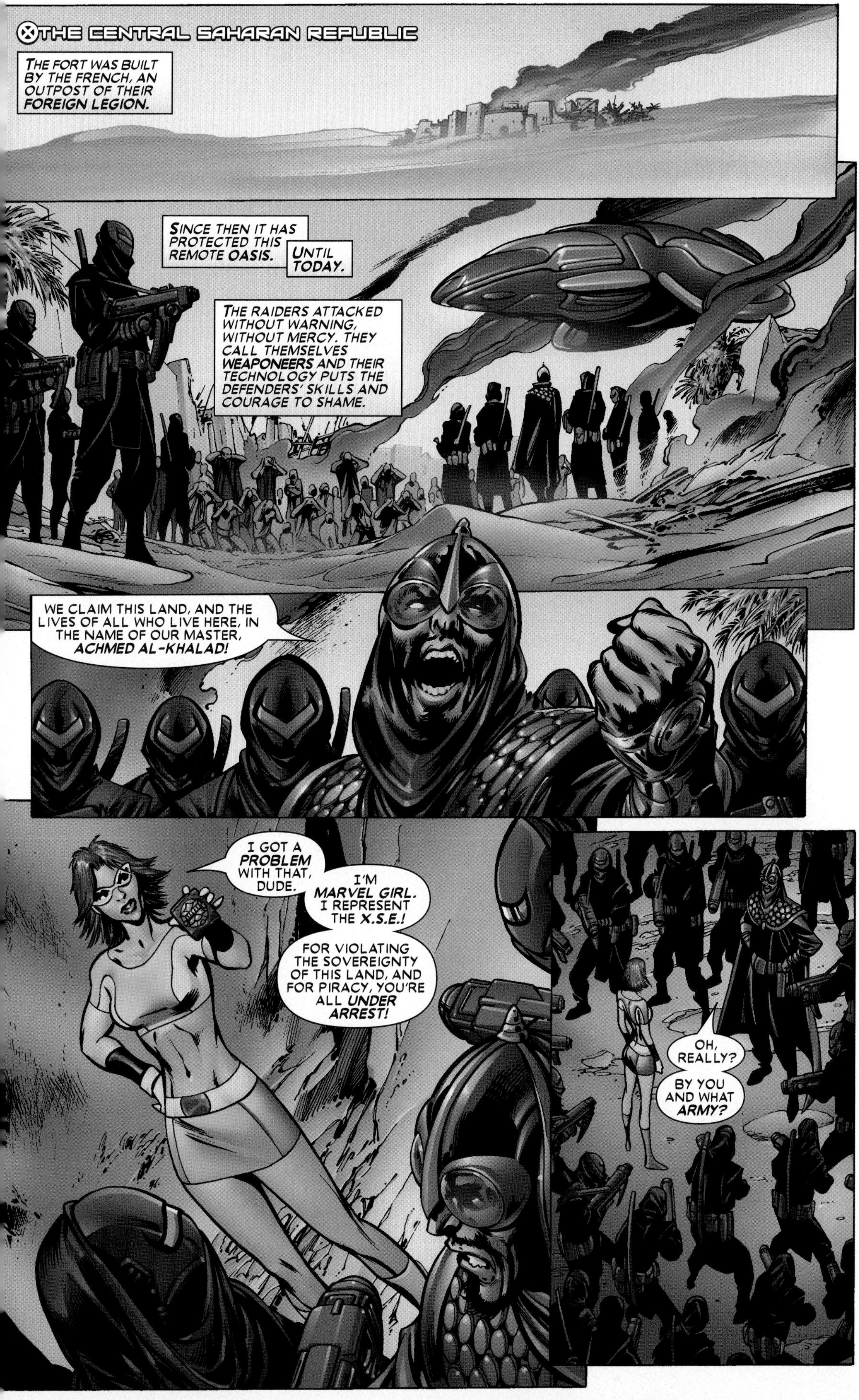

THE CENTRAL SAHARAN REPUBLIC
THE FORT WAS BUILT BY THE FRENCH, AN OUTPOST OF THEIR FOREIGN LEGION.
SINCE THEN IT HAS PROTECTED THIS REMOTE OASIS.
UNTIL TODAY.
THE RAIDERS ATTACKED WITHOUT WARNING, WITHOUT MERCY. THEY CALL THEMSELVES WEAPONEERS AND THEIR TECHNOLOGY PUTS THE DEFENDERS' SKILLS AND COURAGE TO SHAME.
WE CLAIM THIS LAND, AND THE LIVES OF ALL WHO LIVE HERE, IN THE NAME OF OUR MASTER, ACHMED AL-KHALAD!
I GOT A PROBLEM WITH THAT, DUDE.
I'M MARVEL GIRL. I REPRESENT THE X.S.E.!
FOR VIOLATING THE SOVEREIGNTY OF THIS LAND, AND FOR PIRACY, YOU'RE ALL UNDER ARREST!
OH, REALLY?
BY YOU AND WHAT ARMY?

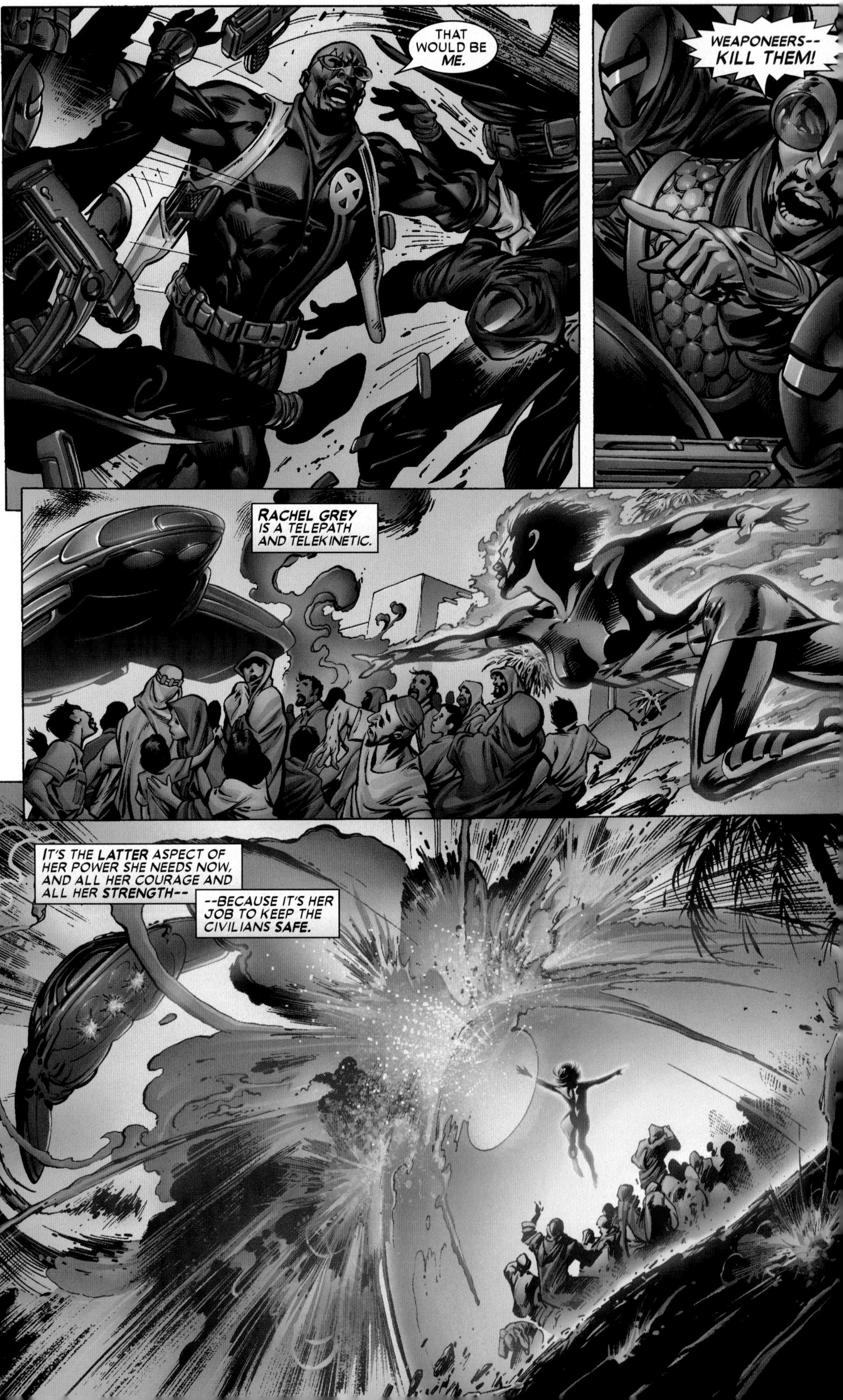

THAT WOULD BE ME.
WEAPONEERS-- KILL THEM!
RACHEL GREY IS A TELEPATH AND TELEKINETIC.
IT'S THE LATTER ASPECT OF HER POWER SHE NEEDS NOW, AND ALL HER COURAGE AND ALL HER STRENGTH--
--BECAUSE IT'S HER JOB TO KEEP THE CIVILIANS SAFE.

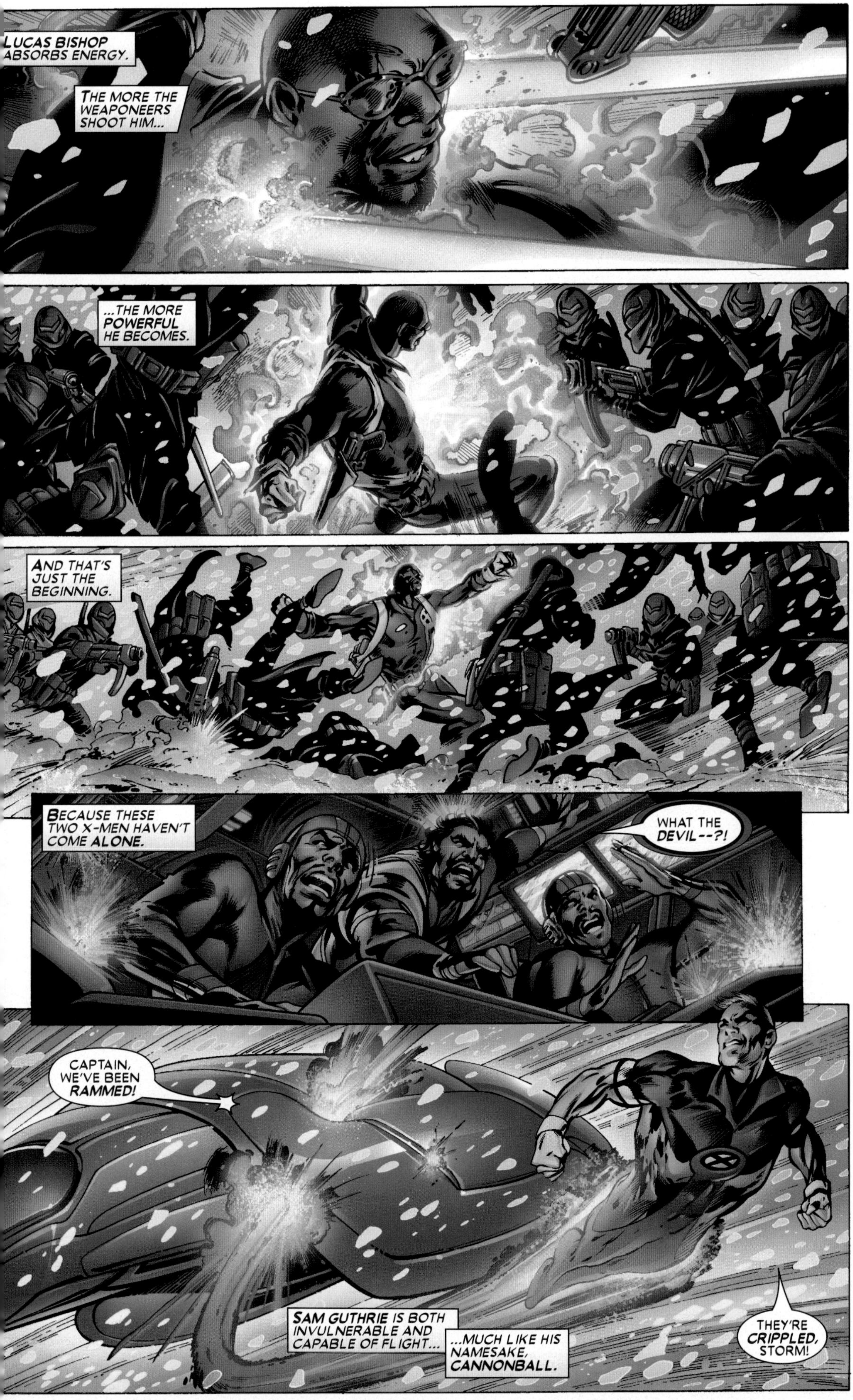
LUCAS BISHOP ABSORBS ENERGY.
THE MORE THE WEAPONEERS SHOOT HIM...
...THE MORE POWERFUL HE BECOMES.
AND THAT'S JUST THE BEGINNING.
BECAUSE THESE TWO X-MEN HAVEN'T COME ALONE.
WHAT THE DEVIL--?!
CAPTAIN, WE'VE BEEN RAMMED!
SAM GUTHRIE IS BOTH INVULNERABLE AND CAPABLE OF FLIGHT...
...MUCH LIKE HIS NAMESAKE, CANNONBALL.
THEY'RE CRIPPLED, STORM!

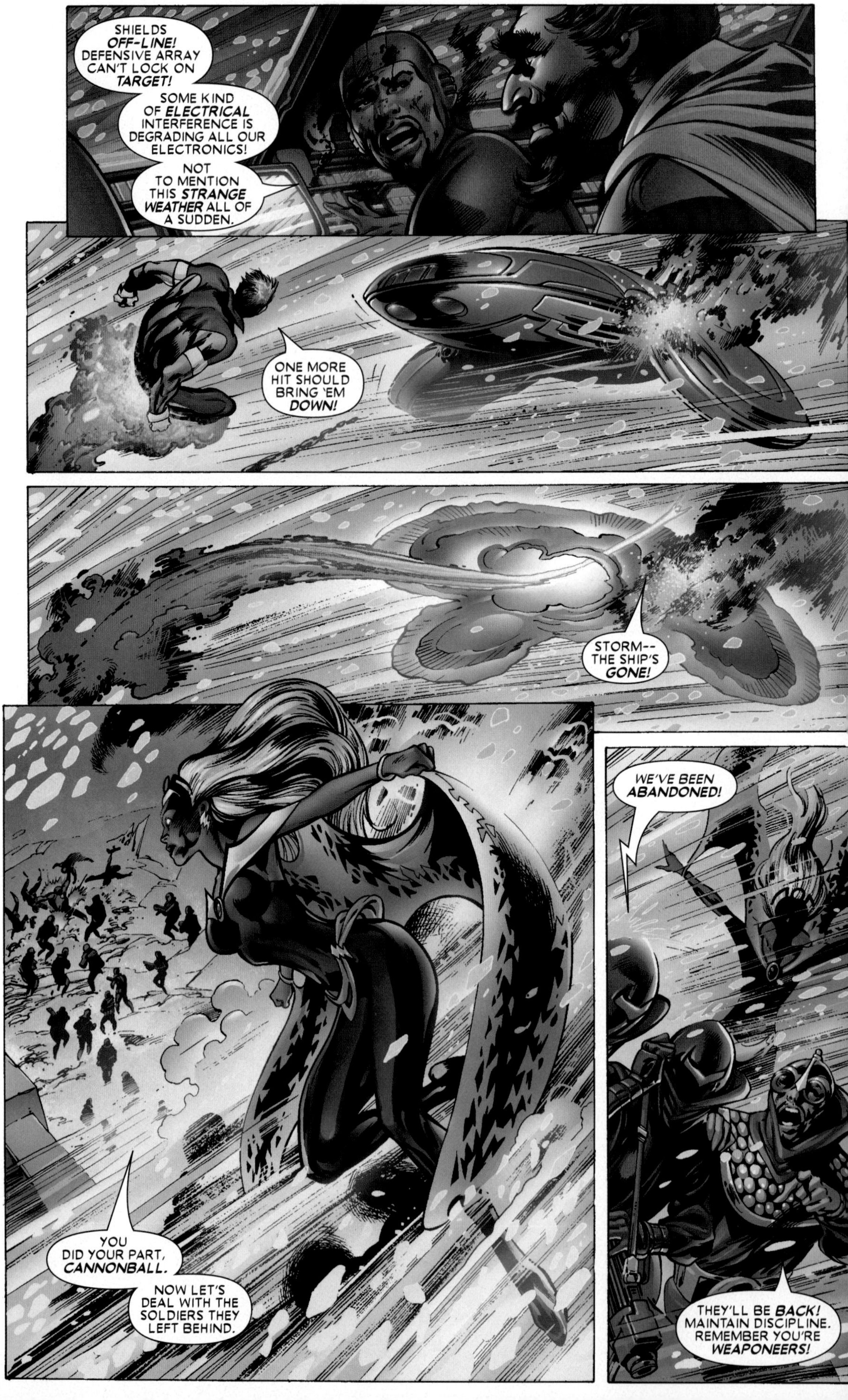
SHIELDS OFF-LINE! DEFENSIVE ARRAY CAN'T LOCK ON TARGET!
SOME KIND OF ELECTRICAL INTERFERENCE IS DEGRADING ALL OUR ELECTRONICS!
NOT TO MENTION THIS STRANGE WEATHER ALL OF A SUDDEN.
ONE MORE HIT SHOULD BRING 'EM DOWN!
STORM-- THE SHIP'S GONE!
YOU DID YOUR PART, CANNONBALL.
NOW LET'S DEAL WITH THE SOLDIERS THEY LEFT BEHIND.
WE'VE BEEN ABANDONED!
THEY'LL BE BACK! MAINTAIN DISCIPLINE. REMEMBER YOU'RE WEAPONEERS!

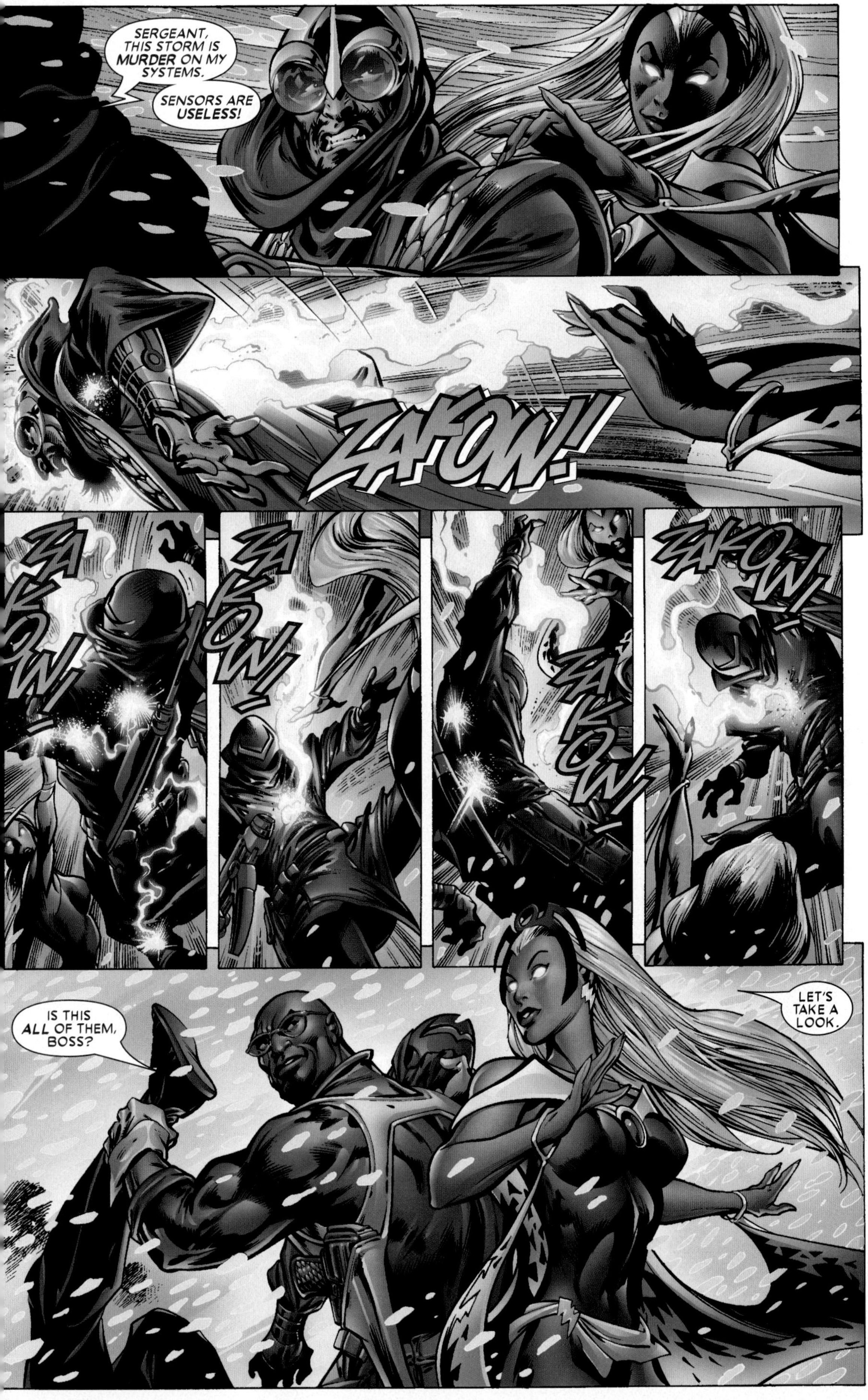
SERGEANT, THIS STORM IS MURDER ON MY SYSTEMS.
SENSORS ARE USELESS!
ZAKOW!
ZAKOW!
ZAKOW!
ZAKOW!
ZAKOW!
IS THIS ALL OF THEM, BOSS?
LET'S TAKE A LOOK.

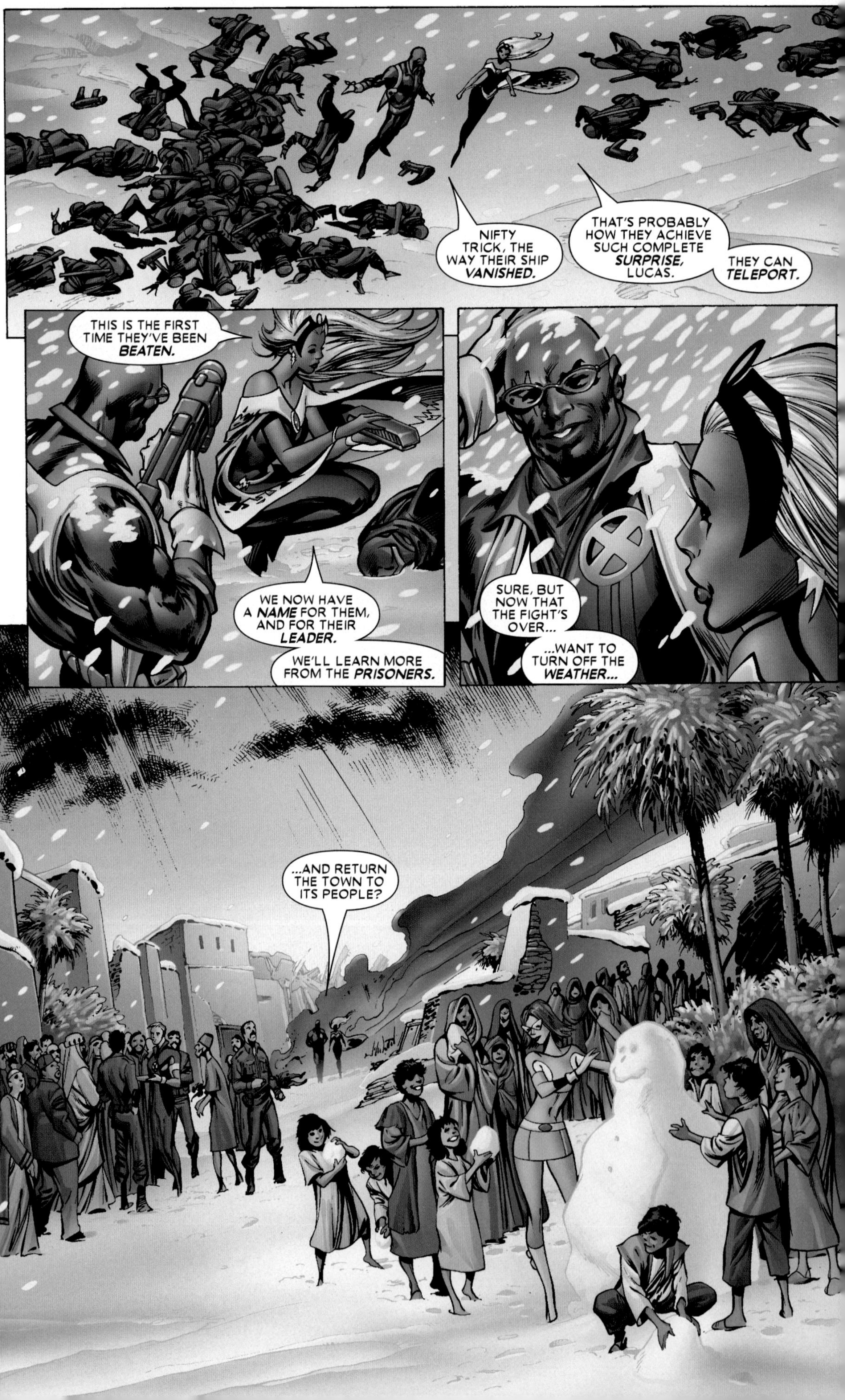
NIFTY TRICK, THE WAY THEIR SHIP VANISHED.
THAT'S PROBABLY HOW THEY ACHIEVE SUCH COMPLETE SURPRISE, LUCAS.
THEY CAN TELEPORT.
THIS IS THE FIRST TIME THEY'VE BEEN BEATEN.
WE NOW HAVE A NAME FOR THEM, AND FOR THEIR LEADER.
WE'LL LEARN MORE FROM THE PRISONERS.
SURE, BUT NOW THAT THE FIGHT'S OVER...
...WANT TO TURN OFF THE WEATHER...
...AND RETURN THE TOWN TO ITS PEOPLE?

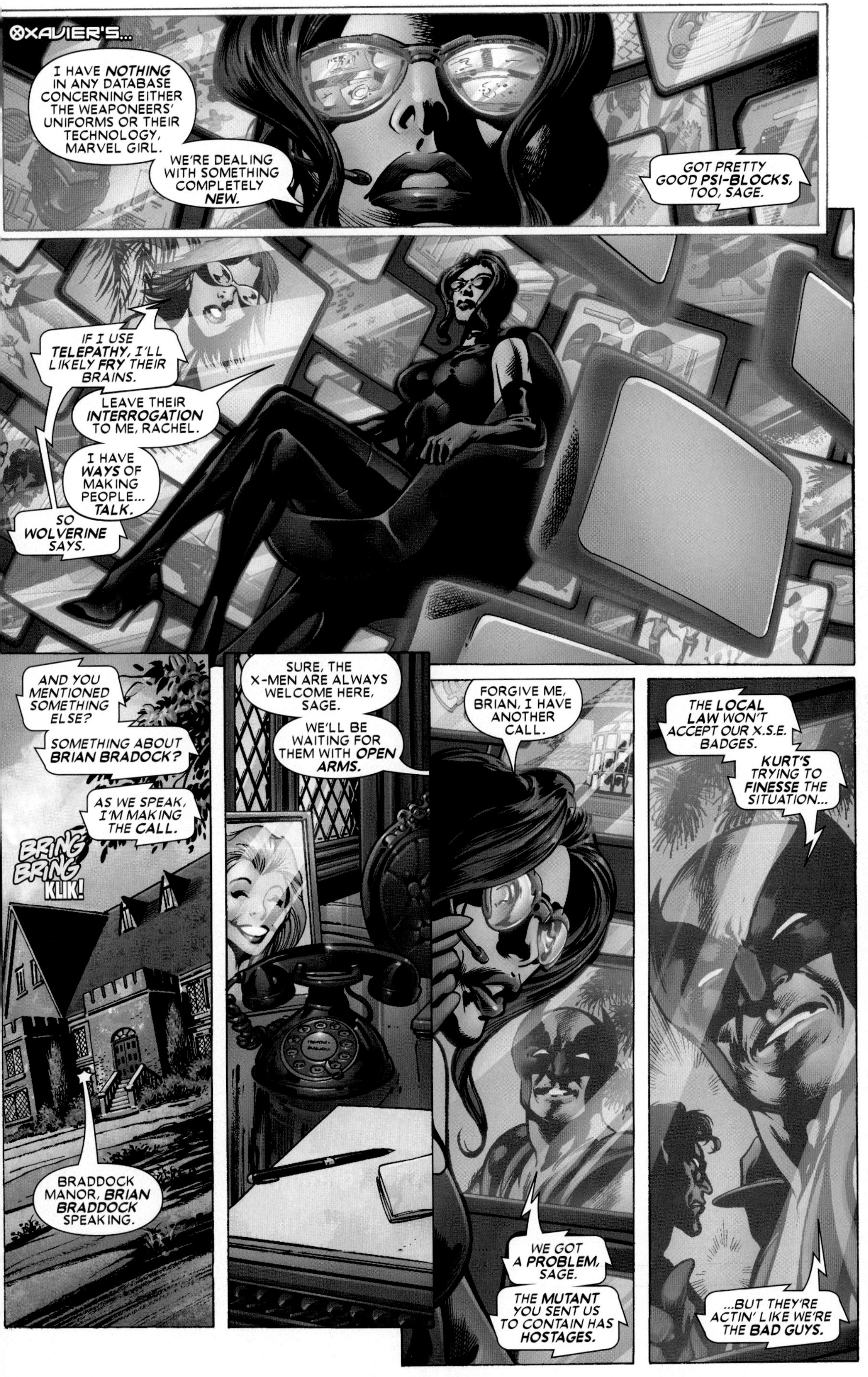
XAVIER'S...
I HAVE NOTHING IN ANY DATABASE CONCERNING EITHER THE WEAPONEERS' UNIFORMS OR THEIR TECHNOLOGY, MARVEL GIRL.
WE'RE DEALING WITH SOMETHING COMPLETELY NEW.
GOT PRETTY GOOD PSI-BLOCKS, TOO, SAGE.
IF I USE TELEPATHY, I'LL LIKELY FRY THEIR BRAINS.
LEAVE THEIR INTERROGATION TO ME, RACHEL.
I HAVE WAYS OF MAKING PEOPLE... TALK.
SO WOLVERINE SAYS.
AND YOU MENTIONED SOMETHING ELSE?
SOMETHING ABOUT BRIAN BRADOCK?
AS WE SPEAK, I'M MAKING THE CALL.
BRING BRING
KLIK!
BRADDOCK MANOR, BRIAN BRADDOCK SPEAKING.
SURE, THE X-MEN ARE ALWAYS WELCOME HERE, SAGE.
WE'LL BE WAITING FOR THEM WITH OPEN ARMS.
FORGIVE ME, BRIAN, I HAVE ANOTHER CALL.
WE GOT A PROBLEM, SAGE.
THE MUTANT YOU SENT US TO CONTAIN HAS HOSTAGES.
THE LOCAL LAW WON'T ACCEPT OUR X.S.E. BADGES.
KURT'S TRYING TO FINESSE THE SITUATION...
...BUT THEY'RE ACTIN' LIKE WE'RE THE BAD GUYS.

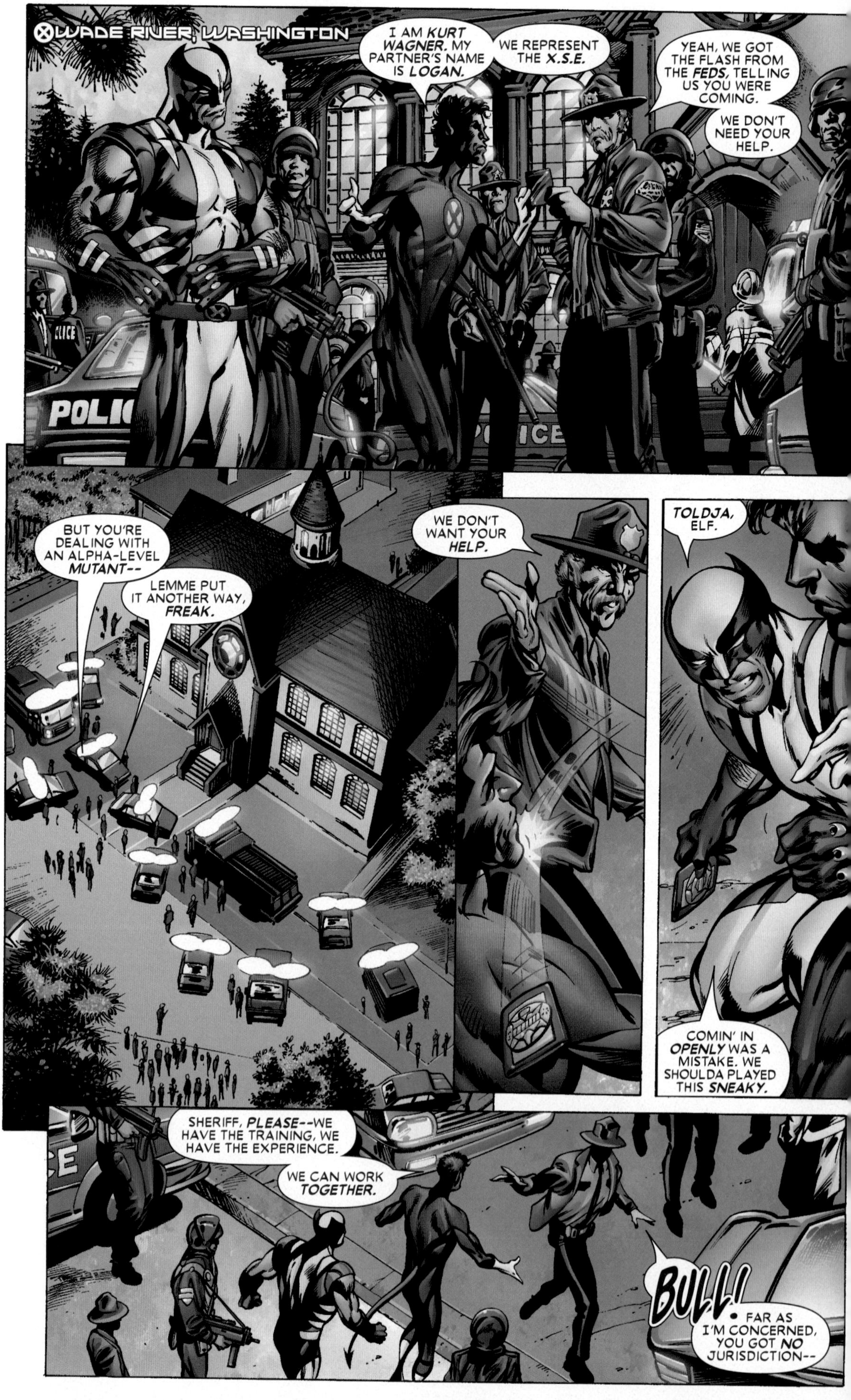
WADE RIVER, WASHINGTON
I AM KURT WAGNER. MY PARTNER'S NAME IS LOGAN.
WE REPRESENT THE X.S.E.
YEAH, WE GOT THE FLASH FROM THE FEDS, TELLING US YOU WERE COMING.
WE DON'T NEED YOUR HELP.
POLIC
BUT YOU'RE DEALING WITH AN ALPHA-LEVEL MUTANT--
LEMME PUT IT ANOTHER WAY, FREAK.
WE DON'T WANT YOUR HELP.
TOLDJA, ELF.
COMIN' IN OPENLY WAS A MISTAKE. WE SHOULDA PLAYED THIS SNEAKY.
SHERIFF, PLEASE--WE HAVE THE TRAINING, WE HAVE THE EXPERIENCE.
WE CAN WORK TOGETHER.
BULL!
FAR AS I'M CONCERNED, YOU GOT NO JURISDICTION--

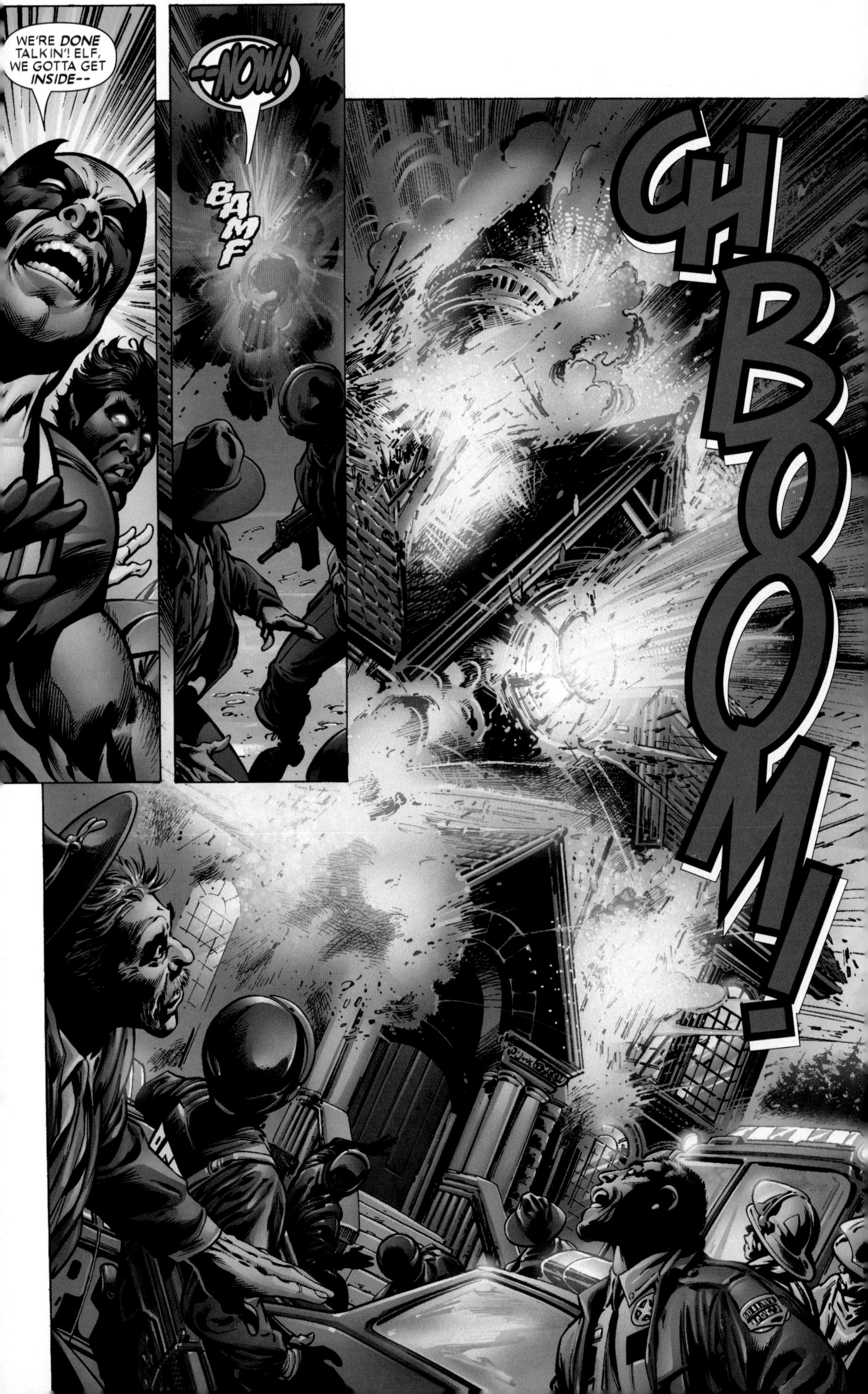
WE'RE DONE TALKIN'! ELF, WE GOTTA GET INSIDE--
--NOW!
BAMF
CHBOOM!

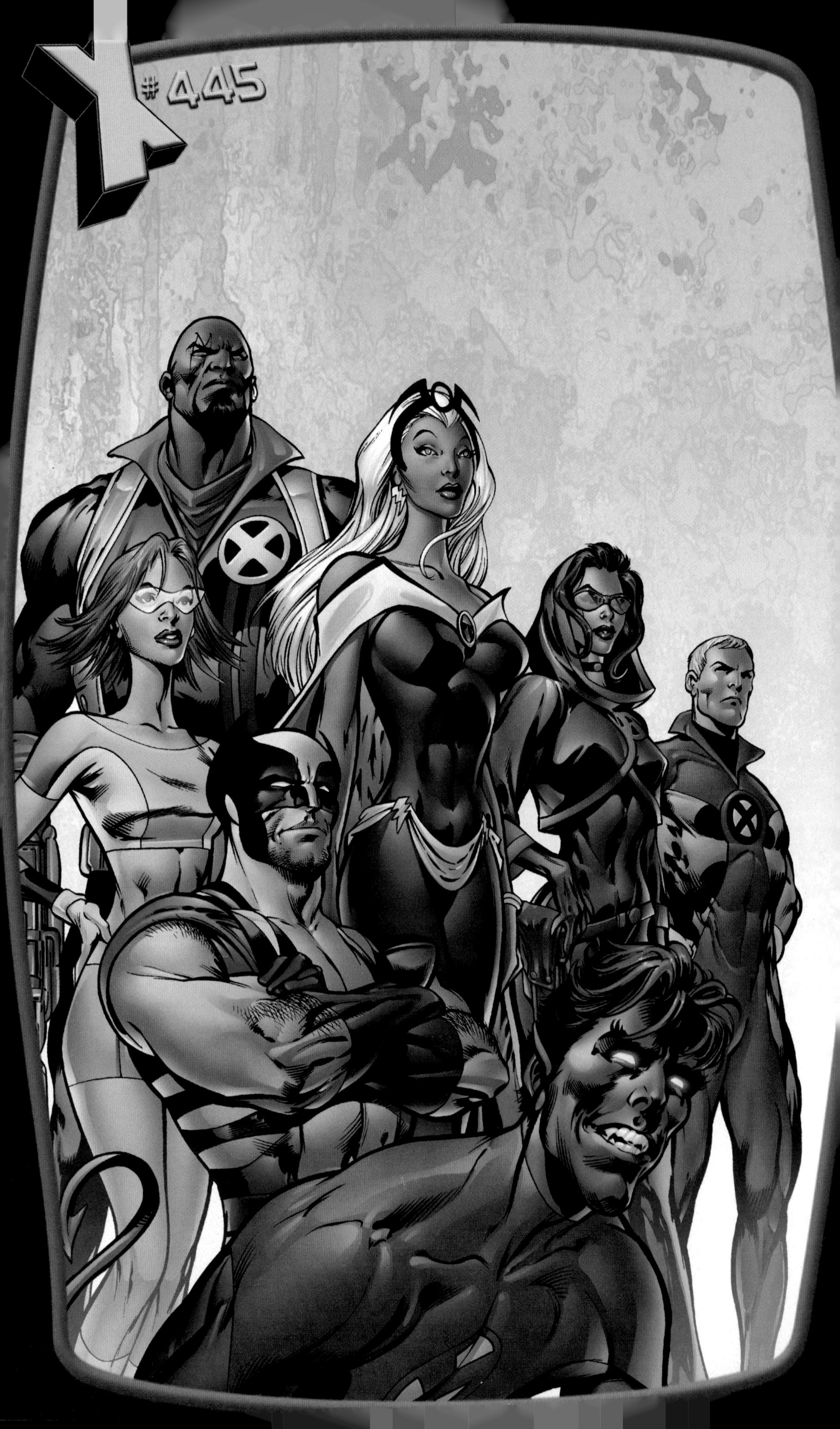
#445

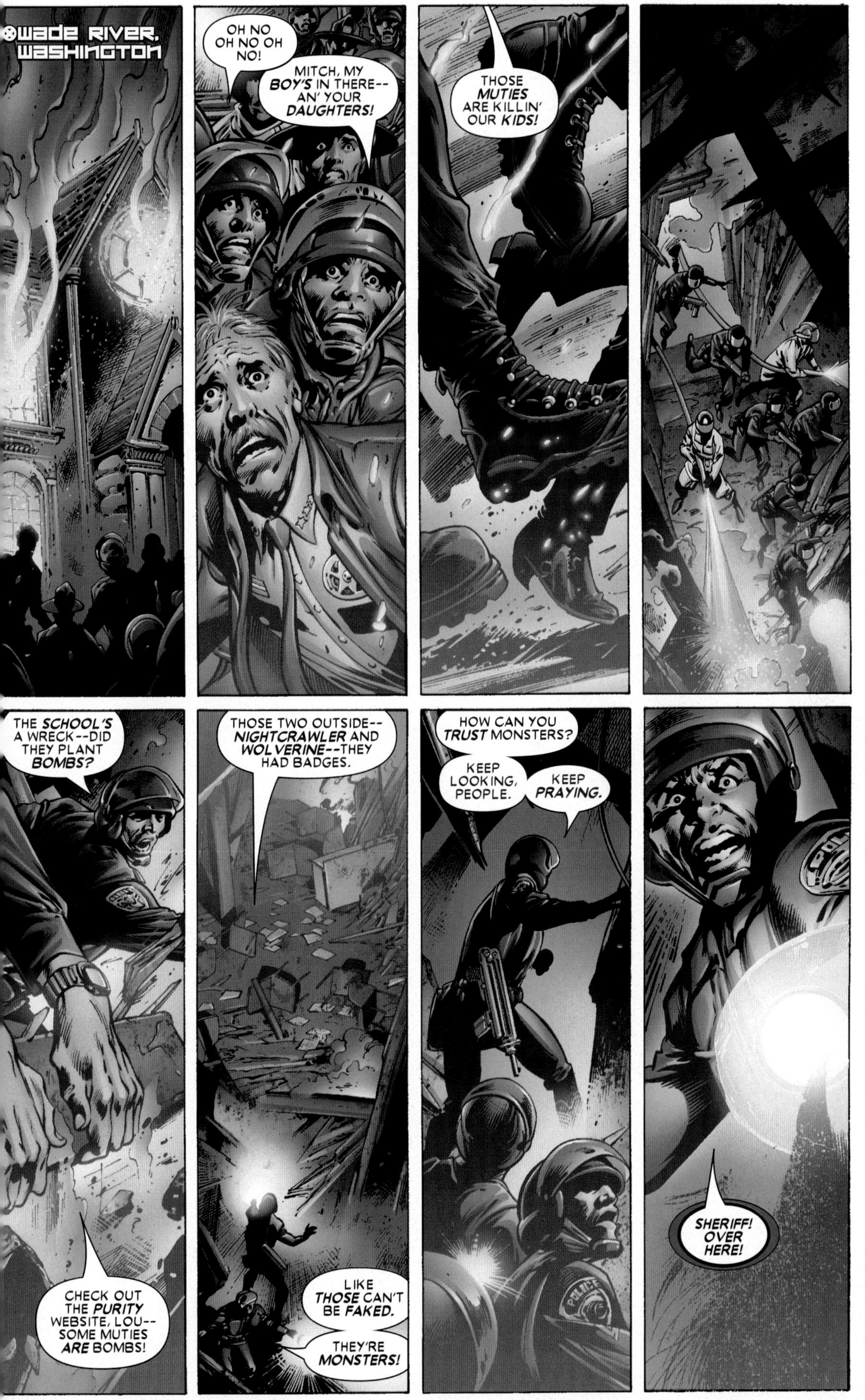
WADE RIVER, WASHINGTON
OH NO OH NO OH NO!
MITCH, MY BOY'S IN THERE-- AN' YOUR DAUGHTERS!
THOSE MUTIES ARE KILLIN' OUR KIDS!
THE SCHOOL'S A WRECK--DID THEY PLANT BOMBS?
CHECK OUT THE PURITY WEBSITE, LOU-- SOME MUTIES ARE BOMBS!
THOSE TWO OUTSIDE-- NIGHTCRAWLER AND WOLVERINE--THEY HAD BADGES.
LIKE THOSE CAN'T BE FAKED.
THEY'RE MONSTERS!
HOW CAN YOU TRUST MONSTERS?
KEEP LOOKING, PEOPLE.
KEEP PRAYING.
SHERIFF! OVER HERE!

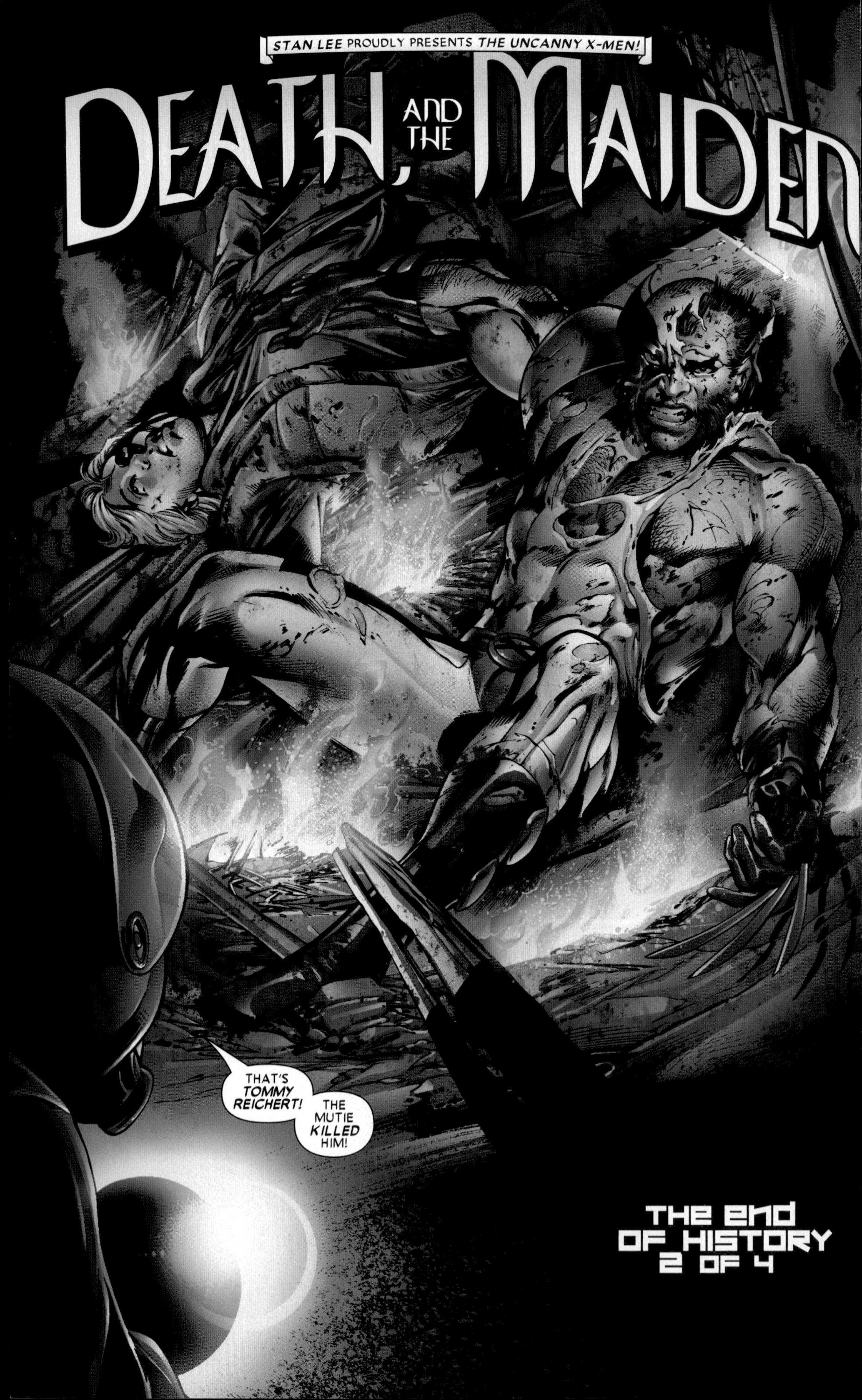
STAN LEE PROUDLY PRESENTS THE UNCANNY X-MEN!
DEATH, AND THE MAIDEN
THAT'S TOMMY REICHERT!
THE MUTIE KILLED HIM!
THE END OF HISTORY 2 OF 4

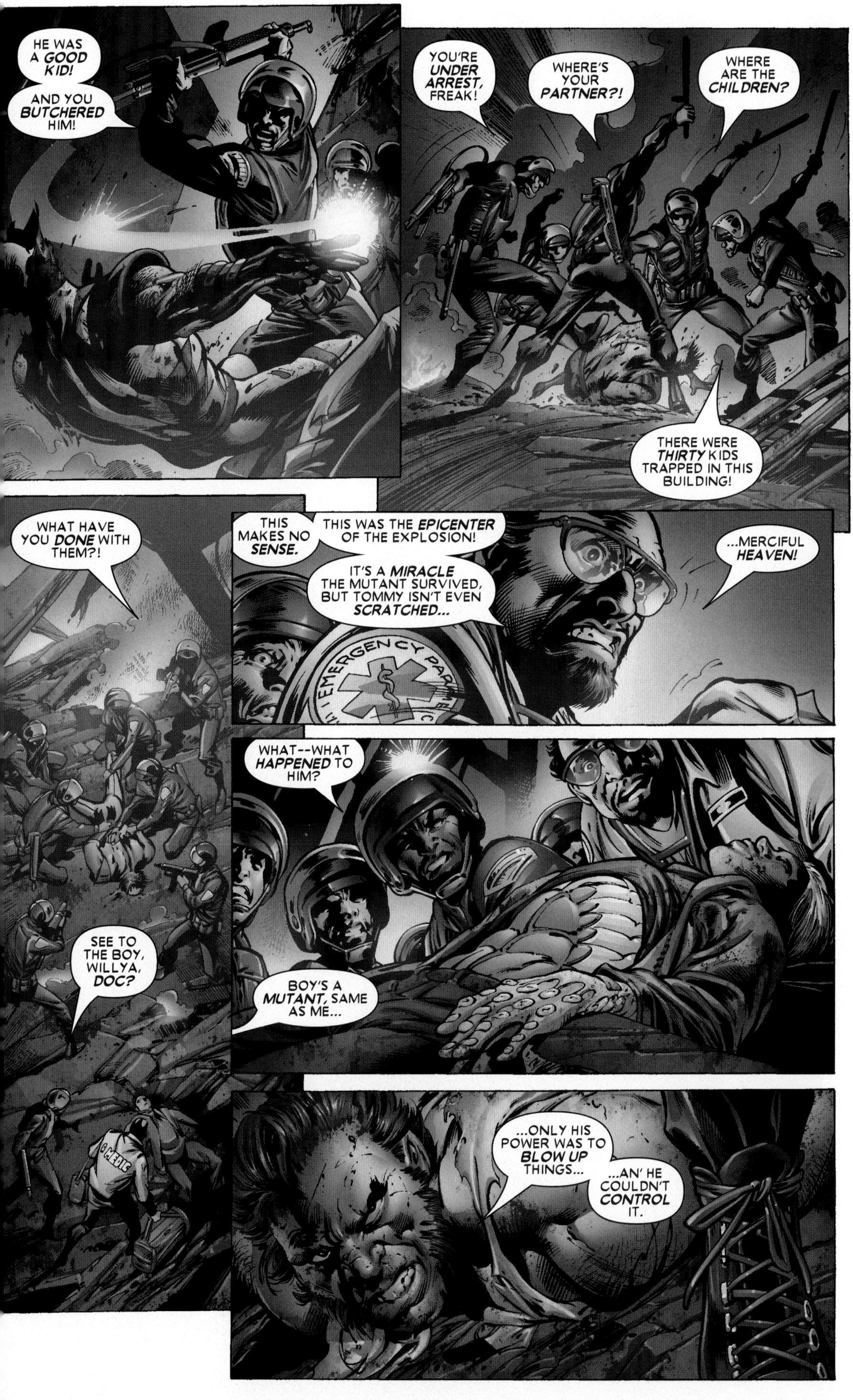
HE WAS A GOOD KID!
AND YOU BUTCHERED HIM!
YOU'RE UNDER ARREST, FREAK!
WHERE'S YOUR PARTNER?!
WHERE ARE THE CHILDREN?
THERE WERE THIRTY KIDS TRAPPED IN THIS BUILDING!
WHAT HAVE YOU DONE WITH THEM?!
THIS MAKES NO SENSE.
THIS WAS THE EPICENTER OF THE EXPLOSION!
IT'S A MIRACLE THE MUTANT SURVIVED, BUT TOMMY ISN'T EVEN SCRATCHED...
...MERCIFUL HEAVEN!
SEE TO THE BOY, WILLYA, DOC?
WHAT--WHAT HAPPENED TO HIM?
BOY'S A MUTANT, SAME AS ME...
...ONLY HIS POWER WAS TO BLOW UP THINGS...
...AN' HE COULDN'T CONTROL IT.

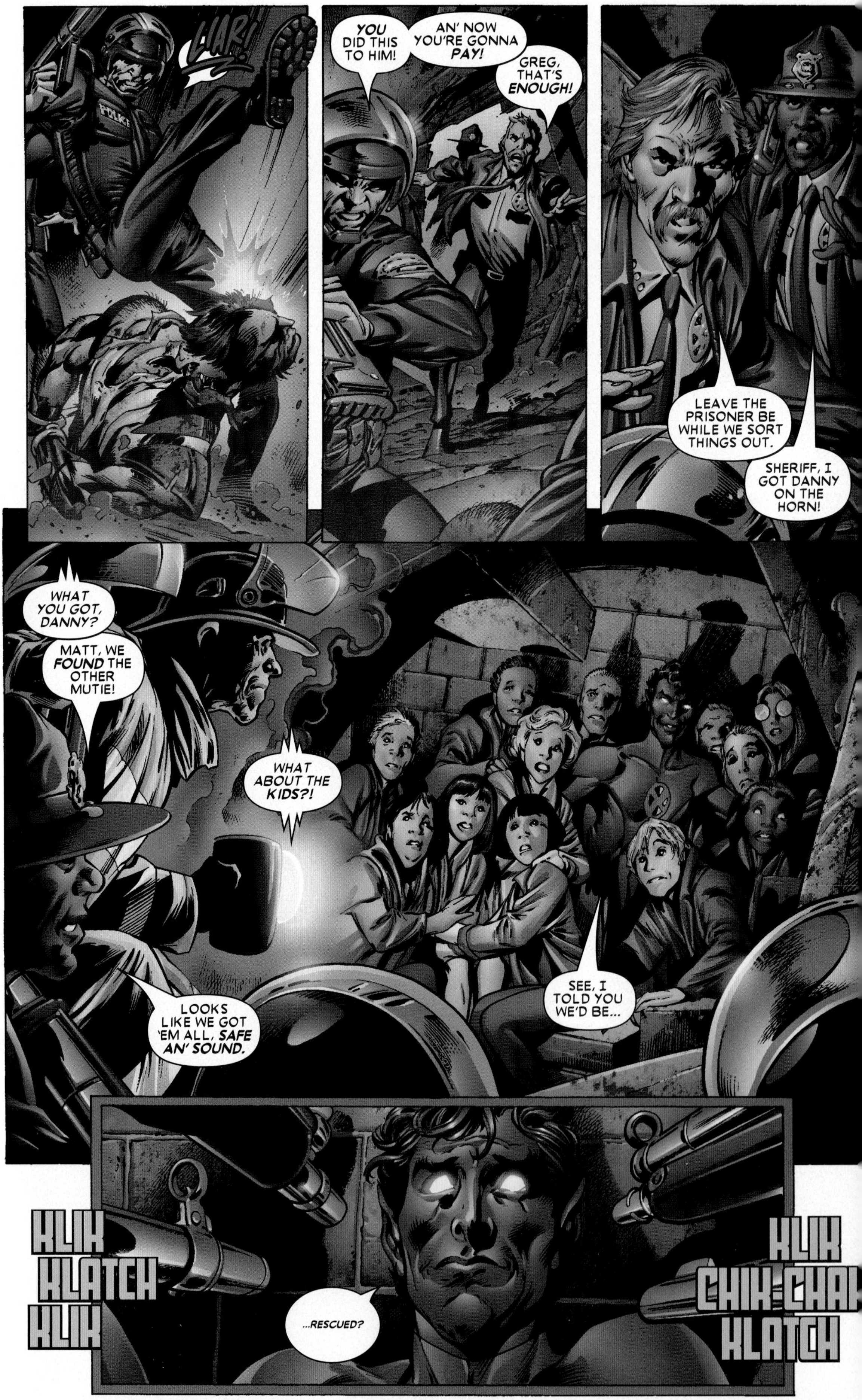
LIAR!
YOU DID THIS TO HIM!
AN' NOW YOU'RE GONNA PAY!
GREG, THAT'S ENOUGH!
LEAVE THE PRISONER BE WHILE WE SORT THINGS OUT.
SHERIFF, I GOT DANNY ON THE HORN!
WHAT YOU GOT, DANNY?
MATT, WE FOUND THE OTHER MUTIE!
WHAT ABOUT THE KIDS?!
LOOKS LIKE WE GOT 'EM ALL, SAFE AN' SOUND.
SEE, I TOLD YOU WE'D BE...
KLIK KLATCH KLIK
KLIK CHIK-CHAK KLATCH
...RESCUED?

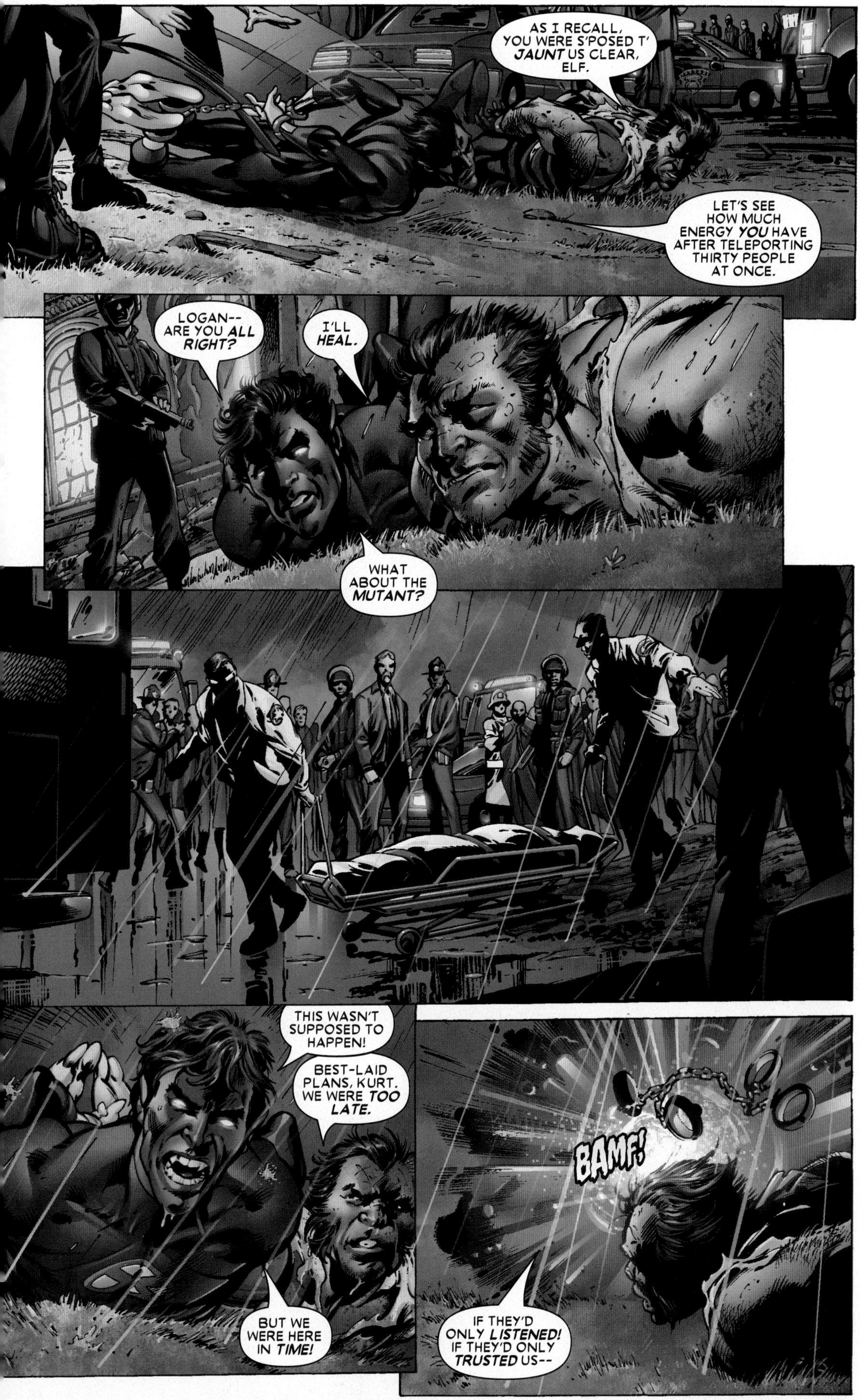
AS I RECALL, YOU WERE S'POSED T' *JAUNT* US CLEAR, ELF.
LET'S SEE HOW MUCH ENERGY *YOU* HAVE AFTER TELEPORTING THIRTY PEOPLE AT ONCE.
LOGAN-- ARE YOU *ALL RIGHT?*
I'LL *HEAL.*
WHAT ABOUT THE *MUTANT?*
THIS WASN'T SUPPOSED TO HAPPEN!
BEST-LAID PLANS, KURT. WE WERE *TOO LATE.*
BUT WE WERE HERE IN *TIME!*
BAMF!
IF THEY'D ONLY *LISTENED!* IF THEY'D ONLY *TRUSTED* US--

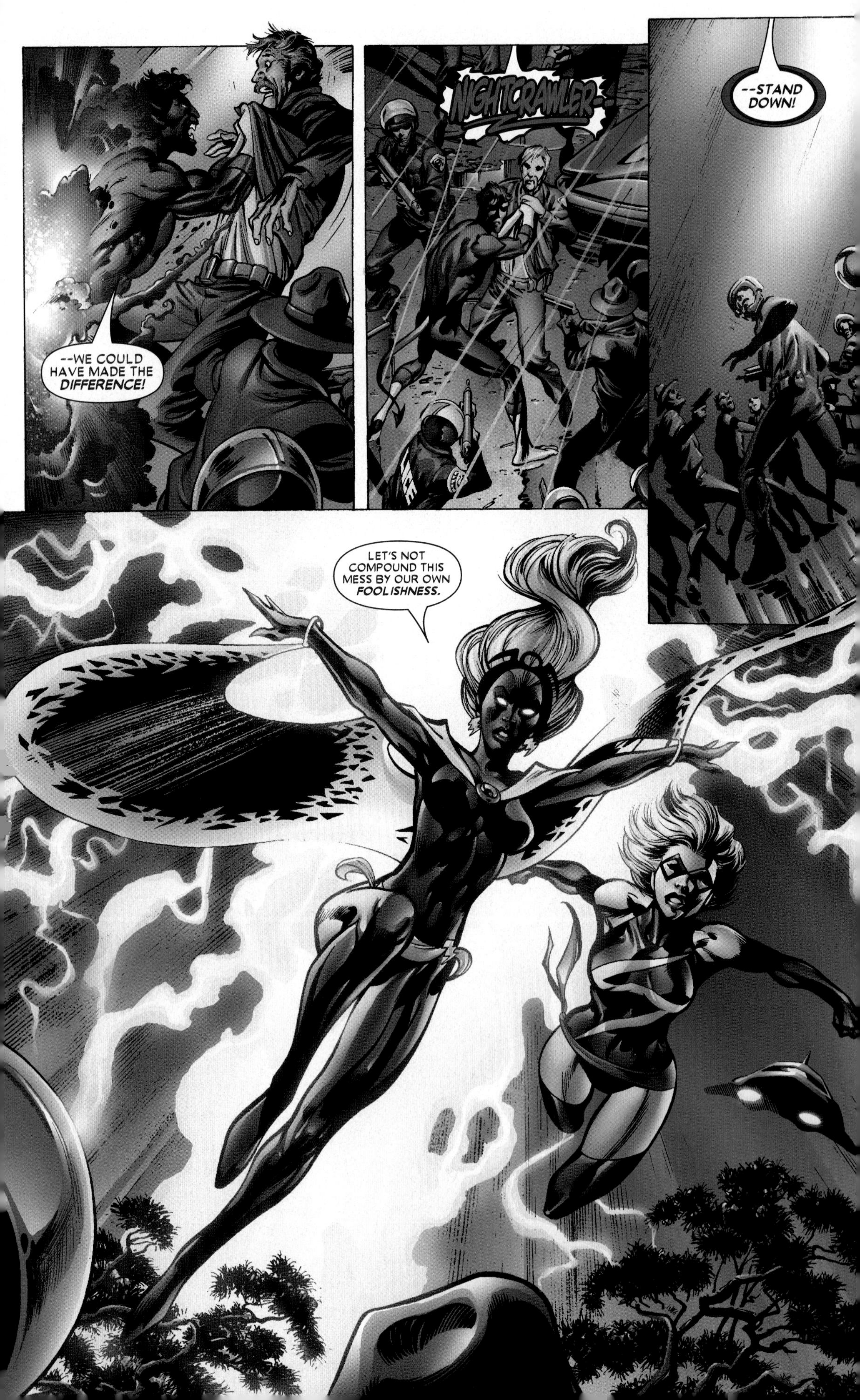
--WE COULD HAVE MADE THE *DIFFERENCE!*
NIGHTCRAWLER--
--STAND DOWN!
LET'S NOT COMPOUND THIS MESS BY OUR OWN *FOOLISHNESS.*

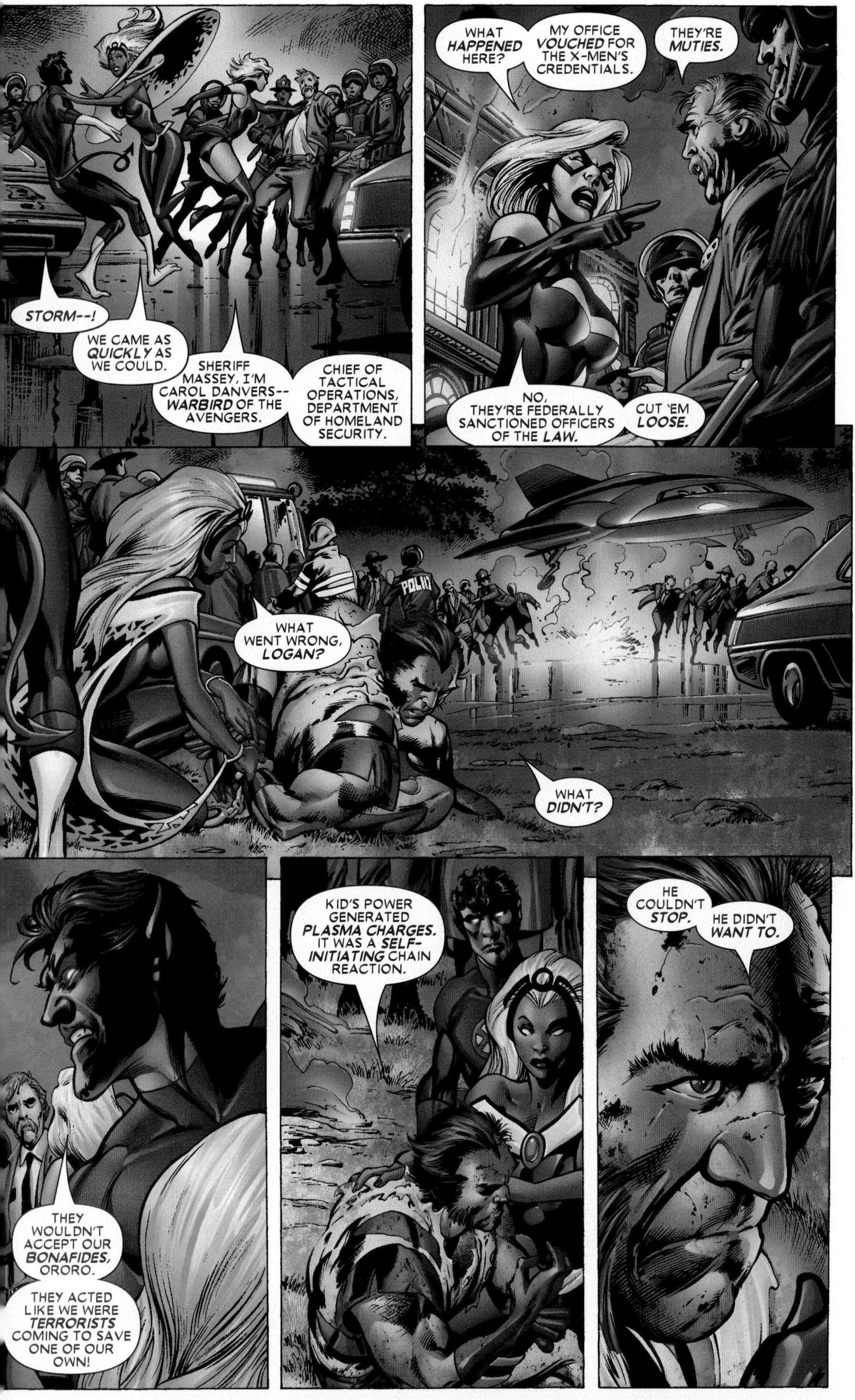
STORM--!
WE CAME AS QUICKLY AS WE COULD.
SHERIFF MASSEY, I'M CAROL DANVERS-- WARBIRD OF THE AVENGERS.
CHIEF OF TACTICAL OPERATIONS, DEPARTMENT OF HOMELAND SECURITY.
WHAT HAPPENED HERE?
MY OFFICE VOUCHED FOR THE X-MEN'S CREDENTIALS.
THEY'RE MUTIES.
NO, THEY'RE FEDERALLY SANCTIONED OFFICERS OF THE LAW.
CUT 'EM LOOSE.
POLICE
WHAT WENT WRONG, LOGAN?
WHAT DIDN'T?
THEY WOULDN'T ACCEPT OUR BONAFIDES, ORORO.
THEY ACTED LIKE WE WERE TERRORISTS COMING TO SAVE ONE OF OUR OWN!
KID'S POWER GENERATED PLASMA CHARGES. IT WAS A SELF-INITIATING CHAIN REACTION.
HE COULDN'T STOP.
HE DIDN'T WANT TO.

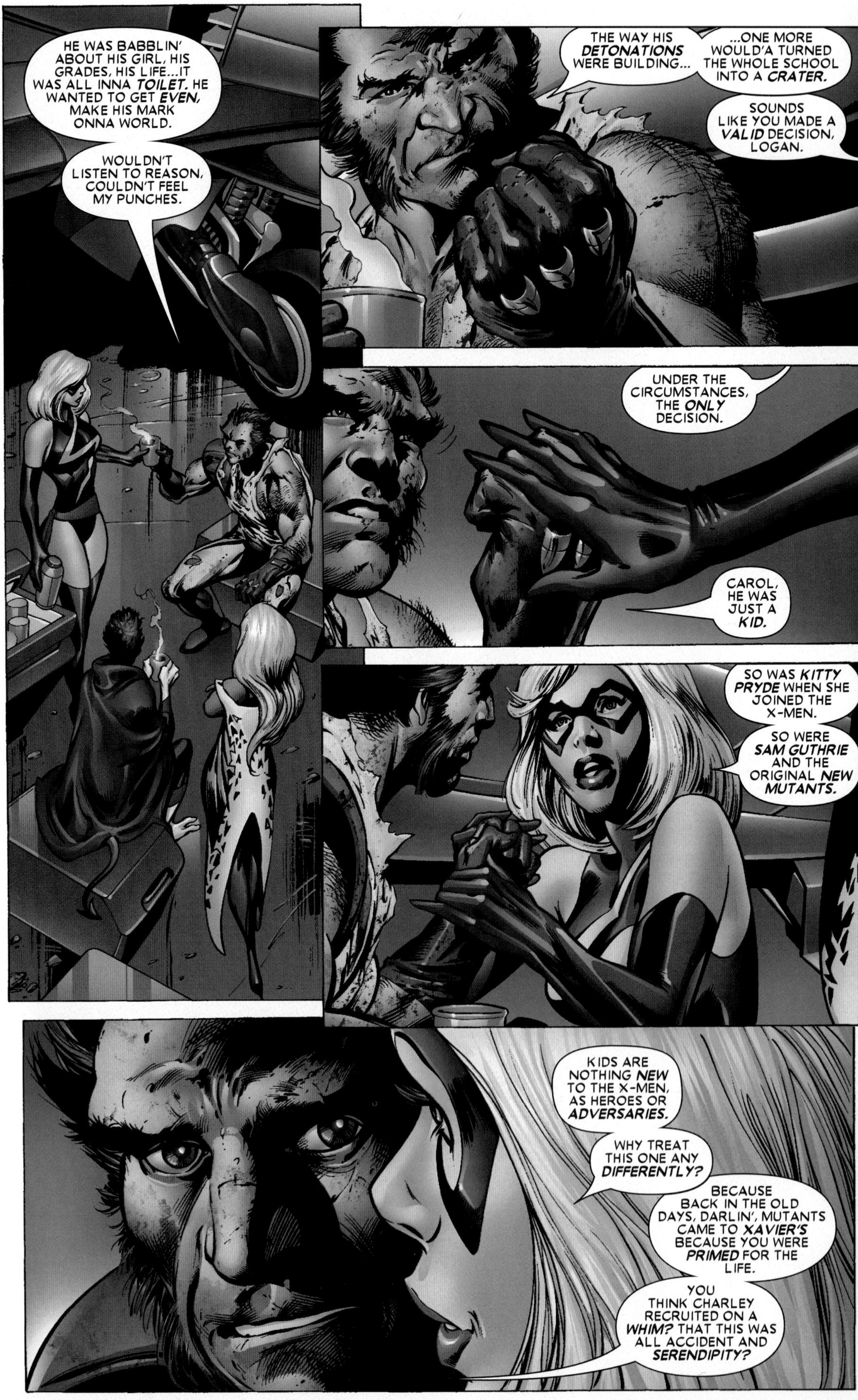
HE WAS BABBLIN' ABOUT HIS GIRL, HIS GRADES, HIS LIFE...IT WAS ALL INNA TOILET. HE WANTED TO GET EVEN, MAKE HIS MARK ONNA WORLD.
WOULDN'T LISTEN TO REASON, COULDN'T FEEL MY PUNCHES.
THE WAY HIS DETONATIONS WERE BUILDING...
...ONE MORE WOULD'A TURNED THE WHOLE SCHOOL INTO A CRATER.
SOUNDS LIKE YOU MADE A VALID DECISION, LOGAN.
UNDER THE CIRCUMSTANCES, THE ONLY DECISION.
CAROL, HE WAS JUST A KID.
SO WAS KITTY PRYDE WHEN SHE JOINED THE X-MEN.
SO WERE SAM GUTHRIE AND THE ORIGINAL NEW MUTANTS.
KIDS ARE NOTHING NEW TO THE X-MEN, AS HEROES OR ADVERSARIES.
WHY TREAT THIS ONE ANY DIFFERENTLY?
BECAUSE BACK IN THE OLD DAYS, DARLIN', MUTANTS CAME TO XAVIER'S BECAUSE YOU WERE PRIMED FOR THE LIFE.
YOU THINK CHARLEY RECRUITED ON A WHIM? THAT THIS WAS ALL ACCIDENT AND SERENDIPITY?

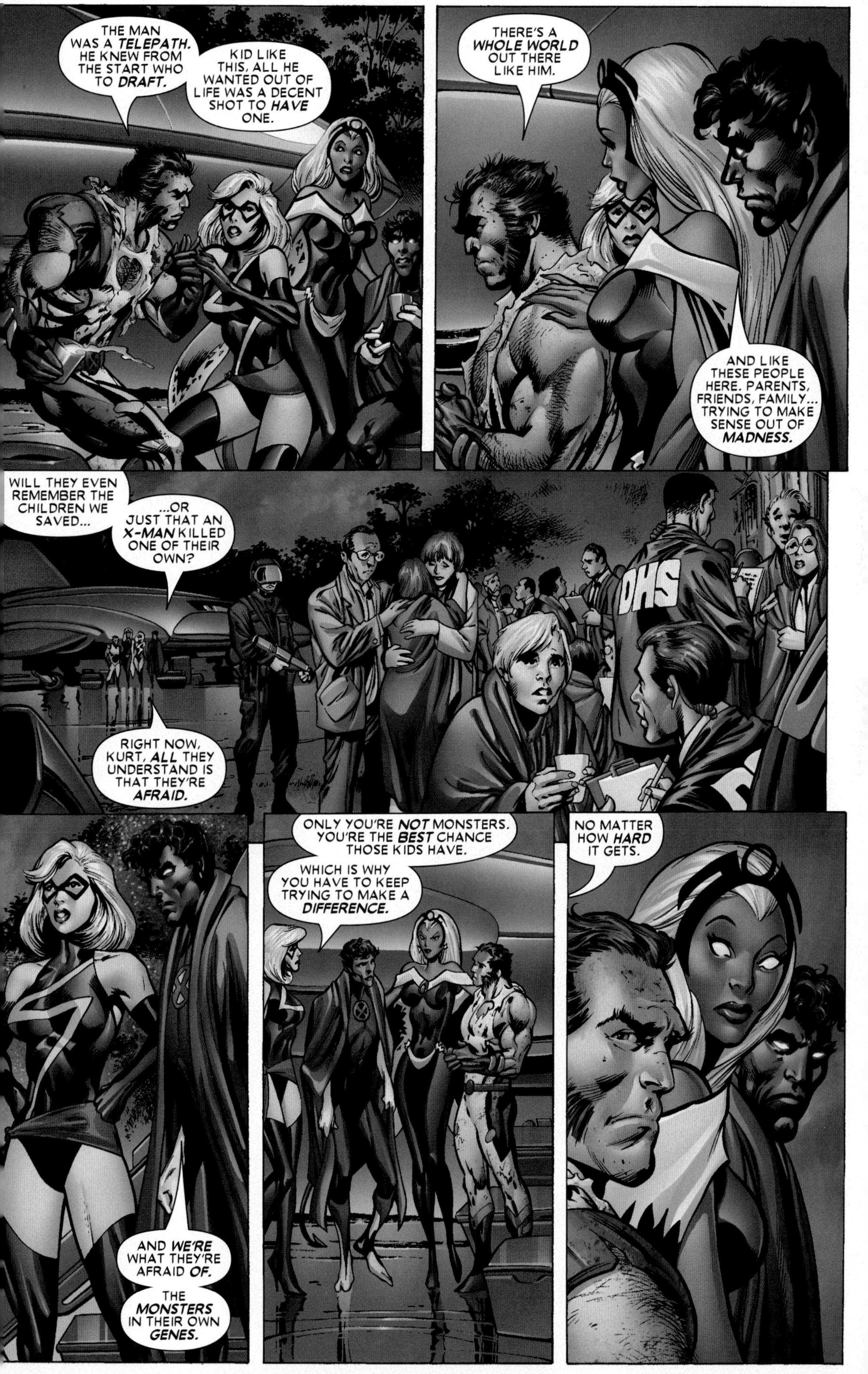
THE MAN WAS A *TELEPATH.* HE KNEW FROM THE START WHO TO *DRAFT.*
KID LIKE THIS, ALL HE WANTED OUT OF LIFE WAS A DECENT SHOT TO *HAVE* ONE.
THERE'S A *WHOLE WORLD* OUT THERE LIKE HIM.
AND LIKE THESE PEOPLE HERE. PARENTS, FRIENDS, FAMILY... TRYING TO MAKE SENSE OUT OF *MADNESS.*
WILL THEY EVEN REMEMBER THE CHILDREN WE SAVED...
...OR JUST THAT AN *X-MAN* KILLED ONE OF THEIR OWN?
RIGHT NOW, KURT, *ALL* THEY UNDERSTAND IS THAT THEY'RE *AFRAID.*
DHS
AND *WE'RE* WHAT THEY'RE AFRAID *OF.*
THE *MONSTERS* IN THEIR OWN *GENES.*
ONLY YOU'RE *NOT* MONSTERS. YOU'RE THE *BEST* CHANCE THOSE KIDS HAVE.
WHICH IS WHY YOU HAVE TO KEEP TRYING TO MAKE A *DIFFERENCE.*
NO MATTER HOW *HARD* IT GETS.

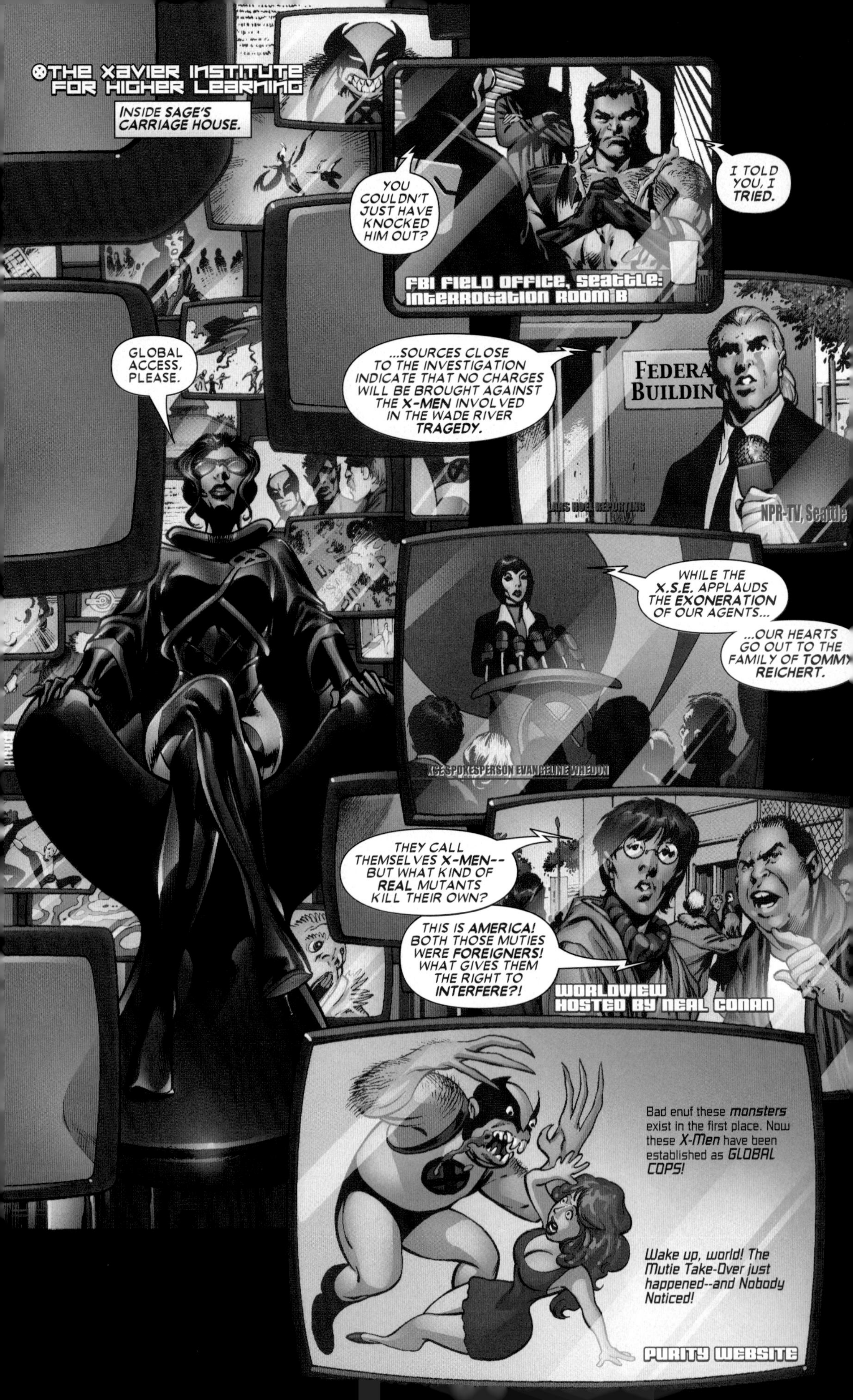
THE XAVIER INSTITUTE FOR HIGHER LEARNING
INSIDE SAGE'S CARRIAGE HOUSE.
YOU COULDN'T JUST HAVE KNOCKED HIM OUT?
I TOLD YOU, I TRIED.
FBI FIELD OFFICE, SEATTLE: INTERROGATION ROOM B
GLOBAL ACCESS, PLEASE.
...SOURCES CLOSE TO THE INVESTIGATION INDICATE THAT NO CHARGES WILL BE BROUGHT AGAINST THE X-MEN INVOLVED IN THE WADE RIVER TRAGEDY.
FEDERA BUILDIN
LARS HOEL REPORTING
NPR-TV, Seattle
WHILE THE X.S.E. APPLAUDS THE EXONERATION OF OUR AGENTS...
...OUR HEARTS GO OUT TO THE FAMILY OF TOMMY REICHERT.
XSE SPOKESPERSON EVANGELINE WHEDON
THEY CALL THEMSELVES X-MEN-- BUT WHAT KIND OF REAL MUTANTS KILL THEIR OWN?
THIS IS AMERICA! BOTH THOSE MUTIES WERE FOREIGNERS! WHAT GIVES THEM THE RIGHT TO INTERFERE?!
WORLDVIEW HOSTED BY NEAL CONAN
Bad enuf these monsters exist in the first place. Now these X-Men have been established as GLOBAL COPS!
Wake up, world! The Mutie Take-Over just happened--and Nobody Noticed!
PURITY WEBSITE

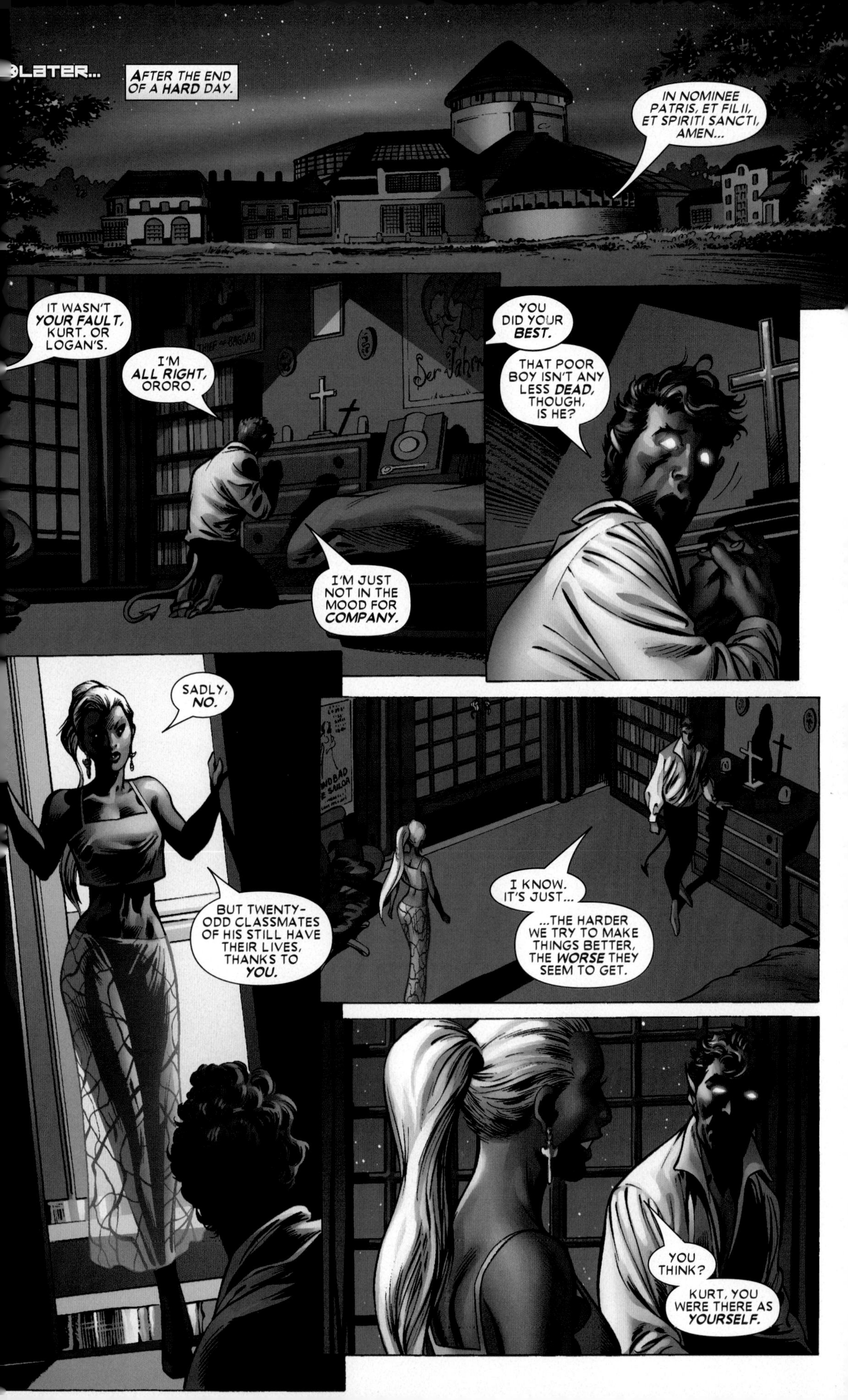
LATER...
AFTER THE END OF A HARD DAY.
IN NOMINEE PATRIS, ET FILII, ET SPIRITI SANCTI, AMEN...
IT WASN'T YOUR FAULT, KURT. OR LOGAN'S.
I'M ALL RIGHT, ORORO.
I'M JUST NOT IN THE MOOD FOR COMPANY.
YOU DID YOUR BEST.
THAT POOR BOY ISN'T ANY LESS DEAD, THOUGH, IS HE?
SADLY, NO.
BUT TWENTY-ODD CLASSMATES OF HIS STILL HAVE THEIR LIVES, THANKS TO YOU.
I KNOW. IT'S JUST...
...THE HARDER WE TRY TO MAKE THINGS BETTER, THE WORSE THEY SEEM TO GET.
YOU THINK?
KURT, YOU WERE THERE AS YOURSELF.

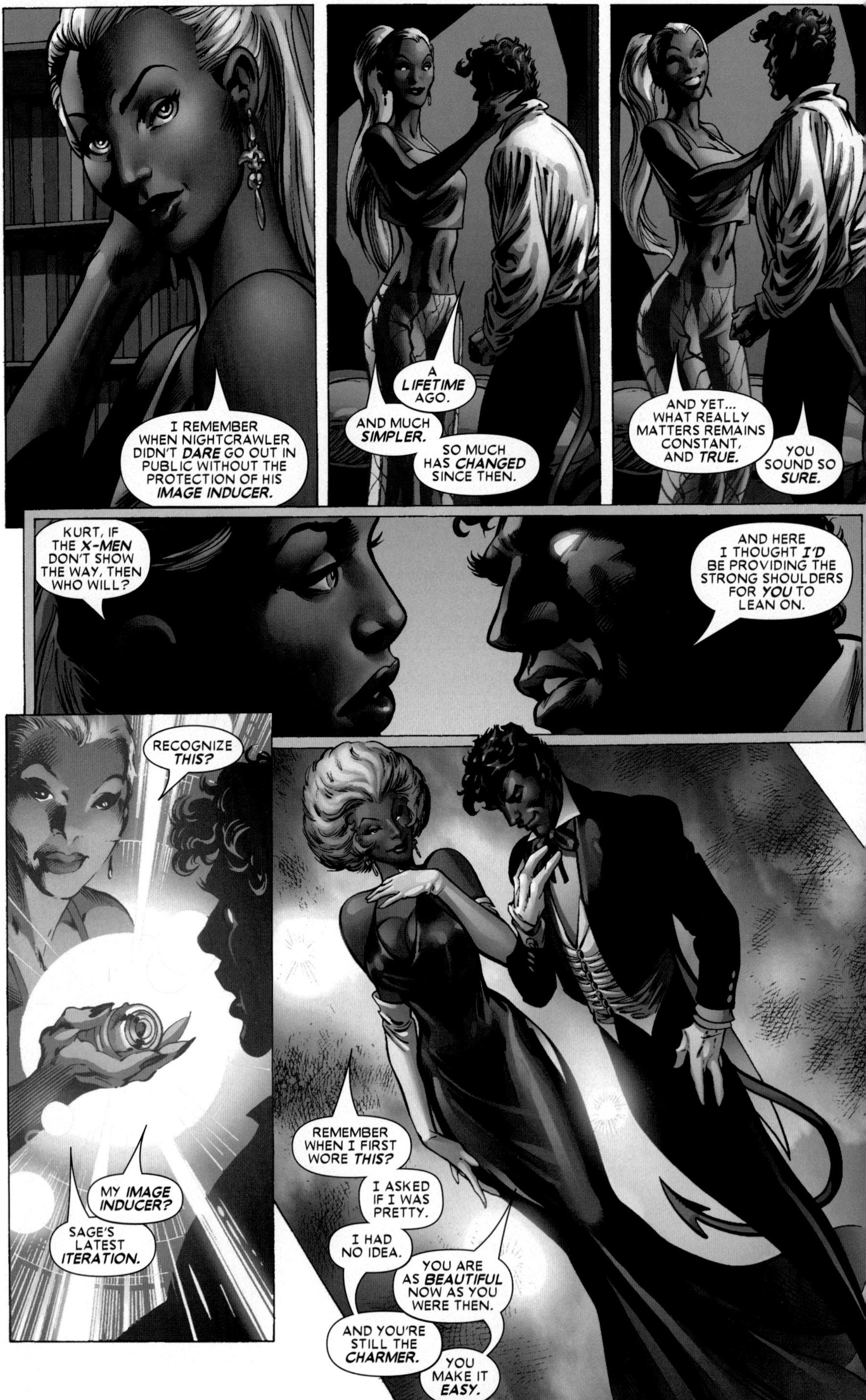
I REMEMBER WHEN NIGHTCRAWLER DIDN'T DARE GO OUT IN PUBLIC WITHOUT THE PROTECTION OF HIS IMAGE INDUCER.
A LIFETIME AGO.
AND MUCH SIMPLER.
SO MUCH HAS CHANGED SINCE THEN.
AND YET... WHAT REALLY MATTERS REMAINS CONSTANT, AND TRUE.
YOU SOUND SO SURE.
KURT, IF THE X-MEN DON'T SHOW THE WAY, THEN WHO WILL?
AND HERE I THOUGHT I'D BE PROVIDING THE STRONG SHOULDERS FOR YOU TO LEAN ON.
RECOGNIZE THIS?
MY IMAGE INDUCER?
SAGE'S LATEST ITERATION.
REMEMBER WHEN I FIRST WORE THIS?
I ASKED IF I WAS PRETTY.
I HAD NO IDEA.
YOU ARE AS BEAUTIFUL NOW AS YOU WERE THEN.
AND YOU'RE STILL THE CHARMER.
YOU MAKE IT EASY.

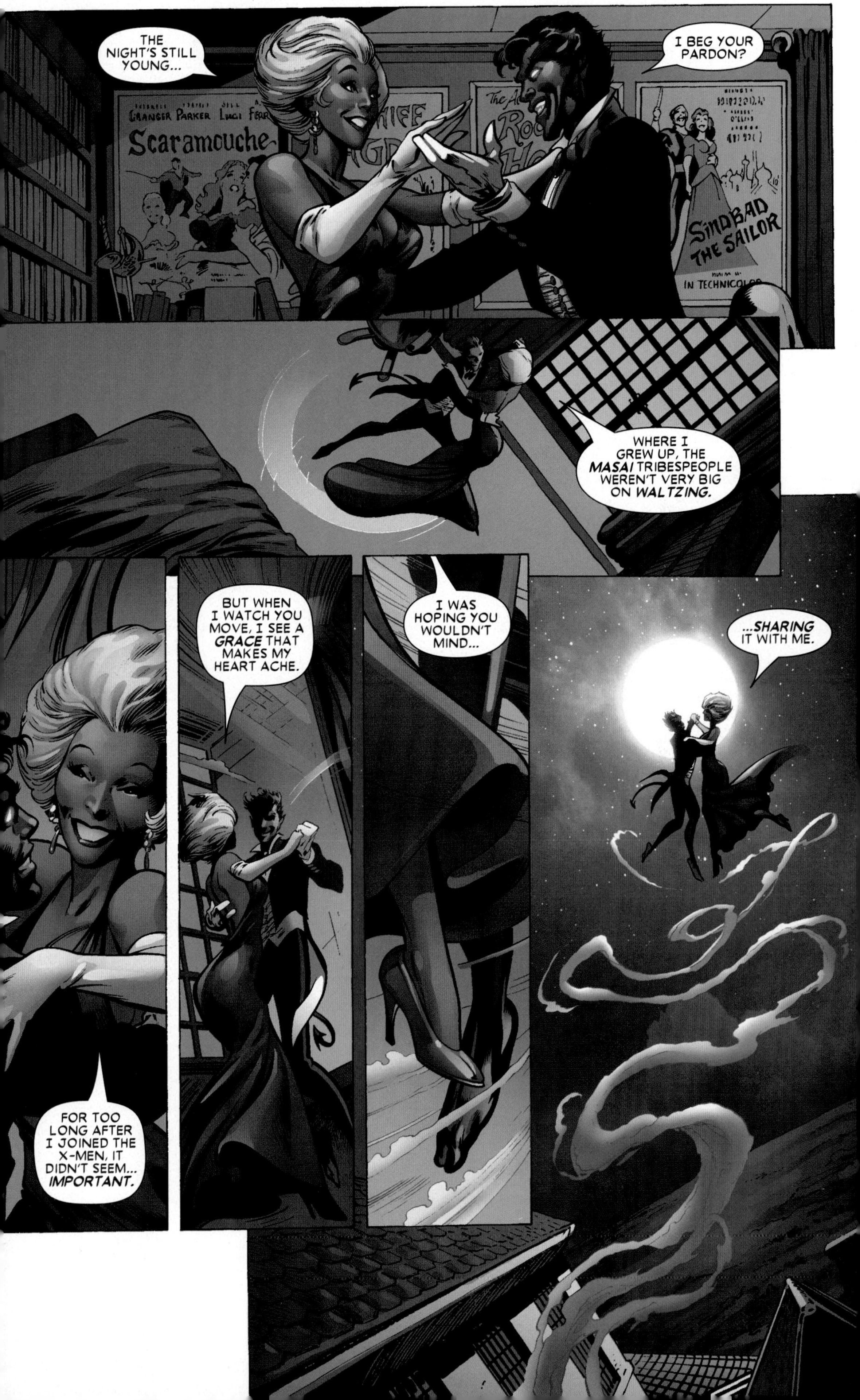
THE NIGHT'S STILL YOUNG...
I BEG YOUR PARDON?
Scaramouche
SINDBAD THE SAILOR
WHERE I GREW UP, THE *MASAI* TRIBESPEOPLE WEREN'T VERY BIG ON *WALTZING.*
FOR TOO LONG AFTER I JOINED THE X-MEN, IT DIDN'T SEEM... ***IMPORTANT.***
BUT WHEN I WATCH YOU MOVE, I SEE A *GRACE* THAT MAKES MY HEART ACHE.
I WAS HOPING YOU WOULDN'T MIND...
...*SHARING* IT WITH ME.

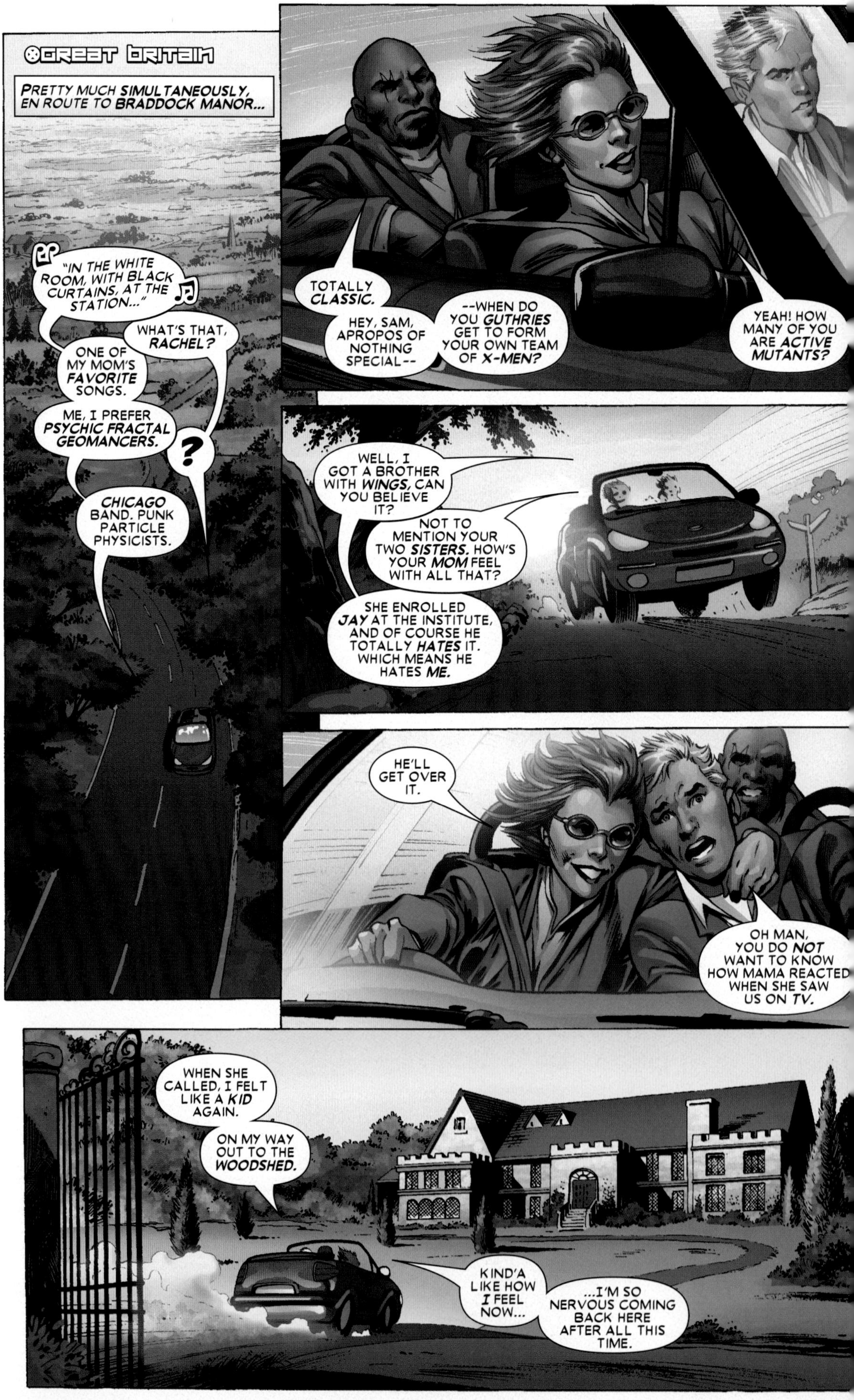
GREAT BRITAIN
PRETTY MUCH SIMULTANEOUSLY, EN ROUTE TO BRADDOCK MANOR...
"IN THE WHITE ROOM, WITH BLACK CURTAINS, AT THE STATION..."
WHAT'S THAT, RACHEL?
ONE OF MY MOM'S FAVORITE SONGS.
ME, I PREFER PSYCHIC FRACTAL GEOMANCERS.
?
CHICAGO BAND. PUNK PARTICLE PHYSICISTS.
TOTALLY CLASSIC.
HEY, SAM, APROPOS OF NOTHING SPECIAL--
--WHEN DO YOU GUTHRIES GET TO FORM YOUR OWN TEAM OF X-MEN?
YEAH! HOW MANY OF YOU ARE ACTIVE MUTANTS?
WELL, I GOT A BROTHER WITH WINGS, CAN YOU BELIEVE IT?
NOT TO MENTION YOUR TWO SISTERS. HOW'S YOUR MOM FEEL WITH ALL THAT?
SHE ENROLLED JAY AT THE INSTITUTE, AND OF COURSE HE TOTALLY HATES IT. WHICH MEANS HE HATES ME.
HE'LL GET OVER IT.
OH MAN, YOU DO NOT WANT TO KNOW HOW MAMA REACTED WHEN SHE SAW US ON TV.
WHEN SHE CALLED, I FELT LIKE A KID AGAIN.
ON MY WAY OUT TO THE WOODSHED.
KIND'A LIKE HOW I FEEL NOW...
...I'M SO NERVOUS COMING BACK HERE AFTER ALL THIS TIME.

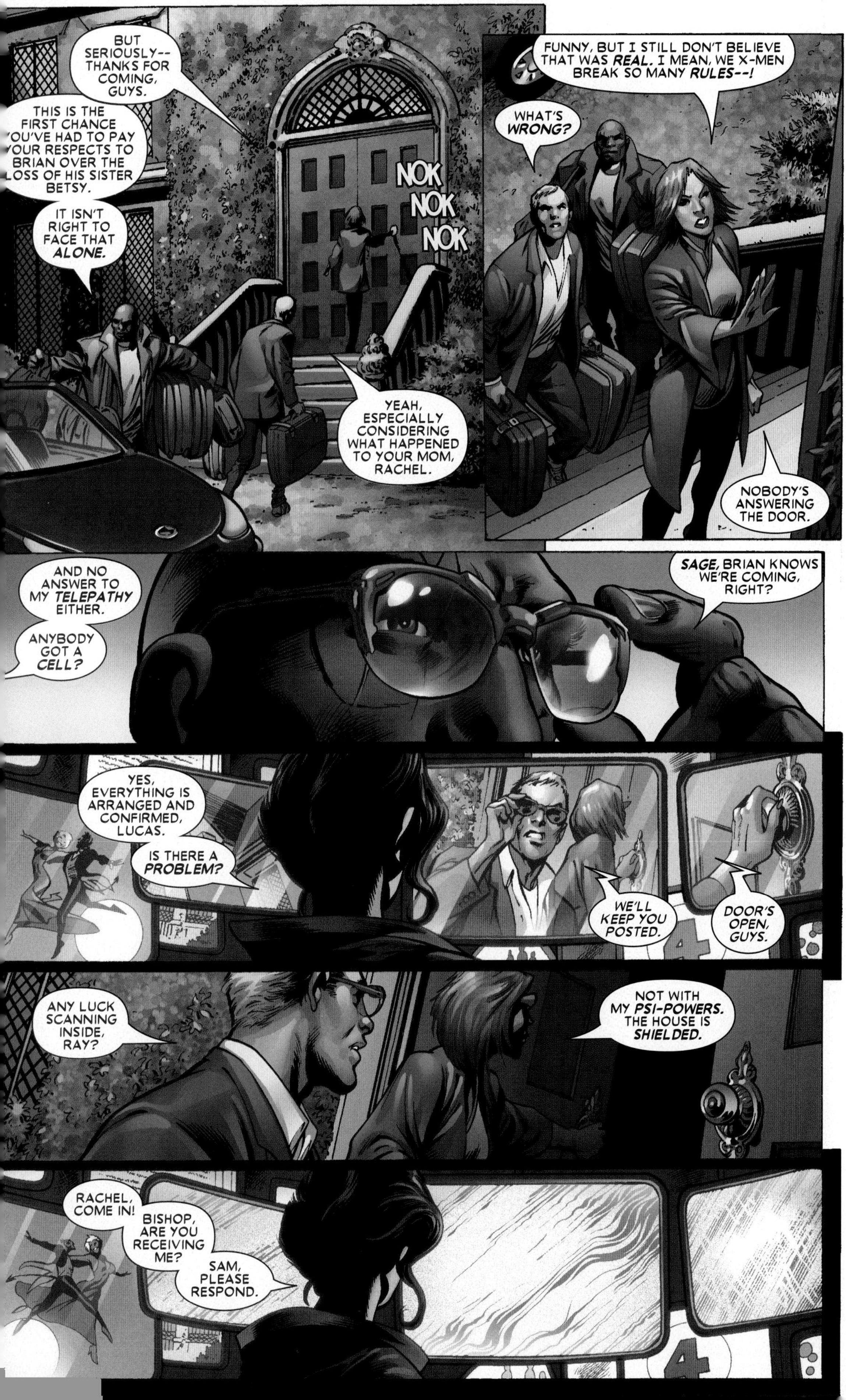
BUT SERIOUSLY--THANKS FOR COMING, GUYS.
THIS IS THE FIRST CHANCE YOU'VE HAD TO PAY YOUR RESPECTS TO BRIAN OVER THE LOSS OF HIS SISTER BETSY.
IT ISN'T RIGHT TO FACE THAT ALONE.
NOK NOK NOK
YEAH, ESPECIALLY CONSIDERING WHAT HAPPENED TO YOUR MOM, RACHEL.
FUNNY, BUT I STILL DON'T BELIEVE THAT WAS REAL. I MEAN, WE X-MEN BREAK SO MANY RULES--!
WHAT'S WRONG?
NOBODY'S ANSWERING THE DOOR.
AND NO ANSWER TO MY TELEPATHY EITHER.
ANYBODY GOT A CELL?
SAGE, BRIAN KNOWS WE'RE COMING, RIGHT?
YES, EVERYTHING IS ARRANGED AND CONFIRMED, LUCAS.
IS THERE A PROBLEM?
WE'LL KEEP YOU POSTED.
DOOR'S OPEN, GUYS.
ANY LUCK SCANNING INSIDE, RAY?
NOT WITH MY PSI-POWERS. THE HOUSE IS SHIELDED.
RACHEL, COME IN!
BISHOP, ARE YOU RECEIVING ME?
SAM, PLEASE RESPOND.

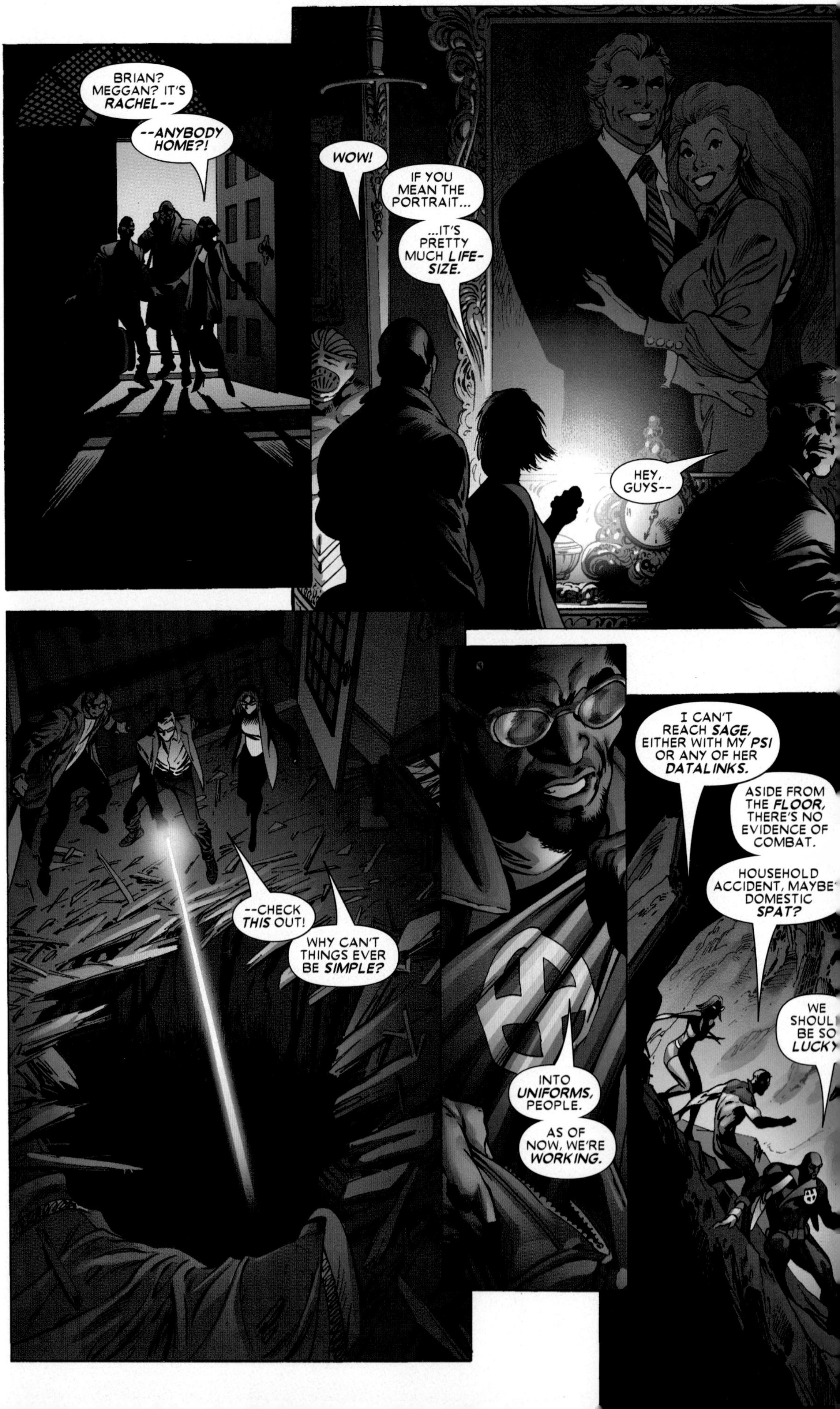
BRIAN? MEGGAN? IT'S RACHEL--
--ANYBODY HOME?!
WOW!
IF YOU MEAN THE PORTRAIT...
...IT'S PRETTY MUCH LIFE-SIZE.
HEY, GUYS--
--CHECK THIS OUT!
WHY CAN'T THINGS EVER BE SIMPLE?
INTO UNIFORMS, PEOPLE.
AS OF NOW, WE'RE WORKING.
I CAN'T REACH SAGE, EITHER WITH MY PSI OR ANY OF HER DATALINKS.
ASIDE FROM THE FLOOR, THERE'S NO EVIDENCE OF COMBAT.
HOUSEHOLD ACCIDENT, MAYBE DOMESTIC SPAT?
WE SHOUL BE SO LUCKY

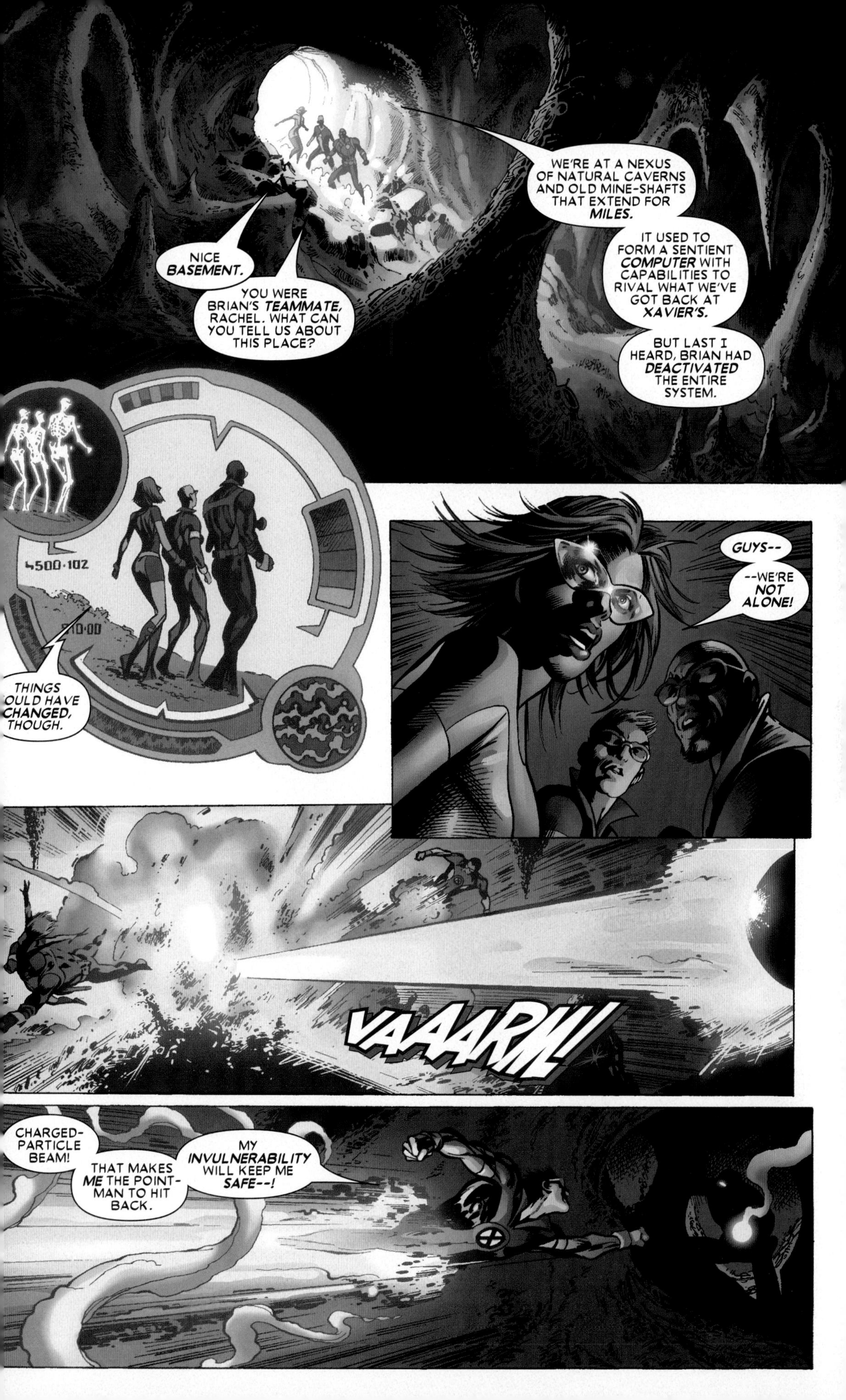
NICE BASEMENT.
YOU WERE BRIAN'S TEAMMATE, RACHEL. WHAT CAN YOU TELL US ABOUT THIS PLACE?
WE'RE AT A NEXUS OF NATURAL CAVERNS AND OLD MINE-SHAFTS THAT EXTEND FOR MILES.
IT USED TO FORM A SENTIENT COMPUTER WITH CAPABILITIES TO RIVAL WHAT WE'VE GOT BACK AT XAVIER'S.
BUT LAST I HEARD, BRIAN HAD DEACTIVATED THE ENTIRE SYSTEM.
4500·102
THINGS OULD HAVE CHANGED, THOUGH.
GUYS--
--WE'RE NOT ALONE!
VAAARM!
CHARGED-PARTICLE BEAM!
THAT MAKES ME THE POINT-MAN TO HIT BACK.
MY INVULNERABILITY WILL KEEP ME SAFE--!

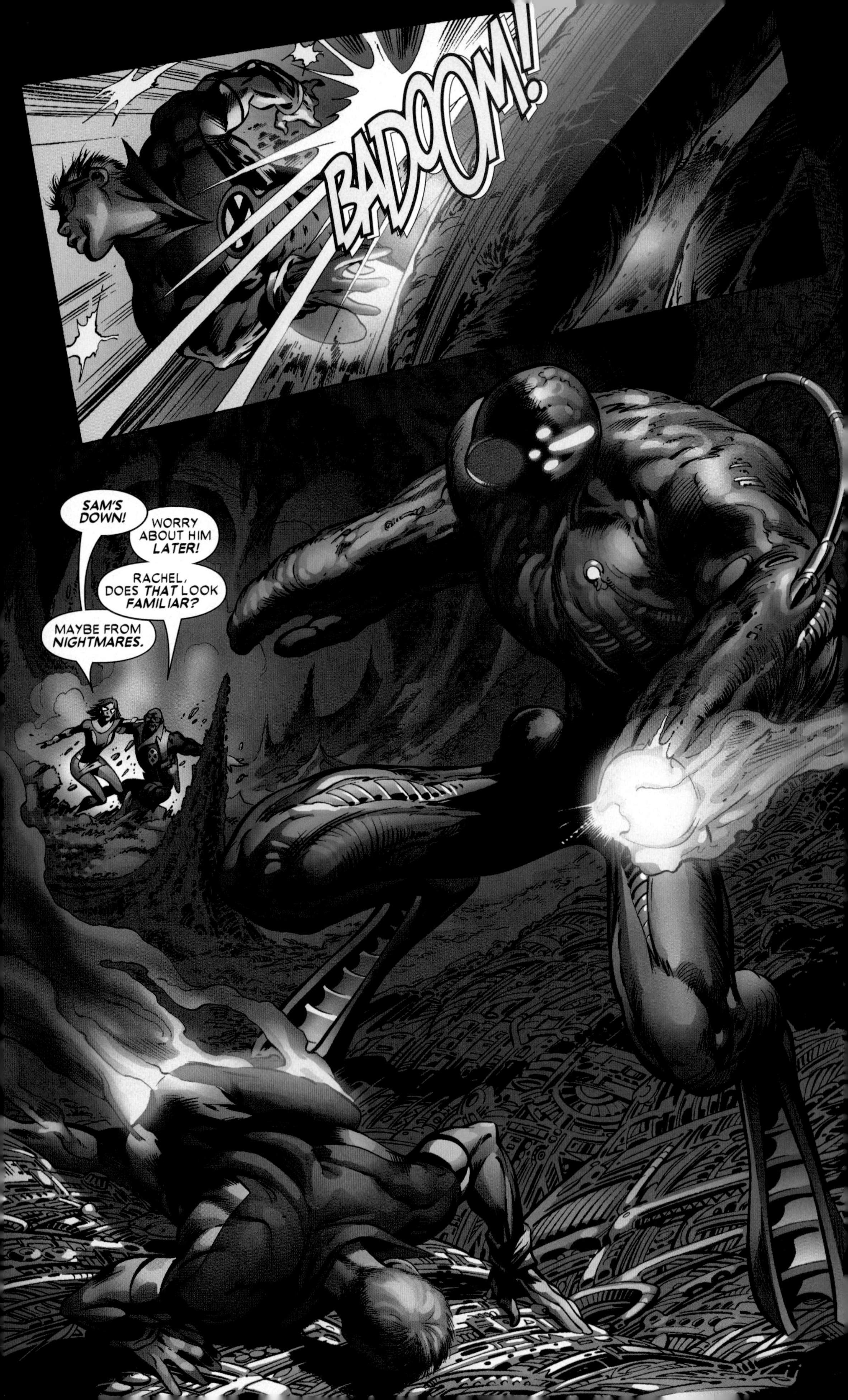

BADOOM!
SAM'S DOWN!
WORRY ABOUT HIM LATER!
RACHEL, DOES THAT LOOK FAMILIAR?
MAYBE FROM NIGHTMARES.

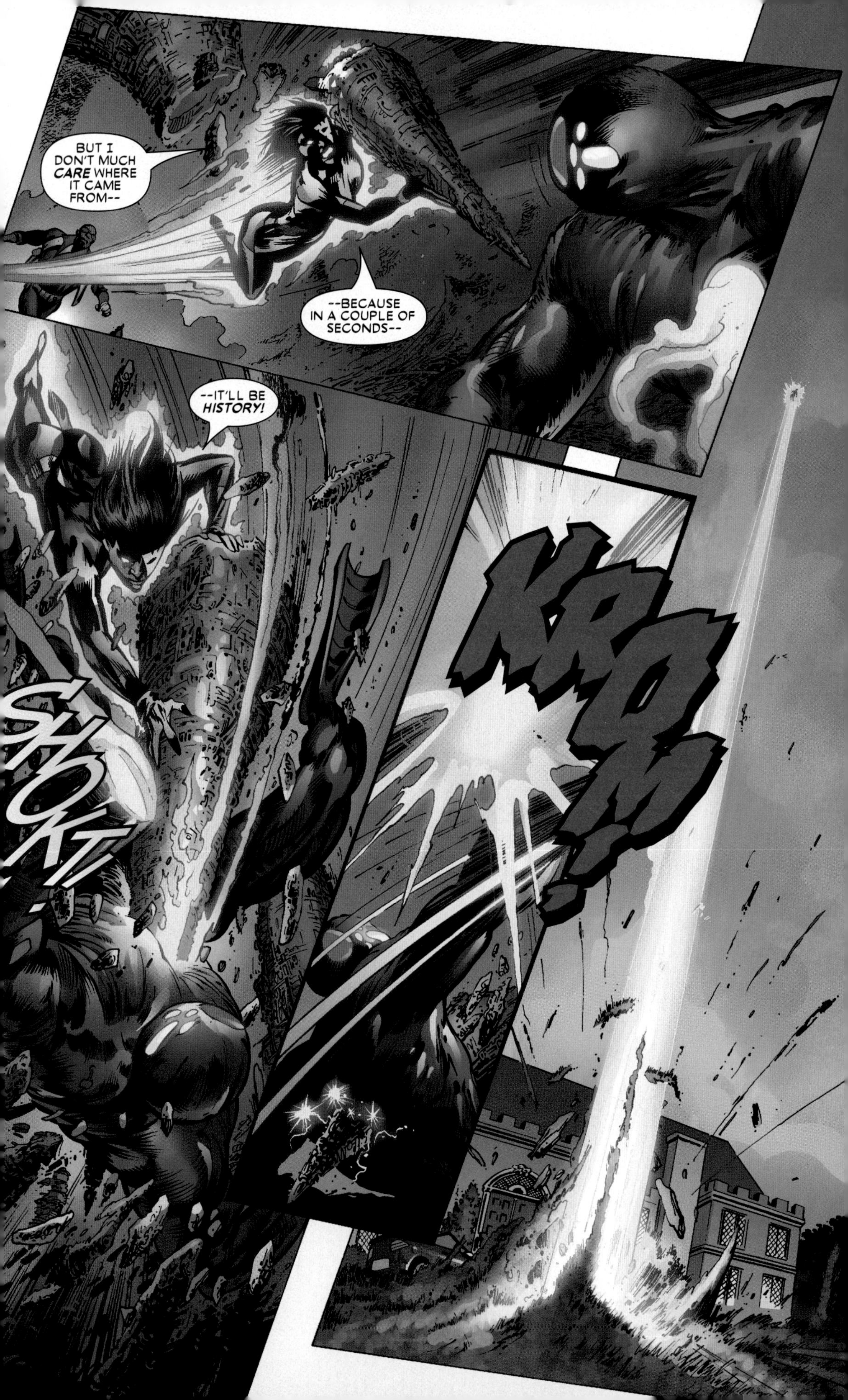
BUT I DON'T MUCH CARE WHERE IT CAME FROM--
--BECAUSE IN A COUPLE OF SECONDS--
--IT'LL BE HISTORY!
SHOK!!
KROOM!!

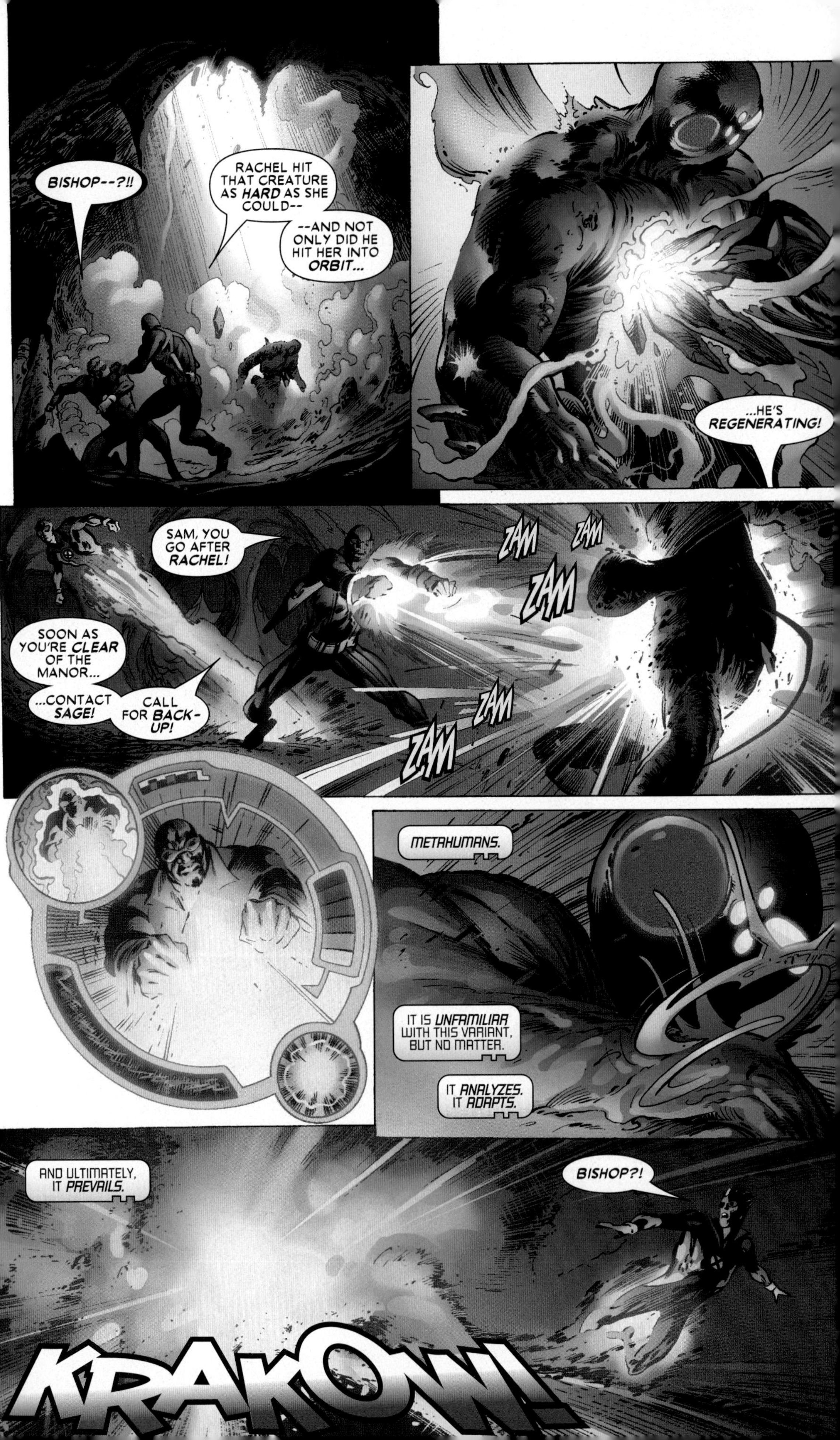
BISHOP--?!!
RACHEL HIT THAT CREATURE AS HARD AS SHE COULD--
--AND NOT ONLY DID HE HIT HER INTO ORBIT...
...HE'S REGENERATING!
SAM, YOU GO AFTER RACHEL!
SOON AS YOU'RE CLEAR OF THE MANOR...
...CONTACT SAGE!
CALL FOR BACK-UP!
ZAM
ZAM
ZAM
ZAM
ZAM
METAHUMANS.
IT IS UNFAMILIAR WITH THIS VARIANT, BUT NO MATTER.
IT ANALYZES. IT ADAPTS.
AND ULTIMATELY, IT PREVAILS.
BISHOP?!
KRAKOW!

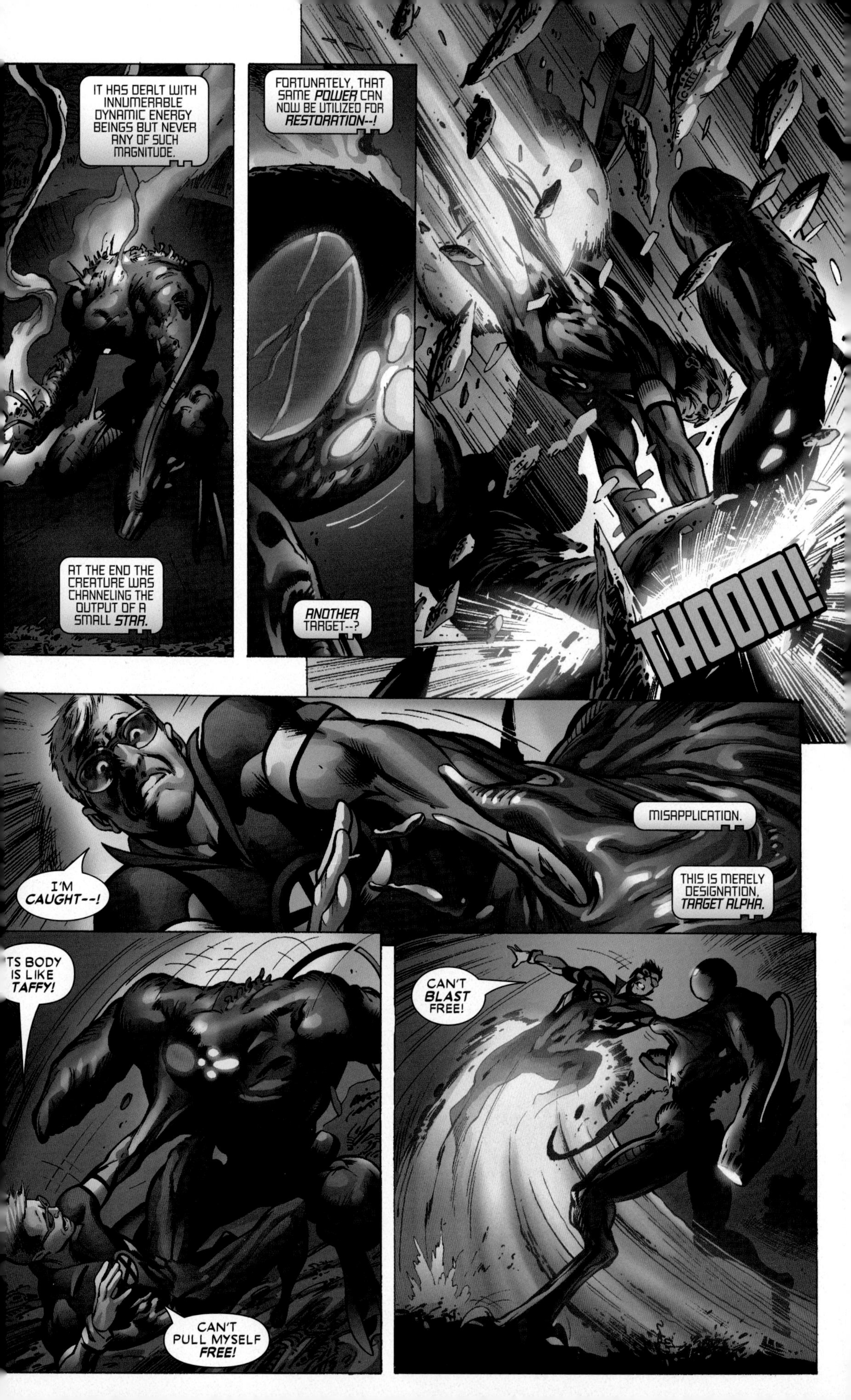
IT HAS DEALT WITH INNUMERABLE DYNAMIC ENERGY BEINGS BUT NEVER ANY OF SUCH MAGNITUDE.
AT THE END THE CREATURE WAS CHANNELING THE OUTPUT OF A SMALL STAR.
FORTUNATELY, THAT SAME POWER CAN NOW BE UTILIZED FOR RESTORATION--!
ANOTHER TARGET--?
THOOM!
I'M CAUGHT--!
MISAPPLICATION.
THIS IS MERELY DESIGNATION, TARGET ALPHA.
TS BODY IS LIKE TAFFY!
CAN'T PULL MYSELF FREE!
CAN'T BLAST FREE!

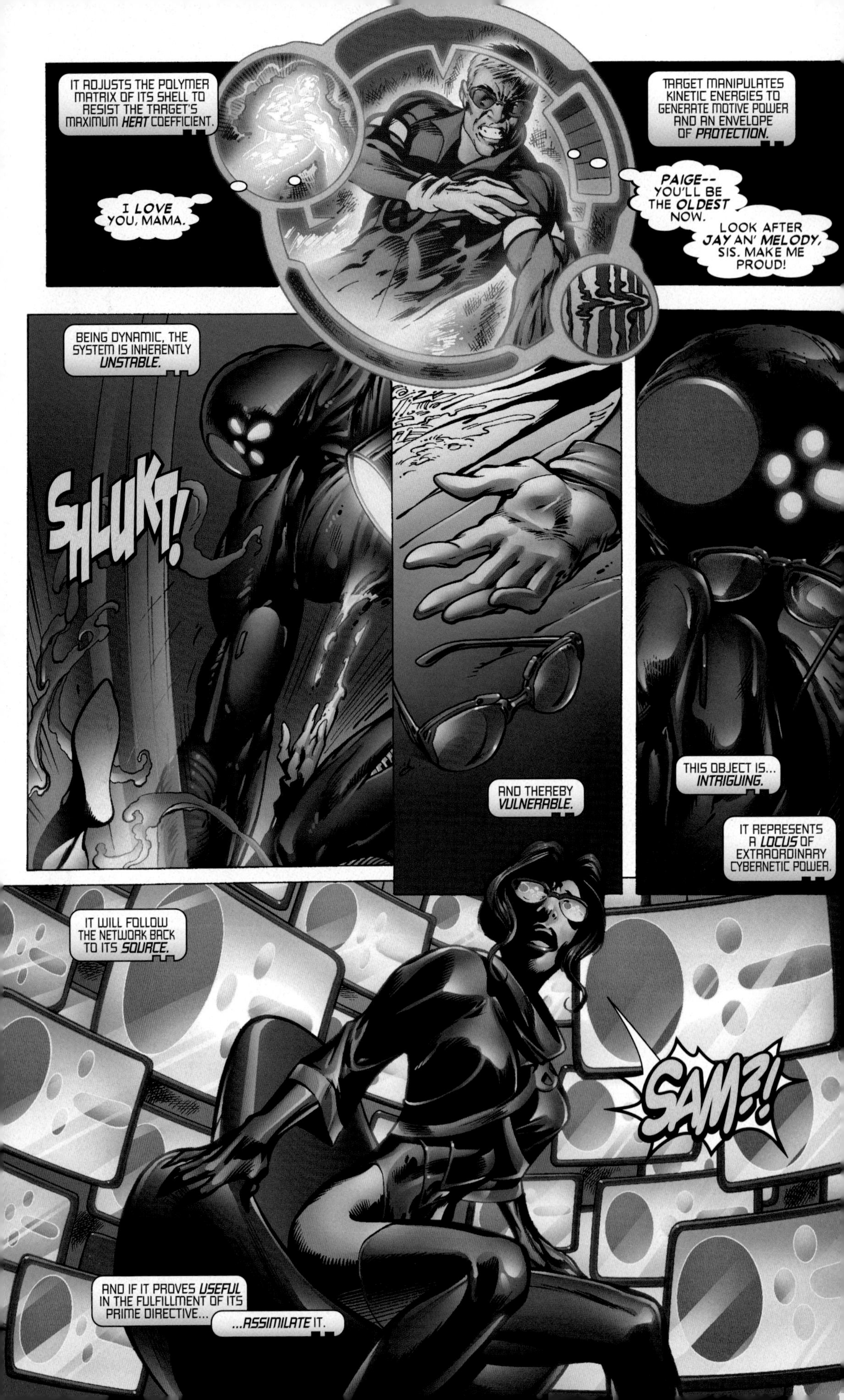
IT ADJUSTS THE POLYMER MATRIX OF ITS SHELL TO RESIST THE TARGET'S MAXIMUM HEAT COEFFICIENT.
TARGET MANIPULATES KINETIC ENERGIES TO GENERATE MOTIVE POWER AND AN ENVELOPE OF PROTECTION.
I LOVE YOU, MAMA.
PAIGE-- YOU'LL BE THE OLDEST NOW.
LOOK AFTER JAY AN' MELODY, SIS. MAKE ME PROUD!
BEING DYNAMIC, THE SYSTEM IS INHERENTLY UNSTABLE.
SHLUKT!
AND THEREBY VULNERABLE.
THIS OBJECT IS... INTRIGUING.
IT REPRESENTS A LOCUS OF EXTRAORDINARY CYBERNETIC POWER.
IT WILL FOLLOW THE NETWORK BACK TO ITS SOURCE.
SAM?!
AND IF IT PROVES USEFUL IN THE FULFILLMENT OF ITS PRIME DIRECTIVE...
...ASSIMILATE IT.

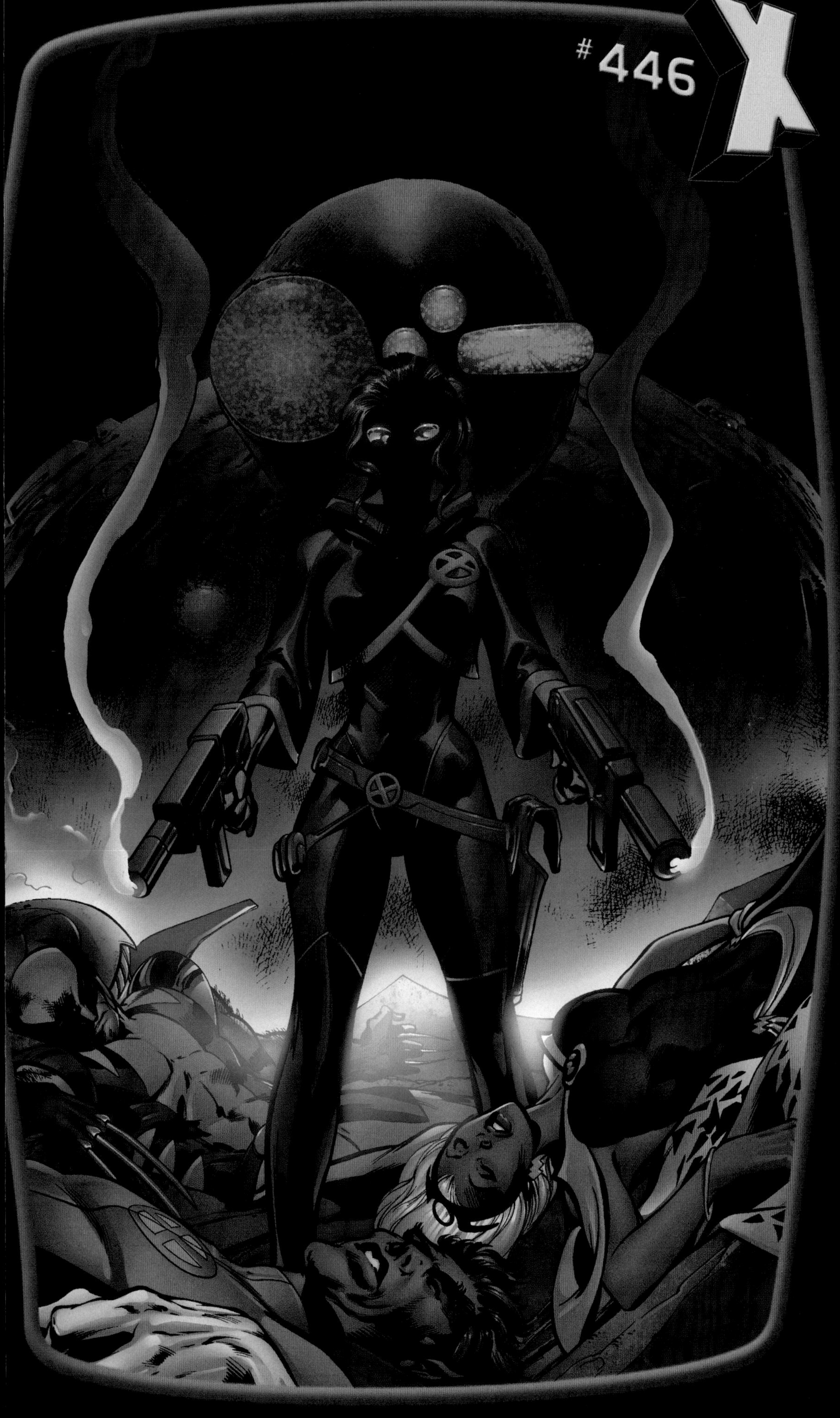
#446

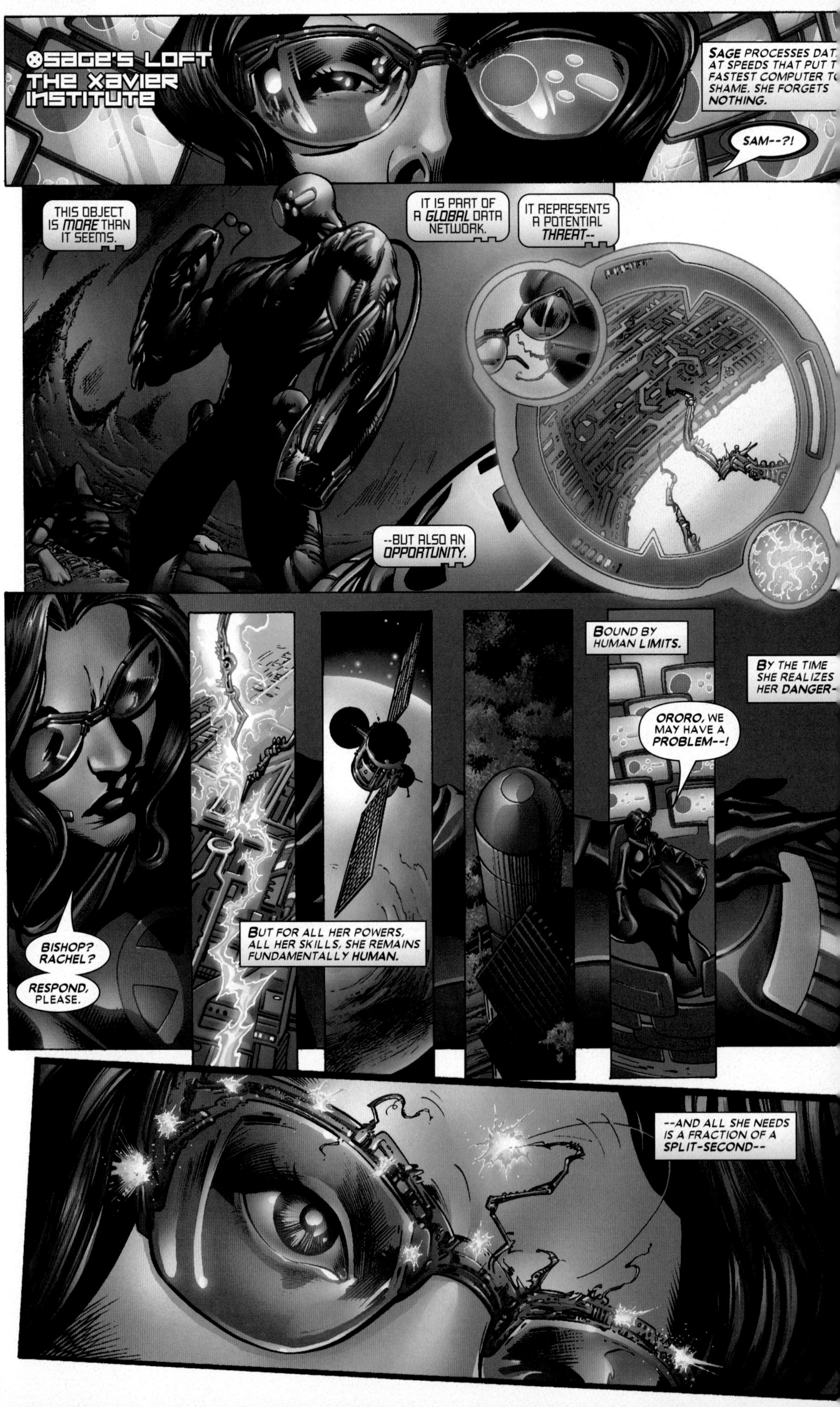
SAGE'S LOFT
THE XAVIER INSTITUTE
SAGE PROCESSES DAT AT SPEEDS THAT PUT T FASTEST COMPUTER T SHAME. SHE FORGETS NOTHING.
SAM--?!
THIS OBJECT IS MORE THAN IT SEEMS.
IT IS PART OF A GLOBAL DATA NETWORK.
IT REPRESENTS A POTENTIAL THREAT--
--BUT ALSO AN OPPORTUNITY.
BISHOP? RACHEL?
RESPOND, PLEASE.
BUT FOR ALL HER POWERS, ALL HER SKILLS, SHE REMAINS FUNDAMENTALLY HUMAN.
BOUND BY HUMAN LIMITS.
ORORO, WE MAY HAVE A PROBLEM--!
BY THE TIME SHE REALIZES HER DANGER-
--AND ALL SHE NEEDS IS A FRACTION OF A SPLIT-SECOND--

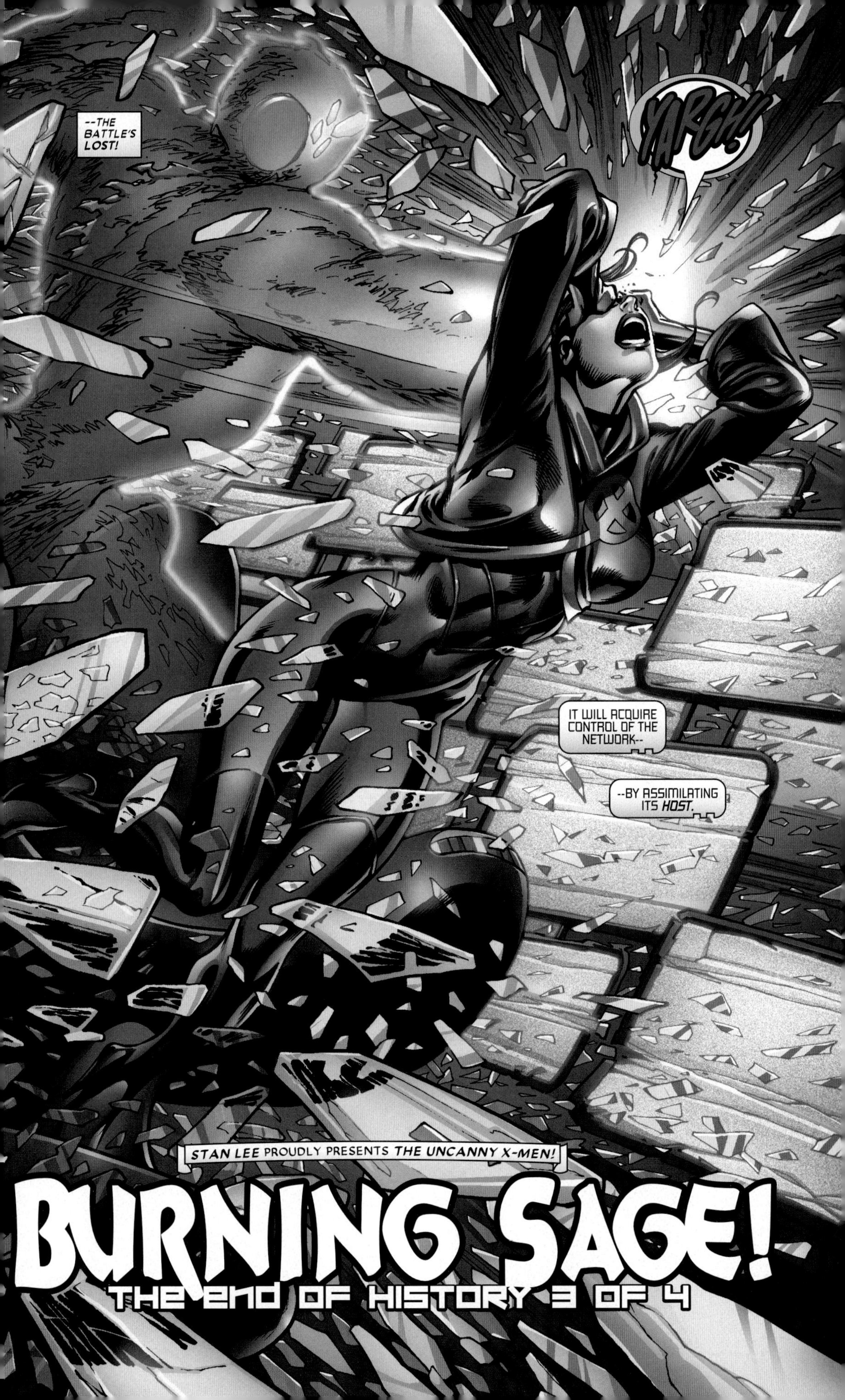

--THE BATTLE'S LOST!
YARGH!
IT WILL ACQUIRE CONTROL OF THE NETWORK--
--BY ASSIMILATING ITS HOST.
STAN LEE PROUDLY PRESENTS THE UNCANNY X-MEN!
BURNING SAGE!
THE END OF HISTORY 3 OF 4

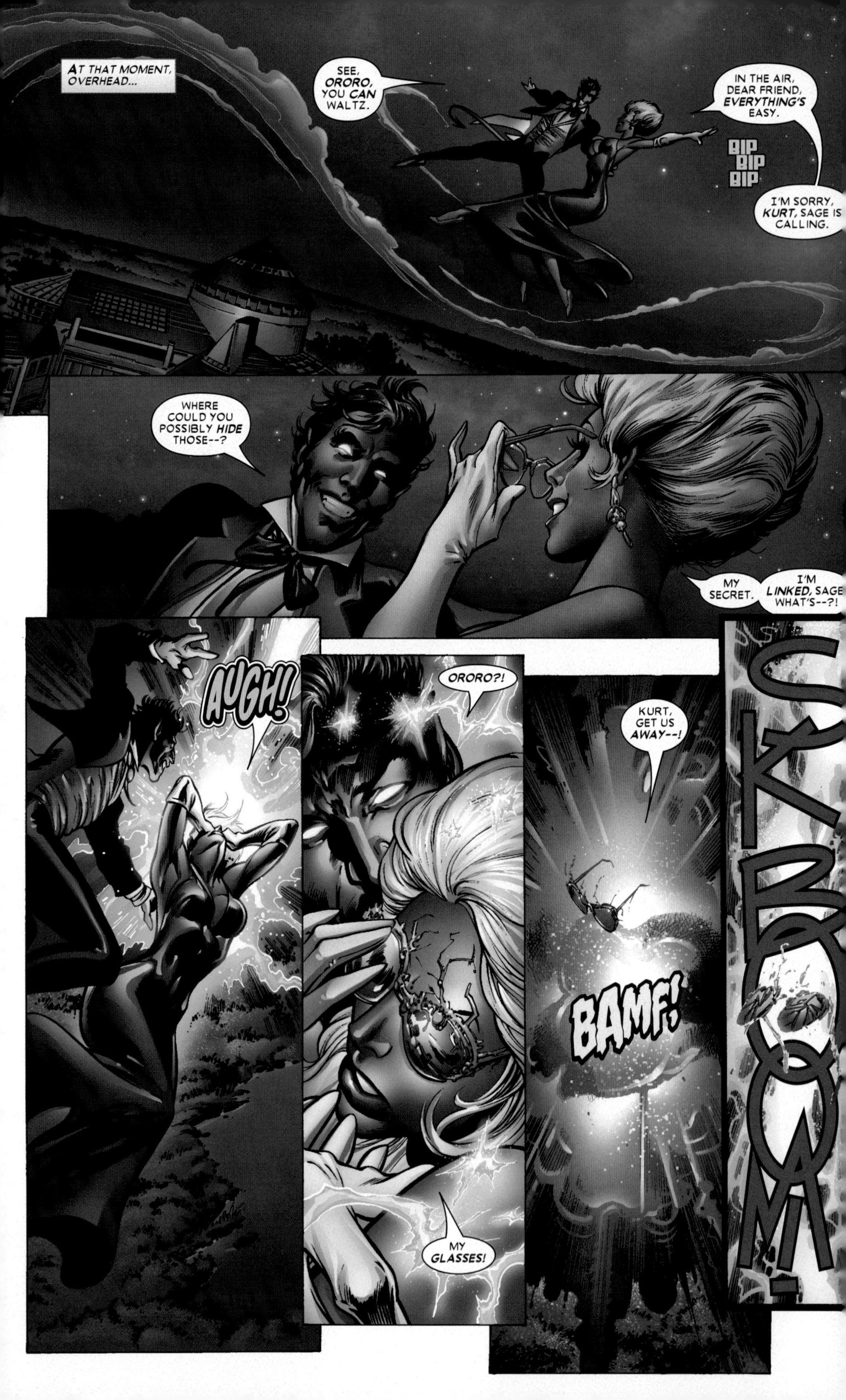
AT THAT MOMENT, OVERHEAD...
SEE, ORORO, YOU CAN WALTZ.
IN THE AIR, DEAR FRIEND, EVERYTHING'S EASY.
BIP BIP BIP
I'M SORRY, KURT, SAGE IS CALLING.
WHERE COULD YOU POSSIBLY HIDE THOSE--?
MY SECRET.
I'M LINKED, SAGE WHAT'S--?!
AUGH!
ORORO?!
MY GLASSES!
KURT, GET US AWAY--!
BAMF!
SKRBOOM!

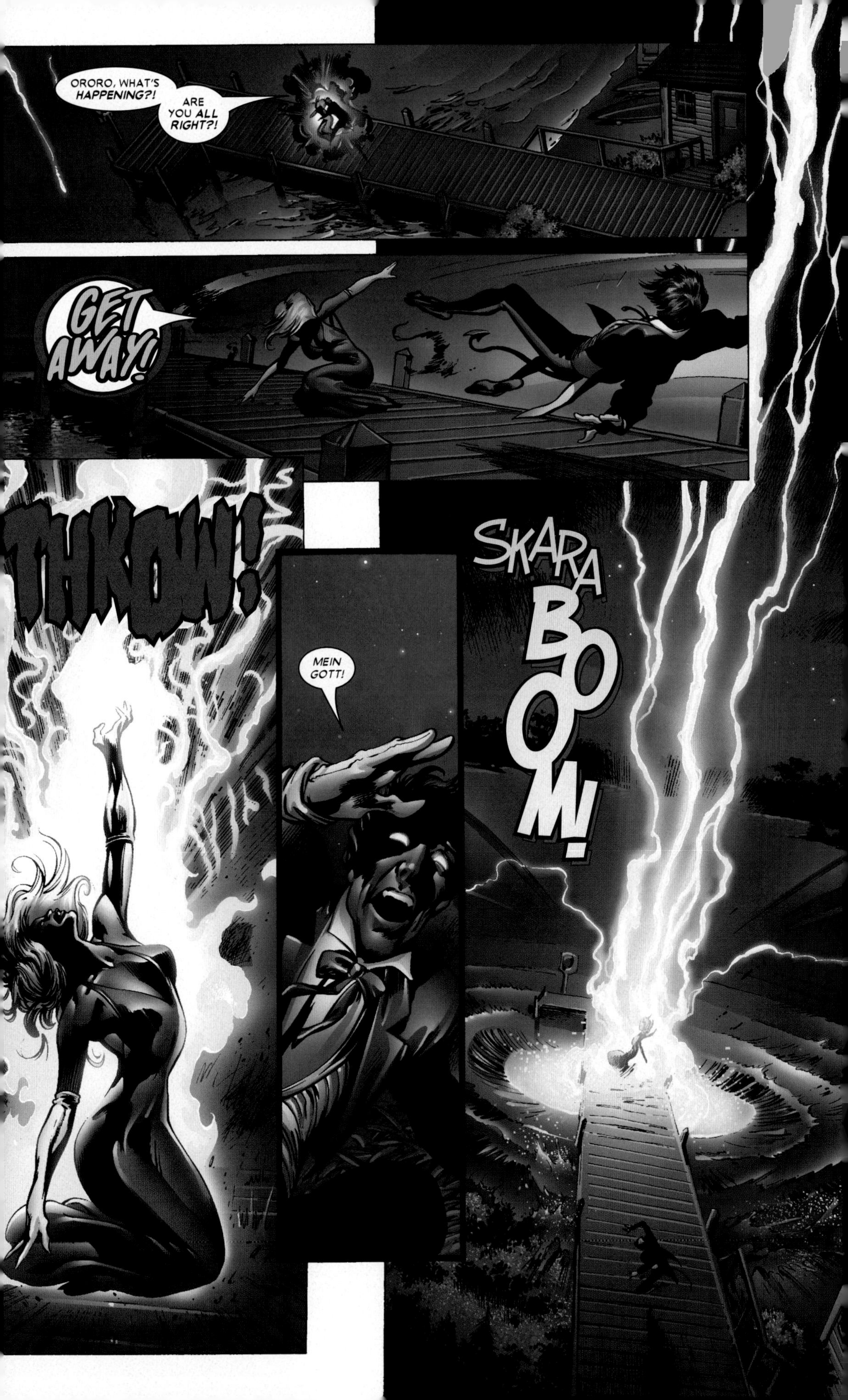
ORORO, WHAT'S HAPPENING?!
ARE YOU ALL RIGHT?!
GET AWAY!
THKOW!
MEIN GOTT!
SKARA BOOM!

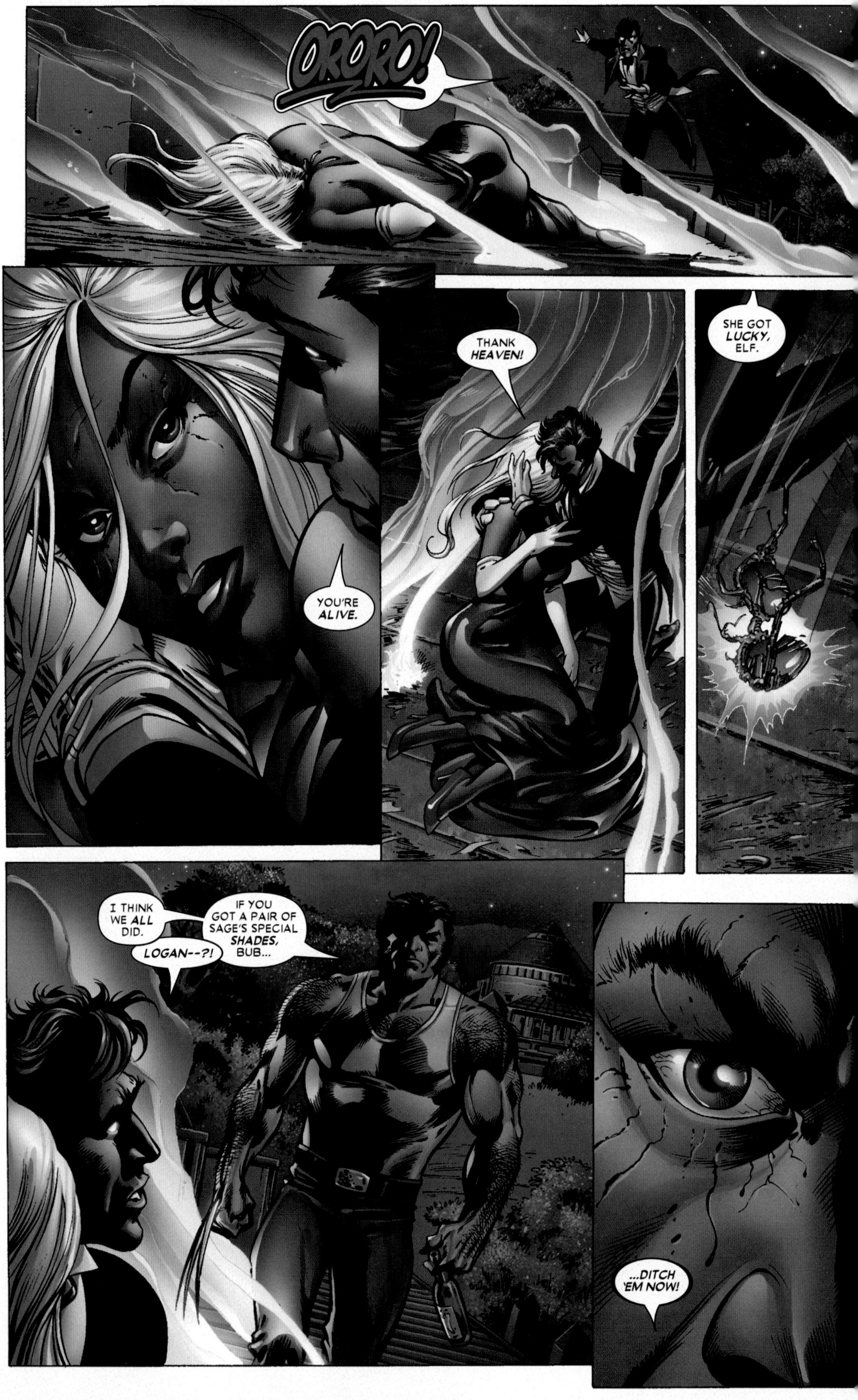

ORORO!
YOU'RE ALIVE.
THANK HEAVEN!
SHE GOT LUCKY, ELF.
I THINK WE ALL DID.
LOGAN--?!
IF YOU GOT A PAIR OF SAGE'S SPECIAL SHADES, BUB...
...DITCH 'EM NOW!

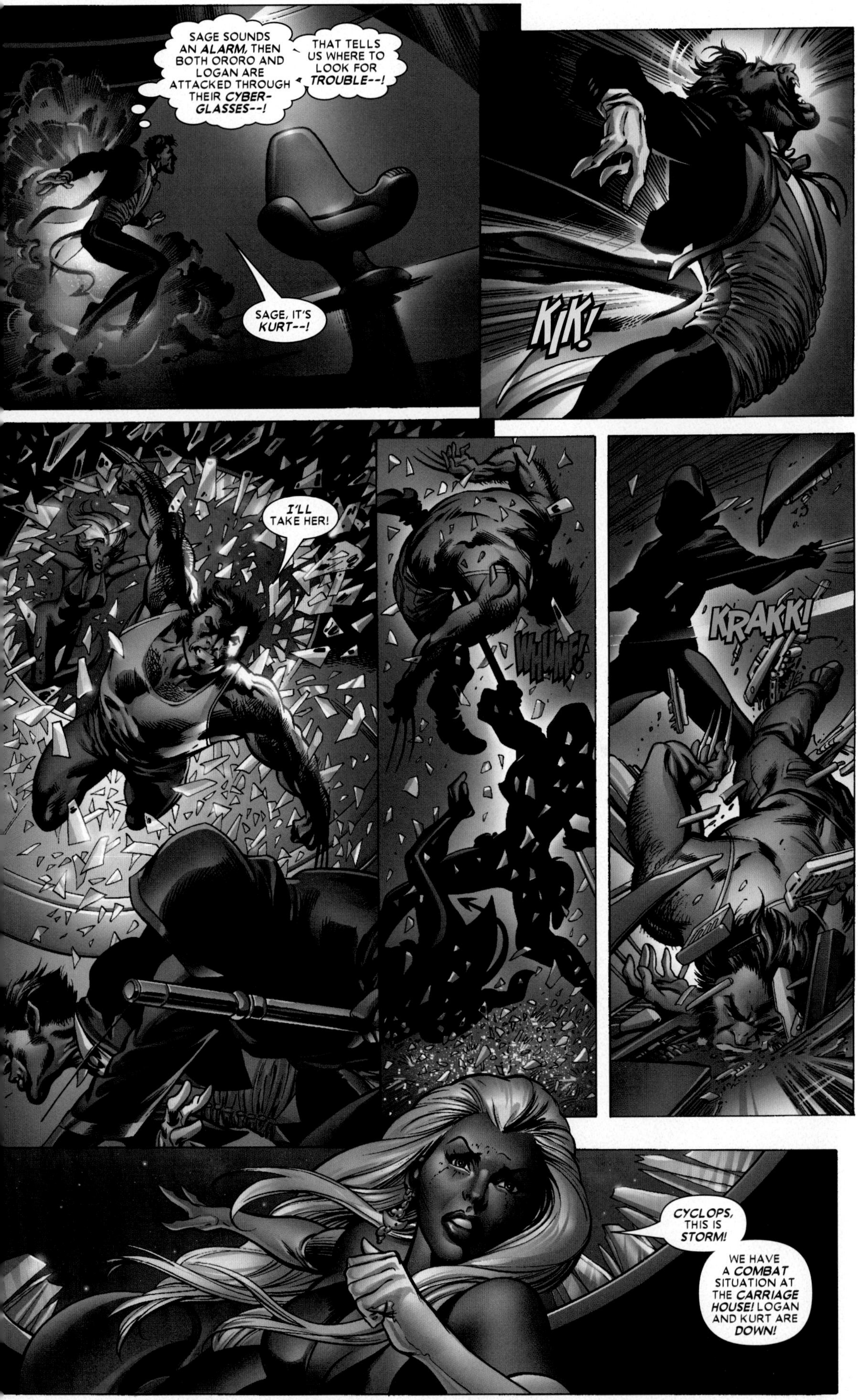
SAGE SOUNDS AN ALARM, THEN BOTH ORORO AND LOGAN ARE ATTACKED THROUGH THEIR CYBER-GLASSES--!
THAT TELLS US WHERE TO LOOK FOR TROUBLE--!
SAGE, IT'S KURT--!
KIK!
I'LL TAKE HER!
WHUMF!
KRAKK!
CYCLOPS, THIS IS STORM!
WE HAVE A COMBAT SITUATION AT THE CARRIAGE HOUSE! LOGAN AND KURT ARE DOWN!

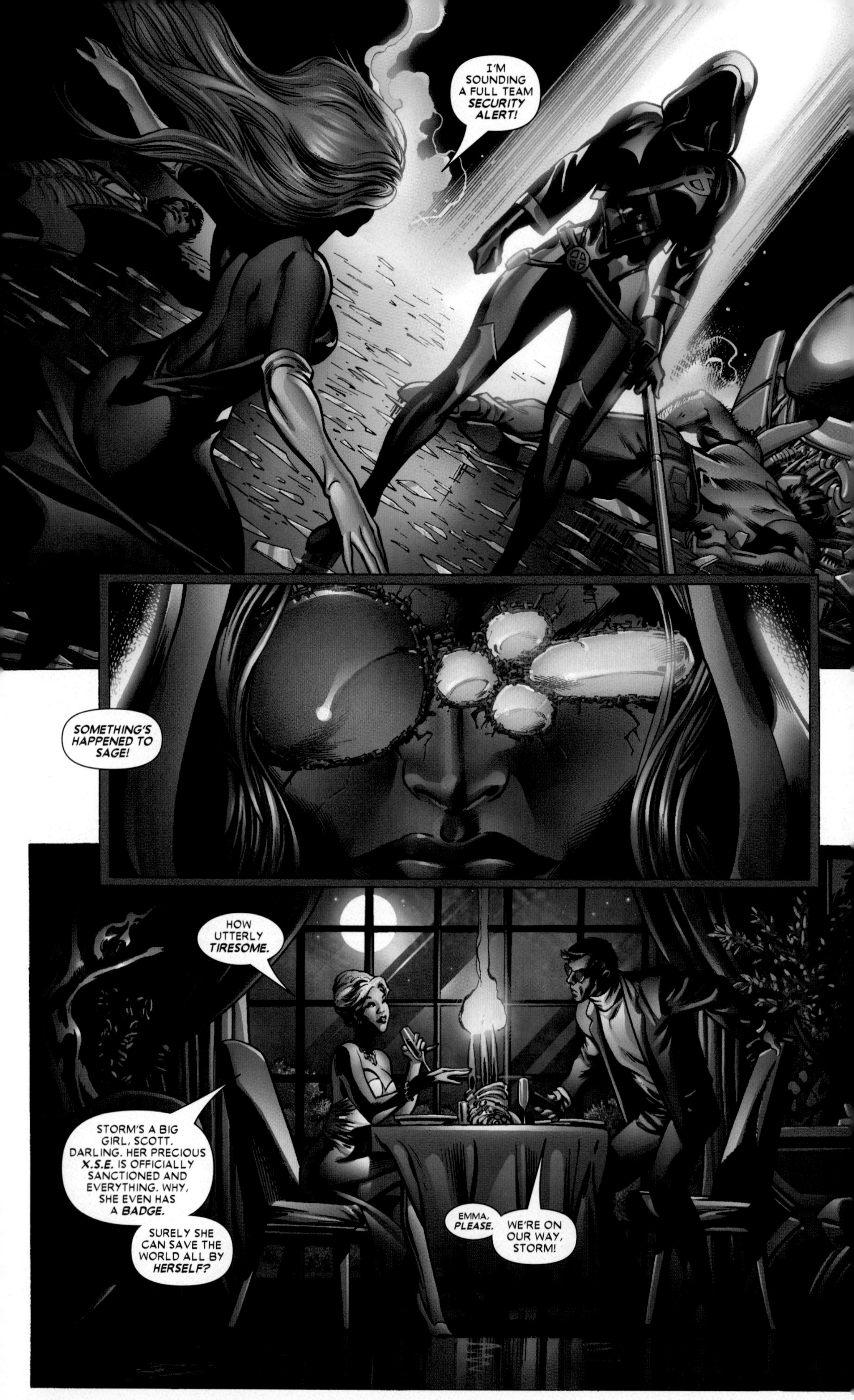
I'M SOUNDING A FULL TEAM SECURITY ALERT!
SOMETHING'S HAPPENED TO SAGE!
HOW UTTERLY TIRESOME.
STORM'S A BIG GIRL, SCOTT. DARLING. HER PRECIOUS X.S.E. IS OFFICIALLY SANCTIONED AND EVERYTHING. WHY, SHE EVEN HAS A BADGE.
SURELY SHE CAN SAVE THE WORLD ALL BY HERSELF?
EMMA, PLEASE.
WE'RE ON OUR WAY, STORM!

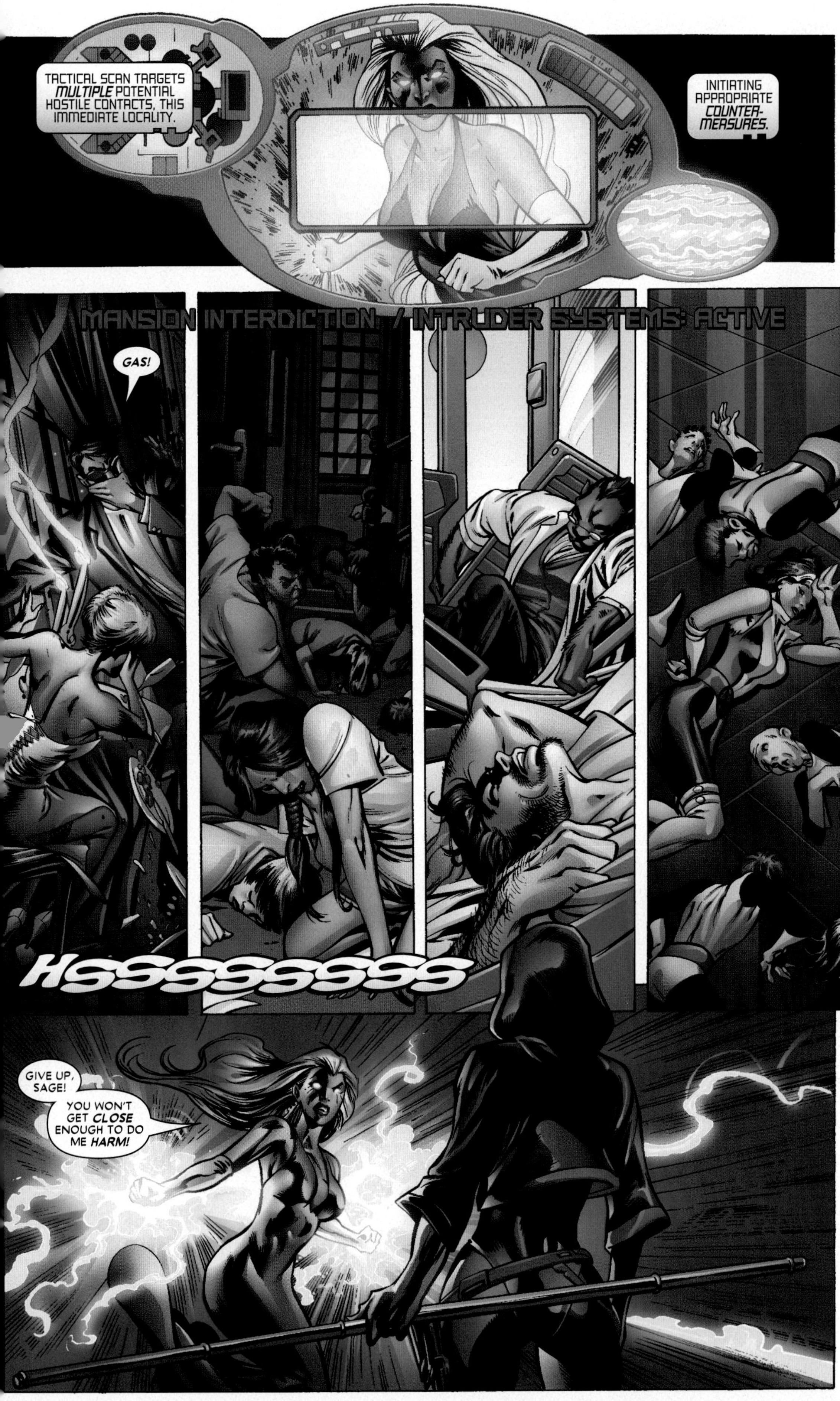
TACTICAL SCAN TARGETS MULTIPLE POTENTIAL HOSTILE CONTACTS, THIS IMMEDIATE LOCALITY.
INITIATING APPROPRIATE COUNTER-MEASURES.
MANSION INTERDICTION / INTRUDER SYSTEMS: ACTIVE
GAS!
HSSSSSSSSS
GIVE UP, SAGE!
YOU WON'T GET CLOSE ENOUGH TO DO ME HARM!

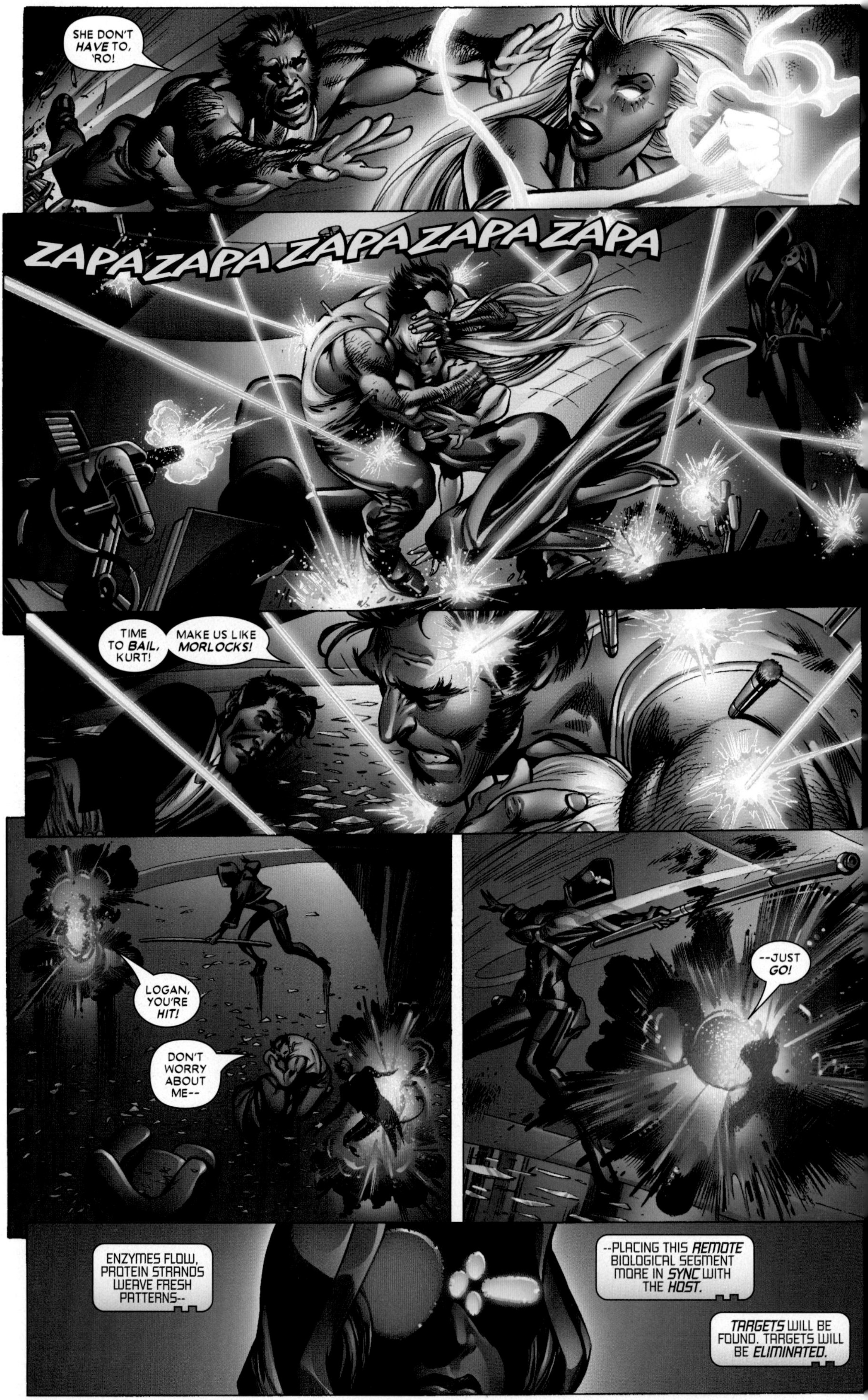
SHE DON'T HAVE TO, 'RO!
ZAPA ZAPA ZAPA ZAPA ZAPA
TIME TO BAIL, KURT!
MAKE US LIKE MORLOCKS!
LOGAN, YOU'RE HIT!
DON'T WORRY ABOUT ME--
--JUST GO!
ENZYMES FLOW, PROTEIN STRANDS WEAVE FRESH PATTERNS--
--PLACING THIS REMOTE BIOLOGICAL SEGMENT MORE IN SYNC WITH THE HOST.
TARGETS WILL BE FOUND. TARGETS WILL BE ELIMINATED.

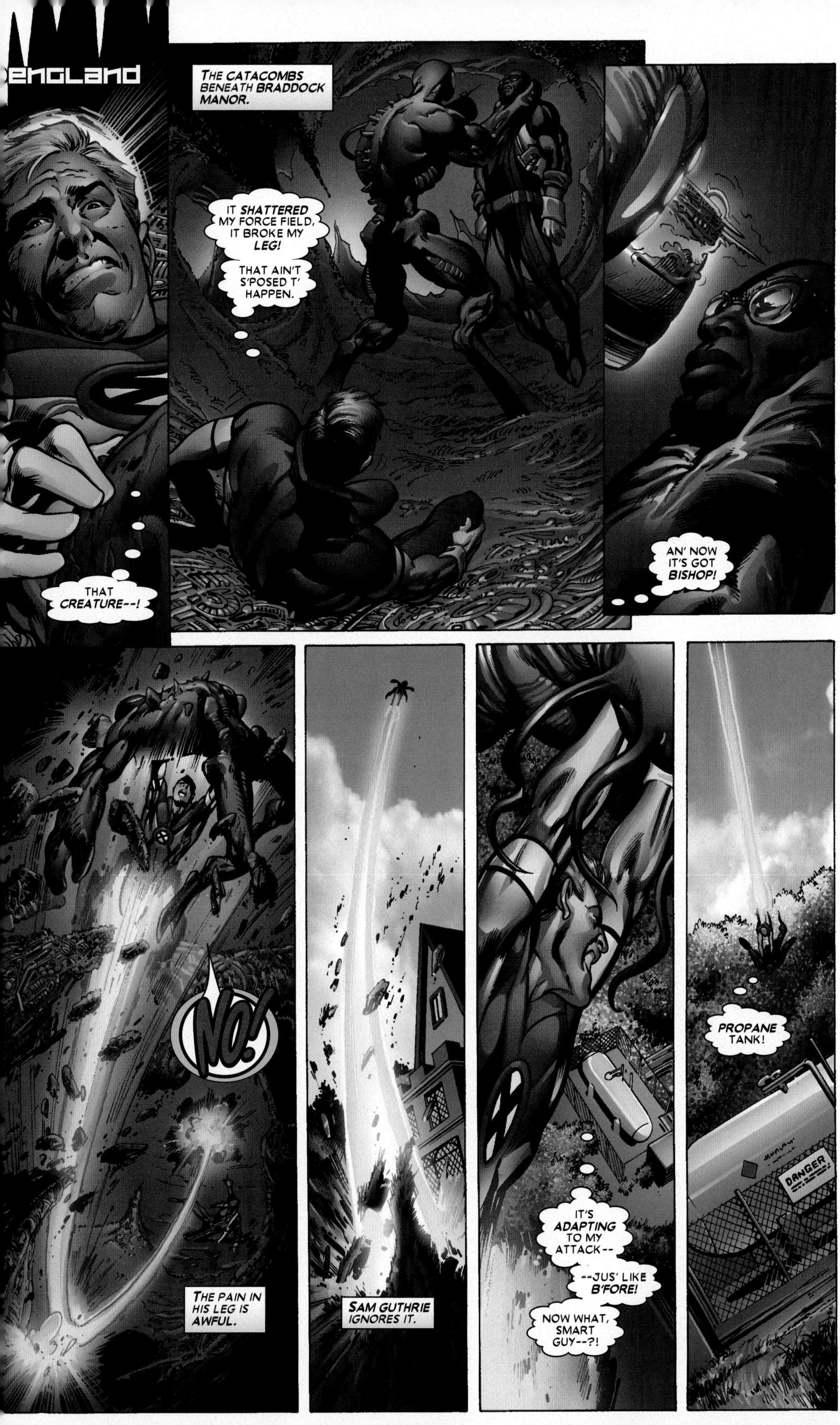

ENGLAND
THE CATACOMBS BENEATH BRADDOCK MANOR.
THAT CREATURE--!
IT SHATTERED MY FORCE FIELD, IT BROKE MY LEG!
THAT AIN'T S'POSED T' HAPPEN.
AN' NOW IT'S GOT BISHOP!
NO!
THE PAIN IN HIS LEG IS AWFUL.
SAM GUTHRIE IGNORES IT.
IT'S ADAPTING TO MY ATTACK--
--JUS' LIKE B'FORE!
NOW WHAT, SMART GUY--?!
PROPANE TANK!
DANGER

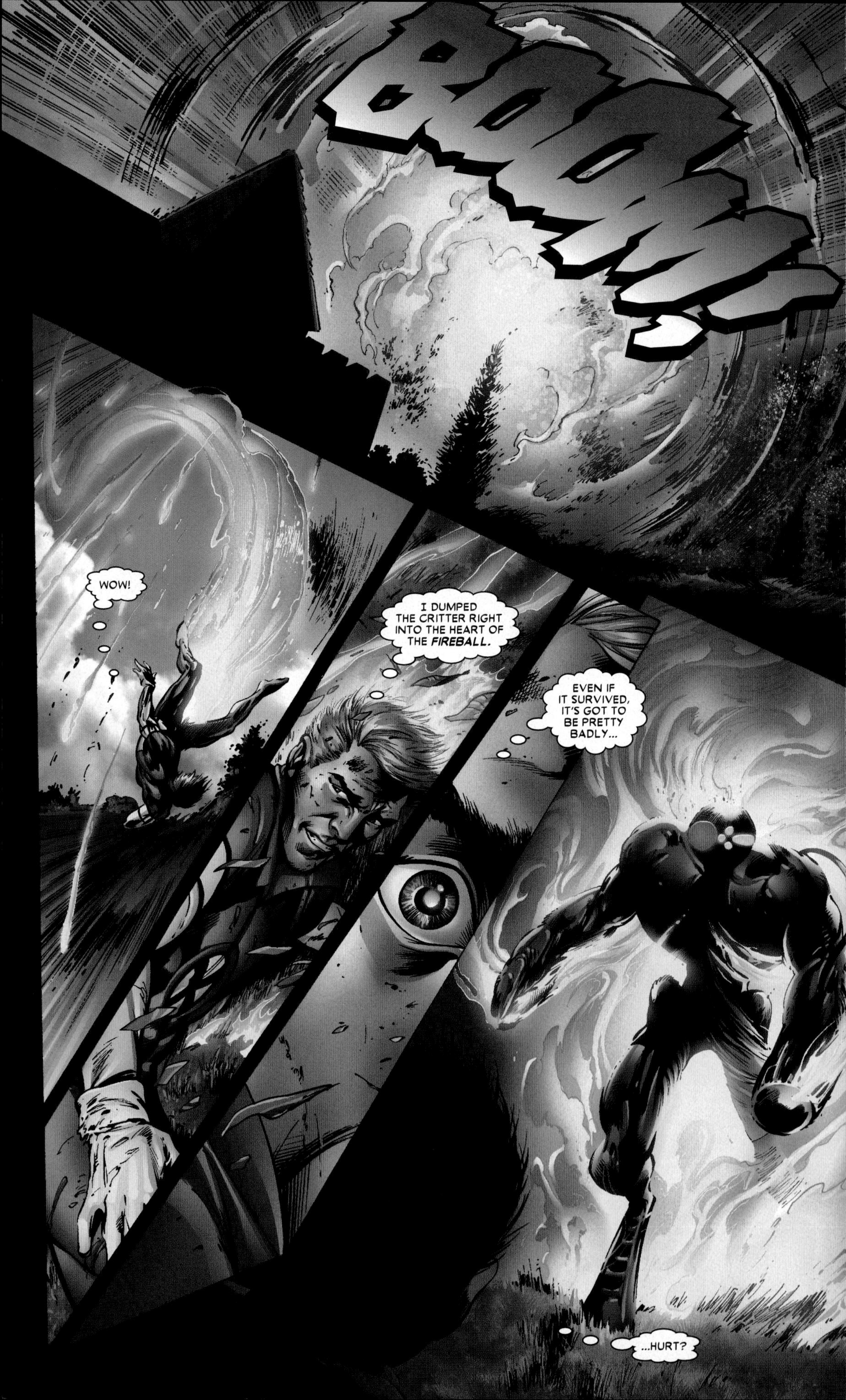
BLAAMM!!
WOW!
I DUMPED THE CRITTER RIGHT INTO THE HEART OF THE FIREBALL.
EVEN IF IT SURVIVED, IT'S GOT TO BE PRETTY BADLY...
...HURT?

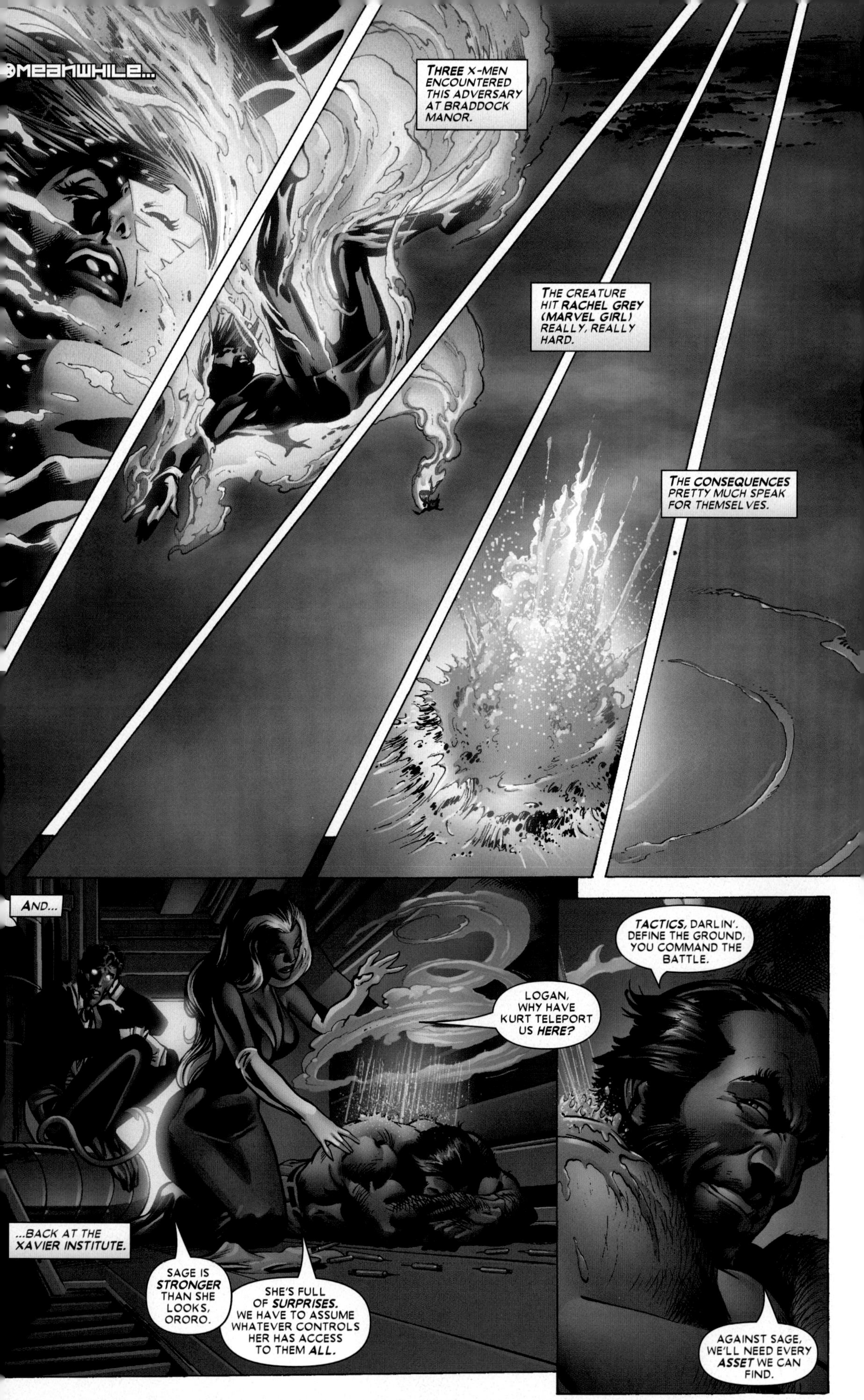
MEANWHILE...
THREE X-MEN ENCOUNTERED THIS ADVERSARY AT BRADDOCK MANOR.
THE CREATURE HIT RACHEL GREY (MARVEL GIRL) REALLY, REALLY HARD.
THE CONSEQUENCES PRETTY MUCH SPEAK FOR THEMSELVES.
AND...
...BACK AT THE XAVIER INSTITUTE.
LOGAN, WHY HAVE KURT TELEPORT US HERE?
SAGE IS STRONGER THAN SHE LOOKS, ORORO.
SHE'S FULL OF SURPRISES. WE HAVE TO ASSUME WHATEVER CONTROLS HER HAS ACCESS TO THEM ALL.
TACTICS, DARLIN'. DEFINE THE GROUND, YOU COMMAND THE BATTLE.
AGAINST SAGE, WE'LL NEED EVERY ASSET WE CAN FIND.

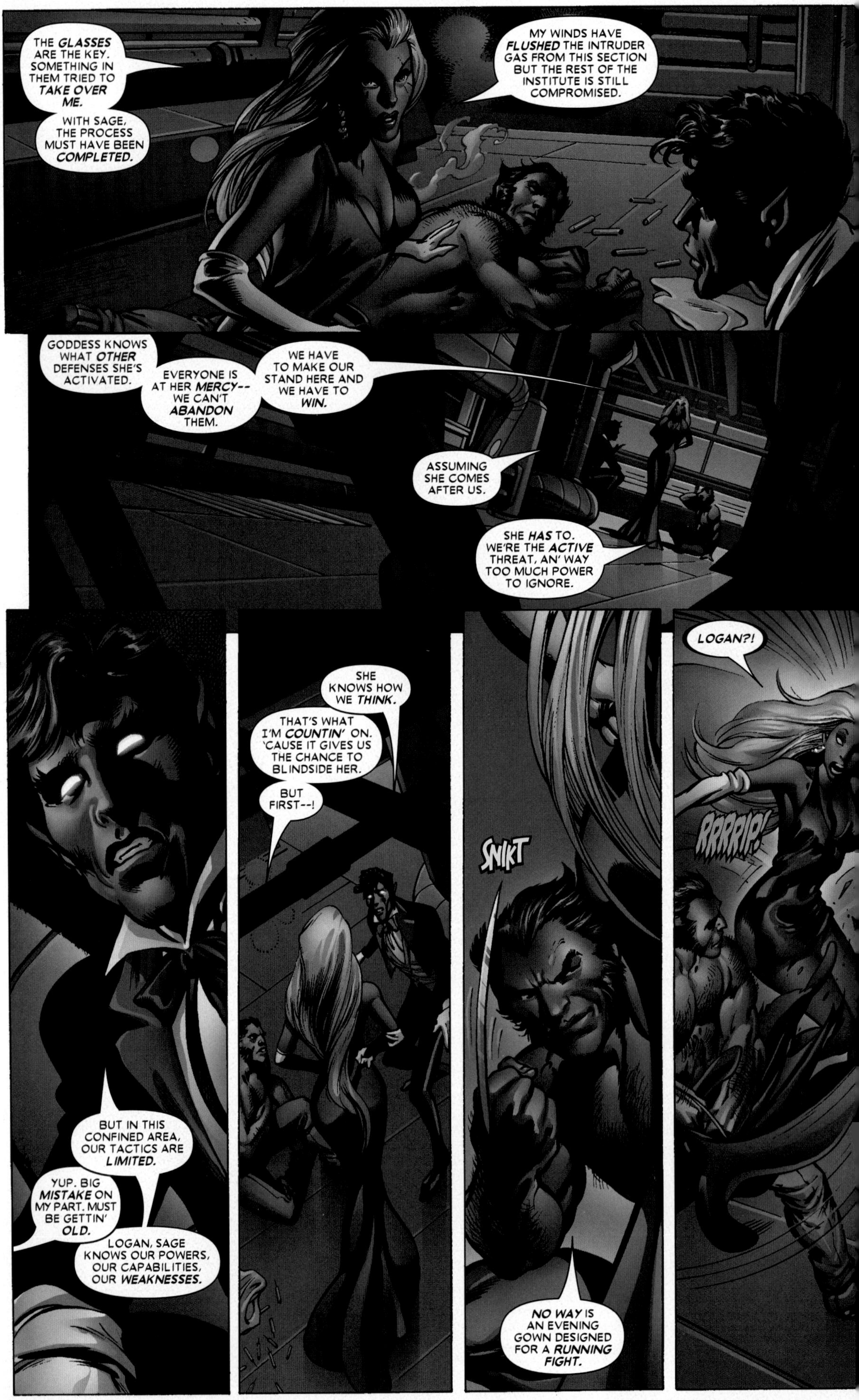
THE GLASSES ARE THE KEY. SOMETHING IN THEM TRIED TO TAKE OVER ME.
WITH SAGE, THE PROCESS MUST HAVE BEEN COMPLETED.
MY WINDS HAVE FLUSHED THE INTRUDER GAS FROM THIS SECTION BUT THE REST OF THE INSTITUTE IS STILL COMPROMISED.
GODDESS KNOWS WHAT OTHER DEFENSES SHE'S ACTIVATED.
EVERYONE IS AT HER MERCY-- WE CAN'T ABANDON THEM.
WE HAVE TO MAKE OUR STAND HERE AND WE HAVE TO WIN.
ASSUMING SHE COMES AFTER US.
SHE HAS TO. WE'RE THE ACTIVE THREAT, AN' WAY TOO MUCH POWER TO IGNORE.
BUT IN THIS CONFINED AREA, OUR TACTICS ARE LIMITED.
YUP. BIG MISTAKE ON MY PART. MUST BE GETTIN' OLD.
LOGAN, SAGE KNOWS OUR POWERS, OUR CAPABILITIES, OUR WEAKNESSES.
SHE KNOWS HOW WE THINK.
THAT'S WHAT I'M COUNTIN' ON. 'CAUSE IT GIVES US THE CHANCE TO BLINDSIDE HER.
BUT FIRST--!
SNIKT
NO WAY IS AN EVENING GOWN DESIGNED FOR A RUNNING FIGHT.
LOGAN?!
RRRRIP!

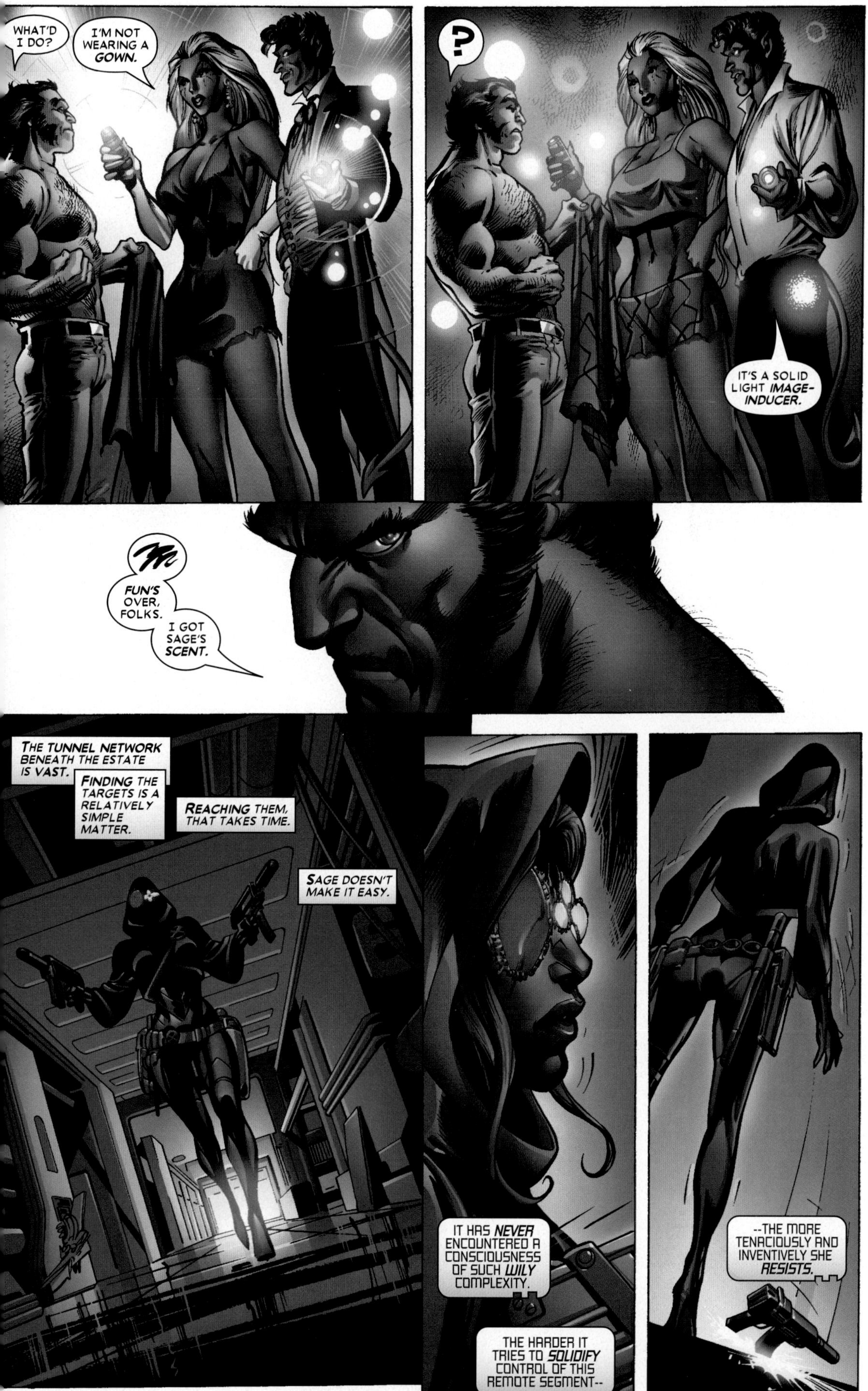
WHAT'D I DO?
I'M NOT WEARING A GOWN.
?
IT'S A SOLID LIGHT IMAGE-INDUCER.
FUN'S OVER, FOLKS.
I GOT SAGE'S SCENT.
THE TUNNEL NETWORK BENEATH THE ESTATE IS VAST.
FINDING THE TARGETS IS A RELATIVELY SIMPLE MATTER.
REACHING THEM, THAT TAKES TIME.
SAGE DOESN'T MAKE IT EASY.
IT HAS NEVER ENCOUNTERED A CONSCIOUSNESS OF SUCH WILY COMPLEXITY.
THE HARDER IT TRIES TO SOLIDIFY CONTROL OF THIS REMOTE SEGMENT--
--THE MORE TENACIOUSLY AND INVENTIVELY SHE RESISTS.

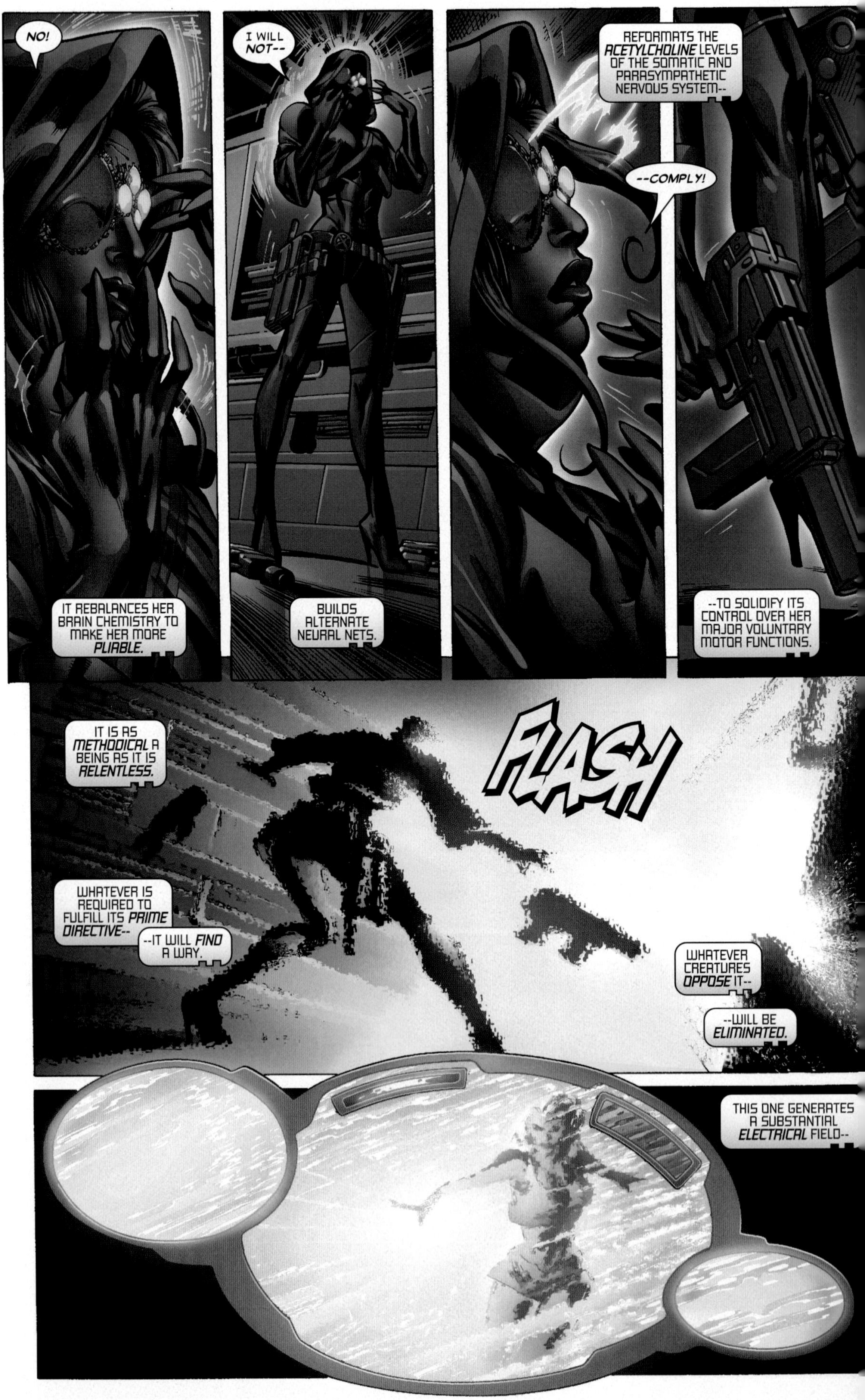
NO!
IT REBALANCES HER BRAIN CHEMISTRY TO MAKE HER MORE PLIABLE.
I WILL NOT--
BUILDS ALTERNATE NEURAL NETS.
REFORMATS THE ACETYLCHOLINE LEVELS OF THE SOMATIC AND PARASYMPATHETIC NERVOUS SYSTEM--
--COMPLY!
--TO SOLIDIFY ITS CONTROL OVER HER MAJOR VOLUNTARY MOTOR FUNCTIONS.
IT IS AS METHODICAL A BEING AS IT IS RELENTLESS.
FLASH
WHATEVER IS REQUIRED TO FULFILL ITS PRIME DIRECTIVE--
--IT WILL FIND A WAY.
WHATEVER CREATURES OPPOSE IT--
--WILL BE ELIMINATED.
THIS ONE GENERATES A SUBSTANTIAL ELECTRICAL FIELD--

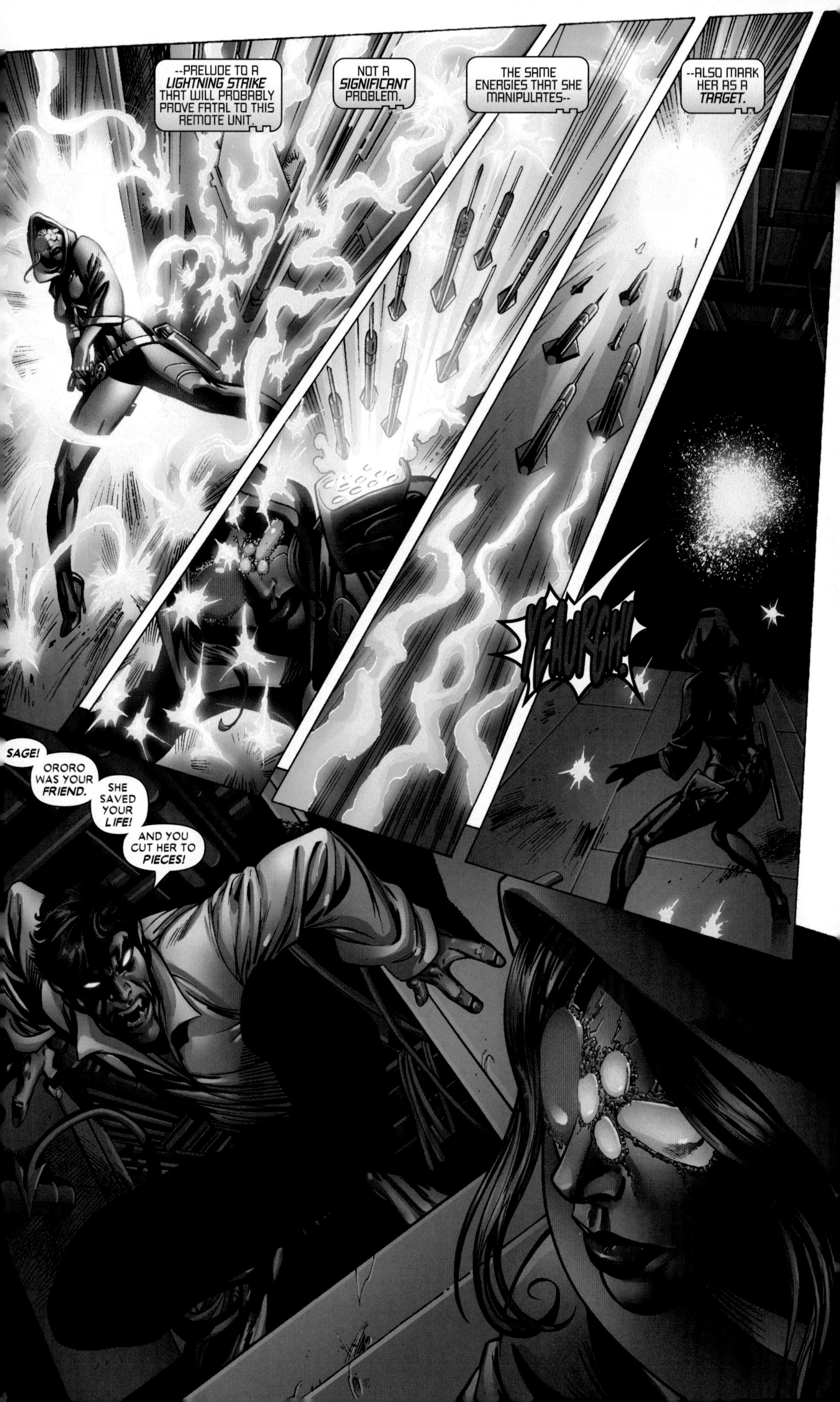
--PRELUDE TO A *LIGHTNING STRIKE* THAT WILL PROBABLY PROVE FATAL TO THIS REMOTE UNIT.
NOT A *SIGNIFICANT* PROBLEM.
THE SAME ENERGIES THAT SHE MANIPULATES--
--ALSO MARK HER AS A *TARGET.*
YEAURGH!
SAGE!
ORORO WAS YOUR *FRIEND.*
SHE SAVED YOUR *LIFE!*
AND YOU CUT HER TO *PIECES!*

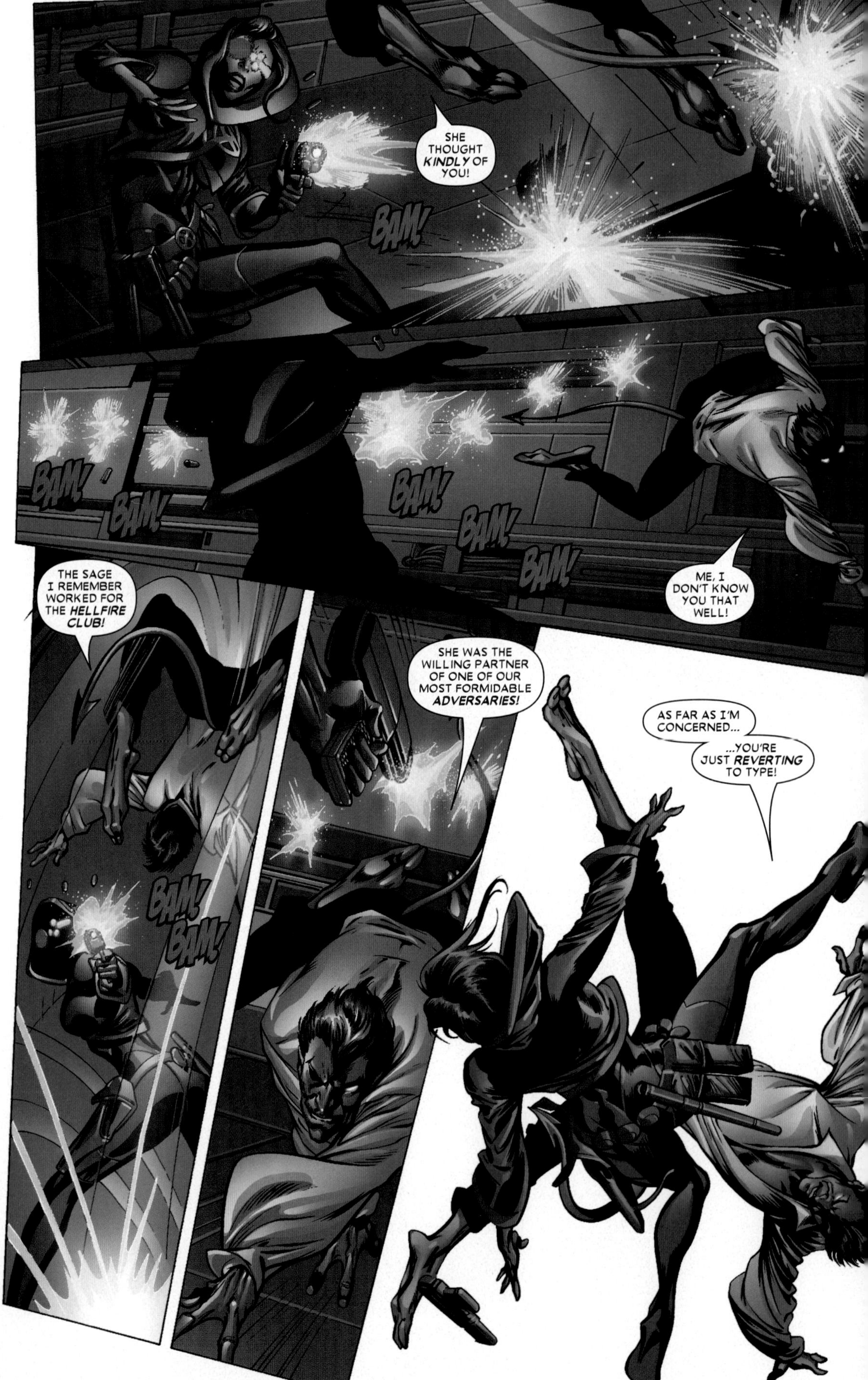
SHE THOUGHT KINDLY OF YOU!
BAM!
BAM!
BAM!
BAM!
BAM!
BAM!
ME, I DON'T KNOW YOU THAT WELL!
THE SAGE I REMEMBER WORKED FOR THE HELLFIRE CLUB!
BAM!
BAM!
SHE WAS THE WILLING PARTNER OF ONE OF OUR MOST FORMIDABLE ADVERSARIES!
AS FAR AS I'M CONCERNED...
...YOU'RE JUST REVERTING TO TYPE!

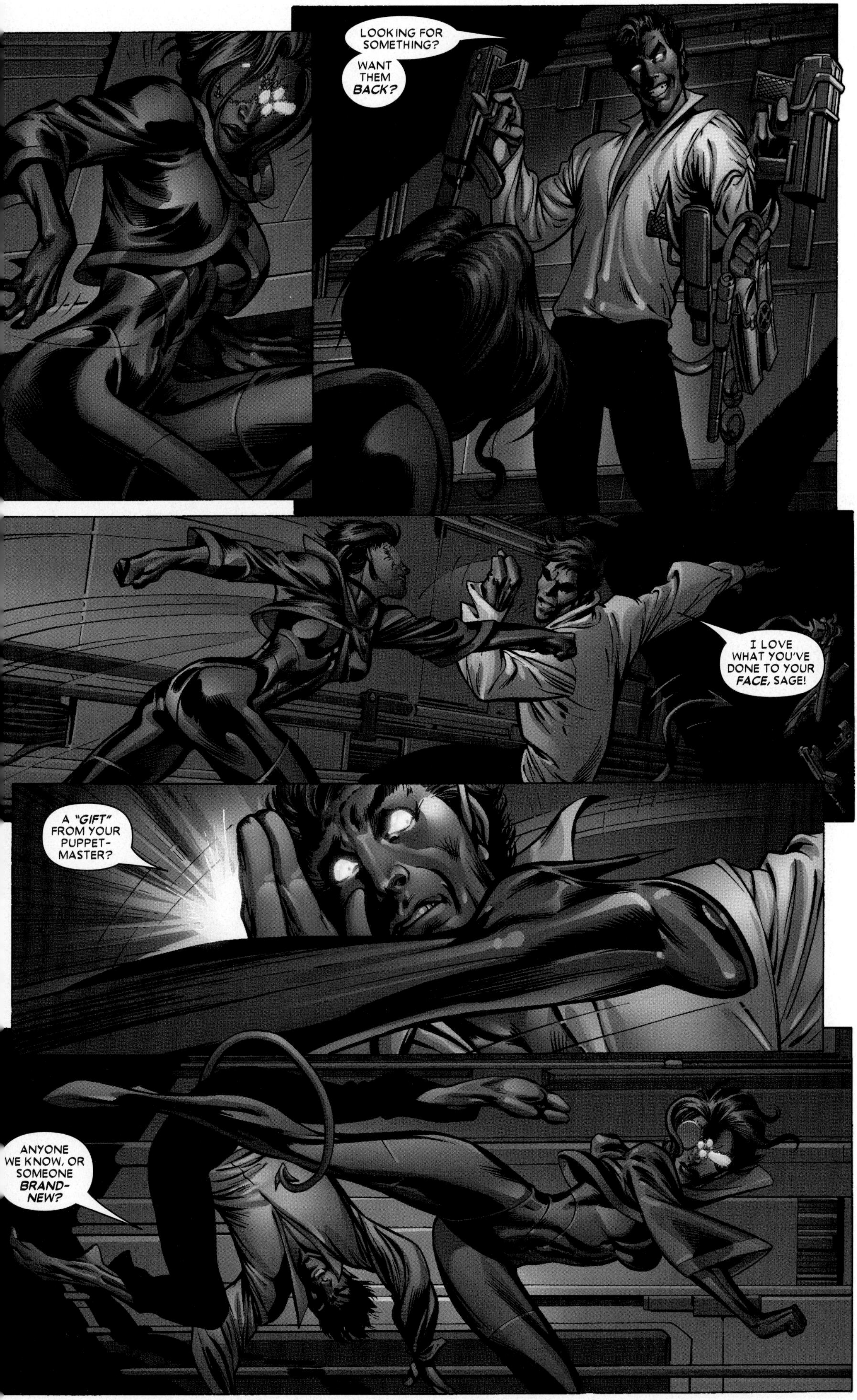
LOOKING FOR SOMETHING?
WANT THEM *BACK?*
I LOVE WHAT YOU'VE DONE TO YOUR *FACE,* SAGE!
A *"GIFT"* FROM YOUR PUPPET-MASTER?
ANYONE WE KNOW, OR SOMEONE *BRAND-NEW?*

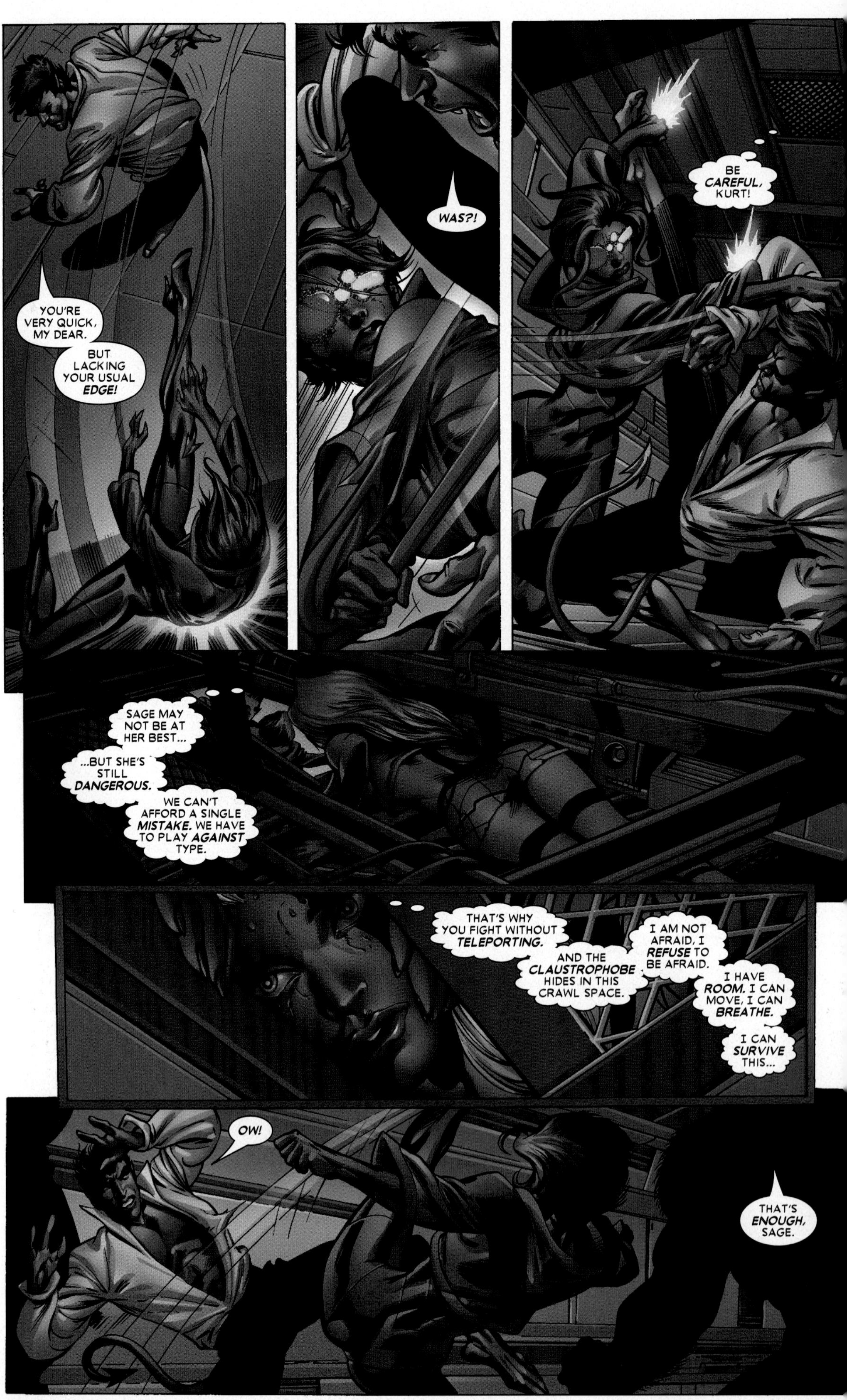
YOU'RE VERY QUICK, MY DEAR.
BUT LACKING YOUR USUAL EDGE!
WAS?!
BE CAREFUL, KURT!
SAGE MAY NOT BE AT HER BEST...
...BUT SHE'S STILL DANGEROUS.
WE CAN'T AFFORD A SINGLE MISTAKE. WE HAVE TO PLAY AGAINST TYPE.
THAT'S WHY YOU FIGHT WITHOUT TELEPORTING.
AND THE CLAUSTROPHOBE HIDES IN THIS CRAWL SPACE.
I AM NOT AFRAID, I REFUSE TO BE AFRAID.
I HAVE ROOM. I CAN MOVE, I CAN BREATHE.
I CAN SURVIVE THIS...
OW!
THAT'S ENOUGH, SAGE.

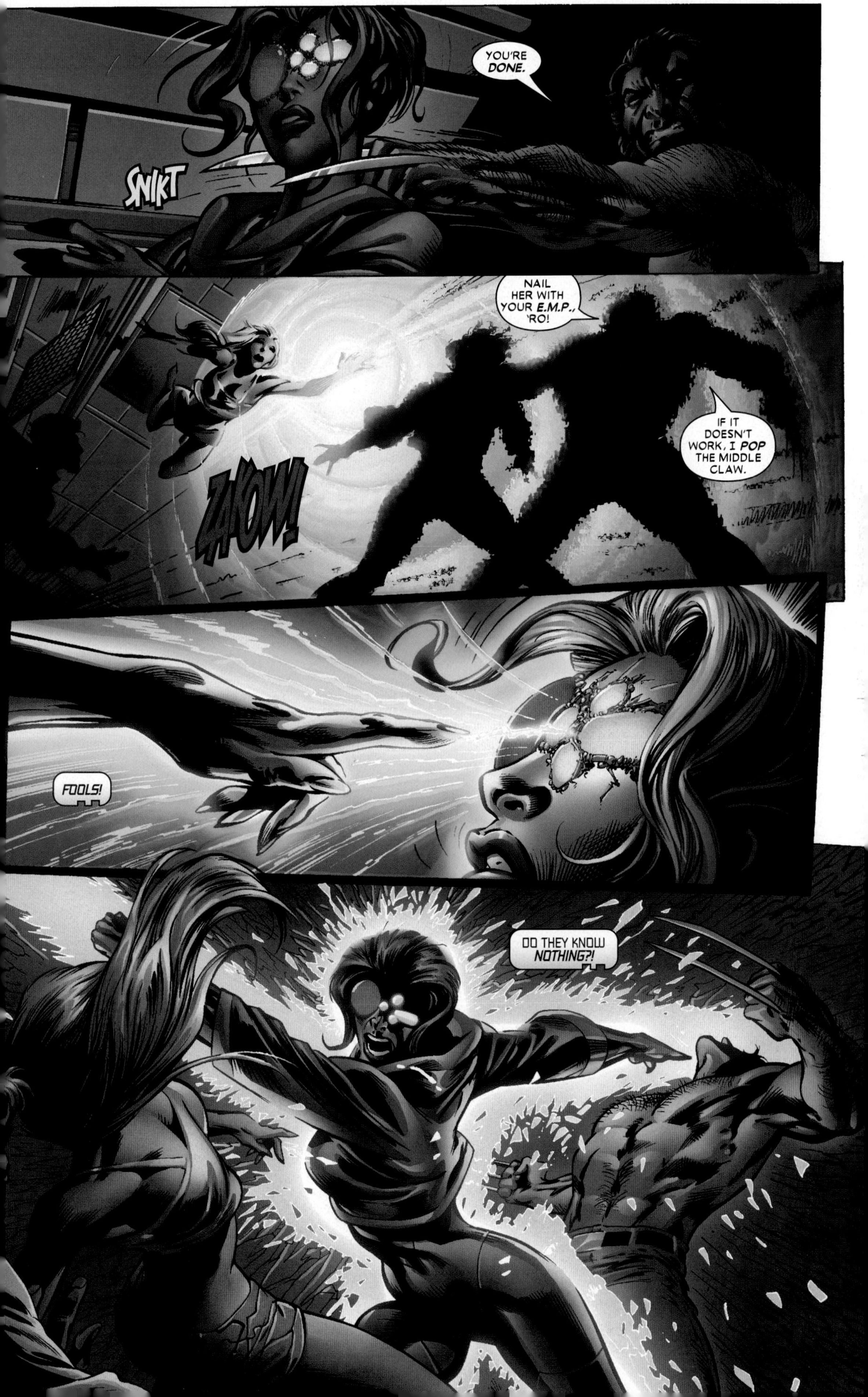
YOU'RE *DONE.*
SNIKT
NAIL HER WITH YOUR *E.M.P.*, 'RO!
IF IT DOESN'T WORK, I *POP* THE MIDDLE CLAW.
ZAKOW!
FOOLS!
DO THEY KNOW *NOTHING?!*

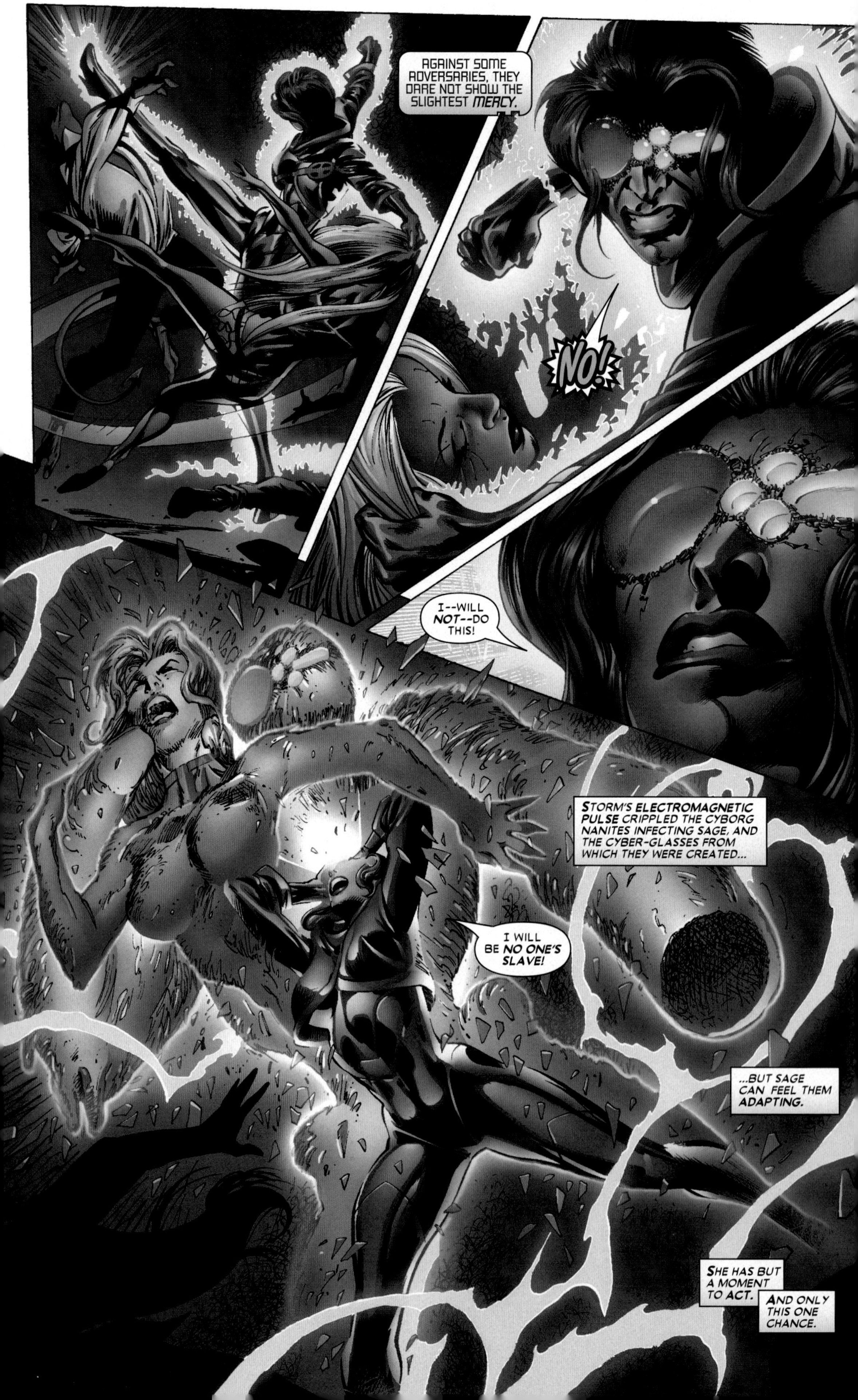
AGAINST SOME ADVERSARIES, THEY DARE NOT SHOW THE SLIGHTEST *MERCY*.
NO!
I--WILL *NOT*--DO THIS!
STORM'S ELECTROMAGNETIC PULSE CRIPPLED THE CYBORG NANITES INFECTING SAGE, AND THE CYBER-GLASSES FROM WHICH THEY WERE CREATED...
I WILL BE *NO ONE'S SLAVE!*
...BUT SAGE CAN FEEL THEM *ADAPTING*.
SHE HAS BUT A MOMENT TO *ACT*.
AND ONLY THIS ONE CHANCE.

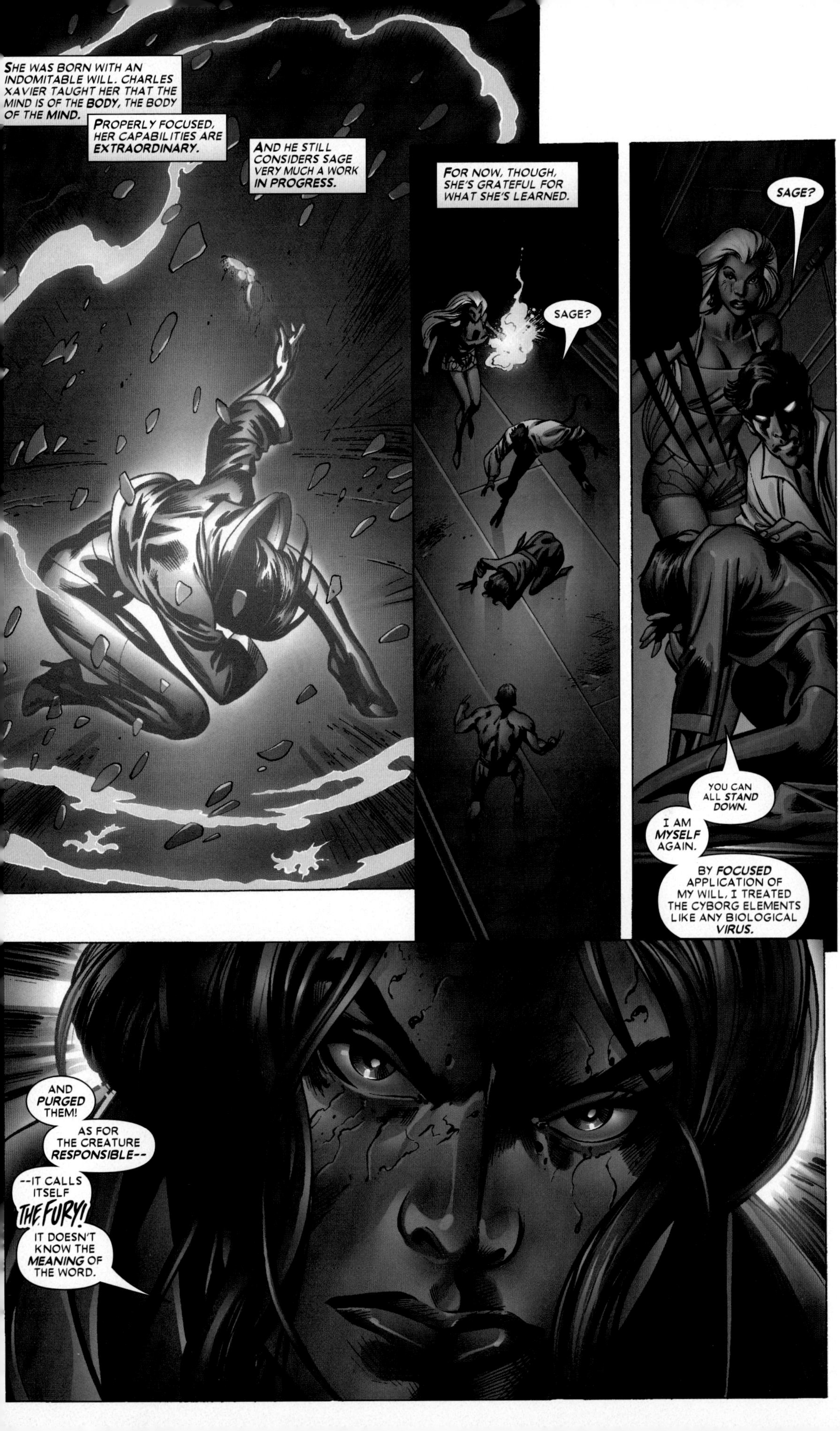
SHE WAS BORN WITH AN INDOMITABLE WILL. CHARLES XAVIER TAUGHT HER THAT THE MIND IS OF THE BODY, THE BODY OF THE MIND.
PROPERLY FOCUSED, HER CAPABILITIES ARE EXTRAORDINARY.
AND HE STILL CONSIDERS SAGE VERY MUCH A WORK IN PROGRESS.
FOR NOW, THOUGH, SHE'S GRATEFUL FOR WHAT SHE'S LEARNED.
SAGE?
SAGE?
YOU CAN ALL STAND DOWN.
I AM MYSELF AGAIN.
BY FOCUSED APPLICATION OF MY WILL, I TREATED THE CYBORG ELEMENTS LIKE ANY BIOLOGICAL VIRUS.
AND PURGED THEM!
AS FOR THE CREATURE RESPONSIBLE--
--IT CALLS ITSELF THE FURY!
IT DOESN'T KNOW THE MEANING OF THE WORD.

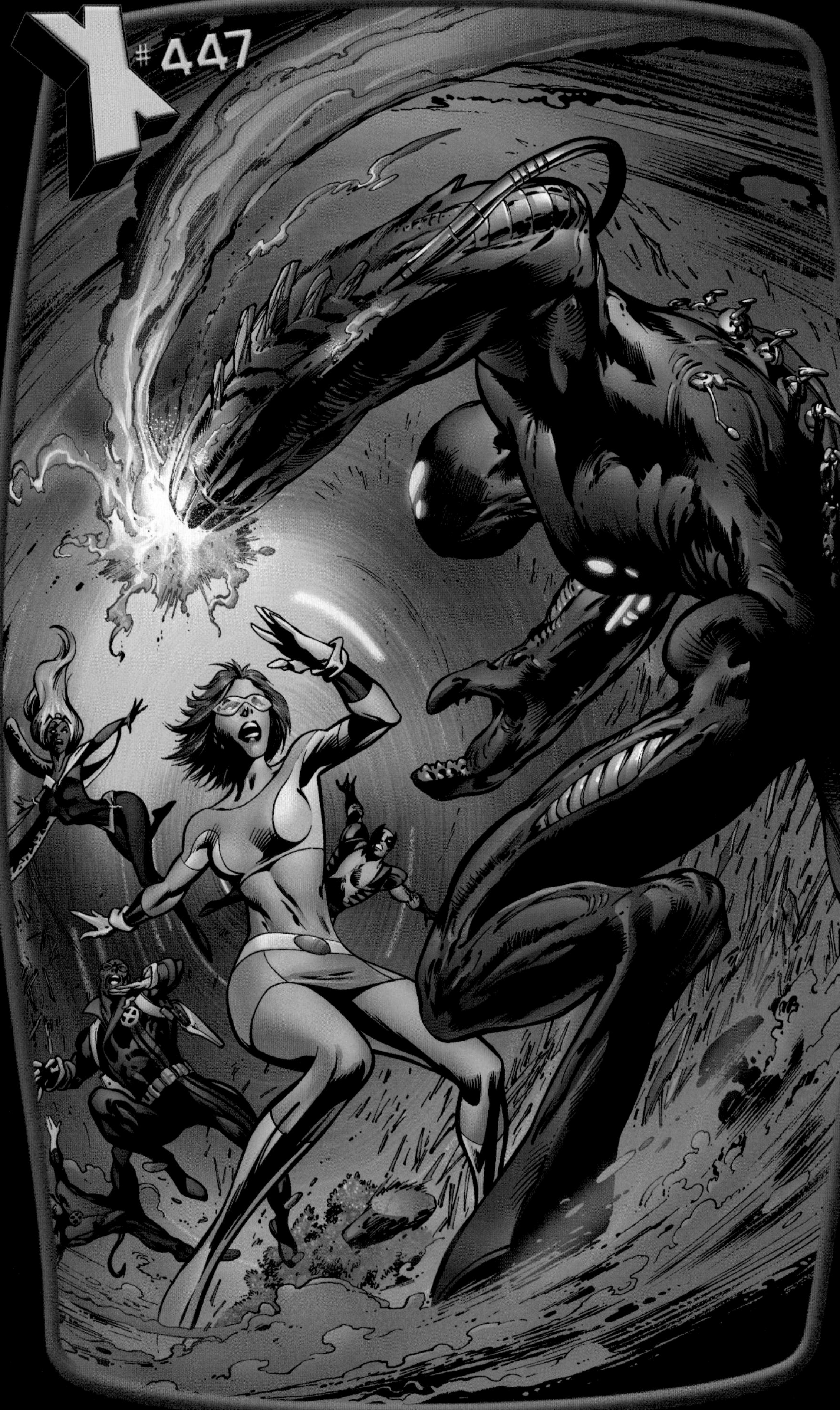

X
447

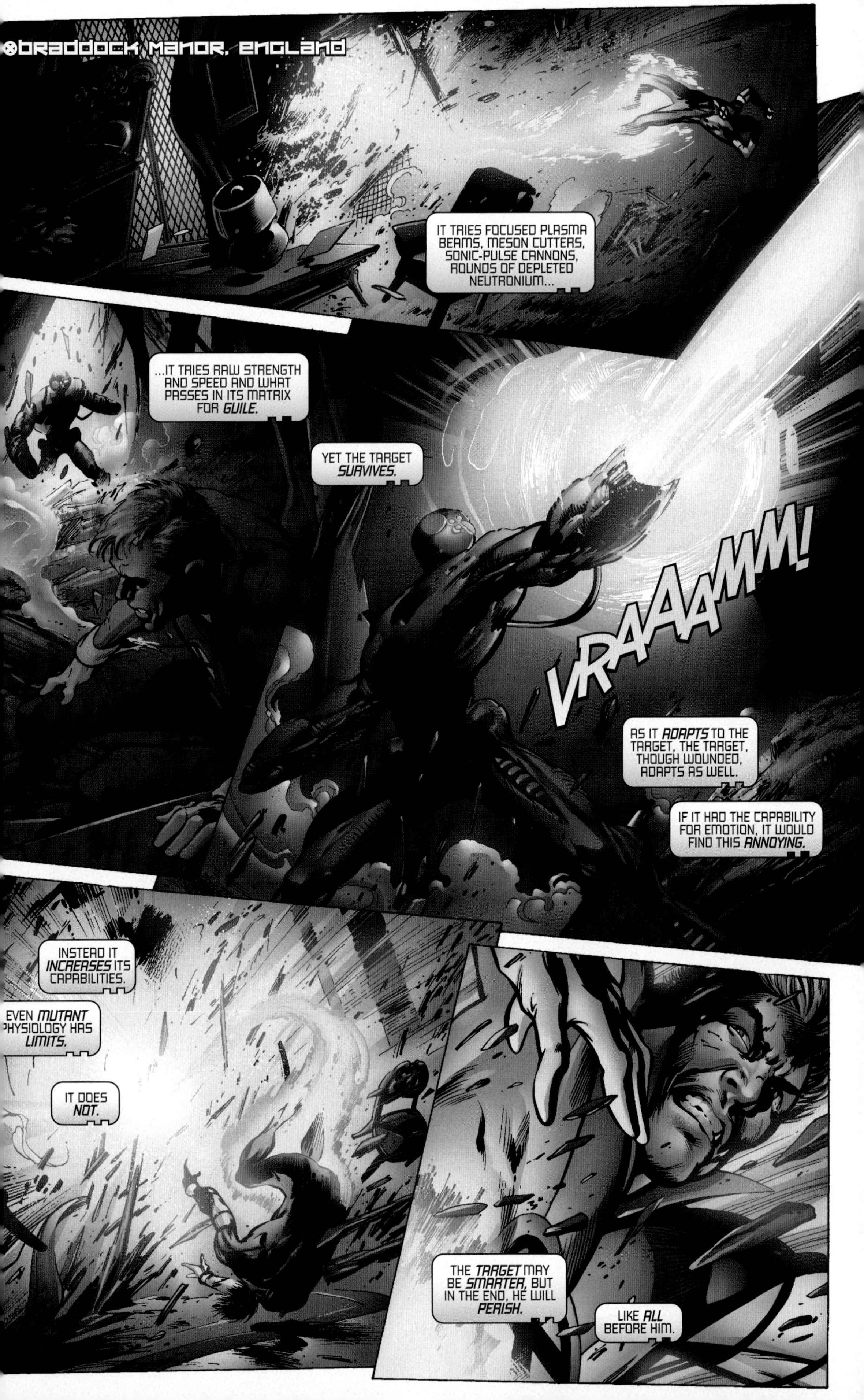
BRADDOCK MANOR, ENGLAND
IT TRIES FOCUSED PLASMA BEAMS, MESON CUTTERS, SONIC-PULSE CANNONS, ROUNDS OF DEPLETED NEUTRONIUM...
...IT TRIES RAW STRENGTH AND SPEED AND WHAT PASSES IN ITS MATRIX FOR GUILE.
YET THE TARGET SURVIVES.
VRAAAAMM!
AS IT ADAPTS TO THE TARGET, THE TARGET, THOUGH WOUNDED, ADAPTS AS WELL.
IF IT HAD THE CAPABILITY FOR EMOTION, IT WOULD FIND THIS ANNOYING.
INSTEAD IT INCREASES ITS CAPABILITIES.
EVEN MUTANT PHYSIOLOGY HAS LIMITS.
IT DOES NOT.
THE TARGET MAY BE SMARTER, BUT IN THE END, HE WILL PERISH.
LIKE ALL BEFORE HIM.

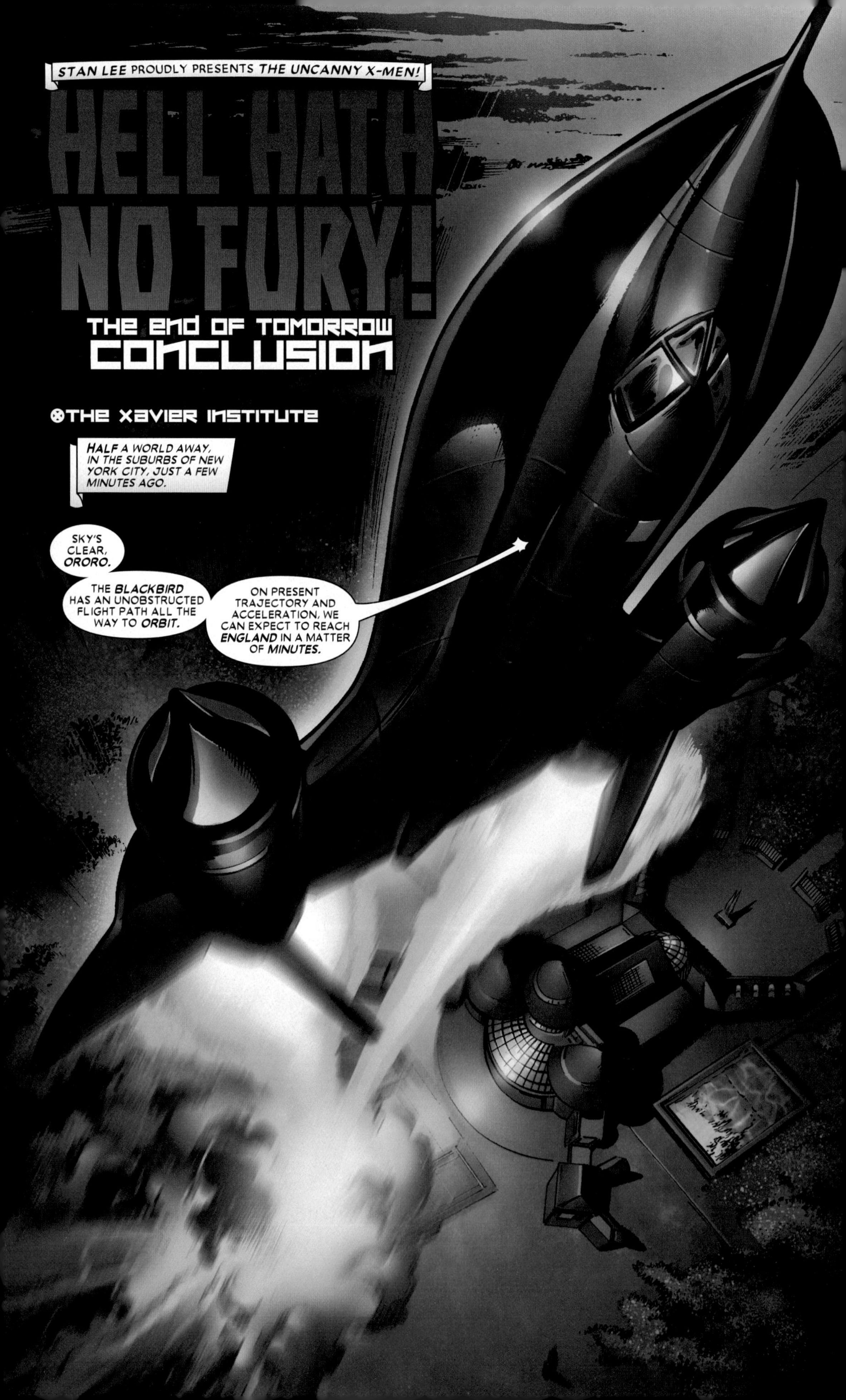
STAN LEE PROUDLY PRESENTS THE UNCANNY X-MEN!
HELL HATH NO FURY!
THE END OF TOMORROW CONCLUSION
THE XAVIER INSTITUTE
HALF A WORLD AWAY, IN THE SUBURBS OF NEW YORK CITY, JUST A FEW MINUTES AGO.
SKY'S CLEAR, ORORO.
THE BLACKBIRD HAS AN UNOBSTRUCTED FLIGHT PATH ALL THE WAY TO ORBIT.
ON PRESENT TRAJECTORY AND ACCELERATION, WE CAN EXPECT TO REACH ENGLAND IN A MATTER OF MINUTES.

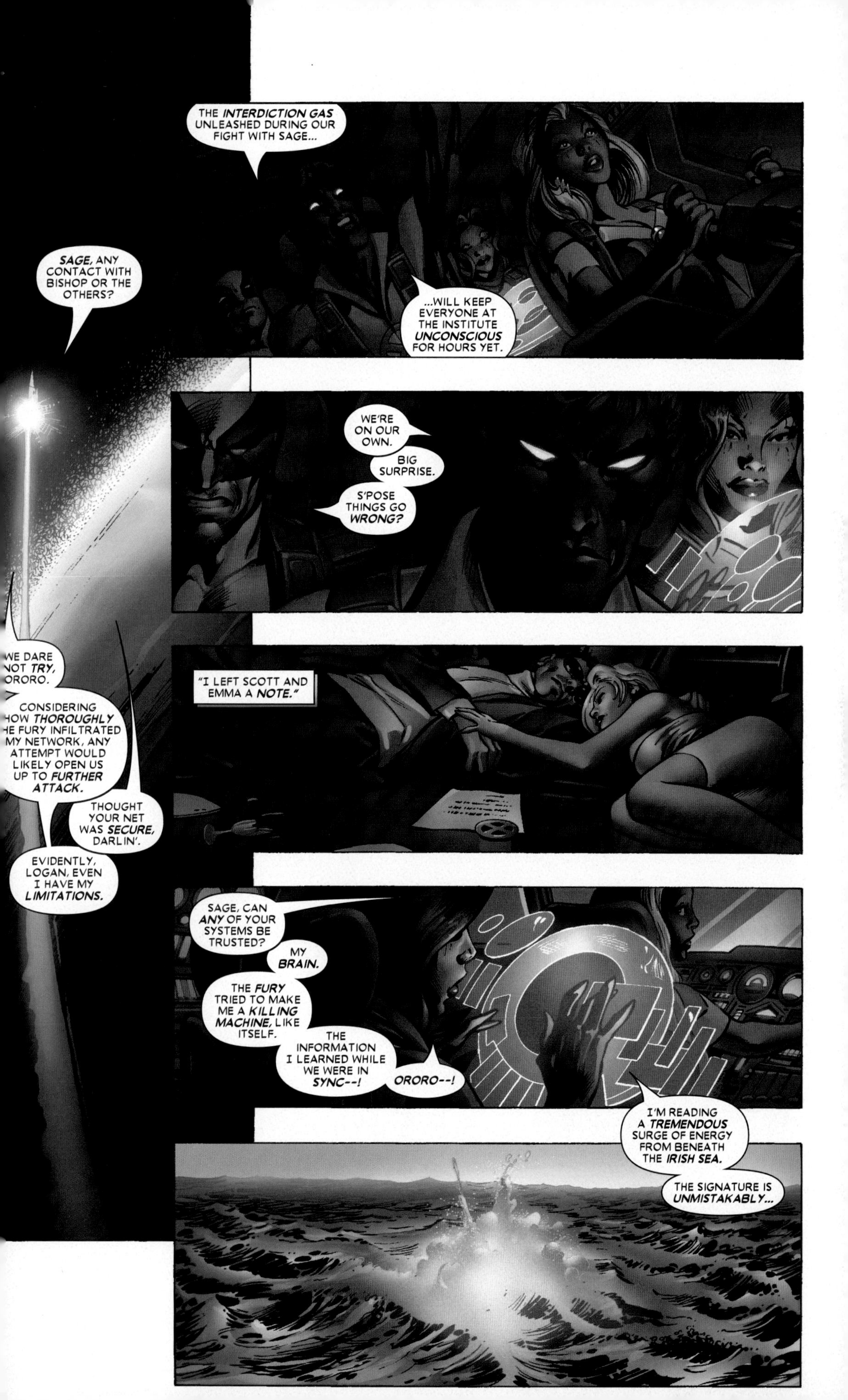
THE INTERDICTION GAS UNLEASHED DURING OUR FIGHT WITH SAGE...
...WILL KEEP EVERYONE AT THE INSTITUTE UNCONSCIOUS FOR HOURS YET.
SAGE, ANY CONTACT WITH BISHOP OR THE OTHERS?
WE'RE ON OUR OWN.
BIG SURPRISE.
S'POSE THINGS GO WRONG?
WE DARE NOT TRY, ORORO.
CONSIDERING HOW THOROUGHLY THE FURY INFILTRATED MY NETWORK, ANY ATTEMPT WOULD LIKELY OPEN US UP TO FURTHER ATTACK.
THOUGHT YOUR NET WAS SECURE, DARLIN'.
EVIDENTLY, LOGAN, EVEN I HAVE MY LIMITATIONS.
"I LEFT SCOTT AND EMMA A NOTE."
SAGE, CAN ANY OF YOUR SYSTEMS BE TRUSTED?
MY BRAIN.
THE FURY TRIED TO MAKE ME A KILLING MACHINE, LIKE ITSELF.
THE INFORMATION I LEARNED WHILE WE WERE IN SYNC--!
ORORO--!
I'M READING A TREMENDOUS SURGE OF ENERGY FROM BENEATH THE IRISH SEA.
THE SIGNATURE IS UNMISTAKABLY...

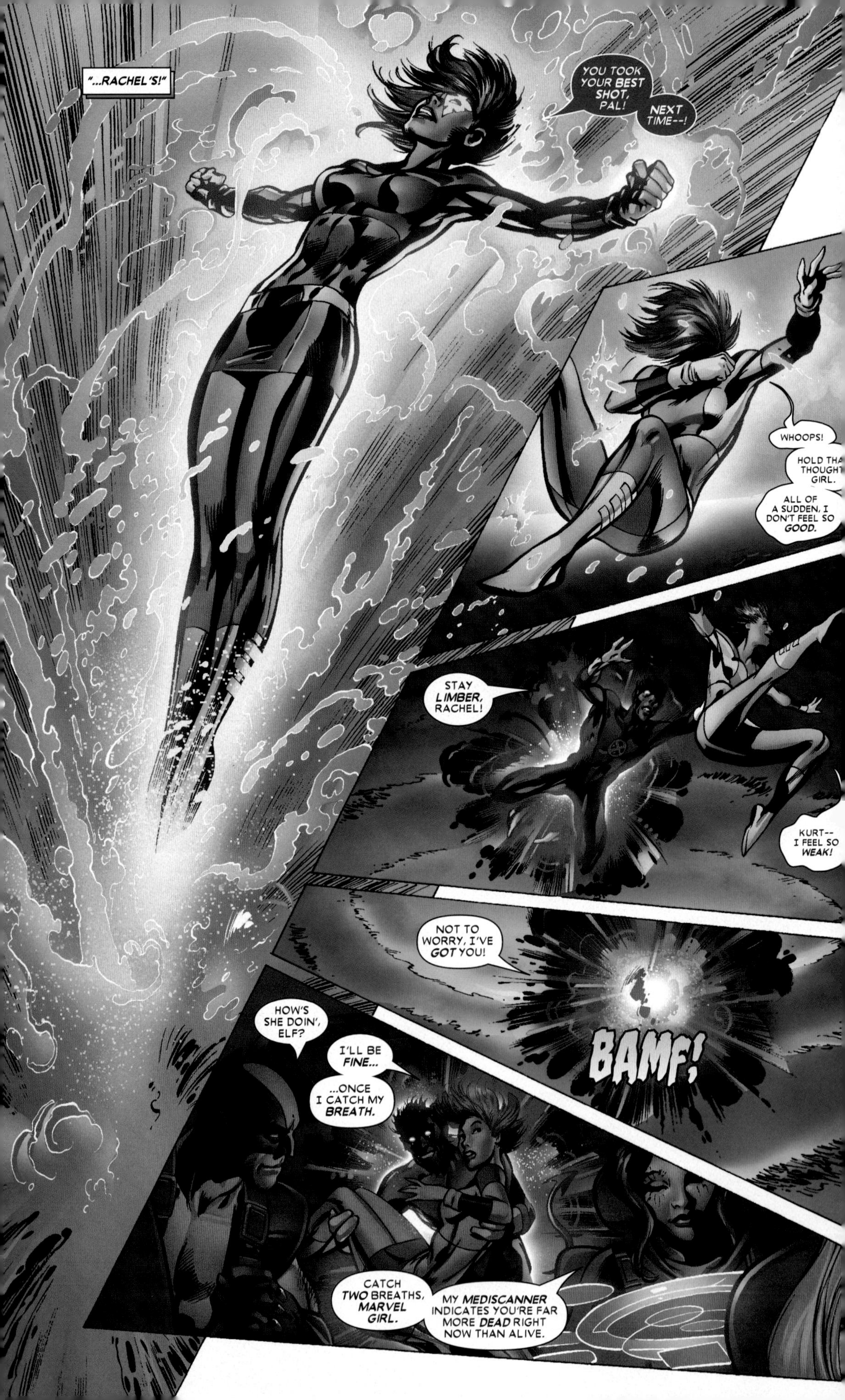
"...RACHEL'S!"
YOU TOOK YOUR BEST SHOT, PAL!
NEXT TIME--!
WHOOPS!
HOLD THA THOUGHT GIRL.
ALL OF A SUDDEN, I DON'T FEEL SO GOOD.
STAY LIMBER, RACHEL!
KURT-- I FEEL SO WEAK!
NOT TO WORRY, I'VE GOT YOU!
BAMF!
HOW'S SHE DOIN', ELF?
I'LL BE FINE...
...ONCE I CATCH MY BREATH.
CATCH TWO BREATHS, MARVEL GIRL.
MY MEDISCANNER INDICATES YOU'RE FAR MORE DEAD RIGHT NOW THAN ALIVE.

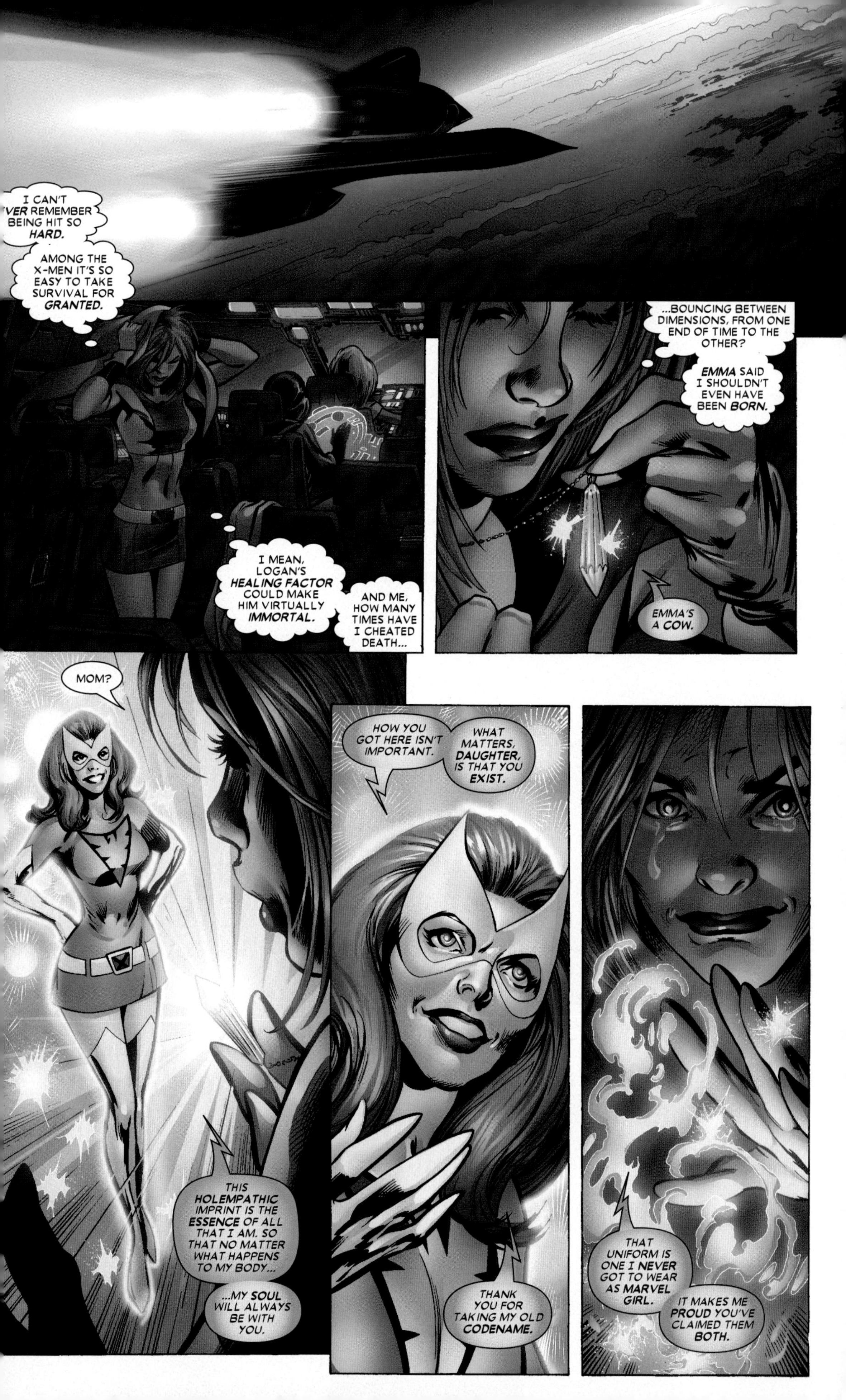
I CAN'T EVER REMEMBER BEING HIT SO HARD.
AMONG THE X-MEN IT'S SO EASY TO TAKE SURVIVAL FOR GRANTED.
I MEAN, LOGAN'S HEALING FACTOR COULD MAKE HIM VIRTUALLY IMMORTAL.
AND ME, HOW MANY TIMES HAVE I CHEATED DEATH...
...BOUNCING BETWEEN DIMENSIONS, FROM ONE END OF TIME TO THE OTHER?
EMMA SAID I SHOULDN'T EVEN HAVE BEEN BORN.
EMMA'S A COW.
MOM?
THIS HOLEMPATHIC IMPRINT IS THE ESSENCE OF ALL THAT I AM. SO THAT NO MATTER WHAT HAPPENS TO MY BODY...
...MY SOUL WILL ALWAYS BE WITH YOU.
HOW YOU GOT HERE ISN'T IMPORTANT.
WHAT MATTERS, DAUGHTER, IS THAT YOU EXIST.
THANK YOU FOR TAKING MY OLD CODENAME.
THAT UNIFORM IS ONE I NEVER GOT TO WEAR AS MARVEL GIRL.
IT MAKES ME PROUD YOU'VE CLAIMED THEM BOTH.

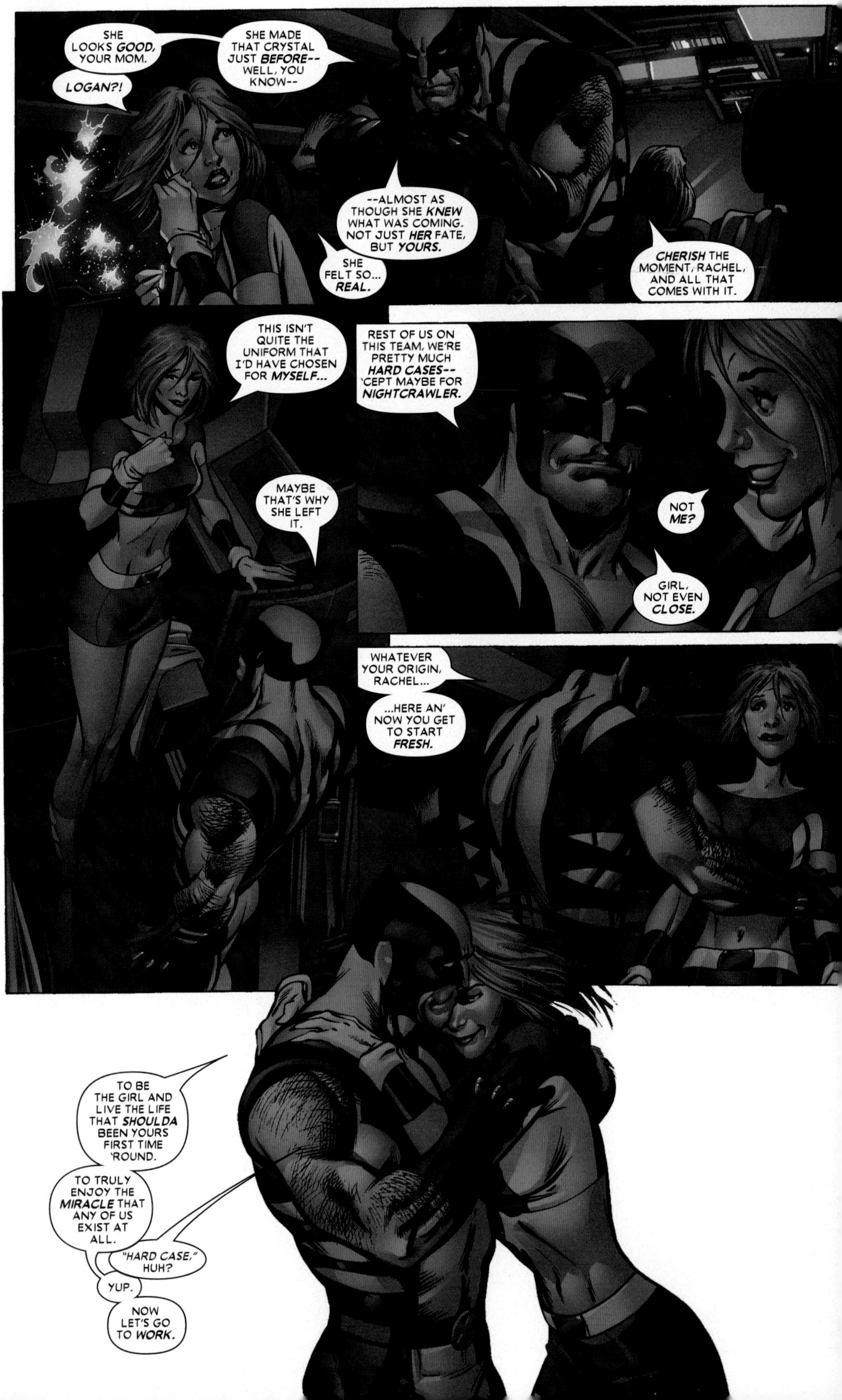
SHE LOOKS GOOD, YOUR MOM.
SHE MADE THAT CRYSTAL JUST BEFORE-- WELL, YOU KNOW--
LOGAN?!
--ALMOST AS THOUGH SHE KNEW WHAT WAS COMING. NOT JUST HER FATE, BUT YOURS.
SHE FELT SO... REAL.
CHERISH THE MOMENT, RACHEL, AND ALL THAT COMES WITH IT.
THIS ISN'T QUITE THE UNIFORM THAT I'D HAVE CHOSEN FOR MYSELF...
MAYBE THAT'S WHY SHE LEFT IT.
REST OF US ON THIS TEAM, WE'RE PRETTY MUCH HARD CASES-- 'CEPT MAYBE FOR NIGHTCRAWLER.
NOT ME?
GIRL, NOT EVEN CLOSE.
WHATEVER YOUR ORIGIN, RACHEL...
...HERE AN' NOW YOU GET TO START FRESH.
TO BE THE GIRL AND LIVE THE LIFE THAT SHOULDA BEEN YOURS FIRST TIME 'ROUND.
TO TRULY ENJOY THE MIRACLE THAT ANY OF US EXIST AT ALL.
"HARD CASE," HUH?
YUP.
NOW LET'S GO TO WORK.

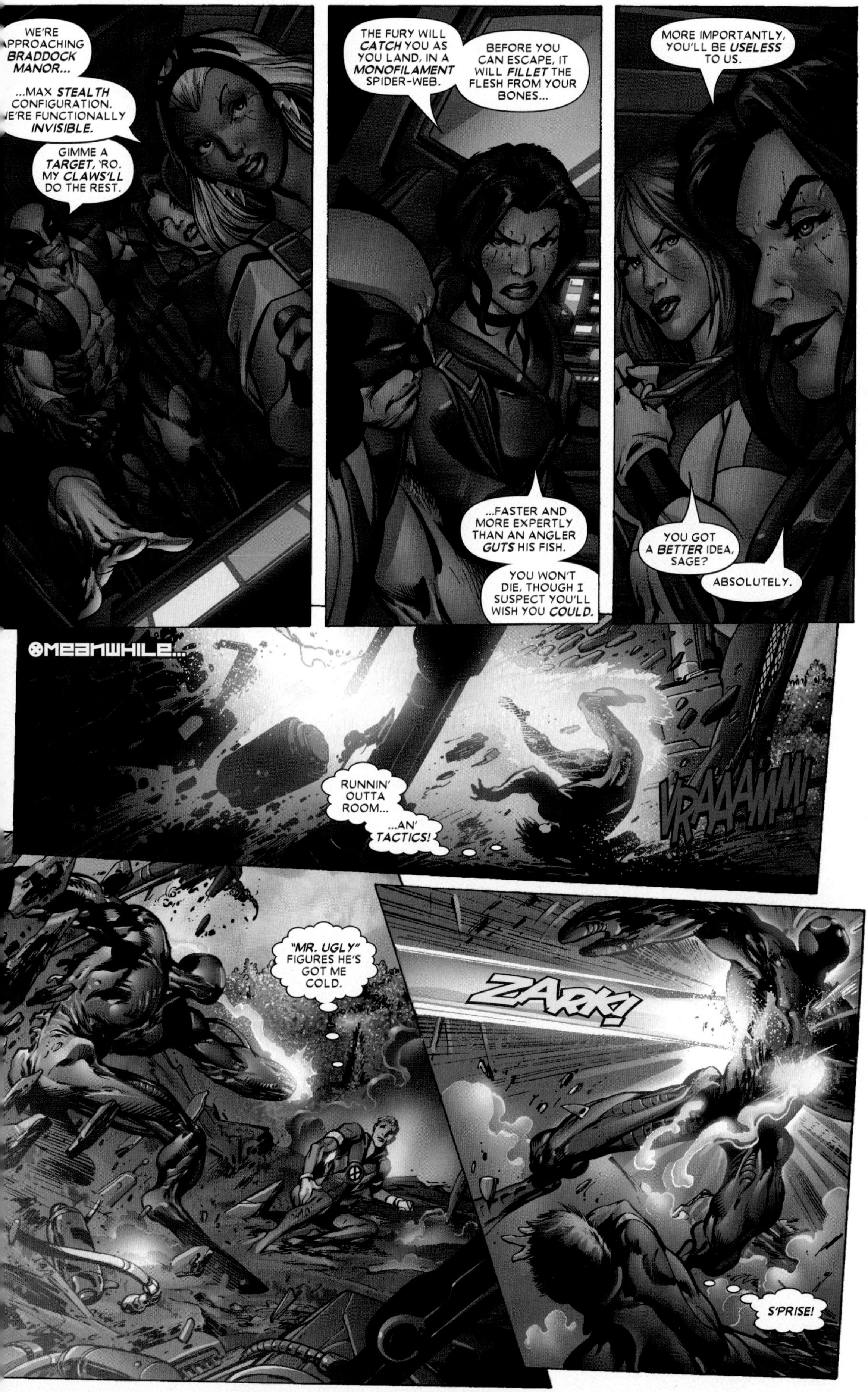
WE'RE APPROACHING BRADDOCK MANOR...
...MAX STEALTH CONFIGURATION. WE'RE FUNCTIONALLY INVISIBLE.
GIMME A TARGET, 'RO. MY CLAWS'LL DO THE REST.
THE FURY WILL CATCH YOU AS YOU LAND, IN A MONOFILAMENT SPIDER-WEB.
BEFORE YOU CAN ESCAPE, IT WILL FILLET THE FLESH FROM YOUR BONES...
...FASTER AND MORE EXPERTLY THAN AN ANGLER GUTS HIS FISH.
YOU WON'T DIE, THOUGH I SUSPECT YOU'LL WISH YOU COULD.
MORE IMPORTANTLY, YOU'LL BE USELESS TO US.
YOU GOT A BETTER IDEA, SAGE?
ABSOLUTELY.
MEANWHILE...
RUNNIN' OUTTA ROOM...
...AN' TACTICS!
VRAAAMM!
"MR. UGLY" FIGURES HE'S GOT ME COLD.
ZARK!
S'PRISE!

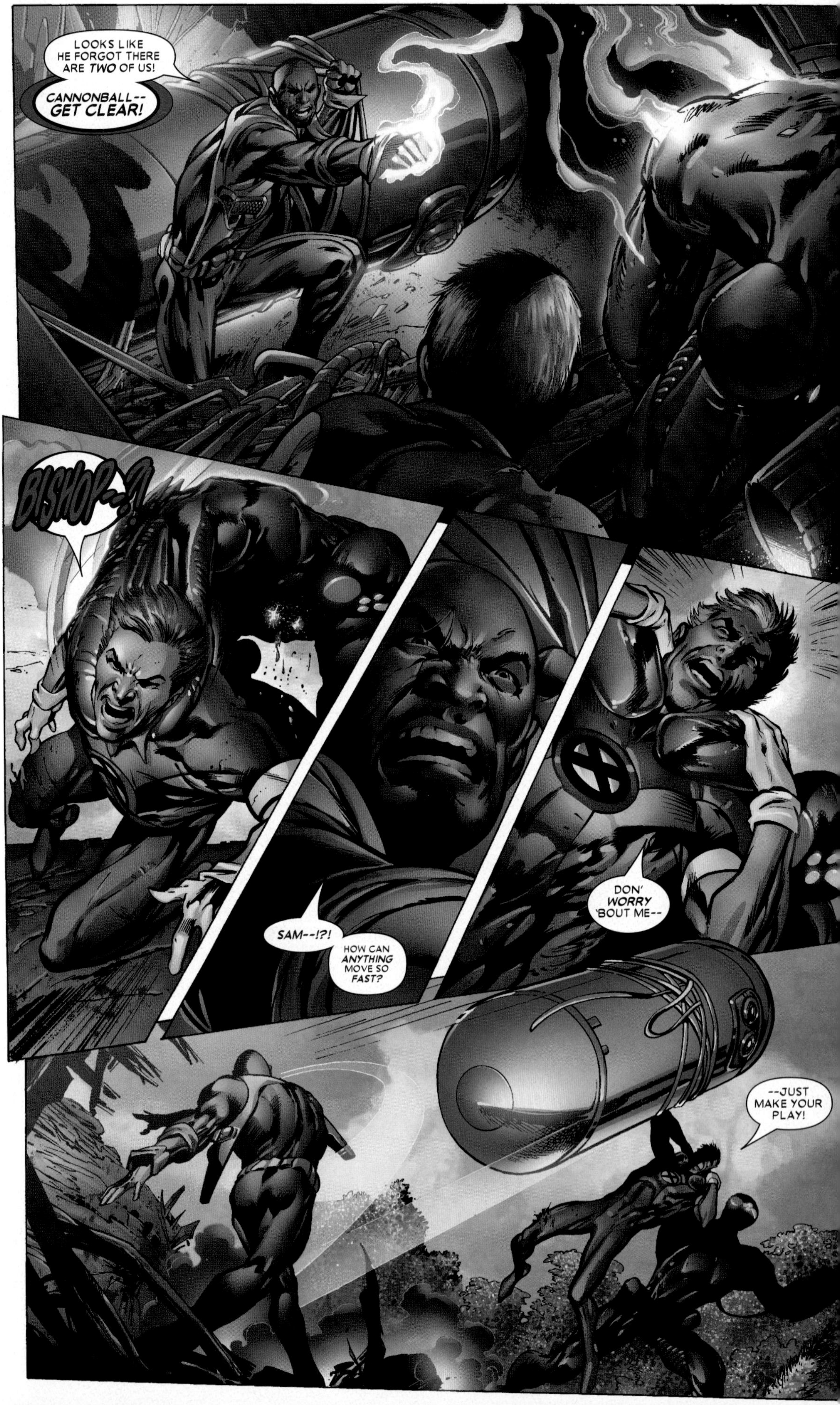
LOOKS LIKE HE FORGOT THERE ARE TWO OF US!
CANNONBALL-- GET CLEAR!
BISHOP--?!
SAM--!?!
HOW CAN ANYTHING MOVE SO FAST?
DON' WORRY 'BOUT ME--
--JUST MAKE YOUR PLAY!

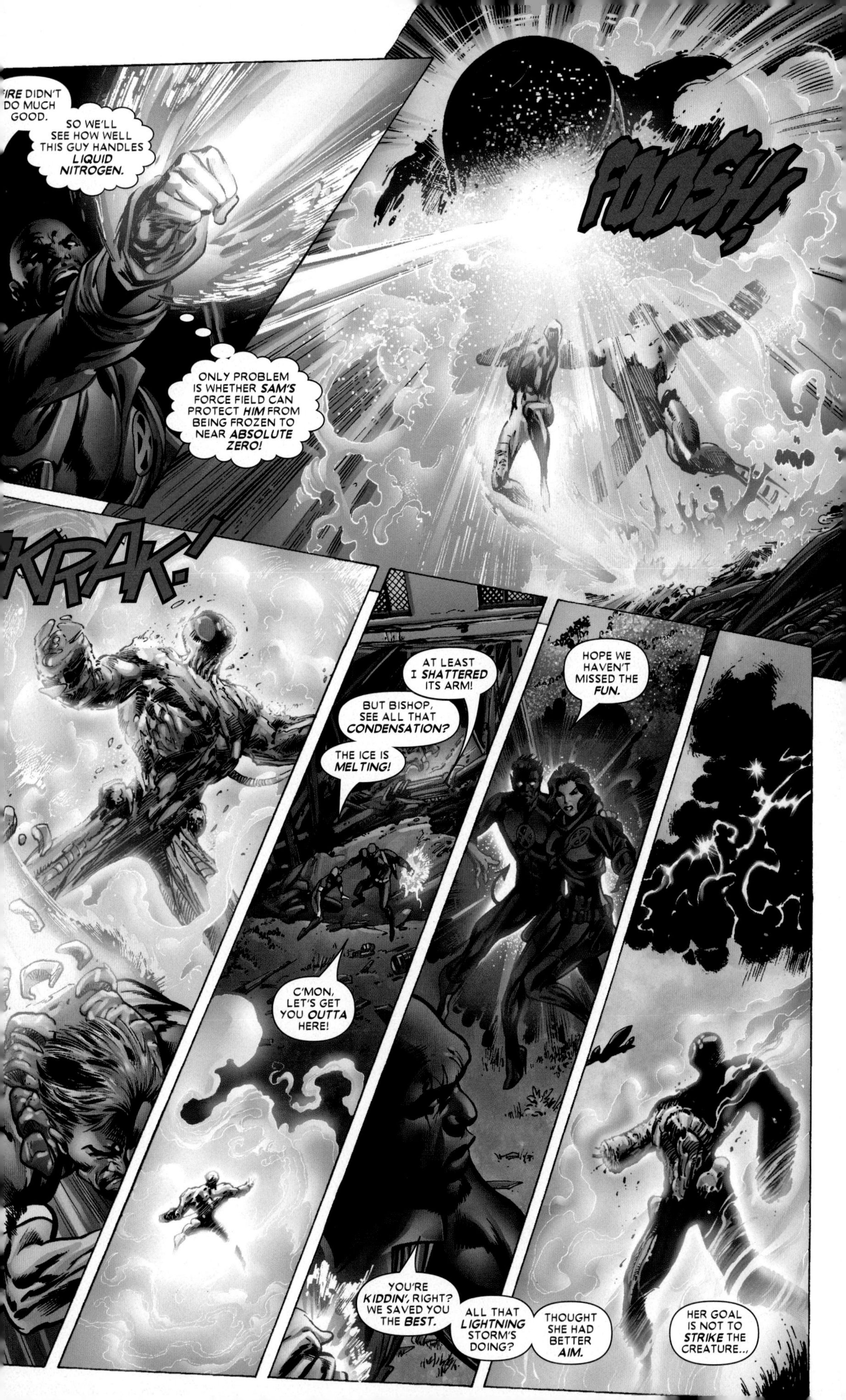

FIRE DIDN'T DO MUCH GOOD.
SO WE'LL SEE HOW WELL THIS GUY HANDLES LIQUID NITROGEN.
ONLY PROBLEM IS WHETHER SAM'S FORCE FIELD CAN PROTECT HIM FROM BEING FROZEN TO NEAR ABSOLUTE ZERO!
FOOSH!
KRAK!
AT LEAST I SHATTERED ITS ARM!
BUT BISHOP, SEE ALL THAT CONDENSATION?
THE ICE IS MELTING!
C'MON, LET'S GET YOU OUTTA HERE!
HOPE WE HAVEN'T MISSED THE FUN.
YOU'RE KIDDIN', RIGHT? WE SAVED YOU THE BEST.
ALL THAT LIGHTNING STORM'S DOING?
THOUGHT SHE HAD BETTER AIM.
HER GOAL IS NOT TO STRIKE THE CREATURE...

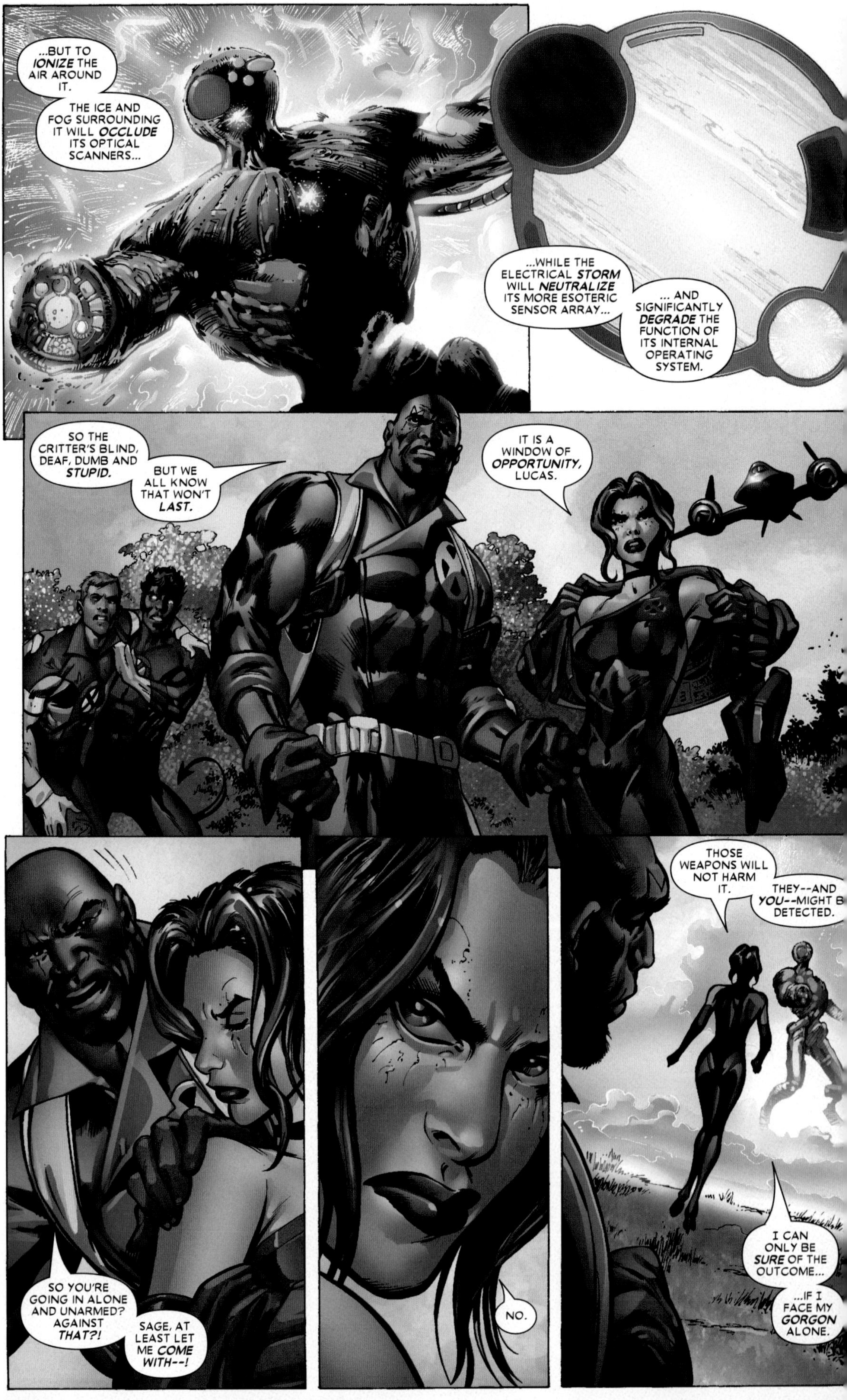
...BUT TO IONIZE THE AIR AROUND IT.
THE ICE AND FOG SURROUNDING IT WILL OCCLUDE ITS OPTICAL SCANNERS...
...WHILE THE ELECTRICAL STORM WILL NEUTRALIZE ITS MORE ESOTERIC SENSOR ARRAY...
... AND SIGNIFICANTLY DEGRADE THE FUNCTION OF ITS INTERNAL OPERATING SYSTEM.
SO THE CRITTER'S BLIND, DEAF, DUMB AND STUPID.
BUT WE ALL KNOW THAT WON'T LAST.
IT IS A WINDOW OF OPPORTUNITY, LUCAS.
SO YOU'RE GOING IN ALONE AND UNARMED? AGAINST THAT?!
SAGE, AT LEAST LET ME COME WITH--!
NO.
THOSE WEAPONS WILL NOT HARM IT.
THEY--AND YOU--MIGHT B DETECTED.
I CAN ONLY BE SURE OF THE OUTCOME...
...IF I FACE MY GORGON ALONE.

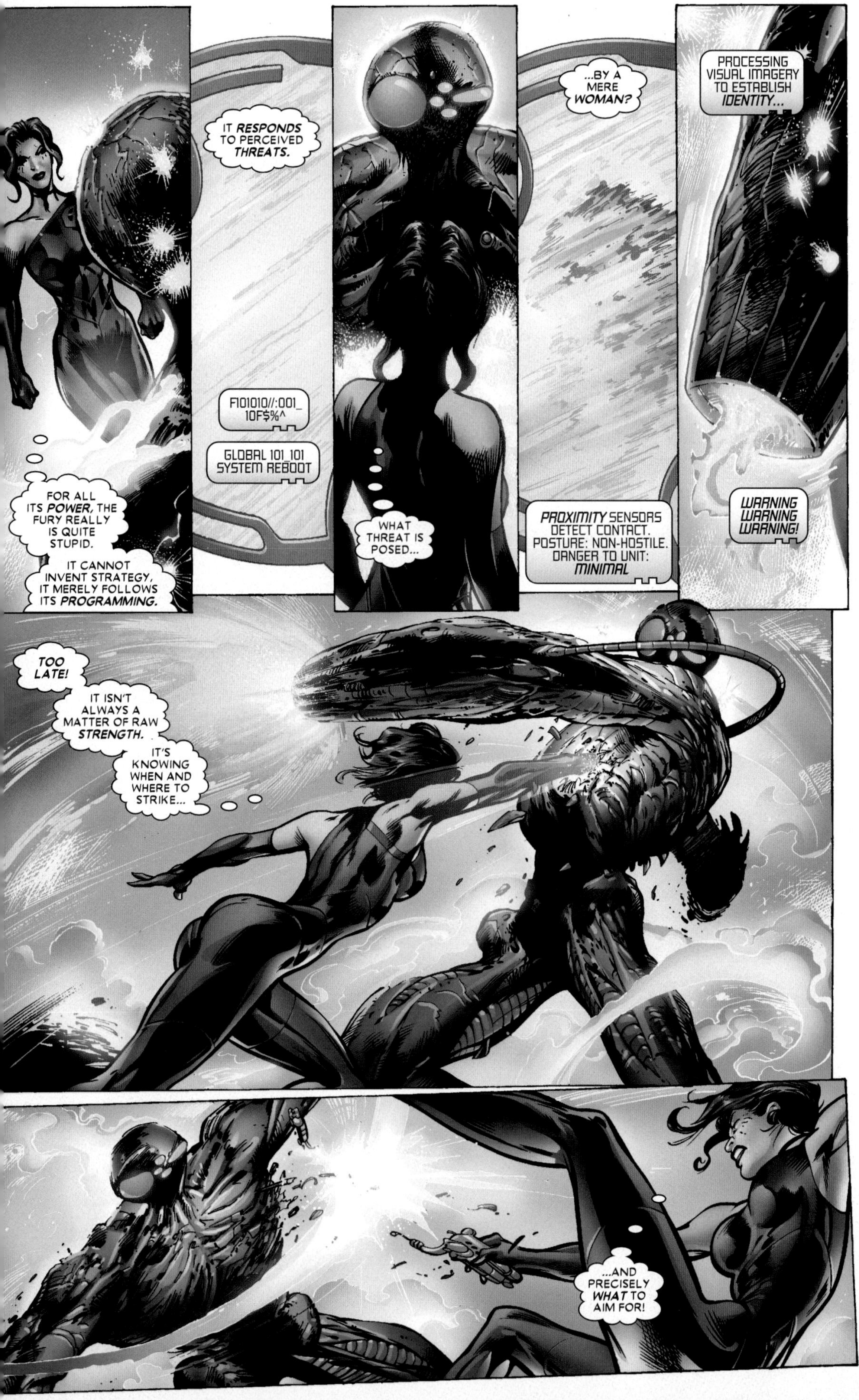

FOR ALL ITS POWER, THE FURY REALLY IS QUITE STUPID.
IT CANNOT INVENT STRATEGY, IT MERELY FOLLOWS ITS PROGRAMMING.
IT RESPONDS TO PERCEIVED THREATS.
F101010//:001_ 10F$%^
GLOBAL 101_101 SYSTEM REBOOT
WHAT THREAT IS POSED...
...BY A MERE WOMAN?
PROXIMITY SENSORS DETECT CONTACT. POSTURE: NON-HOSTILE. DANGER TO UNIT: MINIMAL
PROCESSING VISUAL IMAGERY TO ESTABLISH IDENTITY...
WARNING WARNING WARNING!
TOO LATE!
IT ISN'T ALWAYS A MATTER OF RAW STRENGTH.
IT'S KNOWING WHEN AND WHERE TO STRIKE...
...AND PRECISELY WHAT TO AIM FOR!

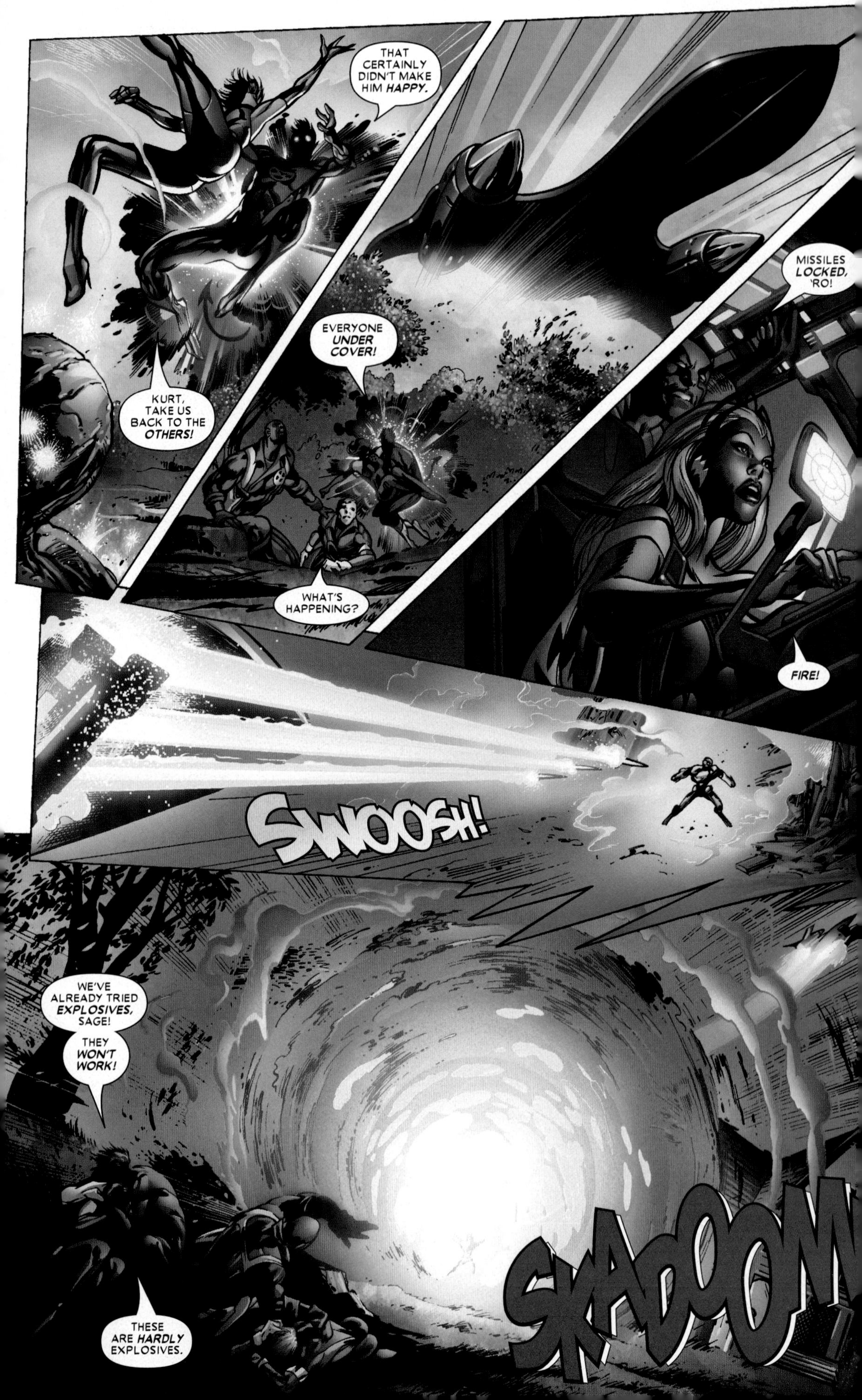
THAT CERTAINLY DIDN'T MAKE HIM HAPPY.
KURT, TAKE US BACK TO THE OTHERS!
EVERYONE UNDER COVER!
WHAT'S HAPPENING?
MISSILES LOCKED, 'RO!
FIRE!
SWOOSH!
WE'VE ALREADY TRIED EXPLOSIVES, SAGE!
THEY WON'T WORK!
THESE ARE HARDLY EXPLOSIVES.
SKADOOOM

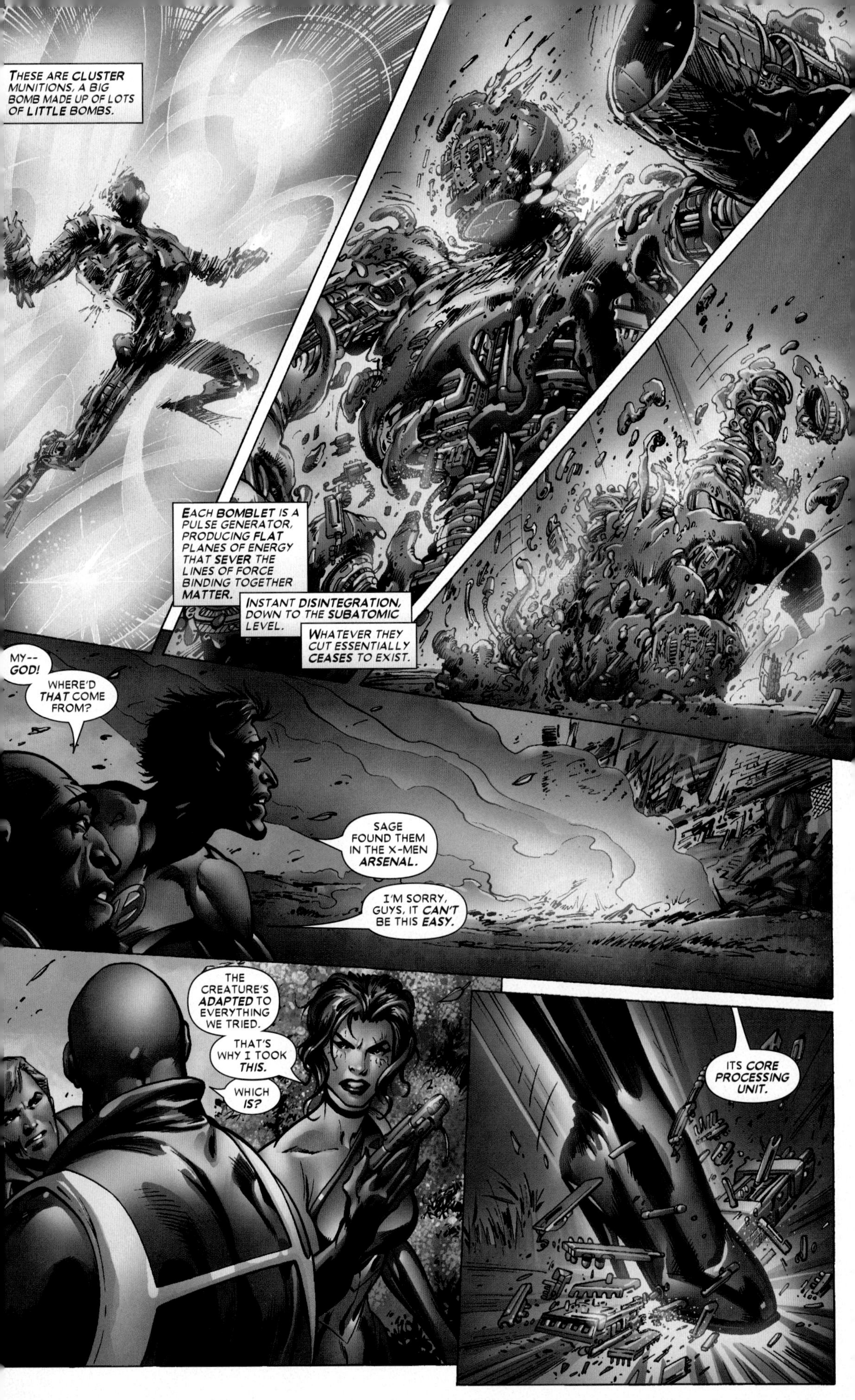
THESE ARE CLUSTER MUNITIONS, A BIG BOMB MADE UP OF LOTS OF LITTLE BOMBS.
EACH BOMBLET IS A PULSE GENERATOR, PRODUCING FLAT PLANES OF ENERGY THAT SEVER THE LINES OF FORCE BINDING TOGETHER MATTER.
INSTANT DISINTEGRATION, DOWN TO THE SUBATOMIC LEVEL.
WHATEVER THEY CUT ESSENTIALLY CEASES TO EXIST.
MY-- GOD!
WHERE'D THAT COME FROM?
SAGE FOUND THEM IN THE X-MEN ARSENAL.
I'M SORRY, GUYS, IT CAN'T BE THIS EASY.
THE CREATURE'S ADAPTED TO EVERYTHING WE TRIED.
THAT'S WHY I TOOK THIS.
WHICH IS?
ITS CORE PROCESSING UNIT.

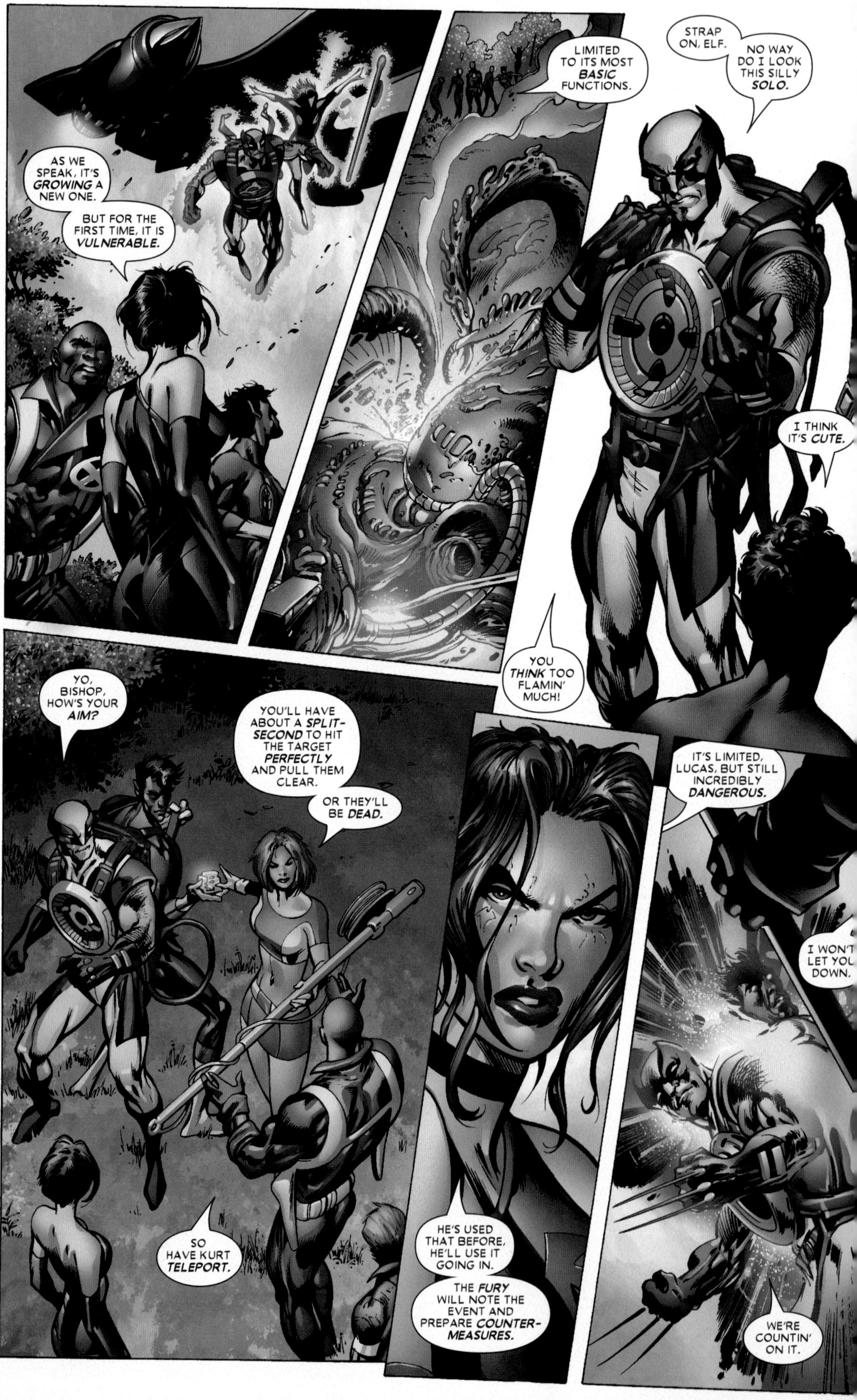
AS WE SPEAK, IT'S GROWING A NEW ONE.
BUT FOR THE FIRST TIME, IT IS VULNERABLE.
LIMITED TO ITS MOST BASIC FUNCTIONS.
STRAP ON, ELF.
NO WAY DO I LOOK THIS SILLY SOLO.
I THINK IT'S CUTE.
YOU THINK TOO FLAMIN' MUCH!
YO, BISHOP, HOW'S YOUR AIM?
YOU'LL HAVE ABOUT A SPLIT-SECOND TO HIT THE TARGET PERFECTLY AND PULL THEM CLEAR.
OR THEY'LL BE DEAD.
SO HAVE KURT TELEPORT.
HE'S USED THAT BEFORE, HE'LL USE IT GOING IN.
THE FURY WILL NOTE THE EVENT AND PREPARE COUNTER-MEASURES.
IT'S LIMITED, LUCAS, BUT STILL INCREDIBLY DANGEROUS.
I WON'T LET YOU DOWN.
WE'RE COUNTIN' ON IT.

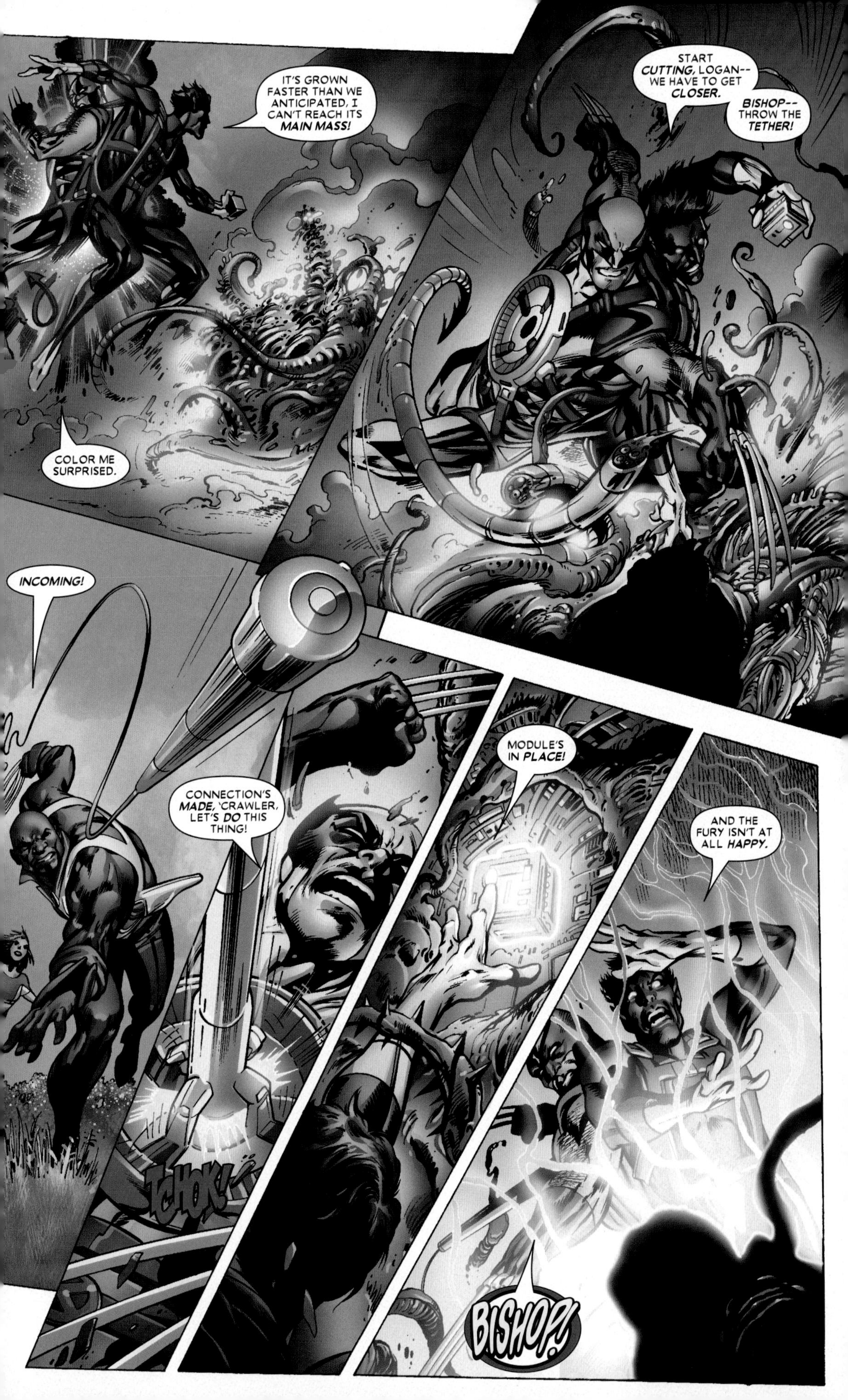
IT'S GROWN FASTER THAN WE ANTICIPATED, I CAN'T REACH ITS *MAIN MASS!*
COLOR ME SURPRISED.
START *CUTTING*, LOGAN-- WE HAVE TO GET *CLOSER.*
BISHOP-- THROW THE *TETHER!*
INCOMING!
CONNECTION'S *MADE*, 'CRAWLER, LET'S *DO* THIS THING!
TCHOK!
MODULE'S IN *PLACE!*
AND THE FURY ISN'T AT ALL *HAPPY.*
BISHOP!

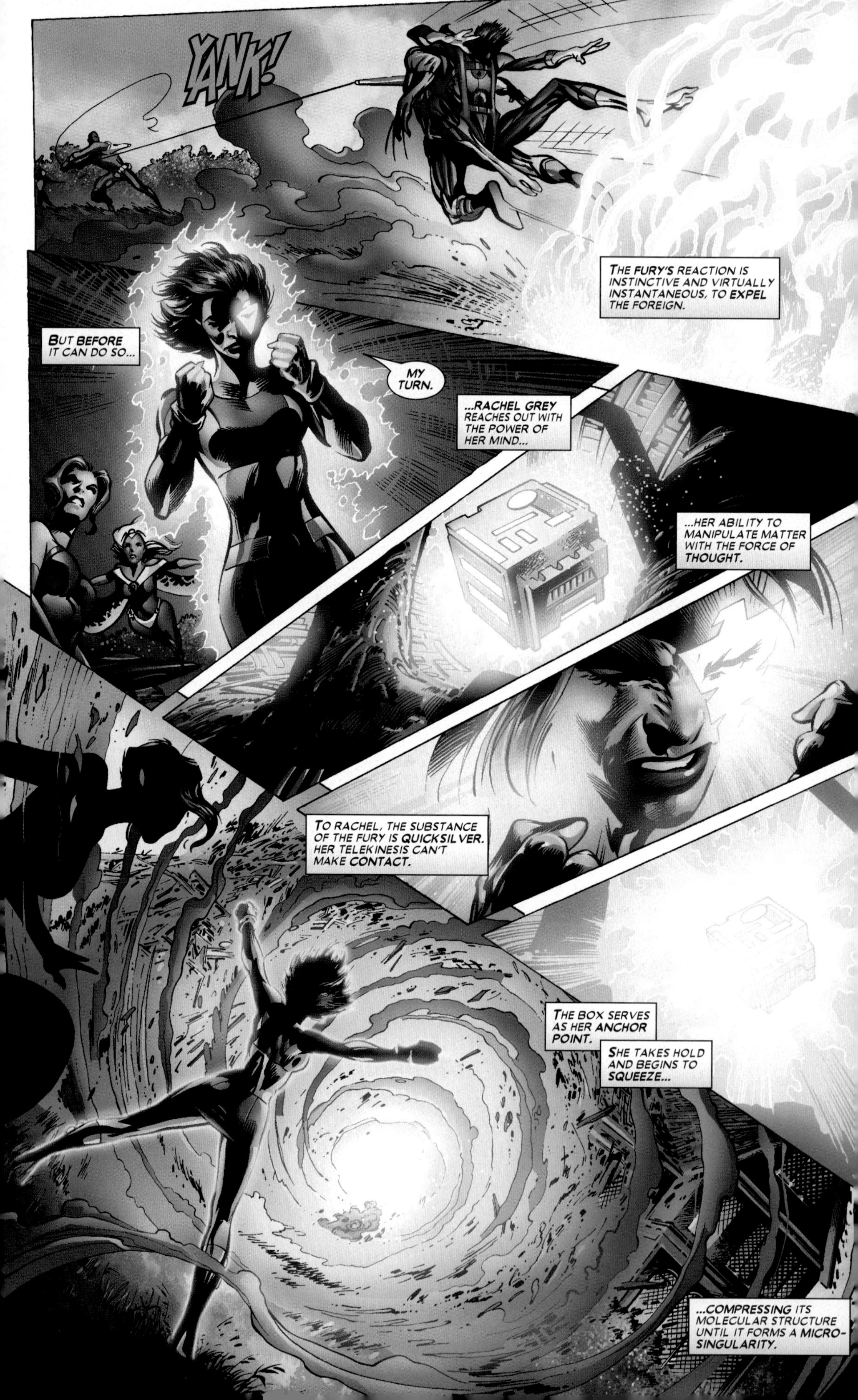
YANK!
THE FURY'S REACTION IS INSTINCTIVE AND VIRTUALLY INSTANTANEOUS, TO EXPEL THE FOREIGN.
BUT BEFORE IT CAN DO SO...
MY TURN.
...RACHEL GREY REACHES OUT WITH THE POWER OF HER MIND...
...HER ABILITY TO MANIPULATE MATTER WITH THE FORCE OF THOUGHT.
TO RACHEL, THE SUBSTANCE OF THE FURY IS QUICKSILVER. HER TELEKINESIS CAN'T MAKE CONTACT.
THE BOX SERVES AS HER ANCHOR POINT.
SHE TAKES HOLD AND BEGINS TO SQUEEZE...
...COMPRESSING ITS MOLECULAR STRUCTURE UNTIL IT FORMS A MICRO-SINGULARITY.

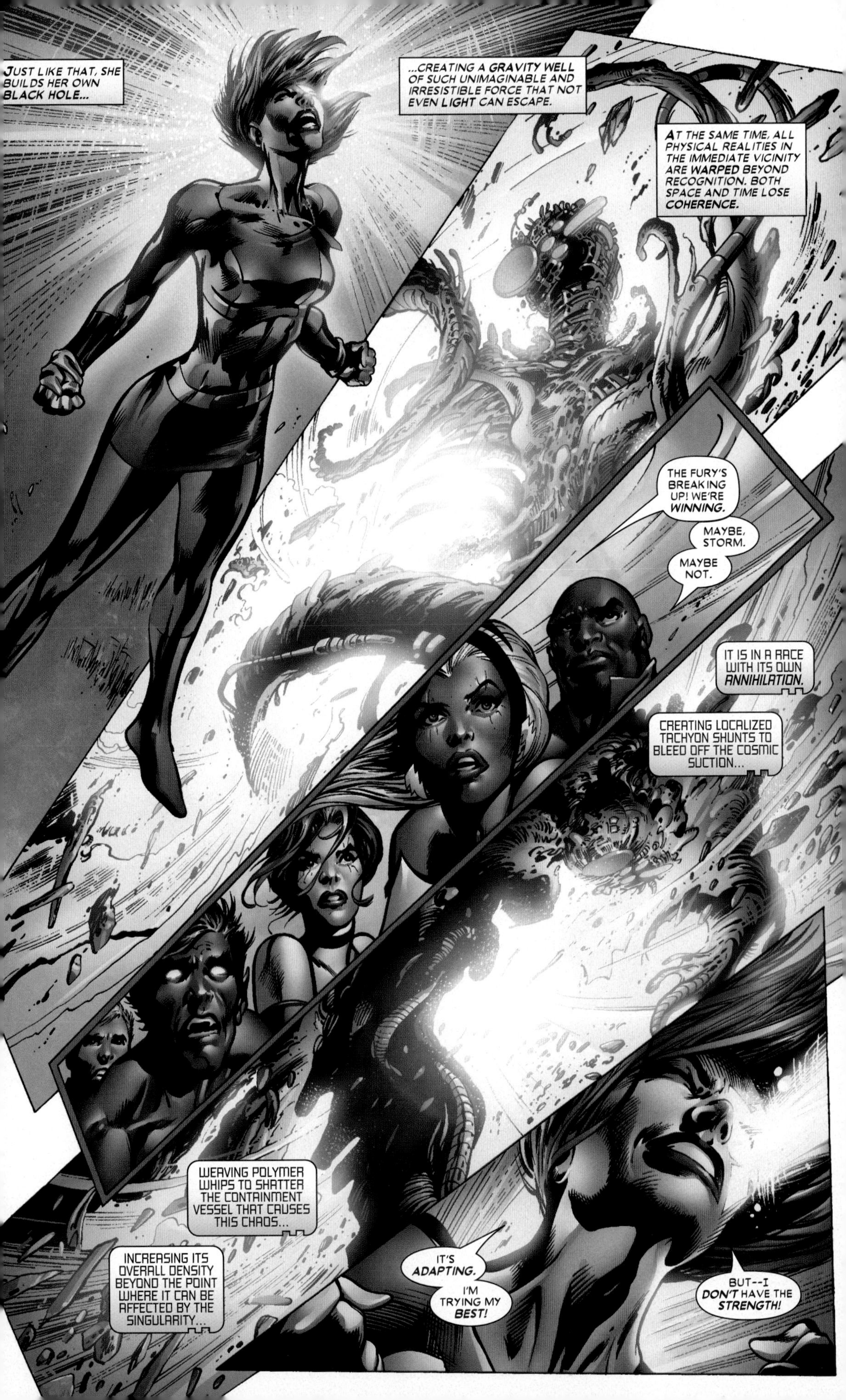
JUST LIKE THAT, SHE BUILDS HER OWN BLACK HOLE...
...CREATING A GRAVITY WELL OF SUCH UNIMAGINABLE AND IRRESISTIBLE FORCE THAT NOT EVEN LIGHT CAN ESCAPE.
AT THE SAME TIME, ALL PHYSICAL REALITIES IN THE IMMEDIATE VICINITY ARE WARPED BEYOND RECOGNITION. BOTH SPACE AND TIME LOSE COHERENCE.
THE FURY'S BREAKING UP! WE'RE WINNING.
MAYBE, STORM.
MAYBE NOT.
IT IS IN A RACE WITH ITS OWN ANNIHILATION.
CREATING LOCALIZED TACHYON SHUNTS TO BLEED OFF THE COSMIC SUCTION...
WEAVING POLYMER WHIPS TO SHATTER THE CONTAINMENT VESSEL THAT CAUSES THIS CHAOS...
INCREASING ITS OVERALL DENSITY BEYOND THE POINT WHERE IT CAN BE AFFECTED BY THE SINGULARITY...
IT'S ADAPTING.
I'M TRYING MY BEST!
BUT--I DON'T HAVE THE STRENGTH!

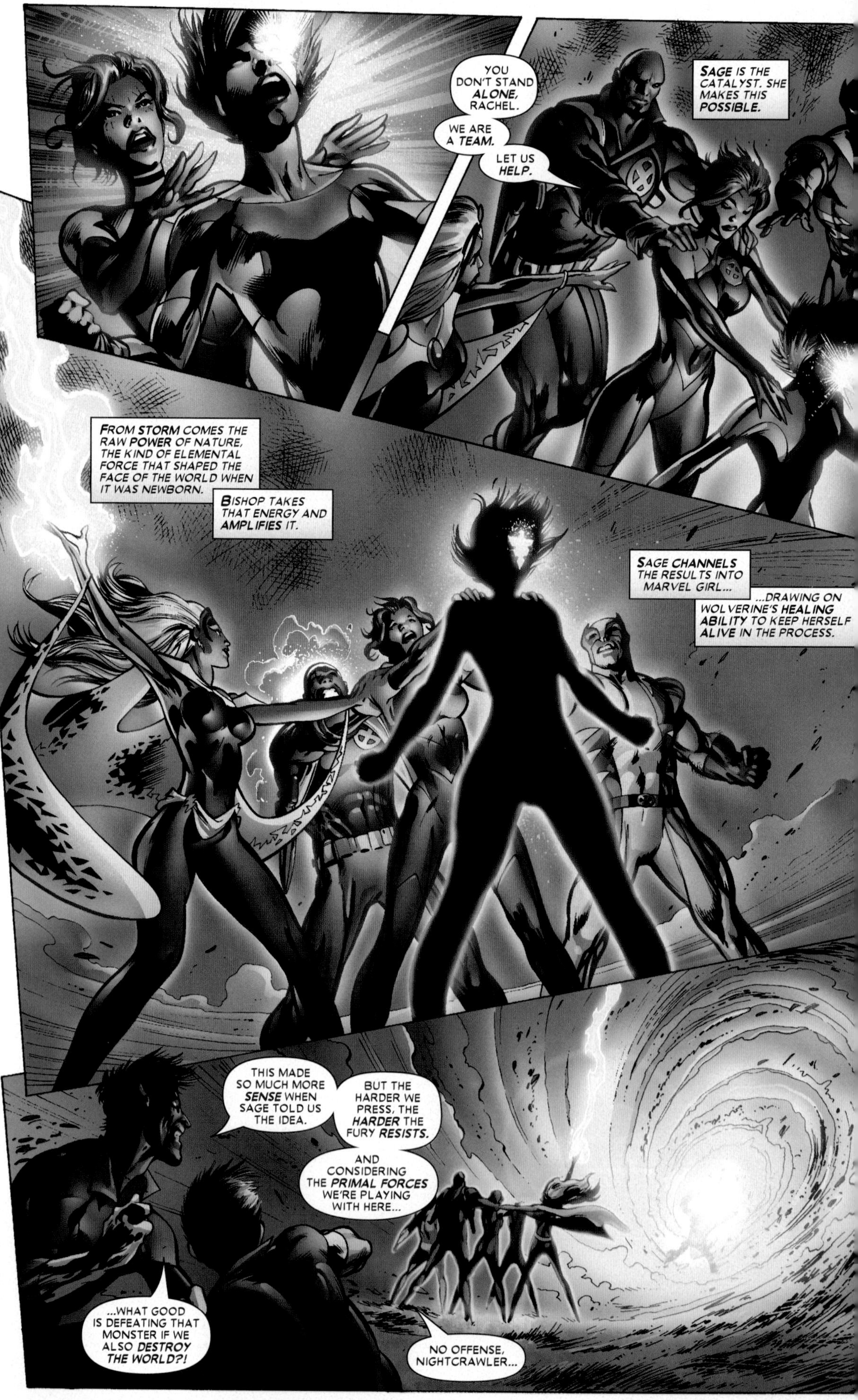
YOU DON'T STAND ALONE, RACHEL.
WE ARE A TEAM.
LET US HELP.
SAGE IS THE CATALYST. SHE MAKES THIS POSSIBLE.
FROM STORM COMES THE RAW POWER OF NATURE, THE KIND OF ELEMENTAL FORCE THAT SHAPED THE FACE OF THE WORLD WHEN IT WAS NEWBORN.
BISHOP TAKES THAT ENERGY AND AMPLIFIES IT.
SAGE CHANNELS THE RESULTS INTO MARVEL GIRL...
...DRAWING ON WOLVERINE'S HEALING ABILITY TO KEEP HERSELF ALIVE IN THE PROCESS.
THIS MADE SO MUCH MORE SENSE WHEN SAGE TOLD US THE IDEA.
BUT THE HARDER WE PRESS, THE HARDER THE FURY RESISTS.
AND CONSIDERING THE PRIMAL FORCES WE'RE PLAYING WITH HERE...
...WHAT GOOD IS DEFEATING THAT MONSTER IF WE ALSO DESTROY THE WORLD?!
NO OFFENSE, NIGHTCRAWLER...

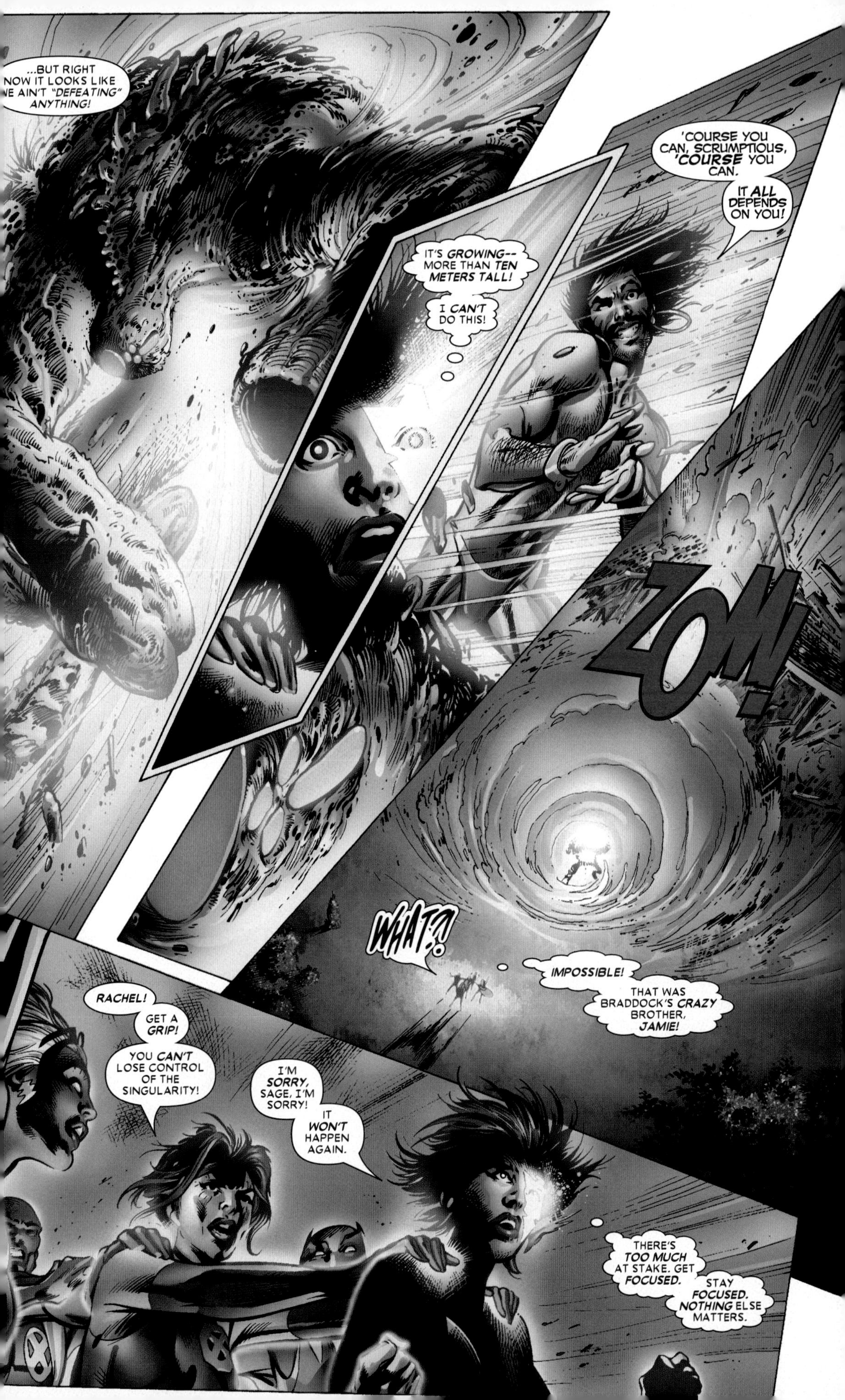
...BUT RIGHT NOW IT LOOKS LIKE WE AIN'T "DEFEATING" ANYTHING!
IT'S GROWING-- MORE THAN TEN METERS TALL!
I CAN'T DO THIS!
'COURSE YOU CAN, SCRUMPTIOUS, 'COURSE YOU CAN.
IT ALL DEPENDS ON YOU!
ZOM!
WHAT?!
IMPOSSIBLE!
THAT WAS BRADDOCK'S CRAZY BROTHER, JAMIE!
RACHEL!
GET A GRIP!
YOU CAN'T LOSE CONTROL OF THE SINGULARITY!
I'M SORRY, SAGE, I'M SORRY!
IT WON'T HAPPEN AGAIN.
THERE'S TOO MUCH AT STAKE. GET FOCUSED.
STAY FOCUSED. NOTHING ELSE MATTERS.

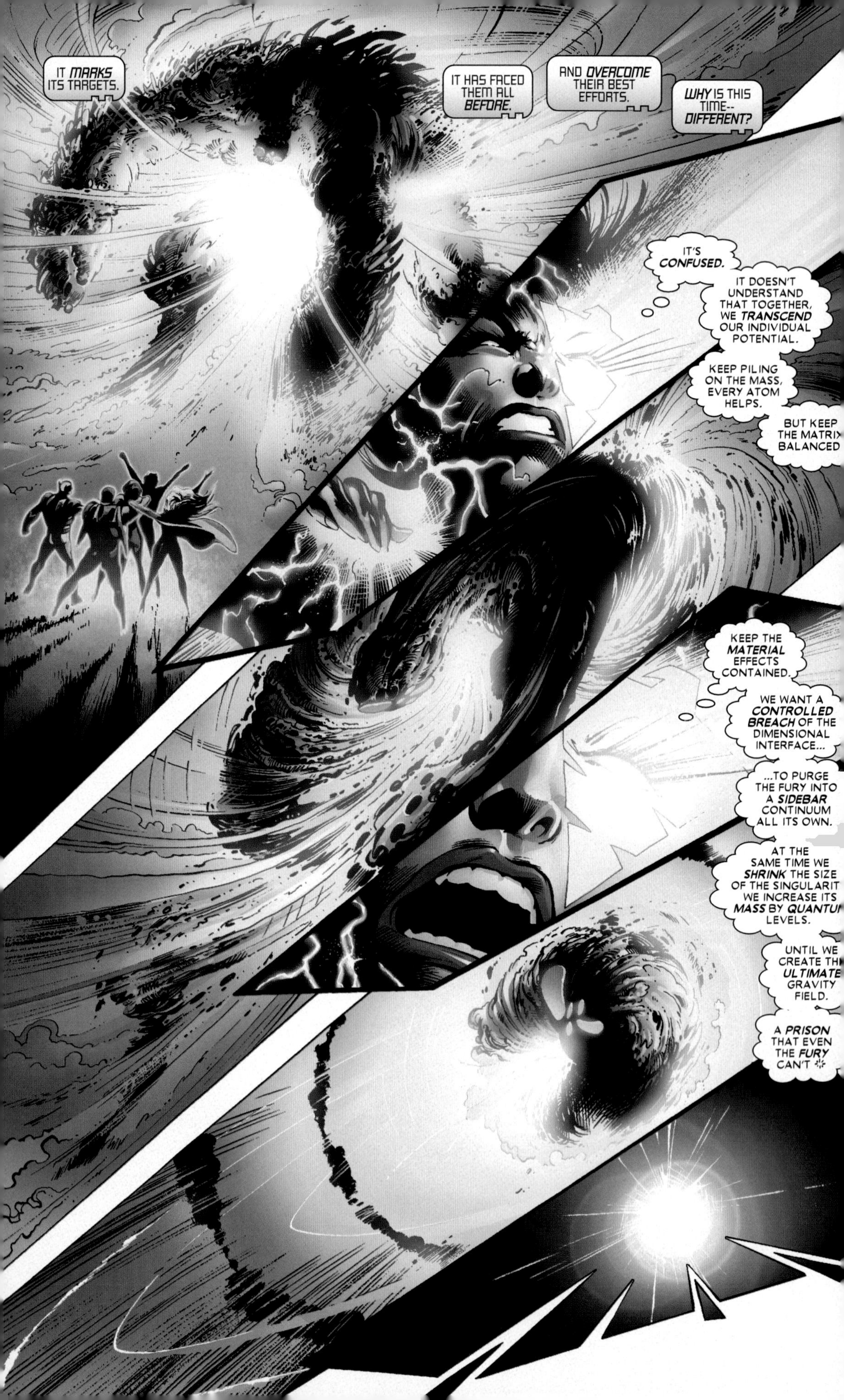
IT MARKS ITS TARGETS.
IT HAS FACED THEM ALL BEFORE.
AND OVERCOME THEIR BEST EFFORTS.
WHY IS THIS TIME-- DIFFERENT?
IT'S CONFUSED.
IT DOESN'T UNDERSTAND THAT TOGETHER, WE TRANSCEND OUR INDIVIDUAL POTENTIAL.
KEEP PILING ON THE MASS, EVERY ATOM HELPS.
BUT KEEP THE MATRI BALANCED
KEEP THE MATERIAL EFFECTS CONTAINED.
WE WANT A CONTROLLED BREACH OF THE DIMENSIONAL INTERFACE...
...TO PURGE THE FURY INTO A SIDEBAR CONTINUUM ALL ITS OWN.
AT THE SAME TIME WE SHRINK THE SIZE OF THE SINGULARIT WE INCREASE ITS MASS BY QUANTU LEVELS.
UNTIL WE CREATE TH ULTIMATE GRAVITY FIELD.
A PRISON THAT EVEN THE FURY CAN'T

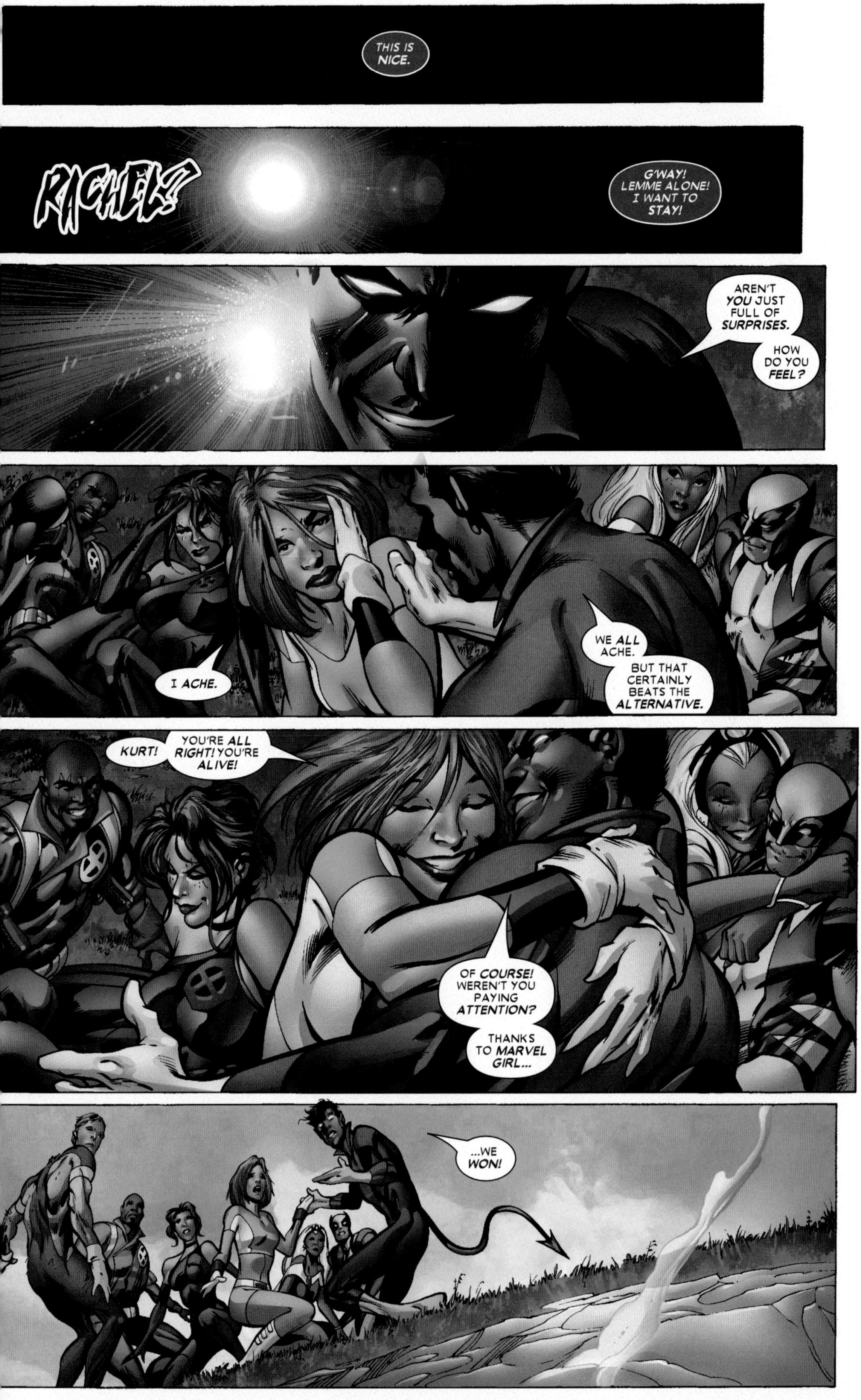
THIS IS NICE.
RACHEL?
G'WAY! LEMME ALONE! I WANT TO STAY!
AREN'T YOU JUST FULL OF SURPRISES.
HOW DO YOU FEEL?
I ACHE.
WE ALL ACHE.
BUT THAT CERTAINLY BEATS THE ALTERNATIVE.
KURT!
YOU'RE ALL RIGHT! YOU'RE ALIVE!
OF COURSE! WEREN'T YOU PAYING ATTENTION?
THANKS TO MARVEL GIRL...
...WE WON!

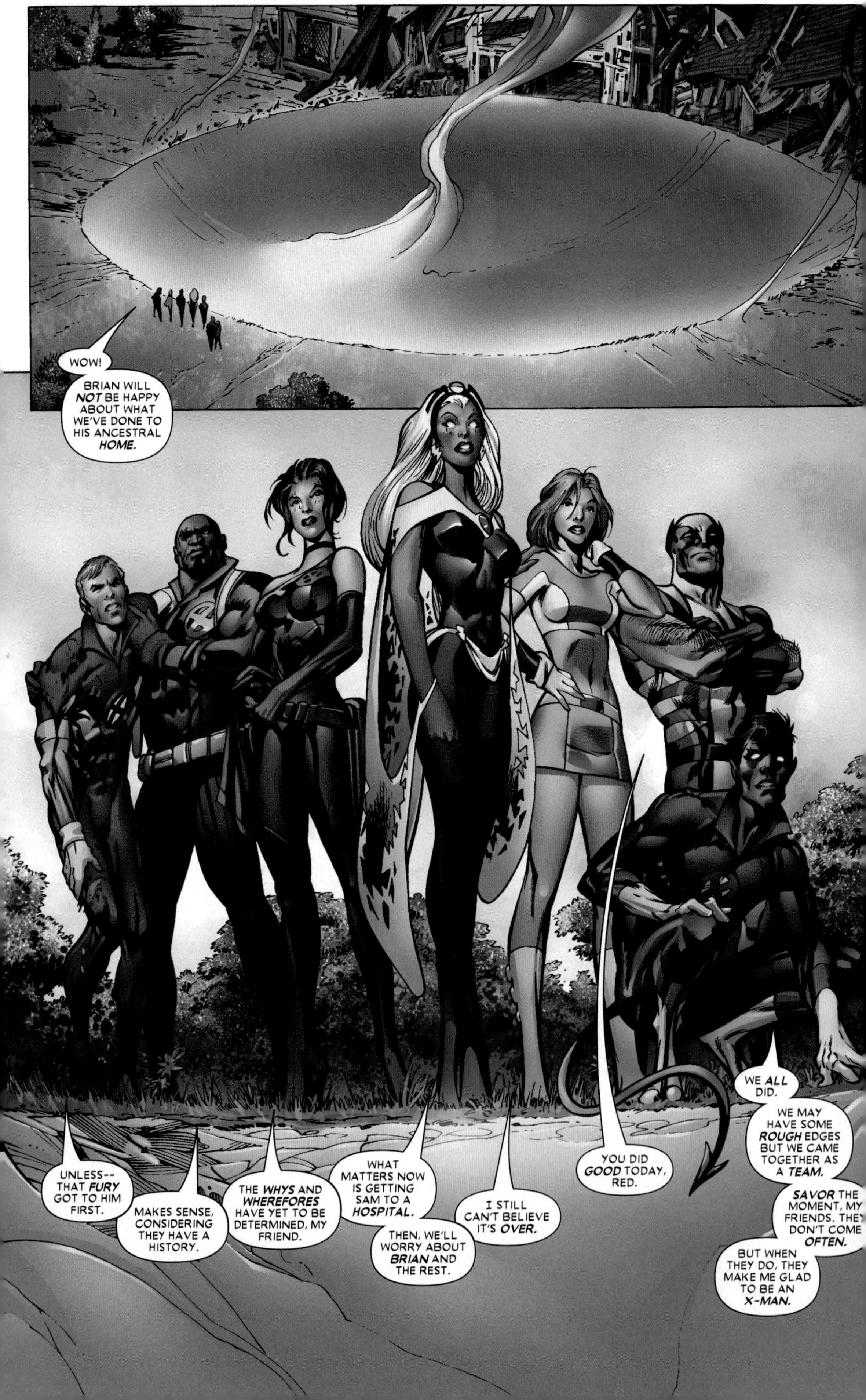

WOW!
BRIAN WILL NOT BE HAPPY ABOUT WHAT WE'VE DONE TO HIS ANCESTRAL HOME.
UNLESS-- THAT FURY GOT TO HIM FIRST.
MAKES SENSE, CONSIDERING THEY HAVE A HISTORY.
THE WHYS AND WHEREFORES HAVE YET TO BE DETERMINED, MY FRIEND.
WHAT MATTERS NOW IS GETTING SAM TO A HOSPITAL.
THEN, WE'LL WORRY ABOUT BRIAN AND THE REST.
I STILL CAN'T BELIEVE IT'S OVER.
YOU DID GOOD TODAY, RED.
WE ALL DID.
WE MAY HAVE SOME ROUGH EDGES BUT WE CAME TOGETHER AS A TEAM.
SAVOR THE MOMENT, MY FRIENDS. THEY DON'T COME OFTEN.
BUT WHEN THEY DO, THEY MAKE ME GLAD TO BE AN X-MAN.

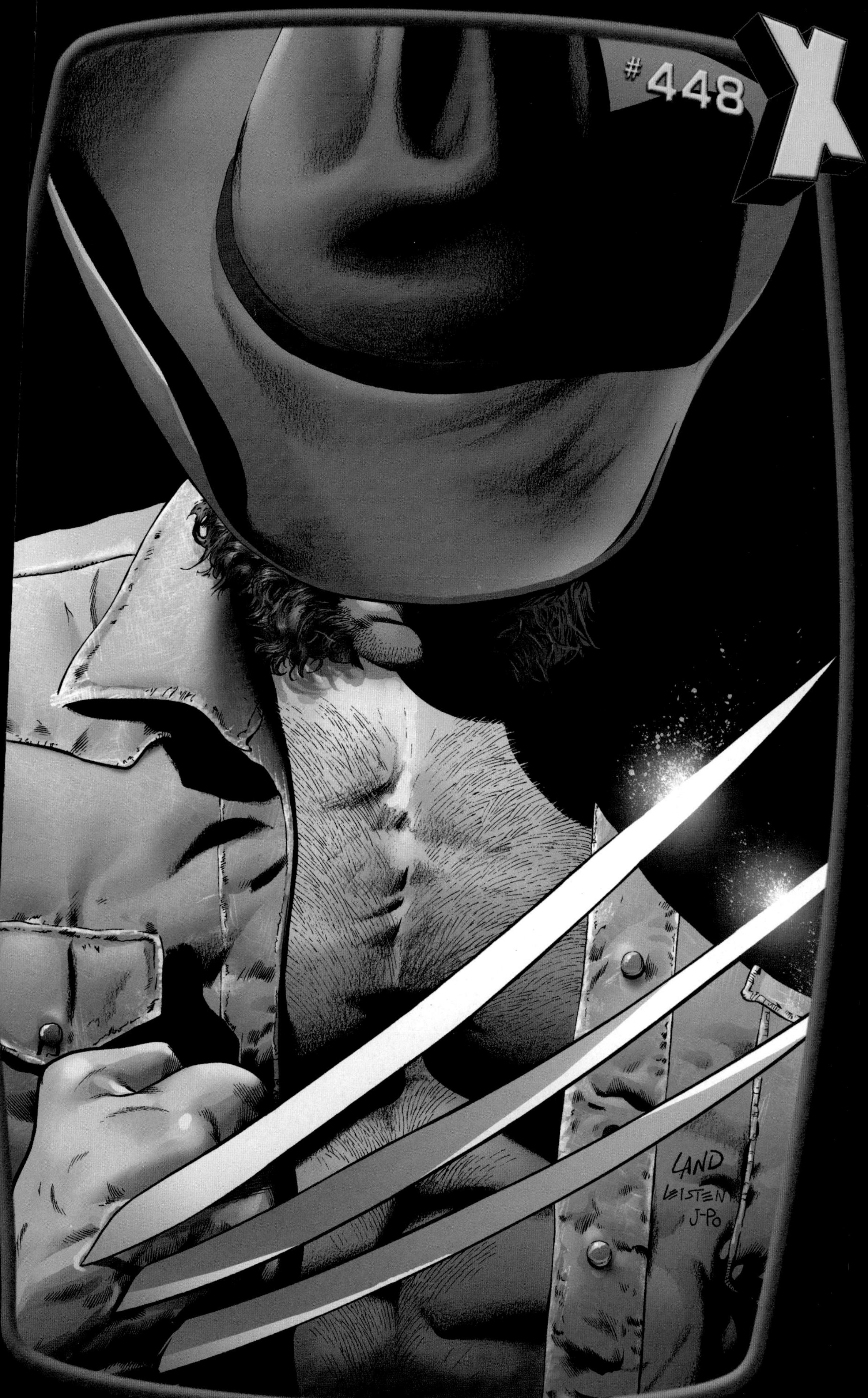
#448
X
LAND
LEISTEN
J-PO

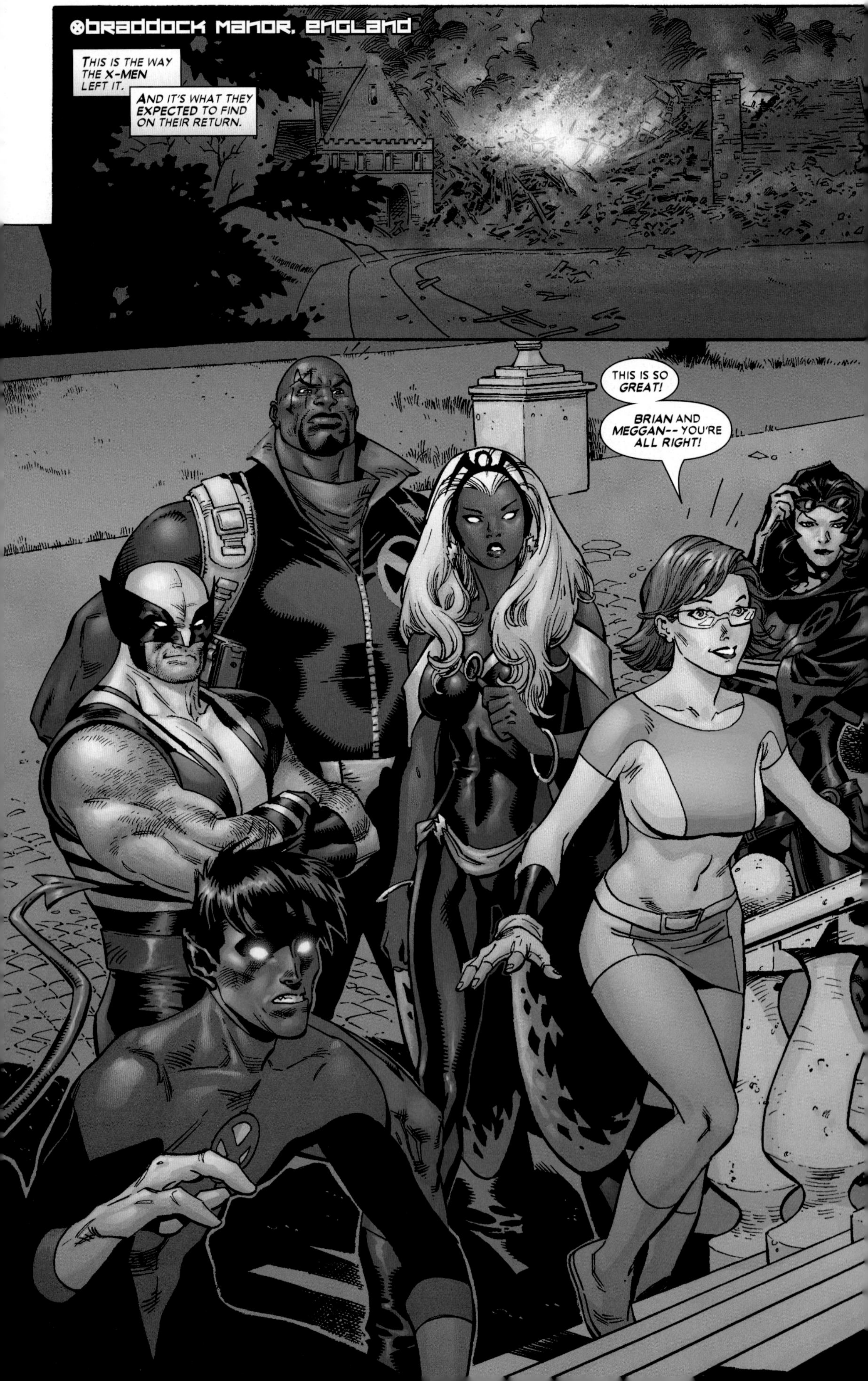
BRADDOCK MANOR, ENGLAND
THIS IS THE WAY THE X-MEN LEFT IT.
AND IT'S WHAT THEY EXPECTED TO FIND ON THEIR RETURN.
THIS IS SO GREAT!
BRIAN AND MEGGAN-- YOU'RE ALL RIGHT!

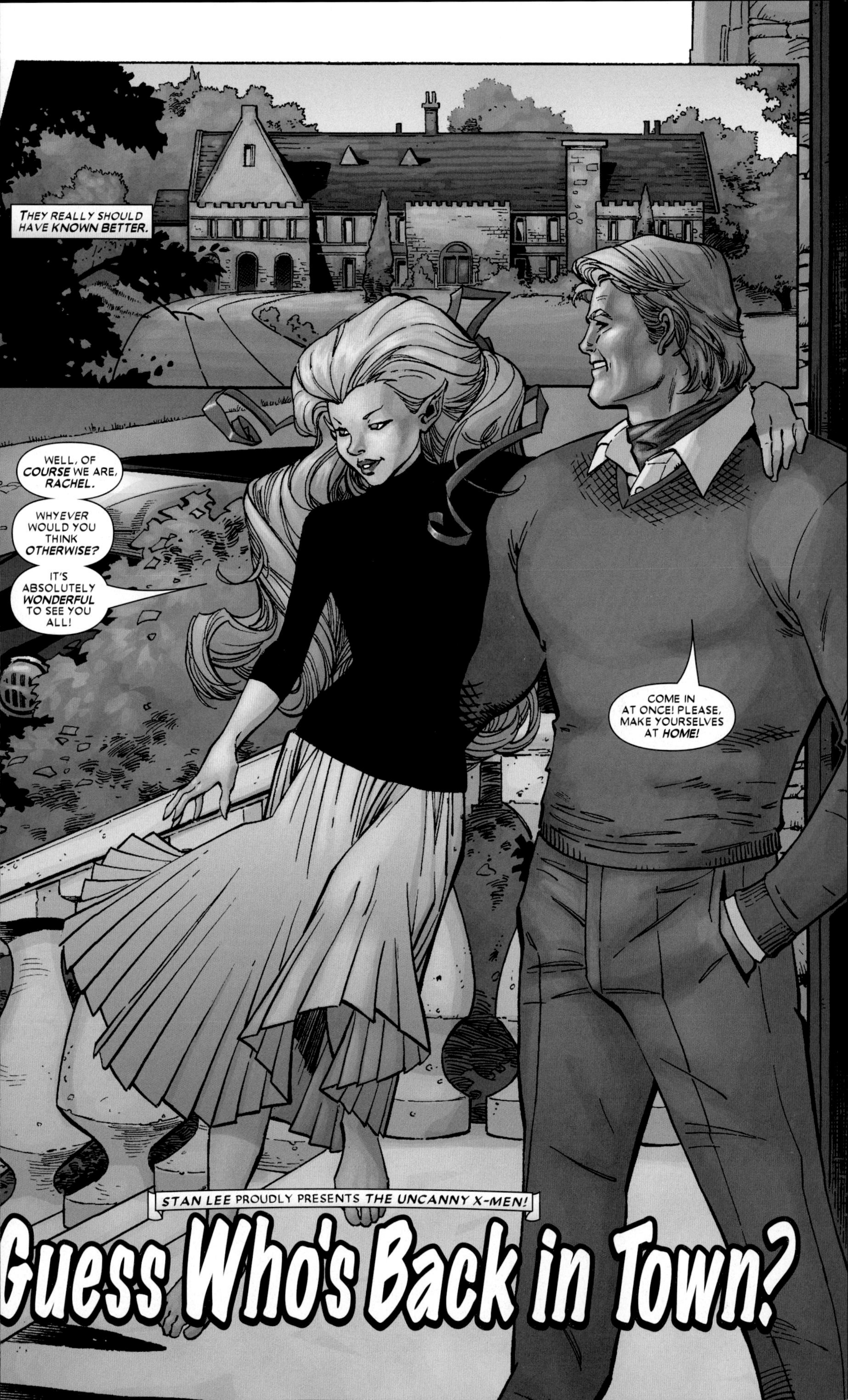
THEY REALLY SHOULD HAVE KNOWN BETTER.
WELL, OF COURSE WE ARE, RACHEL.
WHYEVER WOULD YOU THINK OTHERWISE?
IT'S ABSOLUTELY WONDERFUL TO SEE YOU ALL!
COME IN AT ONCE! PLEASE, MAKE YOURSELVES AT HOME!
STAN LEE PROUDLY PRESENTS THE UNCANNY X-MEN!
Guess Who's Back in Town?

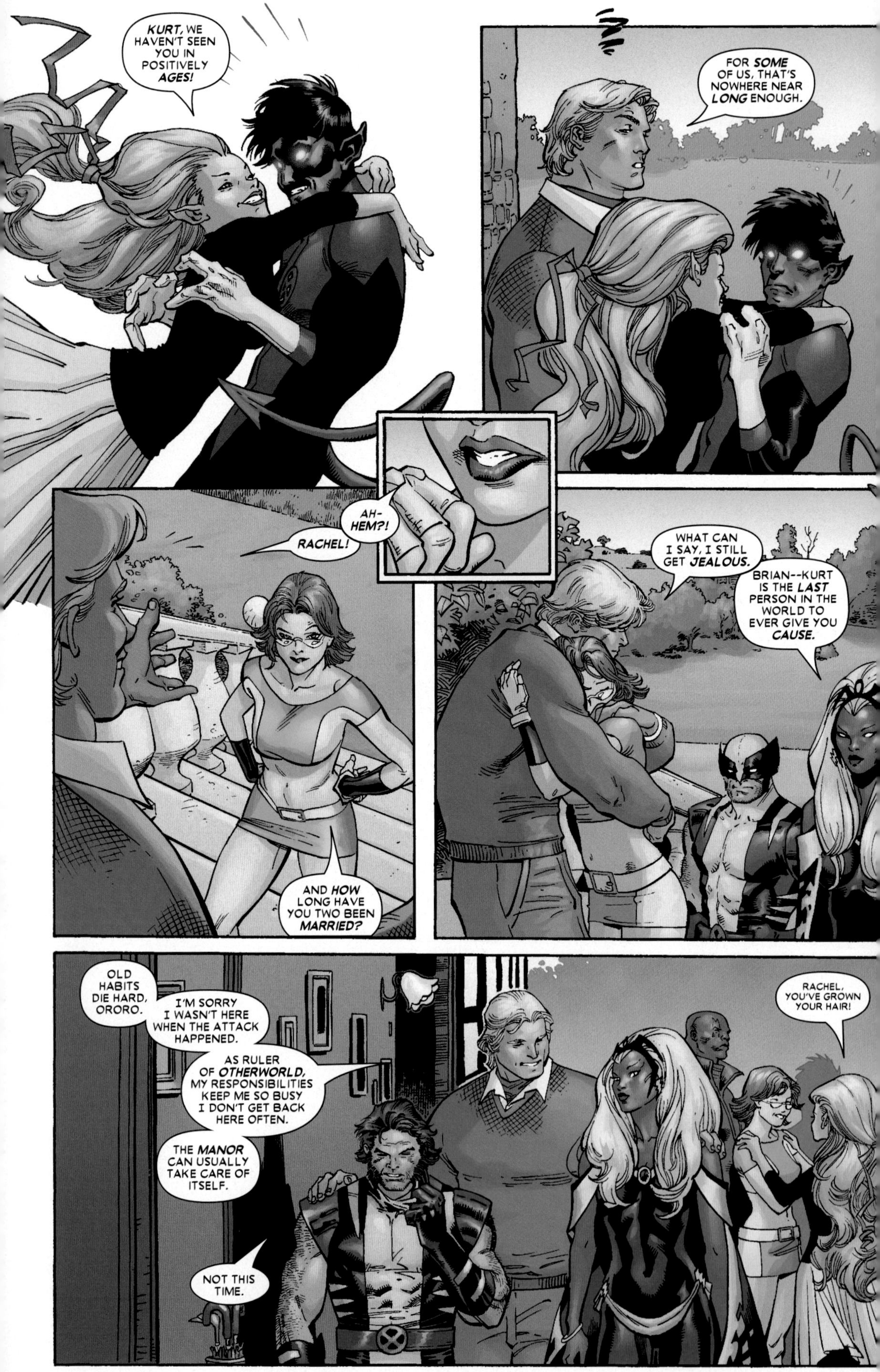
KURT, WE HAVEN'T SEEN YOU IN POSITIVELY AGES!
FOR SOME OF US, THAT'S NOWHERE NEAR LONG ENOUGH.
AH-HEM?!
RACHEL!
AND HOW LONG HAVE YOU TWO BEEN MARRIED?
WHAT CAN I SAY, I STILL GET JEALOUS.
BRIAN--KURT IS THE LAST PERSON IN THE WORLD TO EVER GIVE YOU CAUSE.
OLD HABITS DIE HARD, ORORO.
I'M SORRY I WASN'T HERE WHEN THE ATTACK HAPPENED.
AS RULER OF OTHERWORLD, MY RESPONSIBILITIES KEEP ME SO BUSY I DON'T GET BACK HERE OFTEN.
THE MANOR CAN USUALLY TAKE CARE OF ITSELF.
NOT THIS TIME.
RACHEL, YOU'VE GROWN YOUR HAIR!

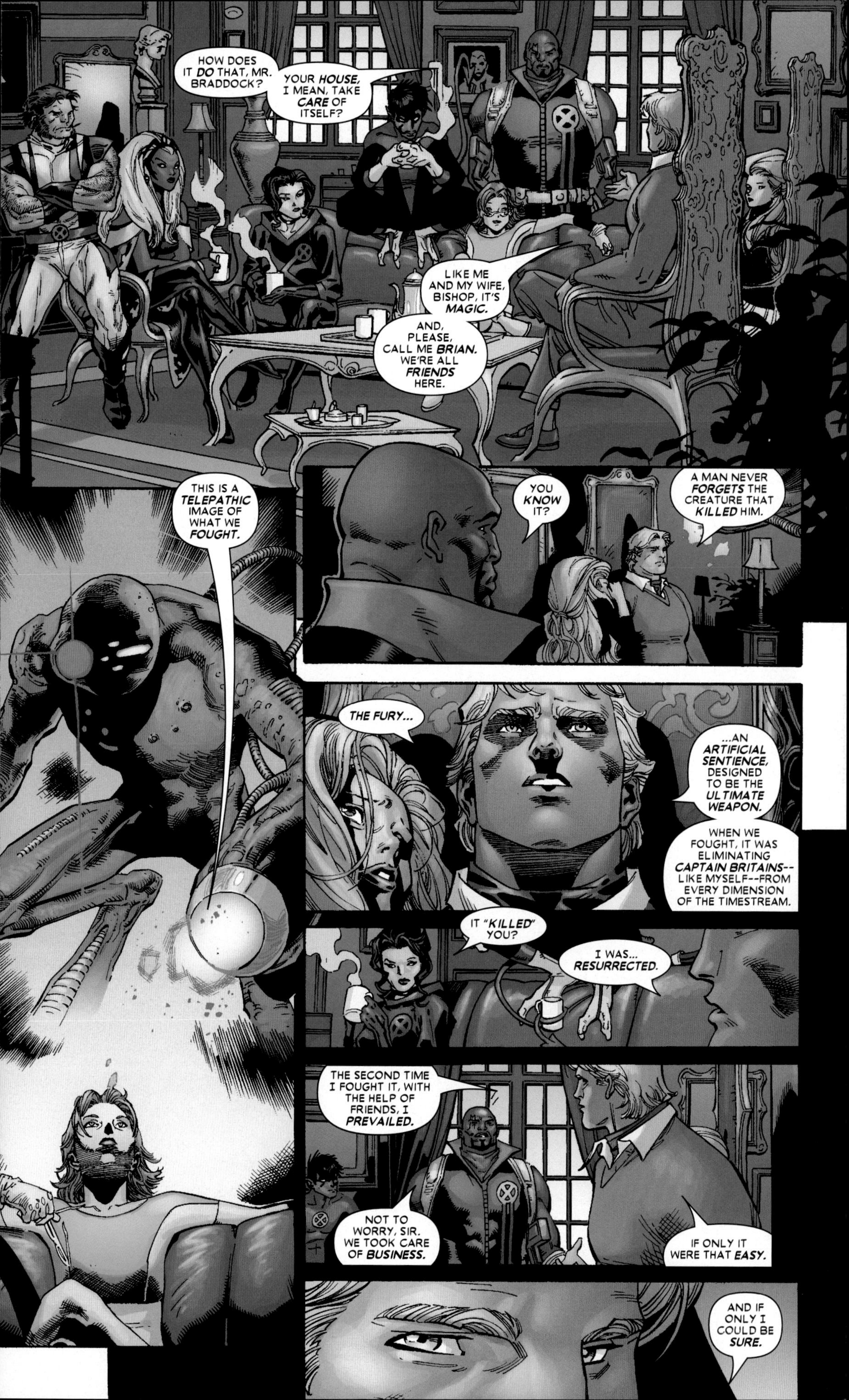

HOW DOES IT DO THAT, MR. BRADDOCK?
YOUR HOUSE, I MEAN, TAKE CARE OF ITSELF?
LIKE ME AND MY WIFE, BISHOP, IT'S MAGIC.
AND, PLEASE, CALL ME BRIAN. WE'RE ALL FRIENDS HERE.
THIS IS A TELEPATHIC IMAGE OF WHAT WE FOUGHT.
YOU KNOW IT?
A MAN NEVER FORGETS THE CREATURE THAT KILLED HIM.
THE FURY...
...AN ARTIFICIAL SENTIENCE, DESIGNED TO BE THE ULTIMATE WEAPON.
WHEN WE FOUGHT, IT WAS ELIMINATING CAPTAIN BRITAINS-- LIKE MYSELF--FROM EVERY DIMENSION OF THE TIMESTREAM.
IT "KILLED" YOU?
I WAS... RESURRECTED.
THE SECOND TIME I FOUGHT IT, WITH THE HELP OF FRIENDS, I PREVAILED.
NOT TO WORRY, SIR. WE TOOK CARE OF BUSINESS.
IF ONLY IT WERE THAT EASY.
AND IF ONLY I COULD BE SURE.

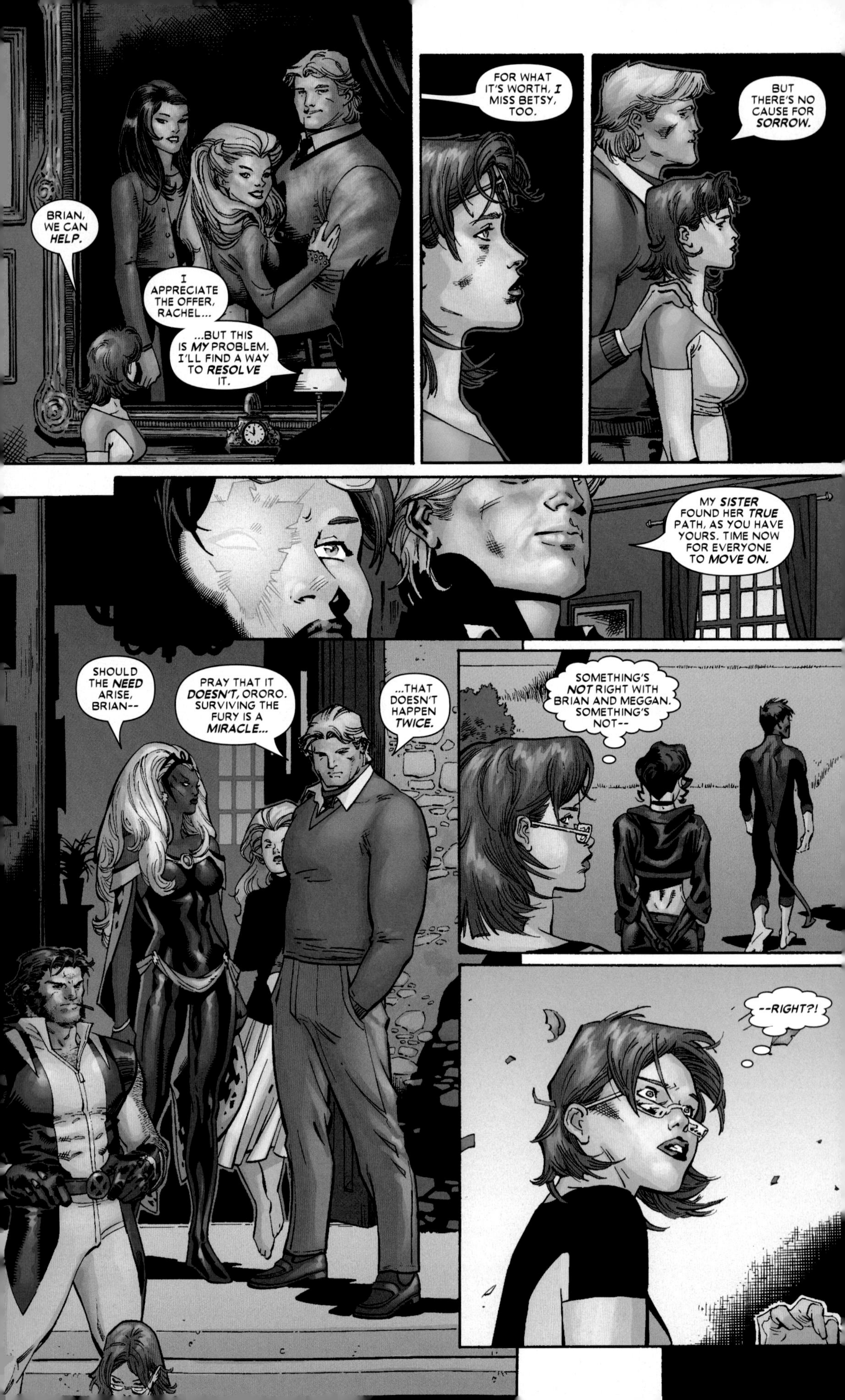
BRIAN, WE CAN HELP.
I APPRECIATE THE OFFER, RACHEL...
...BUT THIS IS MY PROBLEM. I'LL FIND A WAY TO RESOLVE IT.
FOR WHAT IT'S WORTH, I MISS BETSY, TOO.
BUT THERE'S NO CAUSE FOR SORROW.
MY SISTER FOUND HER TRUE PATH, AS YOU HAVE YOURS. TIME NOW FOR EVERYONE TO MOVE ON.
SHOULD THE NEED ARISE, BRIAN--
PRAY THAT IT DOESN'T, ORORO. SURVIVING THE FURY IS A MIRACLE...
...THAT DOESN'T HAPPEN TWICE.
SOMETHING'S NOT RIGHT WITH BRIAN AND MEGGAN. SOMETHING'S NOT--
--RIGHT?!

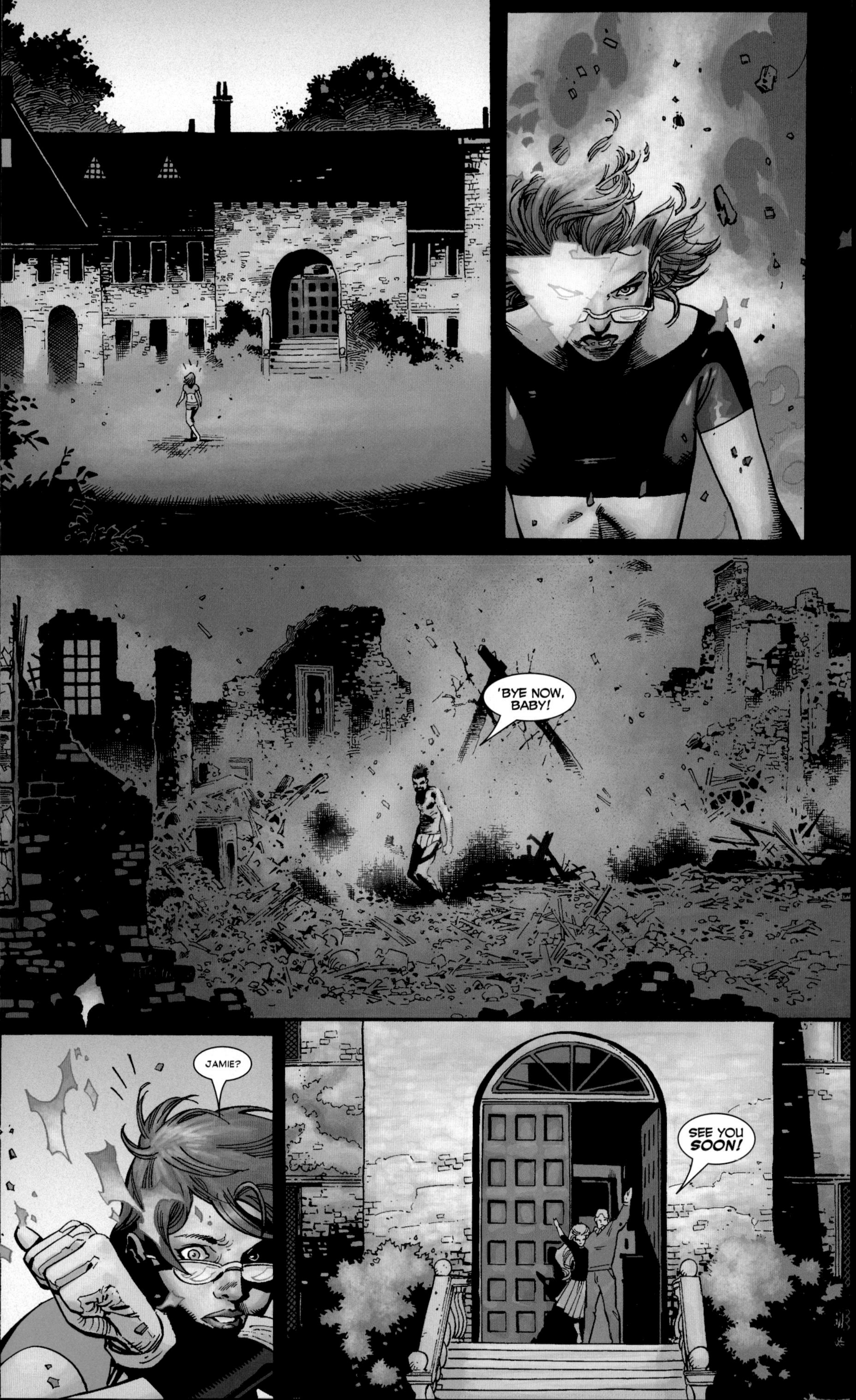
'BYE NOW, BABY!
JAMIE?
SEE YOU SOON!

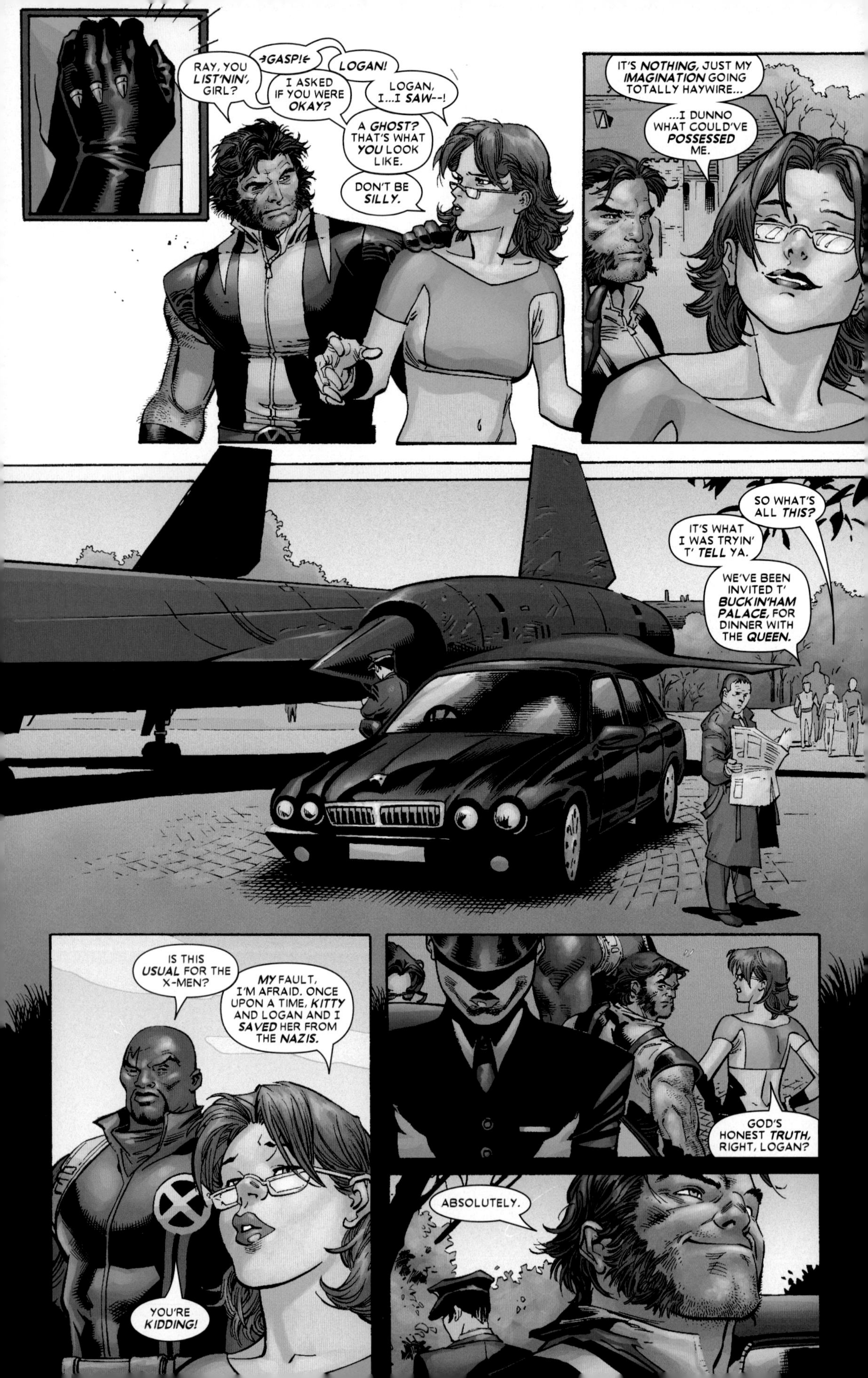
RAY, YOU LIST'NIN', GIRL?
→GASP!←
LOGAN!
I ASKED IF YOU WERE OKAY?
LOGAN, I...I SAW--!
A GHOST? THAT'S WHAT YOU LOOK LIKE.
DON'T BE SILLY.
IT'S NOTHING, JUST MY IMAGINATION GOING TOTALLY HAYWIRE...
...I DUNNO WHAT COULD'VE POSSESSED ME.
SO WHAT'S ALL THIS?
IT'S WHAT I WAS TRYIN' T' TELL YA.
WE'VE BEEN INVITED T' BUCKIN'HAM PALACE, FOR DINNER WITH THE QUEEN.
IS THIS USUAL FOR THE X-MEN?
MY FAULT, I'M AFRAID. ONCE UPON A TIME, KITTY AND LOGAN AND I SAVED HER FROM THE NAZIS.
YOU'RE KIDDING!
GOD'S HONEST TRUTH, RIGHT, LOGAN?
ABSOLUTELY.

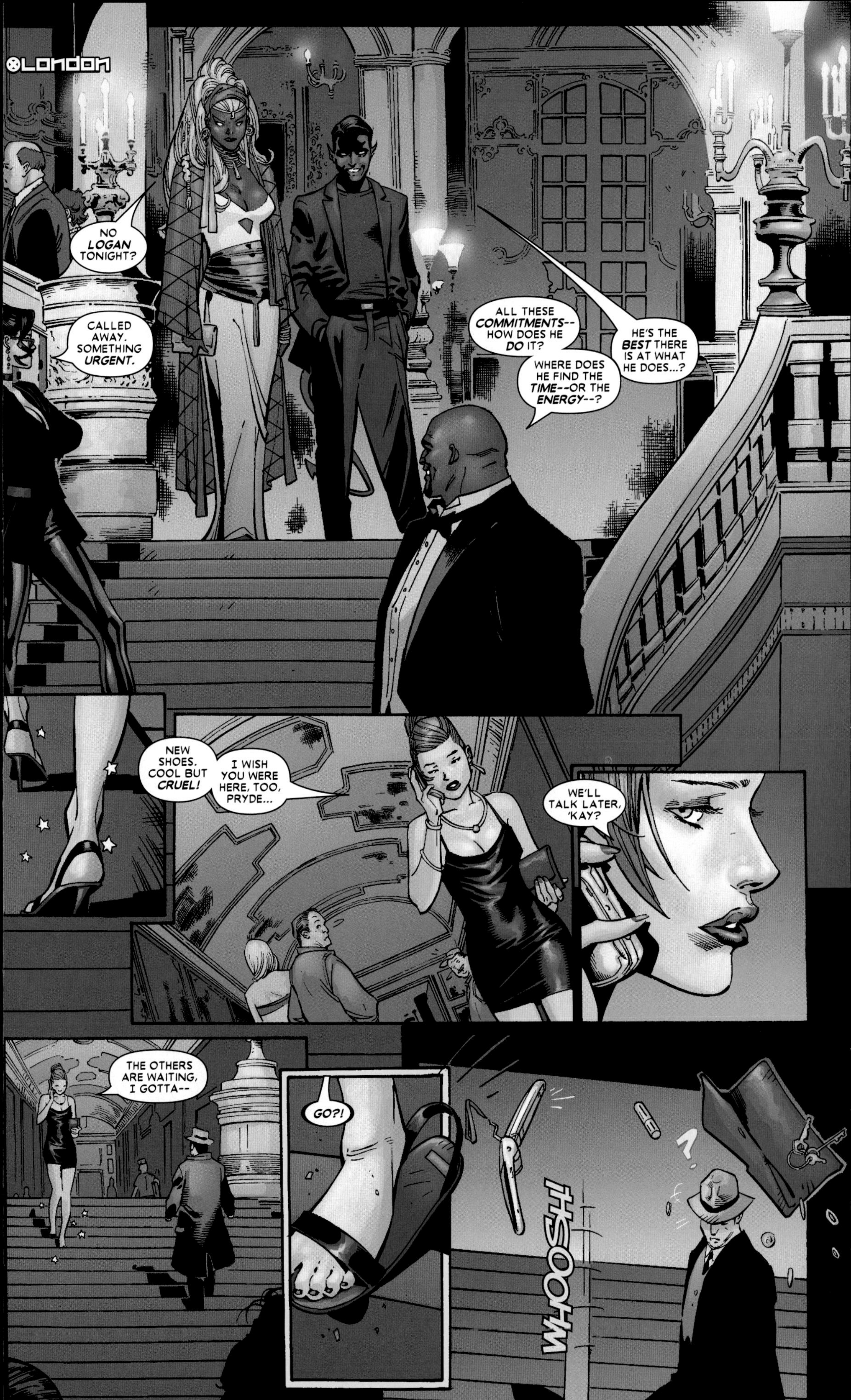
LONDON
NO LOGAN TONIGHT?
CALLED AWAY. SOMETHING URGENT.
ALL THESE COMMITMENTS-- HOW DOES HE DO IT?
WHERE DOES HE FIND THE TIME--OR THE ENERGY--?
HE'S THE BEST THERE IS AT WHAT HE DOES...?
NEW SHOES. COOL BUT CRUEL!
I WISH YOU WERE HERE, TOO, PRYDE...
WE'LL TALK LATER, 'KAY?
THE OTHERS ARE WAITING, I GOTTA--
GO?!
WHOOSH!
?

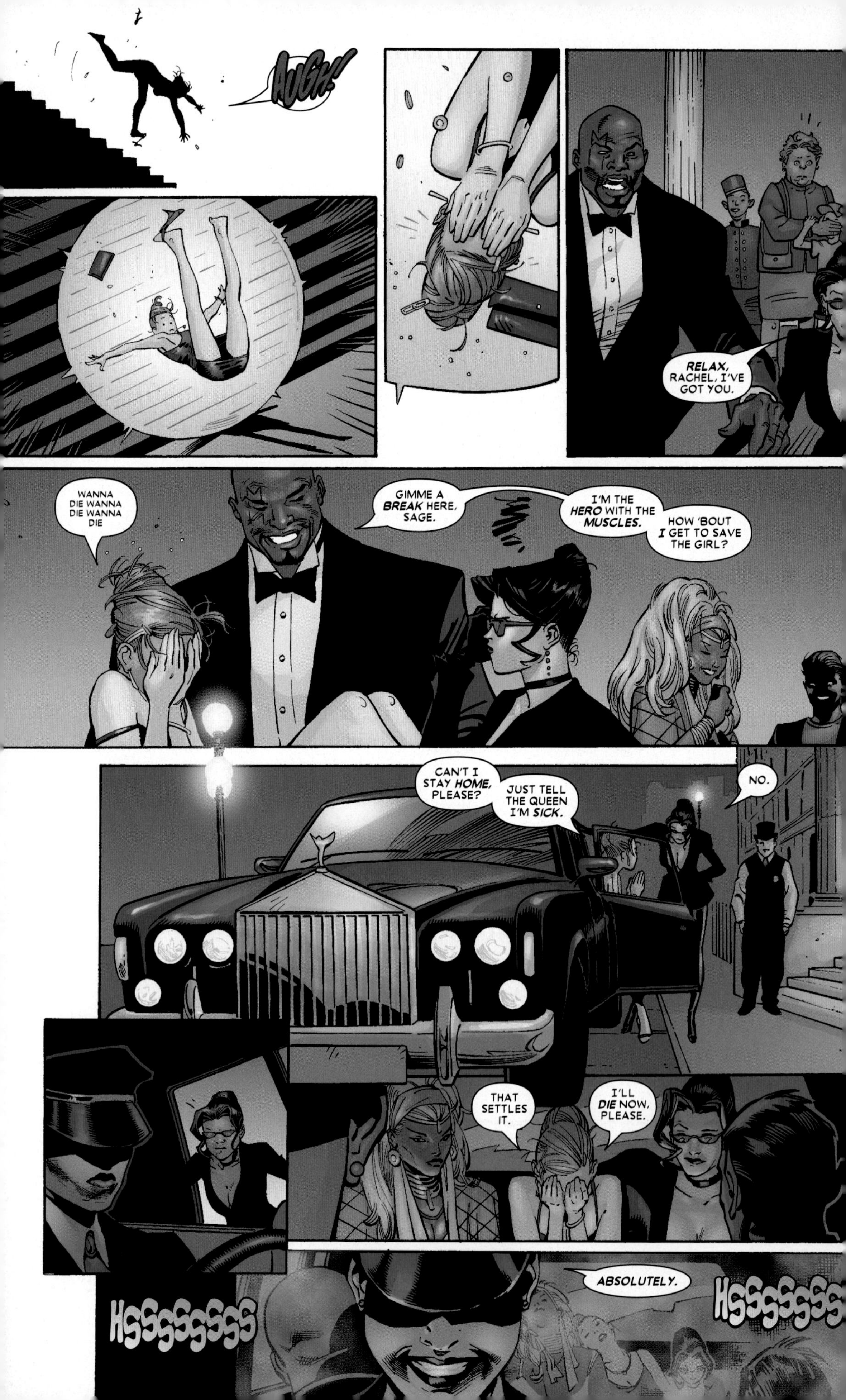
AUGH!
RELAX, RACHEL, I'VE GOT YOU.
WANNA DIE WANNA DIE WANNA DIE
GIMME A BREAK HERE, SAGE.
I'M THE HERO WITH THE MUSCLES.
HOW 'BOUT I GET TO SAVE THE GIRL?
CAN'T I STAY HOME, PLEASE?
JUST TELL THE QUEEN I'M SICK.
NO.
THAT SETTLES IT.
I'LL DIE NOW, PLEASE.
ABSOLUTELY.
HSSSSSSSS
HSSSSSSS

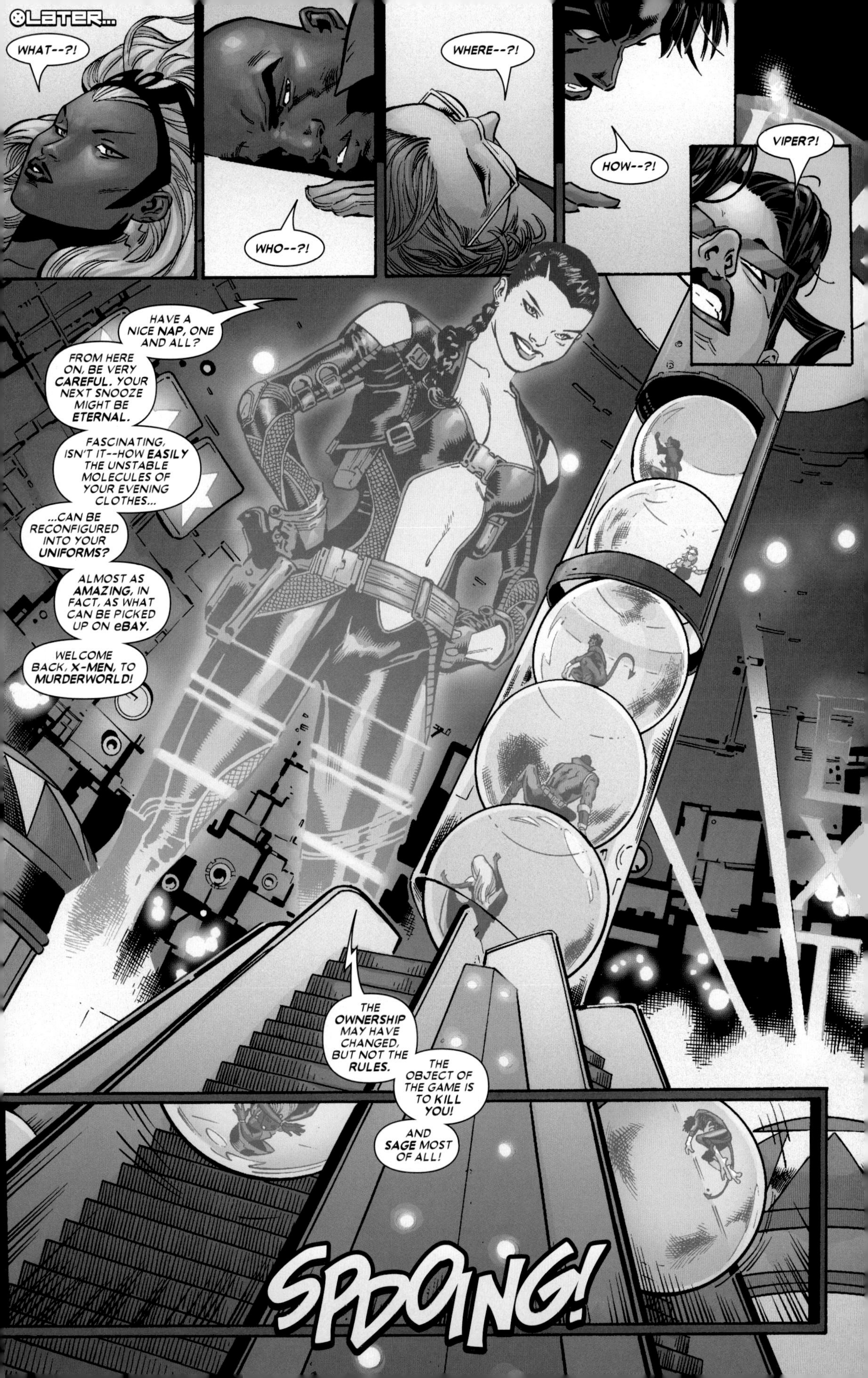
LATER...
WHAT--?!
WHO--?!
WHERE--?!
HOW--?!
VIPER?!
HAVE A NICE NAP, ONE AND ALL?
FROM HERE ON, BE VERY CAREFUL. YOUR NEXT SNOOZE MIGHT BE ETERNAL.
FASCINATING, ISN'T IT--HOW EASILY THE UNSTABLE MOLECULES OF YOUR EVENING CLOTHES...
...CAN BE RECONFIGURED INTO YOUR UNIFORMS?
ALMOST AS AMAZING, IN FACT, AS WHAT CAN BE PICKED UP ON eBAY.
WELCOME BACK, X-MEN, TO MURDERWORLD!
THE OWNERSHIP MAY HAVE CHANGED, BUT NOT THE RULES.
THE OBJECT OF THE GAME IS TO KILL YOU!
AND SAGE MOST OF ALL!
SPDOING!

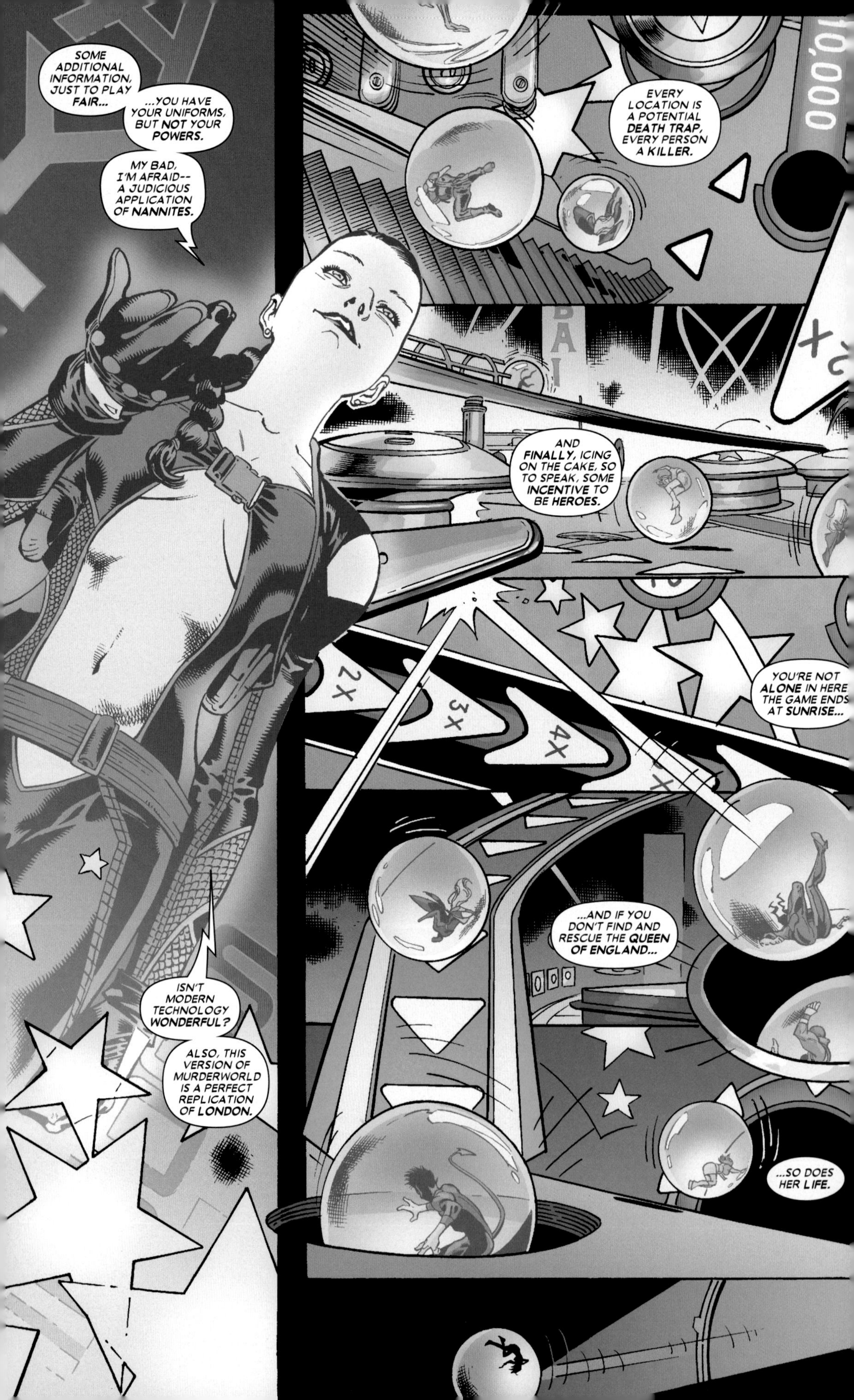

SOME ADDITIONAL INFORMATION, JUST TO PLAY FAIR...
...YOU HAVE YOUR UNIFORMS, BUT NOT YOUR POWERS.
MY BAD, I'M AFRAID-- A JUDICIOUS APPLICATION OF NANNITES.
EVERY LOCATION IS A POTENTIAL DEATH TRAP, EVERY PERSON A KILLER.
10,000
AND FINALLY, ICING ON THE CAKE, SO TO SPEAK, SOME INCENTIVE TO BE HEROES.
YOU'RE NOT ALONE IN HERE THE GAME ENDS AT SUNRISE...
2X
3X
4X
...AND IF YOU DON'T FIND AND RESCUE THE QUEEN OF ENGLAND...
...SO DOES HER LIFE.
ISN'T MODERN TECHNOLOGY WONDERFUL?
ALSO, THIS VERSION OF MURDERWORLD IS A PERFECT REPLICATION OF LONDON.

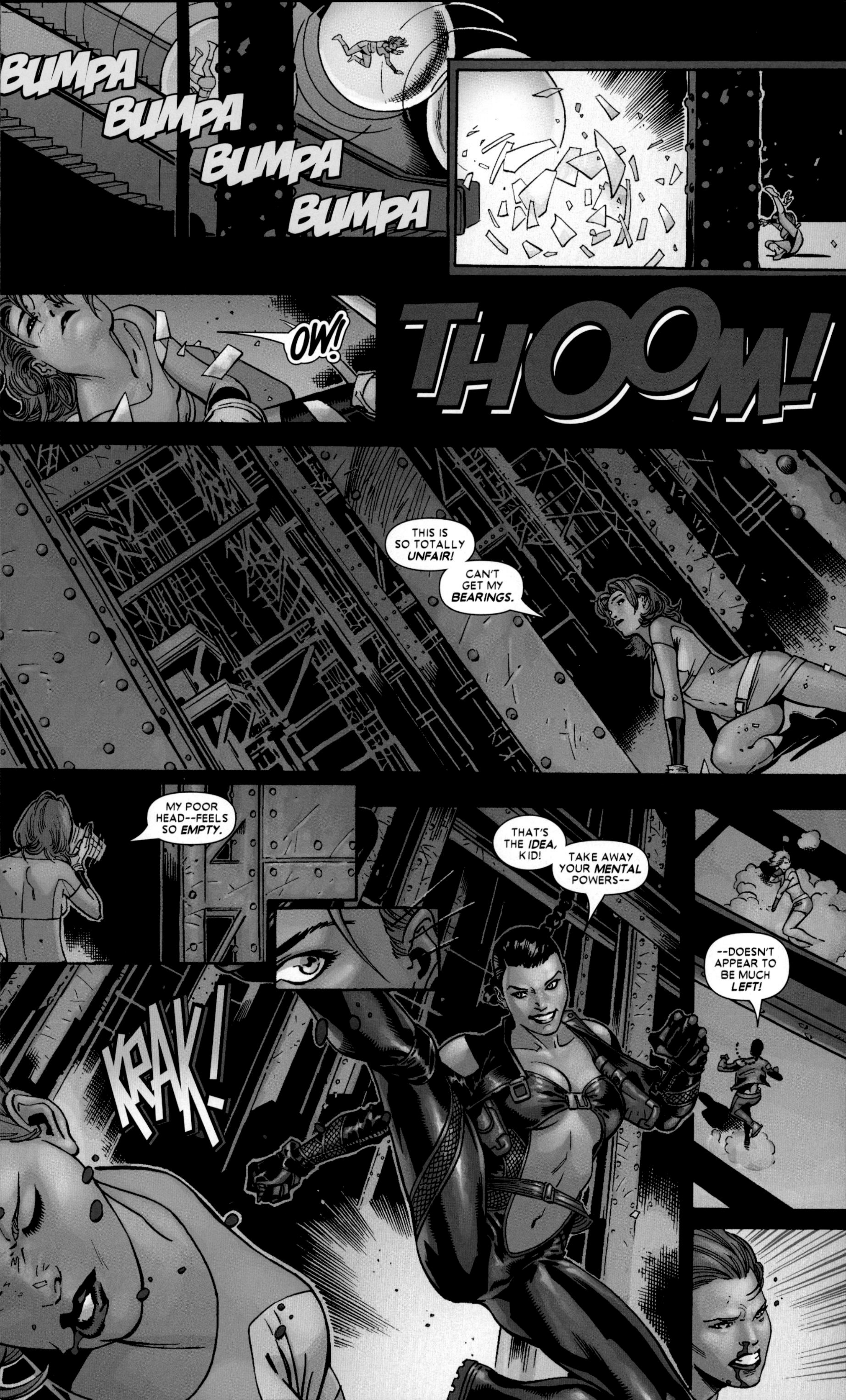
BUMPA
BUMPA
BUMPA
BUMPA
OW!
THOOM!
THIS IS SO TOTALLY UNFAIR!
CAN'T GET MY BEARINGS.
MY POOR HEAD--FEELS SO EMPTY.
THAT'S THE IDEA, KID!
TAKE AWAY YOUR MENTAL POWERS--
--DOESN'T APPEAR TO BE MUCH LEFT!
KRAK!

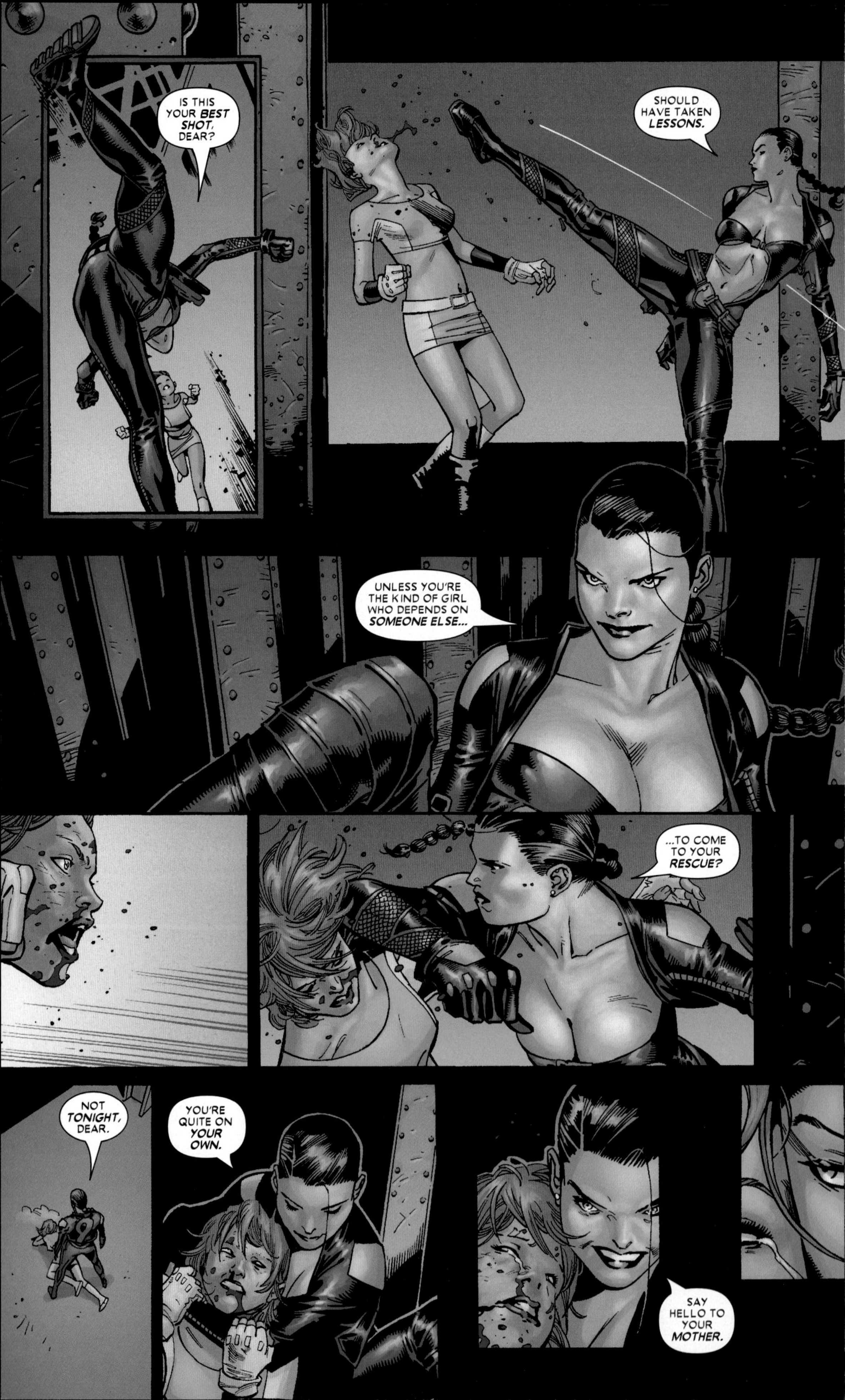
IS THIS YOUR BEST SHOT, DEAR?
SHOULD HAVE TAKEN LESSONS.
UNLESS YOU'RE THE KIND OF GIRL WHO DEPENDS ON SOMEONE ELSE...
...TO COME TO YOUR RESCUE?
NOT TONIGHT, DEAR.
YOU'RE QUITE ON YOUR OWN.
SAY HELLO TO YOUR MOTHER.

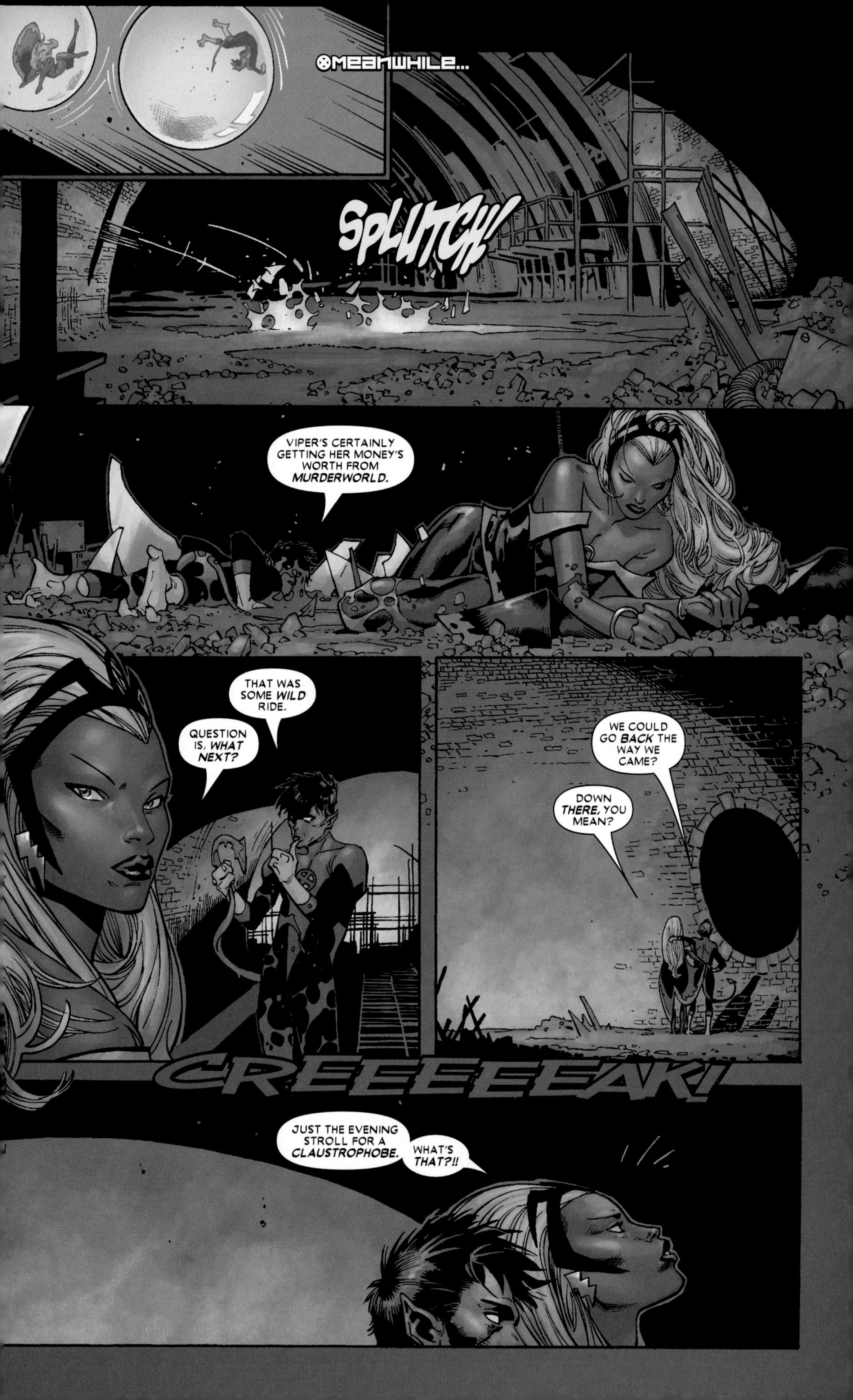
MEANWHILE...
SPLUTCH!
VIPER'S CERTAINLY GETTING HER MONEY'S WORTH FROM *MURDERWORLD.*
THAT WAS SOME *WILD* RIDE.
QUESTION IS, *WHAT NEXT?*
WE COULD GO *BACK* THE WAY WE CAME?
DOWN *THERE,* YOU MEAN?
CREEEEEAK!
JUST THE EVENING STROLL FOR A *CLAUSTROPHOBE.*
WHAT'S *THAT?!!*

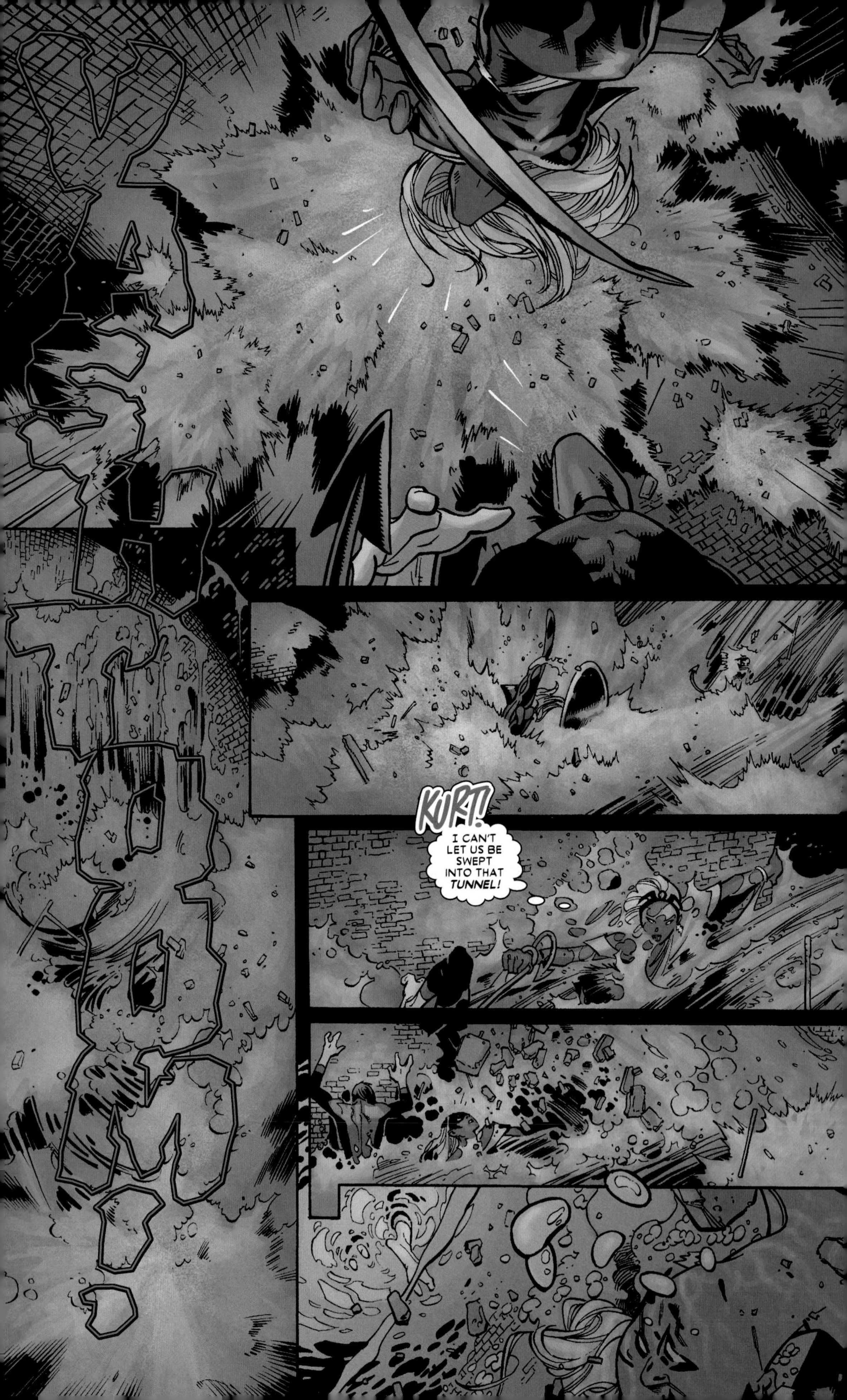
KURT!
I CAN'T LET US BE SWEPT INTO THAT TUNNEL!

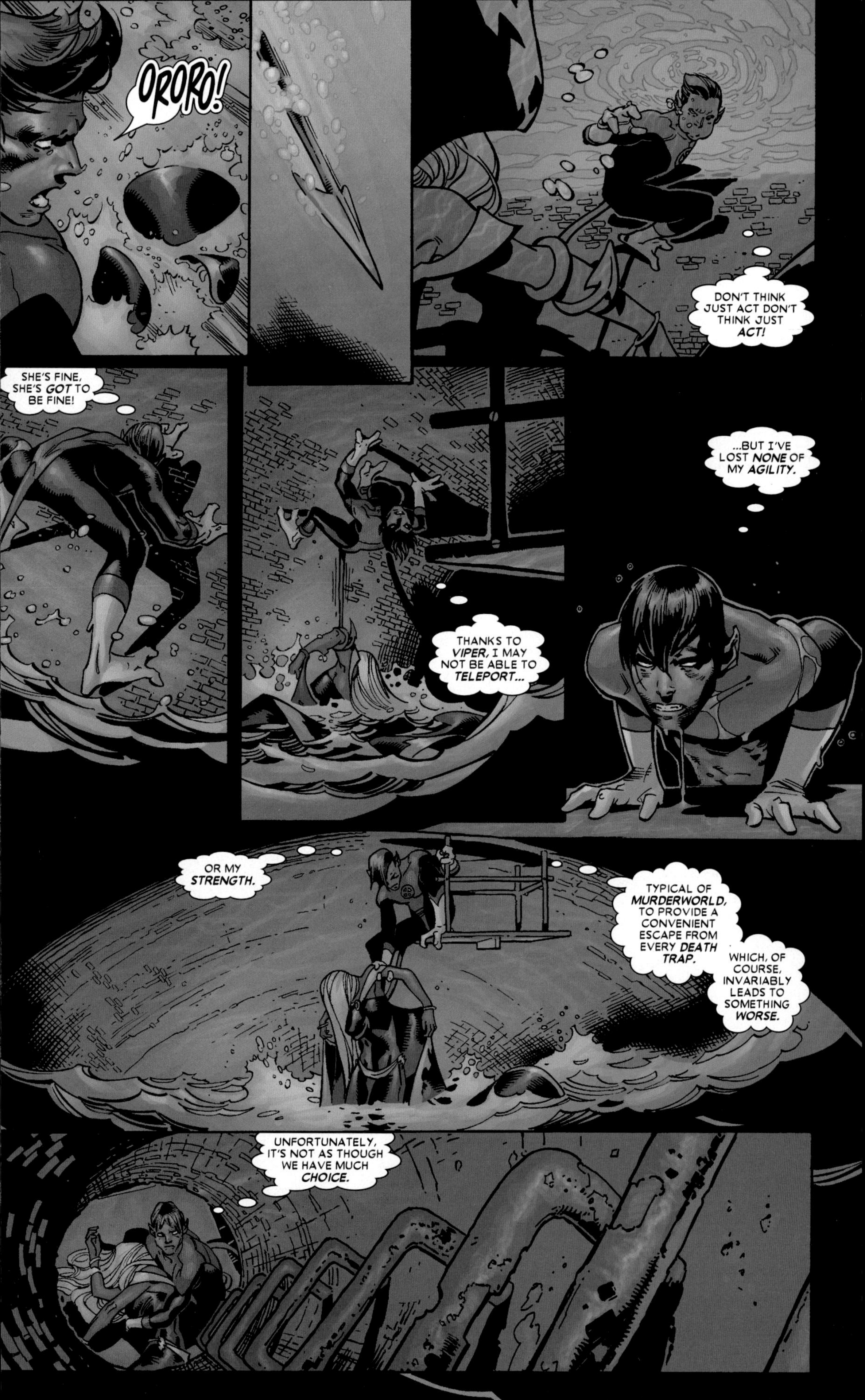
OROROO!
DON'T THINK JUST ACT DON'T THINK JUST ACT!
SHE'S FINE, SHE'S GOT TO BE FINE!
THANKS TO VIPER, I MAY NOT BE ABLE TO TELEPORT...
...BUT I'VE LOST NONE OF MY AGILITY.
OR MY STRENGTH.
TYPICAL OF MURDERWORLD, TO PROVIDE A CONVENIENT ESCAPE FROM EVERY DEATH TRAP.
WHICH, OF COURSE, INVARIABLY LEADS TO SOMETHING WORSE.
UNFORTUNATELY, IT'S NOT AS THOUGH WE HAVE MUCH CHOICE.

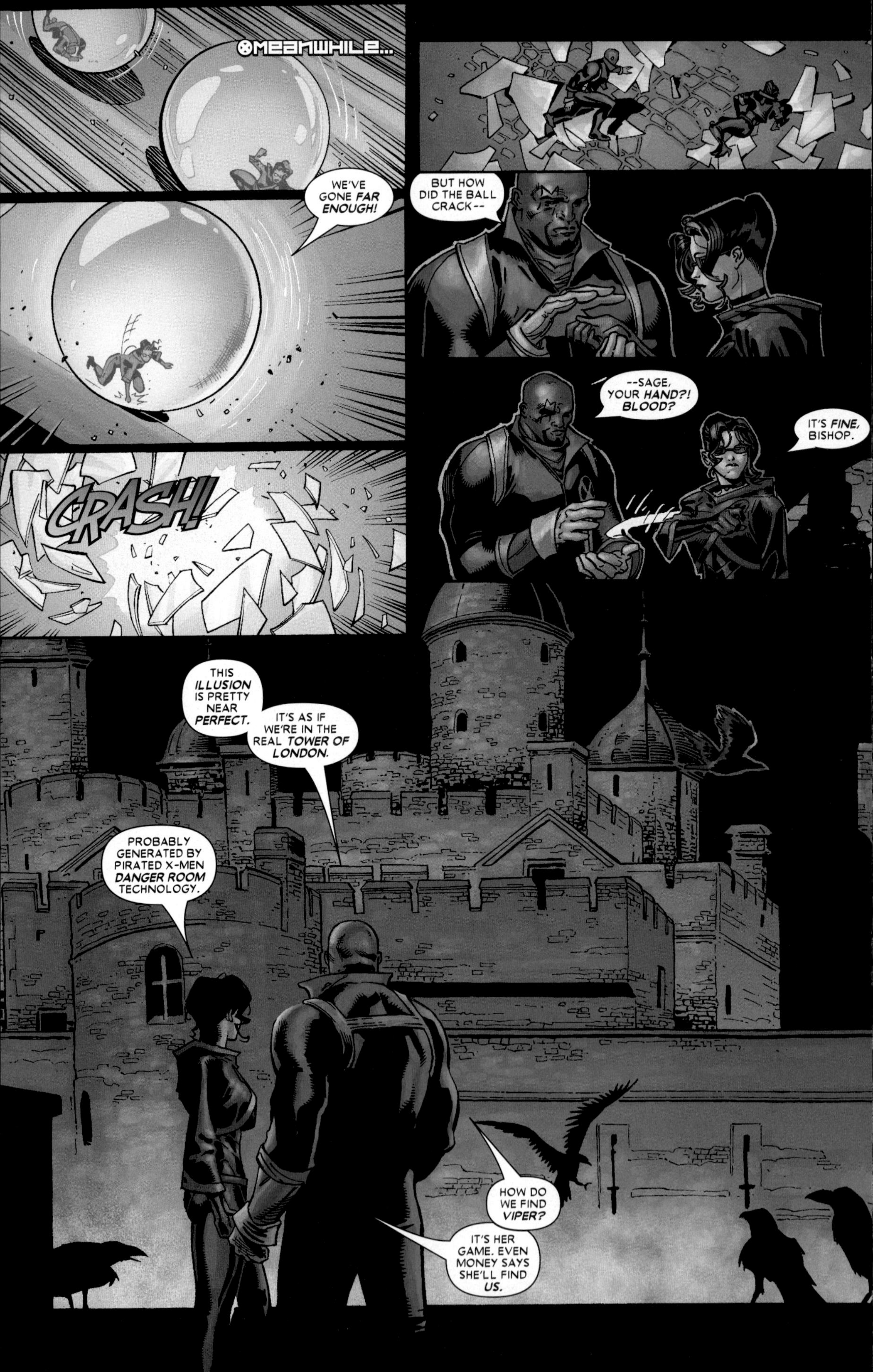
MEANWHILE...
WE'VE GONE FAR ENOUGH!
BUT HOW DID THE BALL CRACK--
CRASH!
--SAGE, YOUR HAND?! BLOOD?
IT'S FINE, BISHOP.
THIS ILLUSION IS PRETTY NEAR PERFECT.
IT'S AS IF WE'RE IN THE REAL TOWER OF LONDON.
PROBABLY GENERATED BY PIRATED X-MEN DANGER ROOM TECHNOLOGY.
HOW DO WE FIND VIPER?
IT'S HER GAME. EVEN MONEY SAYS SHE'LL FIND US.

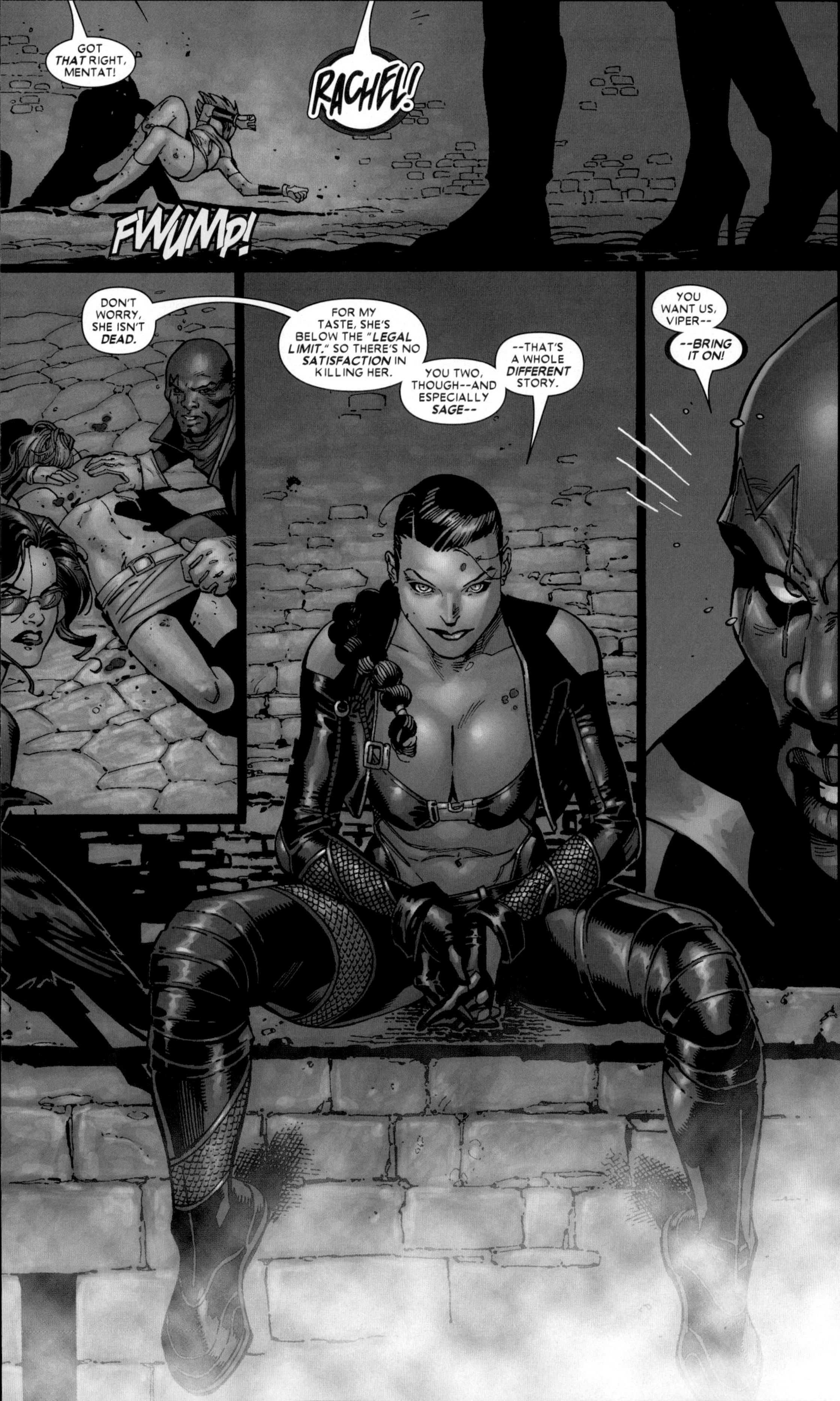
GOT *THAT* RIGHT, MENTAT!
RACHEL!
FWUMP!
DON'T WORRY, SHE ISN'T *DEAD.*
FOR MY TASTE, SHE'S BELOW THE "*LEGAL LIMIT.*" SO THERE'S NO *SATISFACTION* IN KILLING HER.
YOU TWO, THOUGH--AND ESPECIALLY *SAGE*--
--THAT'S A WHOLE *DIFFERENT* STORY.
YOU WANT US, VIPER--
--BRING IT ON!

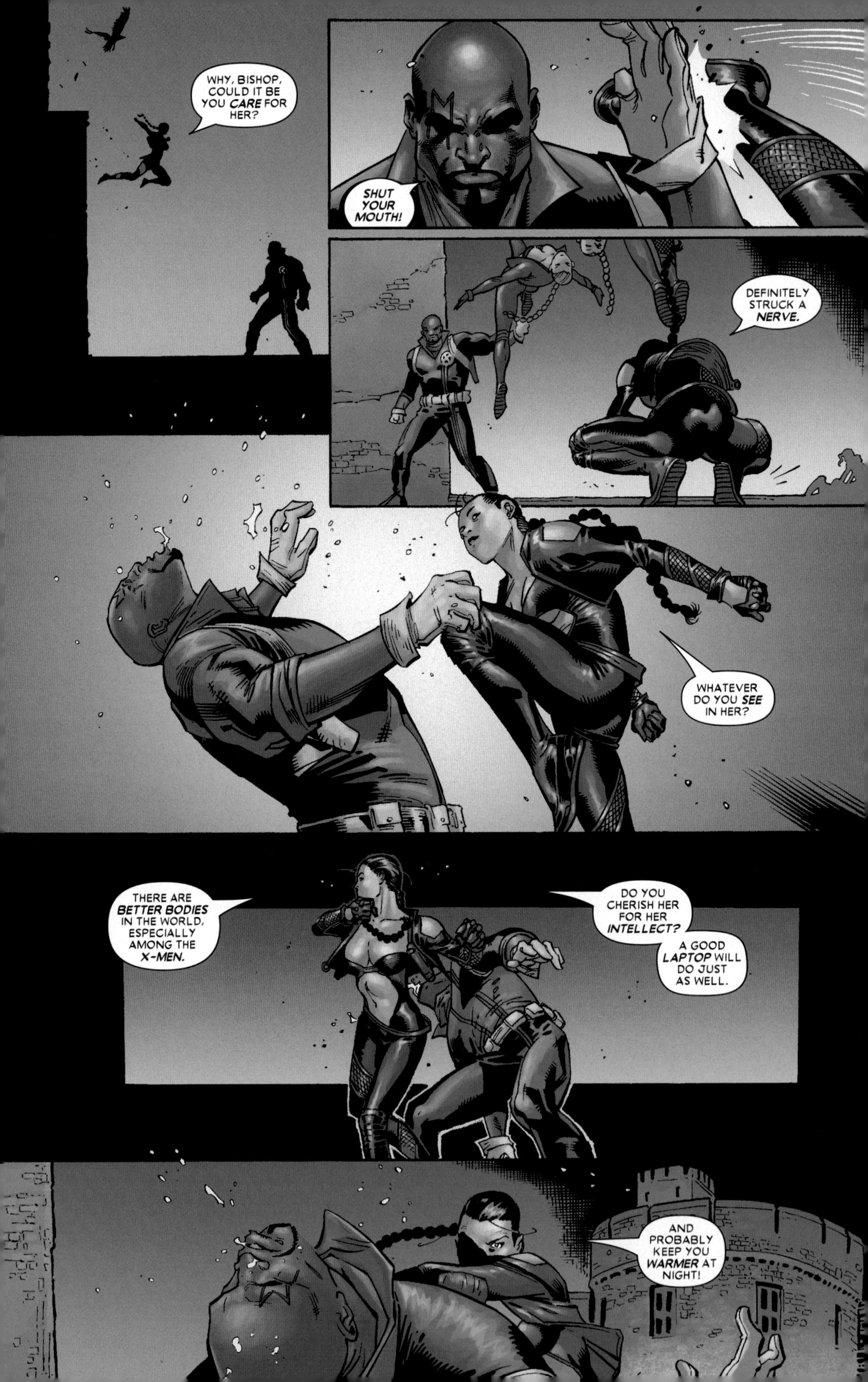
WHY, BISHOP, COULD IT BE YOU CARE FOR HER?
SHUT YOUR MOUTH!
DEFINITELY STRUCK A NERVE.
WHATEVER DO YOU SEE IN HER?
THERE ARE BETTER BODIES IN THE WORLD, ESPECIALLY AMONG THE X-MEN.
DO YOU CHERISH HER FOR HER INTELLECT?
A GOOD LAPTOP WILL DO JUST AS WELL.
AND PROBABLY KEEP YOU WARMER AT NIGHT!

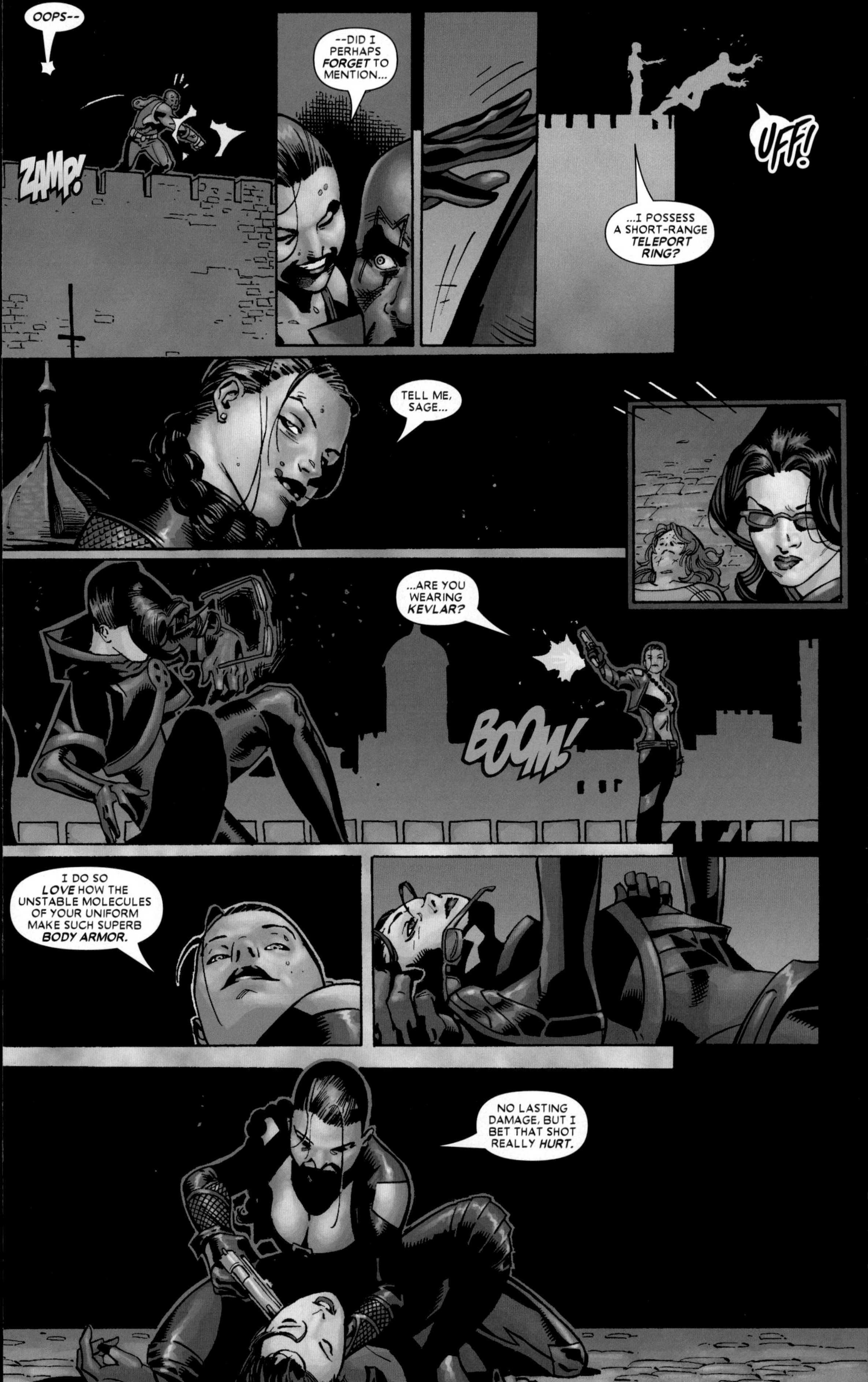
OOPS--
ZAMP!
--DID I PERHAPS FORGET TO MENTION...
...I POSSESS A SHORT-RANGE TELEPORT RING?
UFF!
TELL ME, SAGE...
...ARE YOU WEARING KEVLAR?
BOOM!
I DO SO LOVE HOW THE UNSTABLE MOLECULES OF YOUR UNIFORM MAKE SUCH SUPERB BODY ARMOR.
NO LASTING DAMAGE, BUT I BET THAT SHOT REALLY HURT.

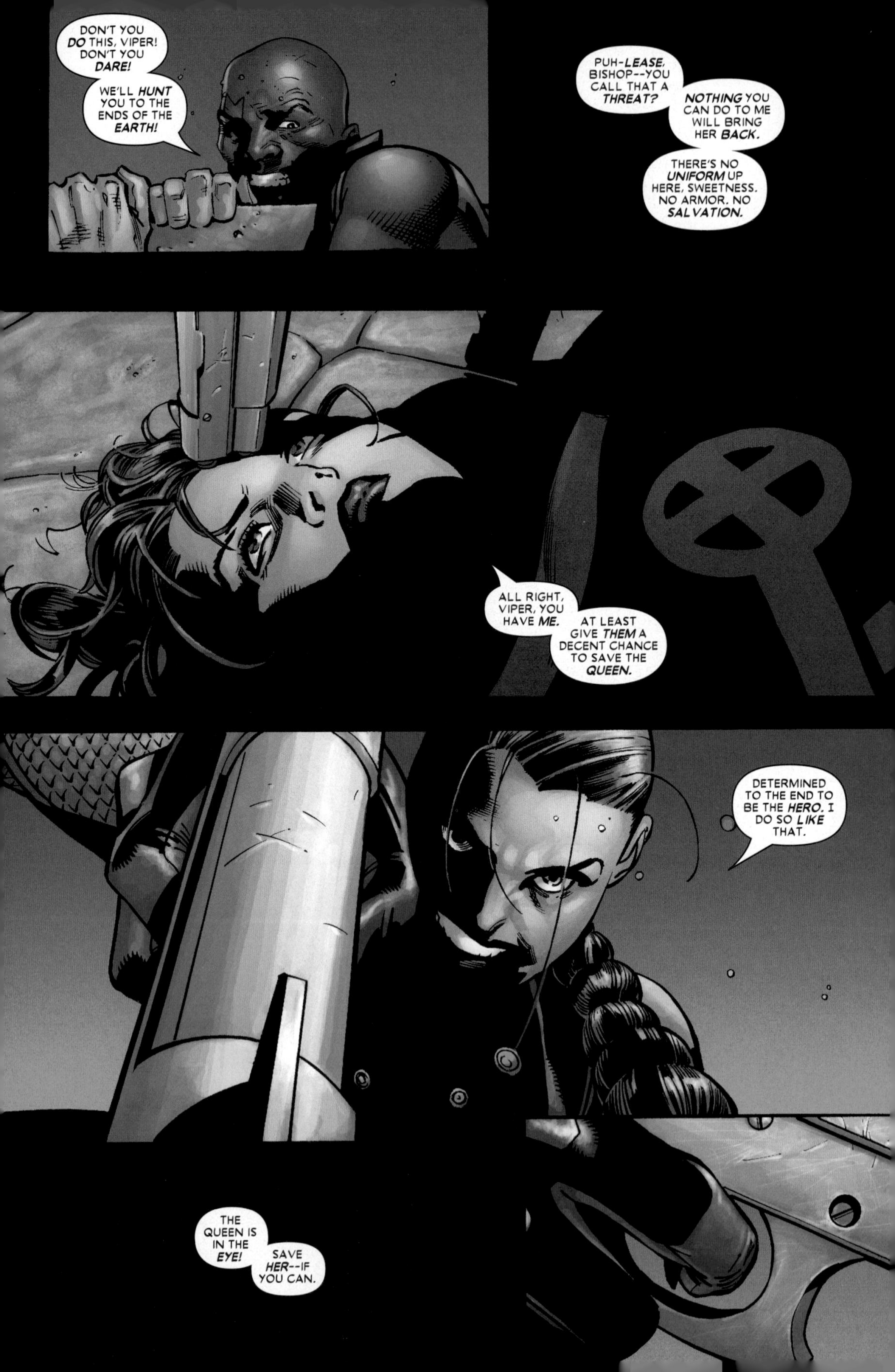
DON'T YOU DO THIS, VIPER! DON'T YOU DARE!
WE'LL HUNT YOU TO THE ENDS OF THE EARTH!
PUH-LEASE, BISHOP--YOU CALL THAT A THREAT?
NOTHING YOU CAN DO TO ME WILL BRING HER BACK.
THERE'S NO UNIFORM UP HERE, SWEETNESS. NO ARMOR. NO SALVATION.
ALL RIGHT, VIPER, YOU HAVE ME.
AT LEAST GIVE THEM A DECENT CHANCE TO SAVE THE QUEEN.
DETERMINED TO THE END TO BE THE HERO. I DO SO LIKE THAT.
THE QUEEN IS IN THE EYE!
SAVE HER--IF YOU CAN.

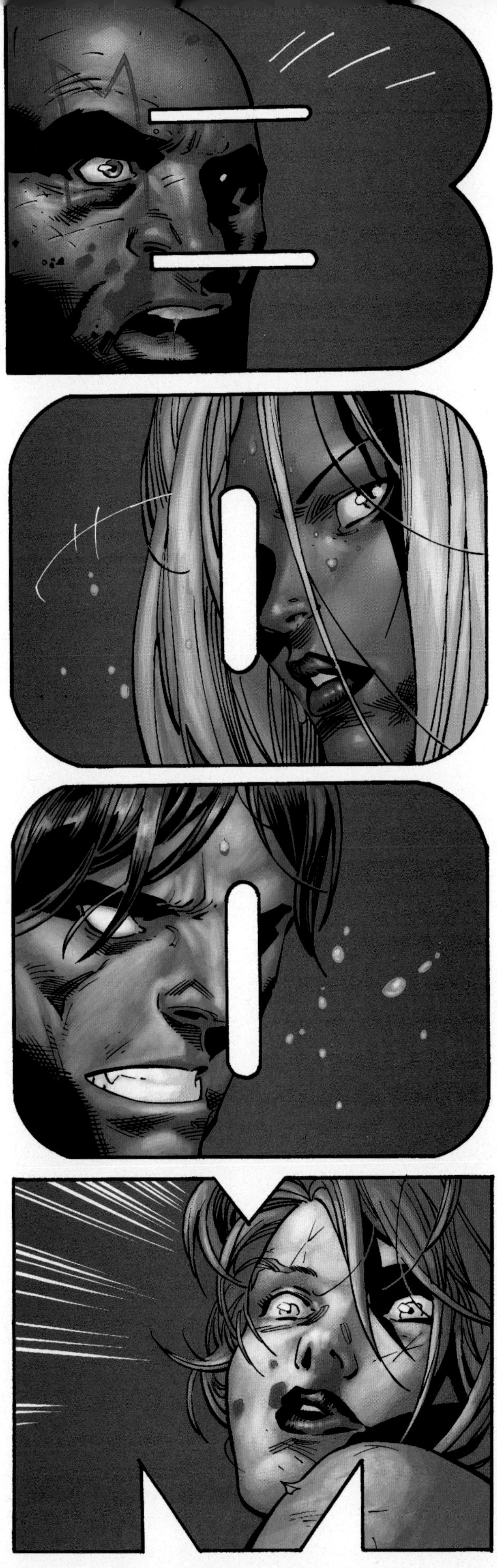
BOOM

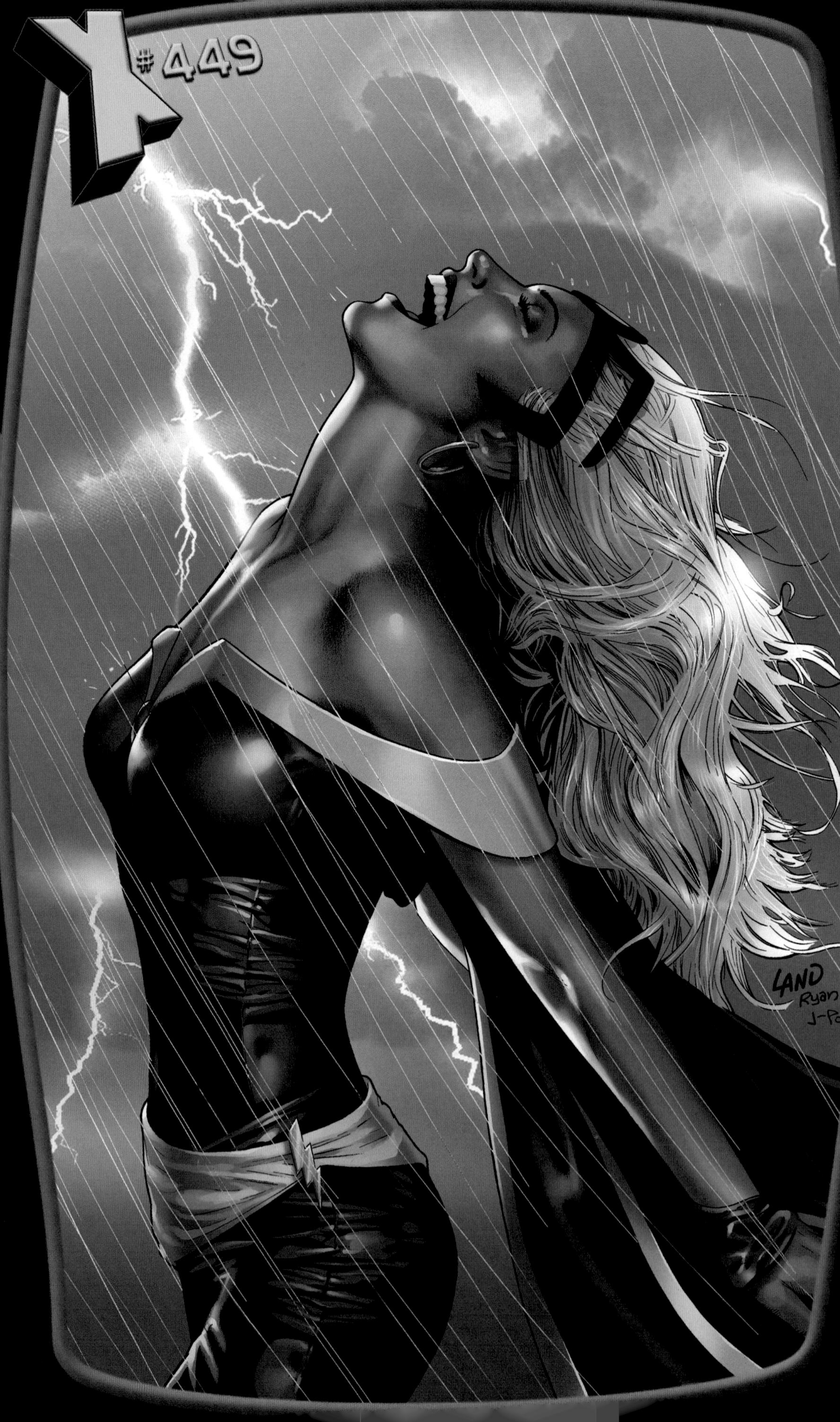
X
#449
LAND
Ryan
J-Po

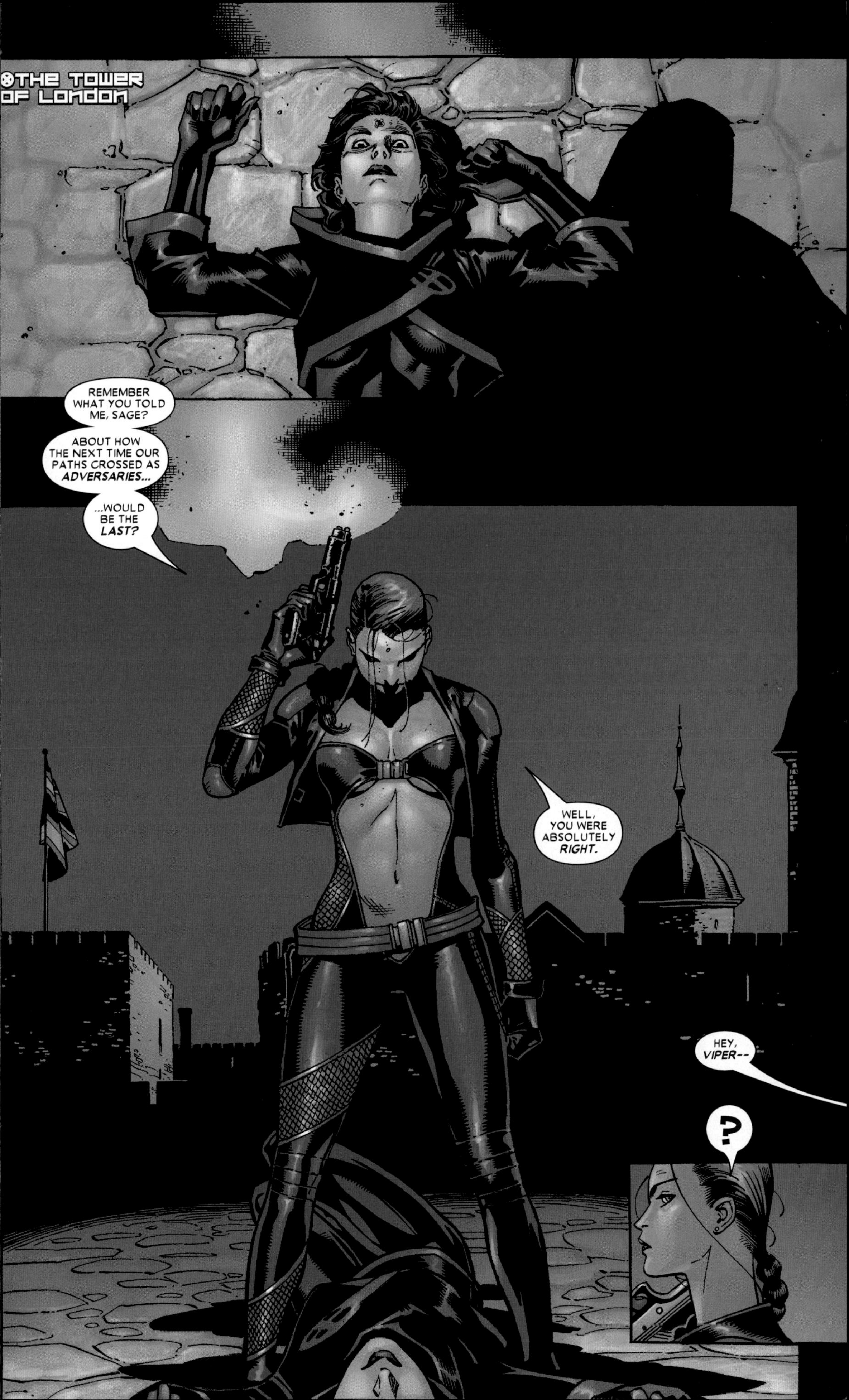
THE TOWER OF LONDON
REMEMBER WHAT YOU TOLD ME, SAGE?
ABOUT HOW THE NEXT TIME OUR PATHS CROSSED AS ADVERSARIES...
...WOULD BE THE LAST?
WELL, YOU WERE ABSOLUTELY RIGHT.
HEY, VIPER--
?

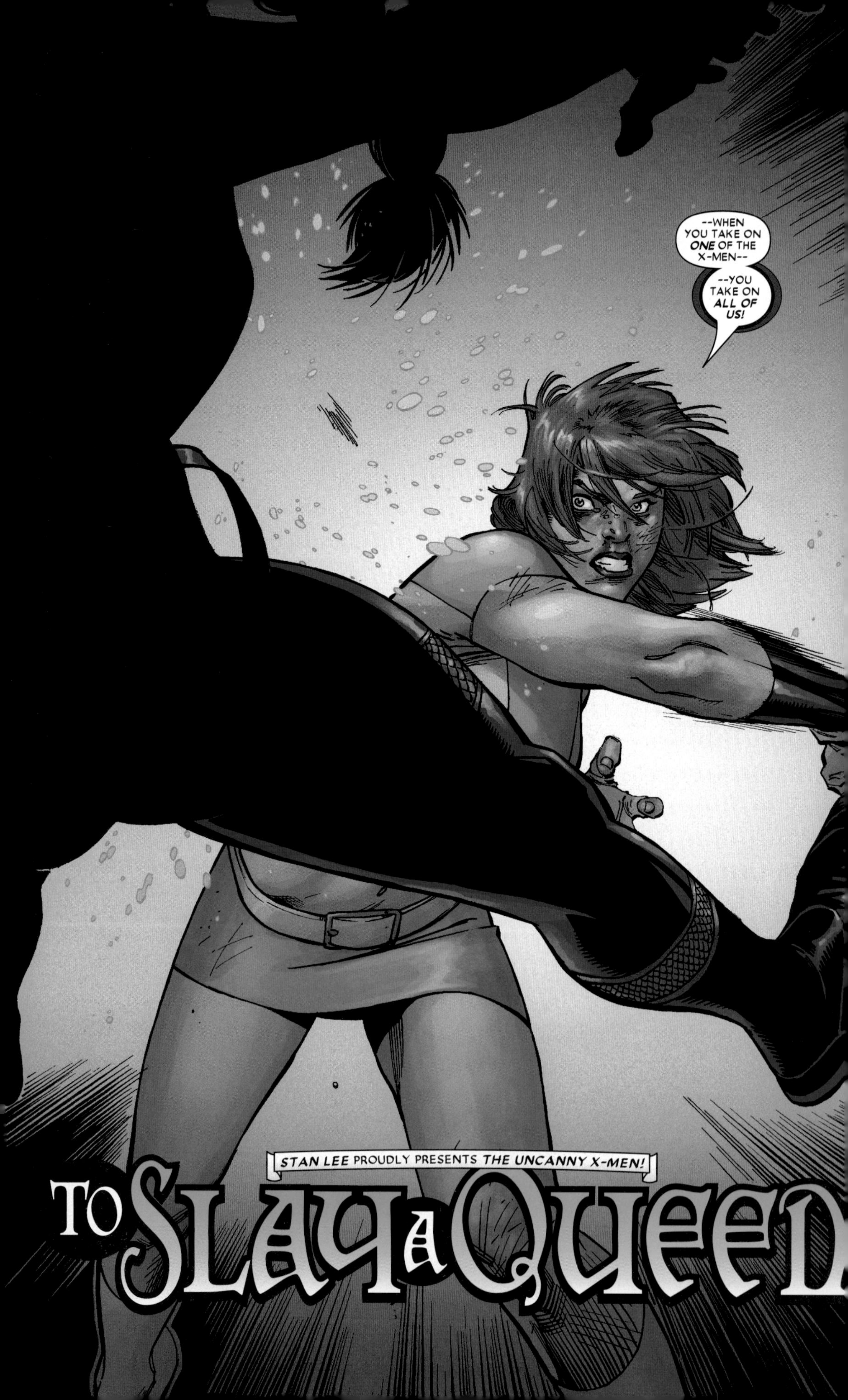
--WHEN YOU TAKE ON ONE OF THE X-MEN--
--YOU TAKE ON ALL OF US!
STAN LEE PROUDLY PRESENTS THE UNCANNY X-MEN!
TO SLAY A QUEEN

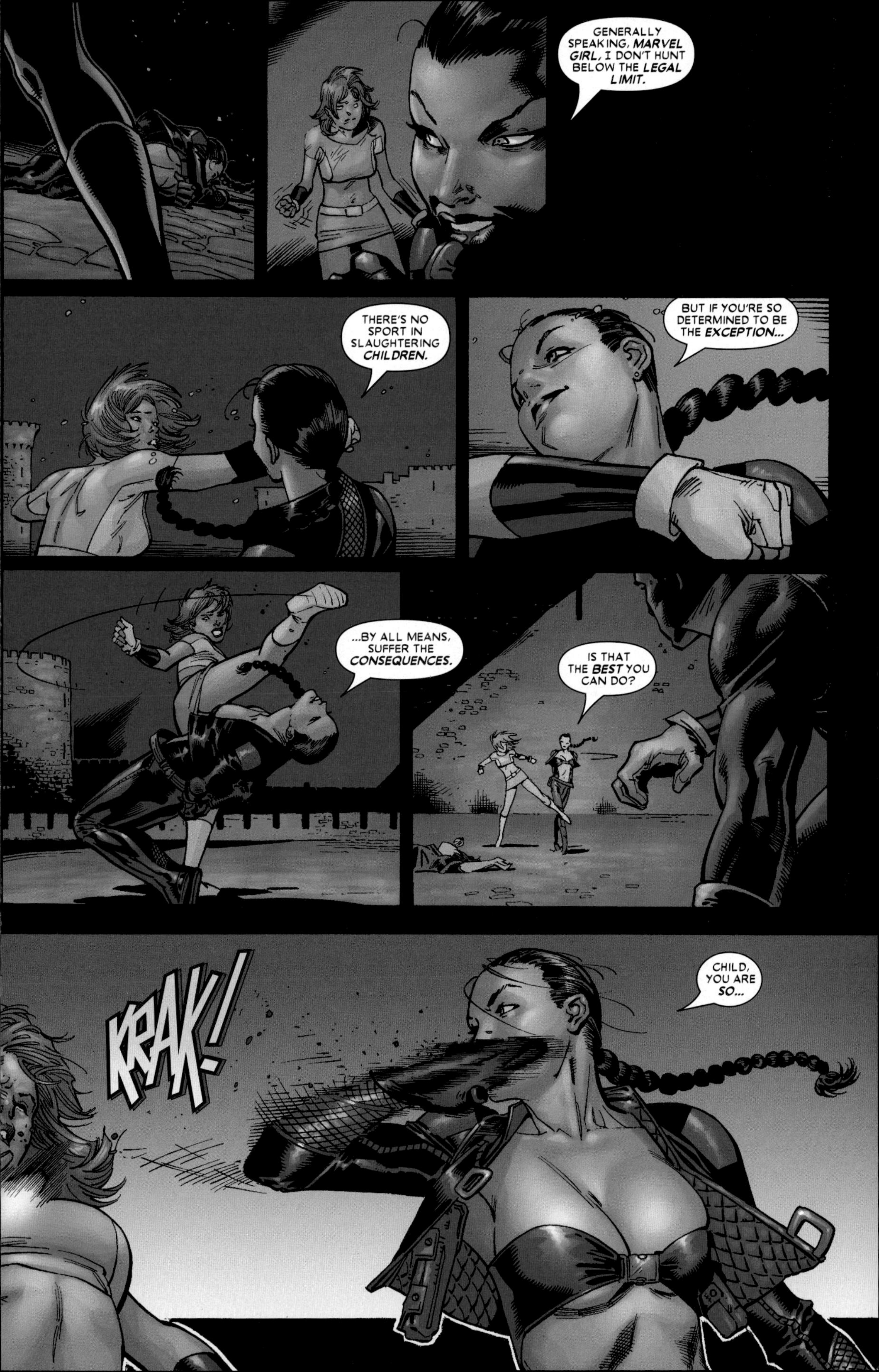
GENERALLY SPEAKING, MARVEL GIRL, I DON'T HUNT BELOW THE LEGAL LIMIT.
THERE'S NO SPORT IN SLAUGHTERING CHILDREN.
BUT IF YOU'RE SO DETERMINED TO BE THE EXCEPTION...
...BY ALL MEANS, SUFFER THE CONSEQUENCES.
IS THAT THE BEST YOU CAN DO?
KRAK!
CHILD, YOU ARE SO...

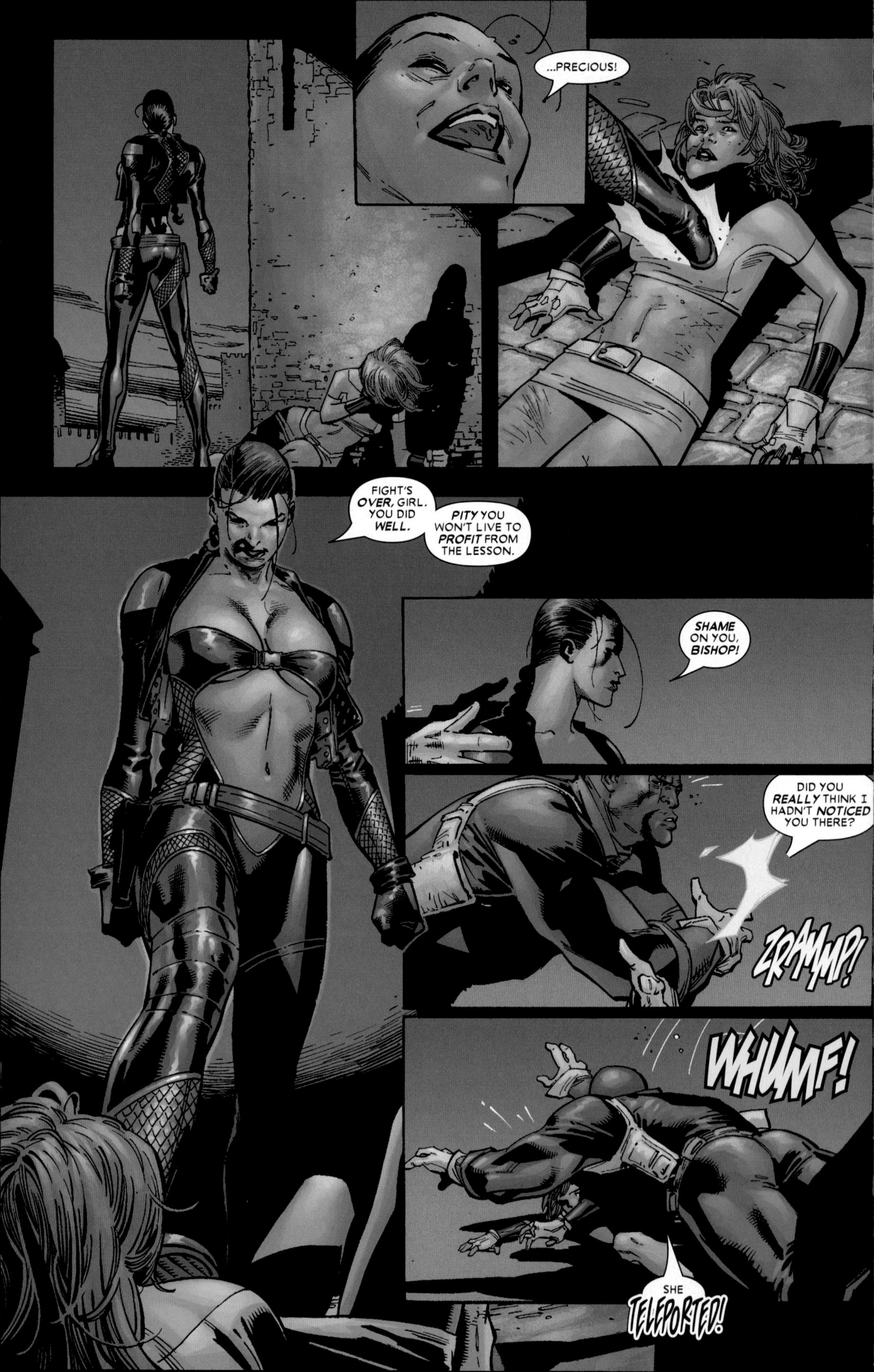

...PRECIOUS!
FIGHT'S OVER, GIRL. YOU DID WELL.
PITY YOU WON'T LIVE TO PROFIT FROM THE LESSON.
SHAME ON YOU, BISHOP!
DID YOU REALLY THINK I HADN'T NOTICED YOU THERE?
ZRAMMP!
WHUMF!
SHE TELEPORTED!

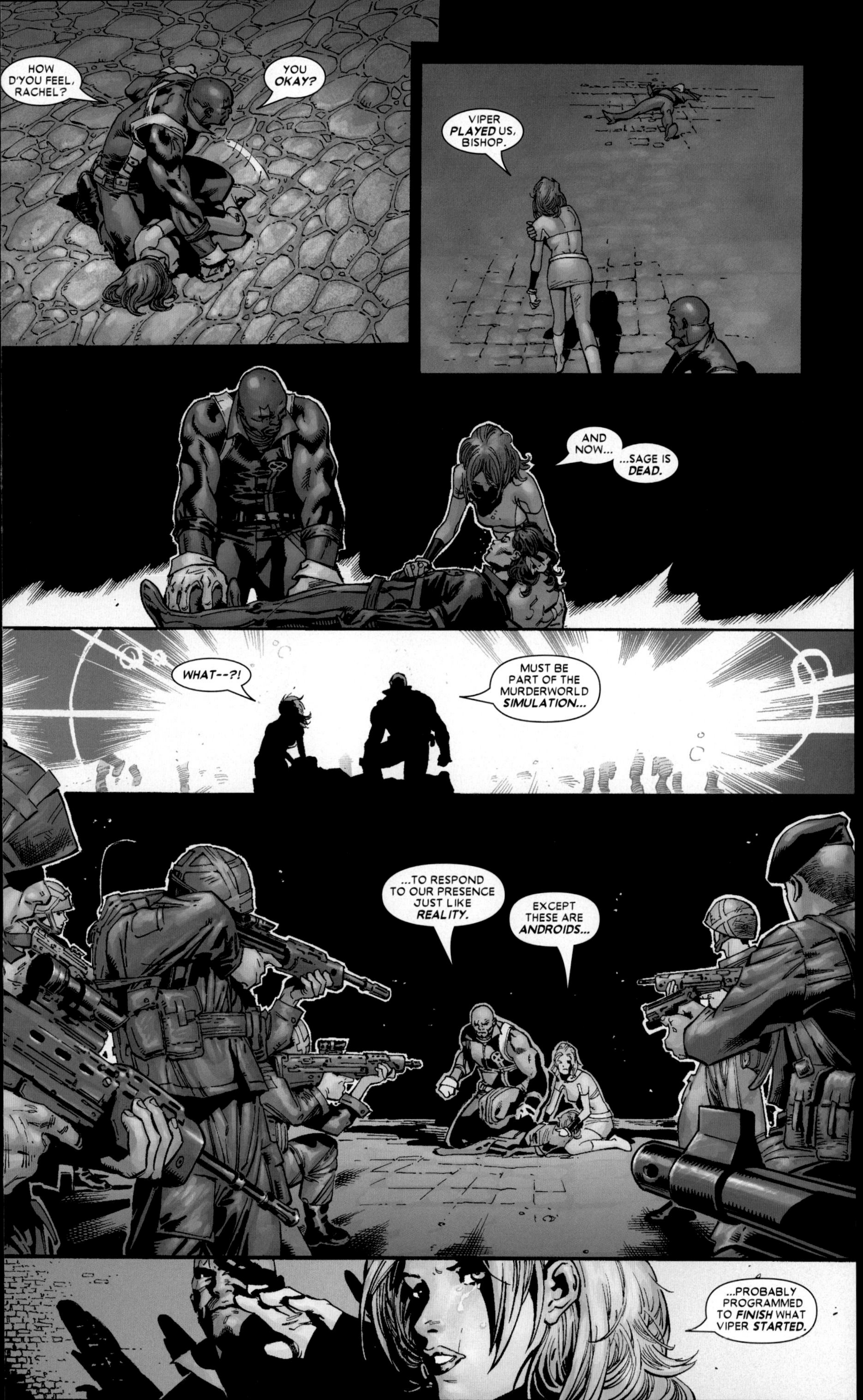
HOW D'YOU FEEL, RACHEL?
YOU OKAY?
VIPER PLAYED US, BISHOP.
AND NOW...
...SAGE IS DEAD.
WHAT--?!
MUST BE PART OF THE MURDERWORLD SIMULATION...
...TO RESPOND TO OUR PRESENCE JUST LIKE REALITY.
EXCEPT THESE ARE ANDROIDS...
...PROBABLY PROGRAMMED TO FINISH WHAT VIPER STARTED.

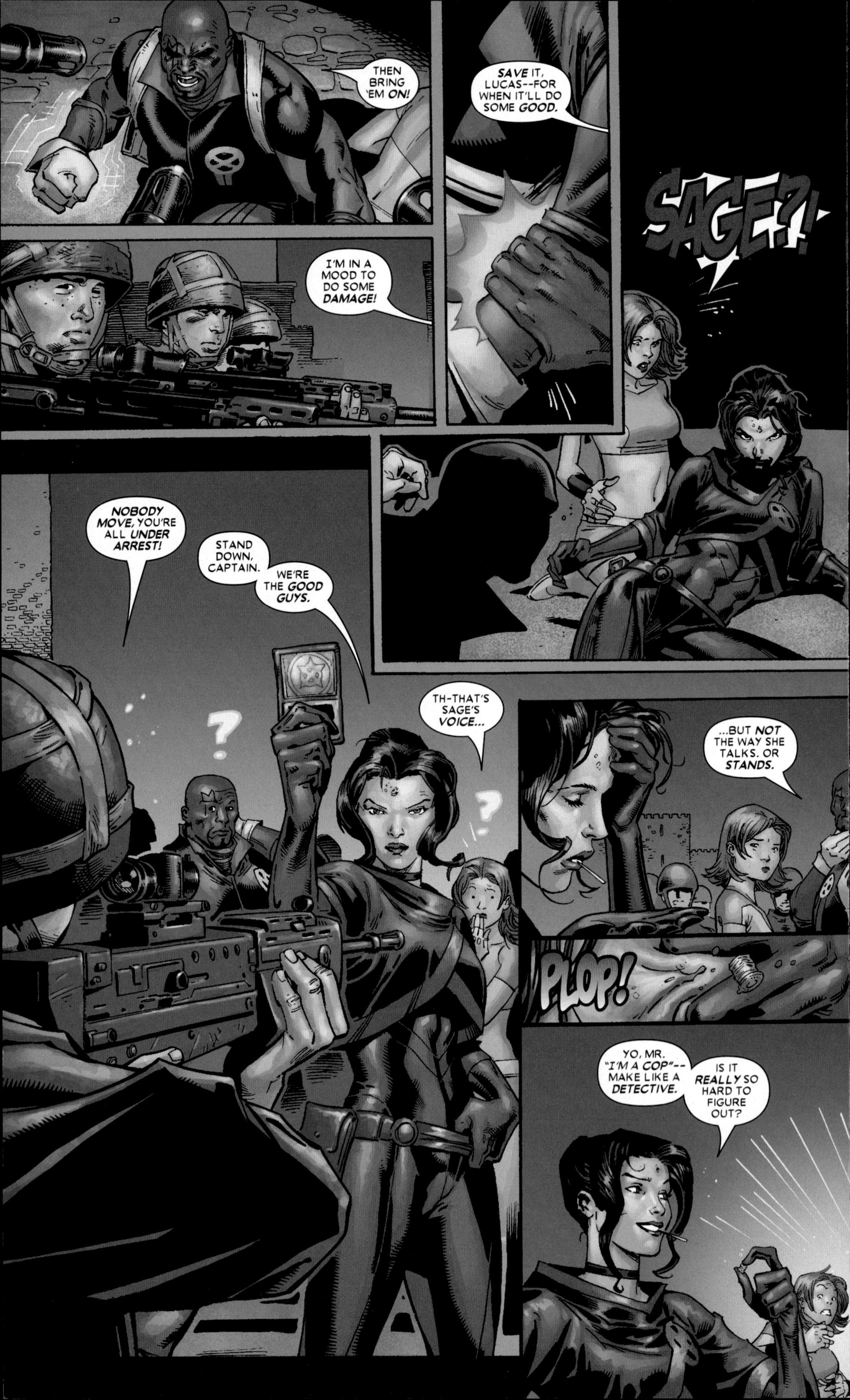
THEN BRING 'EM ON!
SAVE IT, LUCAS--FOR WHEN IT'LL DO SOME GOOD.
I'M IN A MOOD TO DO SOME DAMAGE!
SAGE?!
NOBODY MOVE, YOU'RE ALL UNDER ARREST!
STAND DOWN, CAPTAIN.
WE'RE THE GOOD GUYS.
TH-THAT'S SAGE'S VOICE...
...BUT NOT THE WAY SHE TALKS. OR STANDS.
PLOP!
YO, MR. "I'M A COP"-- MAKE LIKE A DETECTIVE.
IS IT REALLY SO HARD TO FIGURE OUT?

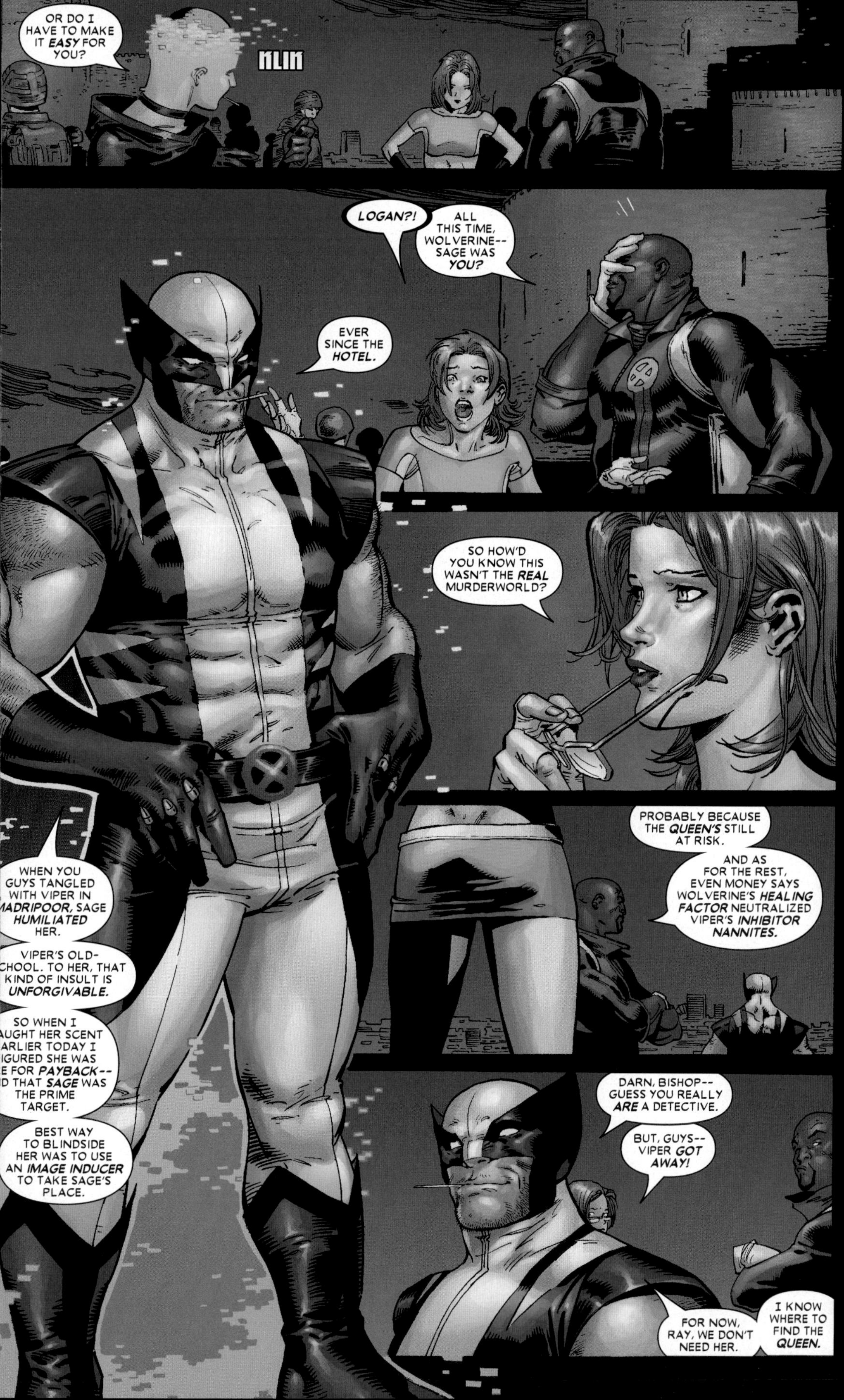
OR DO I HAVE TO MAKE IT EASY FOR YOU?
KLIK
LOGAN?!
ALL THIS TIME, WOLVERINE-- SAGE WAS YOU?
EVER SINCE THE HOTEL.
SO HOW'D YOU KNOW THIS WASN'T THE REAL MURDERWORLD?
WHEN YOU GUYS TANGLED WITH VIPER IN MADRIPOOR, SAGE HUMILIATED HER.
VIPER'S OLD-CHOOL. TO HER, THAT KIND OF INSULT IS UNFORGIVABLE.
SO WHEN I AUGHT HER SCENT ARLIER TODAY I IGURED SHE WAS E FOR PAYBACK-- D THAT SAGE WAS THE PRIME TARGET.
BEST WAY TO BLINDSIDE HER WAS TO USE AN IMAGE INDUCER TO TAKE SAGE'S PLACE.
PROBABLY BECAUSE THE QUEEN'S STILL AT RISK.
AND AS FOR THE REST, EVEN MONEY SAYS WOLVERINE'S HEALING FACTOR NEUTRALIZED VIPER'S INHIBITOR NANNITES.
DARN, BISHOP-- GUESS YOU REALLY ARE A DETECTIVE.
BUT, GUYS-- VIPER GOT AWAY!
FOR NOW, RAY, WE DON'T NEED HER.
I KNOW WHERE TO FIND THE QUEEN.

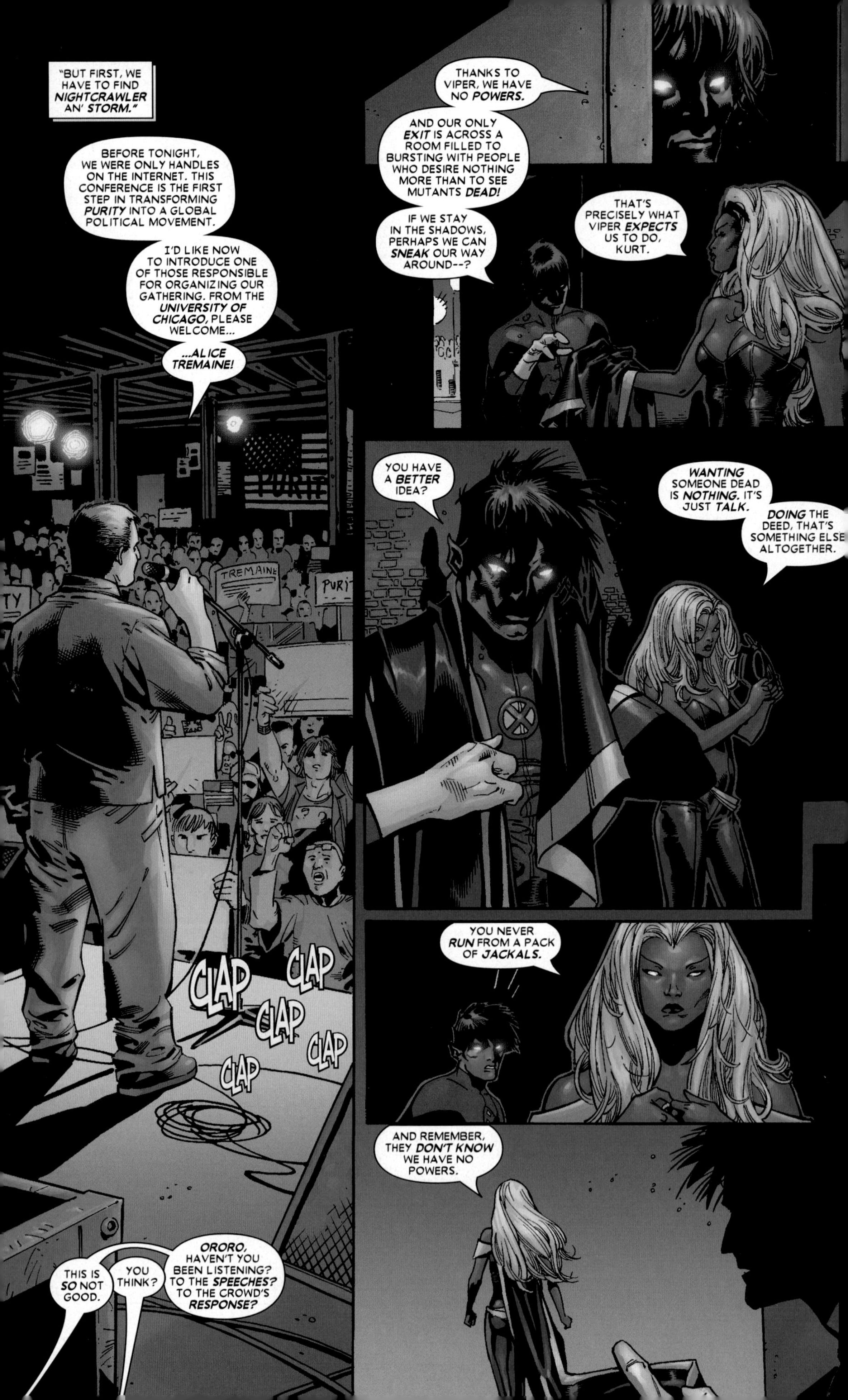
"BUT FIRST, WE HAVE TO FIND NIGHTCRAWLER AN' STORM."
BEFORE TONIGHT, WE WERE ONLY HANDLES ON THE INTERNET. THIS CONFERENCE IS THE FIRST STEP IN TRANSFORMING PURITY INTO A GLOBAL POLITICAL MOVEMENT.
I'D LIKE NOW TO INTRODUCE ONE OF THOSE RESPONSIBLE FOR ORGANIZING OUR GATHERING. FROM THE UNIVERSITY OF CHICAGO, PLEASE WELCOME...
...ALICE TREMAINE!
PURITY
TREMAINE
CLAP
CLAP
CLAP
CLAP
CLAP
THIS IS SO NOT GOOD.
YOU THINK?
ORORO, HAVEN'T YOU BEEN LISTENING? TO THE SPEECHES? TO THE CROWD'S RESPONSE?
THANKS TO VIPER, WE HAVE NO POWERS.
AND OUR ONLY EXIT IS ACROSS A ROOM FILLED TO BURSTING WITH PEOPLE WHO DESIRE NOTHING MORE THAN TO SEE MUTANTS DEAD!
IF WE STAY IN THE SHADOWS, PERHAPS WE CAN SNEAK OUR WAY AROUND--?
THAT'S PRECISELY WHAT VIPER EXPECTS US TO DO, KURT.
YOU HAVE A BETTER IDEA?
WANTING SOMEONE DEAD IS NOTHING. IT'S JUST TALK.
DOING THE DEED, THAT'S SOMETHING ELSE ALTOGETHER.
YOU NEVER RUN FROM A PACK OF JACKALS.
AND REMEMBER, THEY DON'T KNOW WE HAVE NO POWERS.

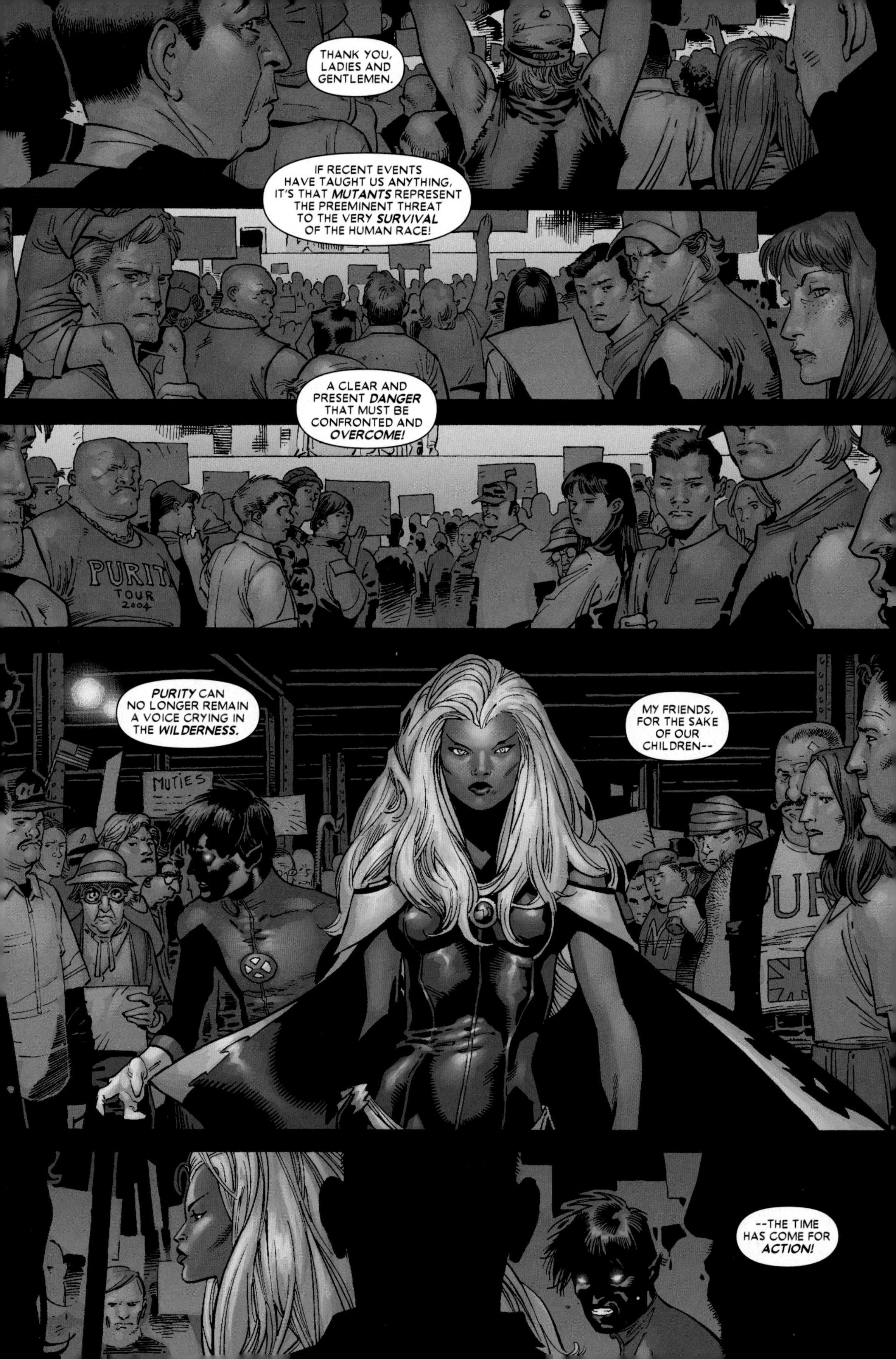

THANK YOU, LADIES AND GENTLEMEN.
IF RECENT EVENTS HAVE TAUGHT US ANYTHING, IT'S THAT MUTANTS REPRESENT THE PREEMINENT THREAT TO THE VERY SURVIVAL OF THE HUMAN RACE!
A CLEAR AND PRESENT DANGER THAT MUST BE CONFRONTED AND OVERCOME!
PURIT
TOUR
2004
PURITY CAN NO LONGER REMAIN A VOICE CRYING IN THE WILDERNESS.
MY FRIENDS, FOR THE SAKE OF OUR CHILDREN--
MUTIES
--THE TIME HAS COME FOR ACTION!

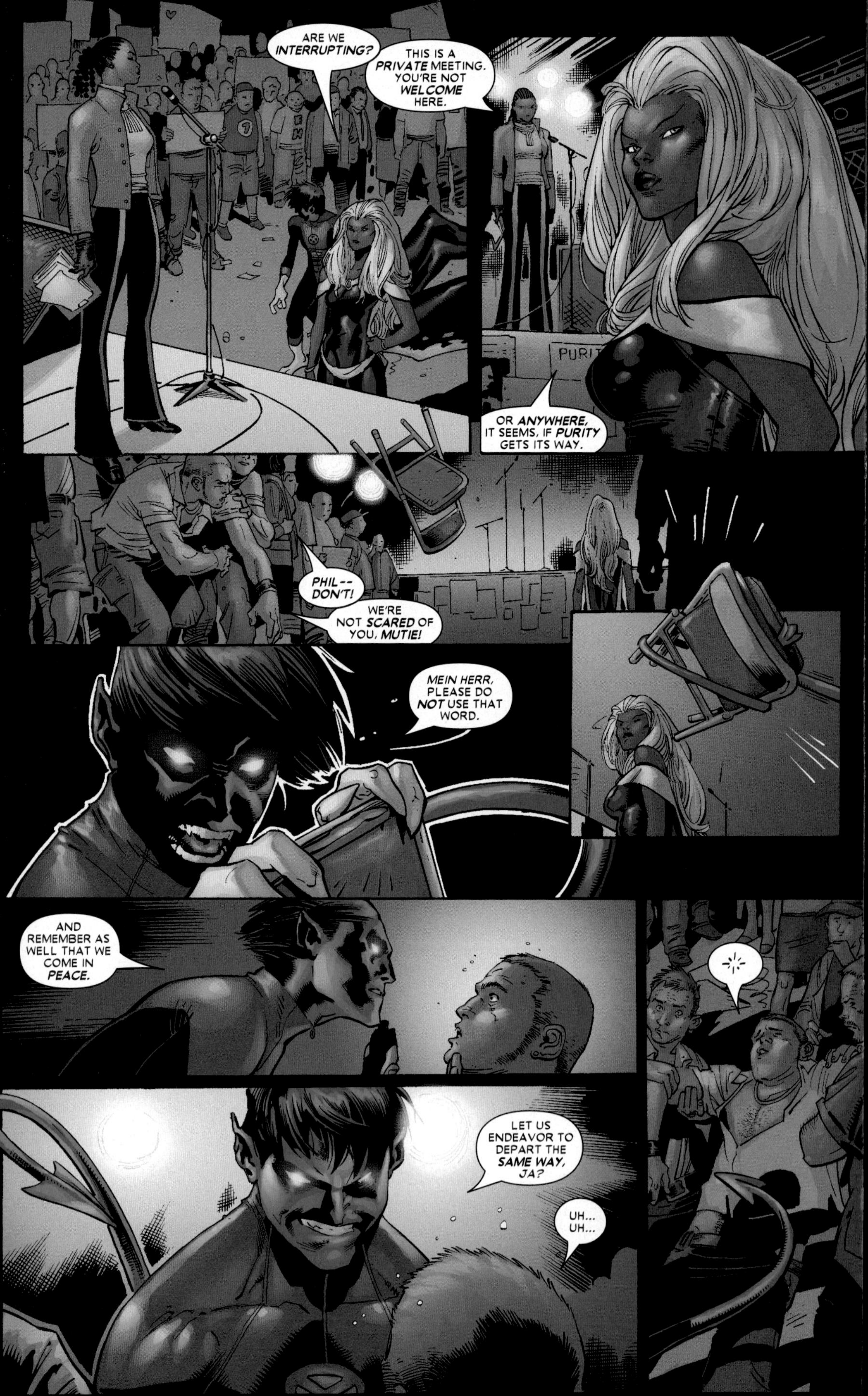
ARE WE INTERRUPTING?
THIS IS A PRIVATE MEETING. YOU'RE NOT WELCOME HERE.
PURIT
OR ANYWHERE, IT SEEMS, IF PURITY GETS ITS WAY.
PHIL-- DON'T!
WE'RE NOT SCARED OF YOU, MUTIE!
MEIN HERR, PLEASE DO NOT USE THAT WORD.
AND REMEMBER AS WELL THAT WE COME IN PEACE.
LET US ENDEAVOR TO DEPART THE SAME WAY, JA?
UH... UH...

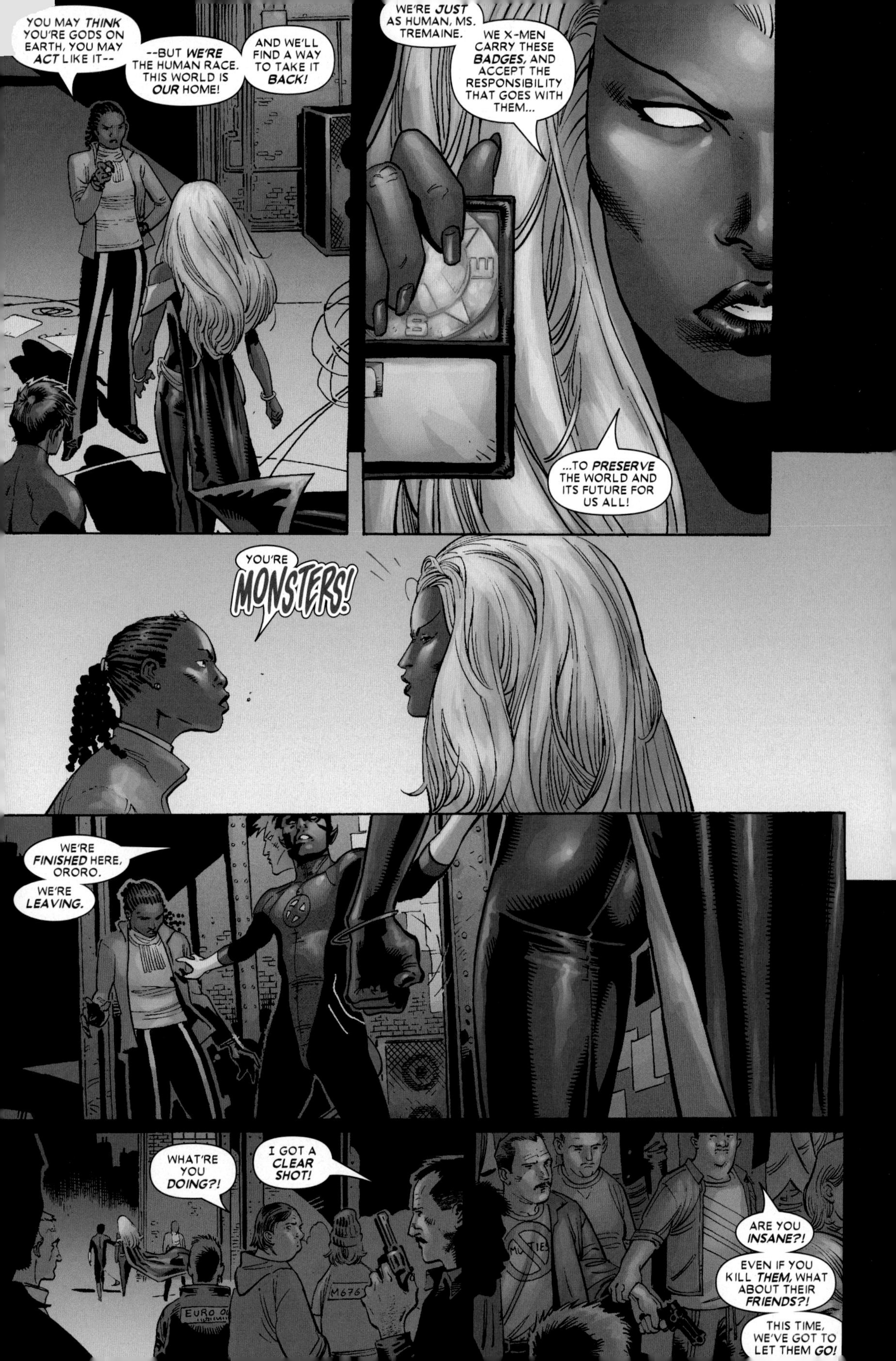
YOU MAY THINK YOU'RE GODS ON EARTH, YOU MAY ACT LIKE IT--
--BUT WE'RE THE HUMAN RACE. THIS WORLD IS OUR HOME!
AND WE'LL FIND A WAY TO TAKE IT BACK!
WE'RE JUST AS HUMAN, MS. TREMAINE.
WE X-MEN CARRY THESE BADGES, AND ACCEPT THE RESPONSIBILITY THAT GOES WITH THEM...
...TO PRESERVE THE WORLD AND ITS FUTURE FOR US ALL!
YOU'RE MONSTERS!
WE'RE FINISHED HERE, ORORO.
WE'RE LEAVING.
WHAT'RE YOU DOING?!
I GOT A CLEAR SHOT!
ARE YOU INSANE?!
EVEN IF YOU KILL THEM, WHAT ABOUT THEIR FRIENDS?!
THIS TIME, WE'VE GOT TO LET THEM GO!

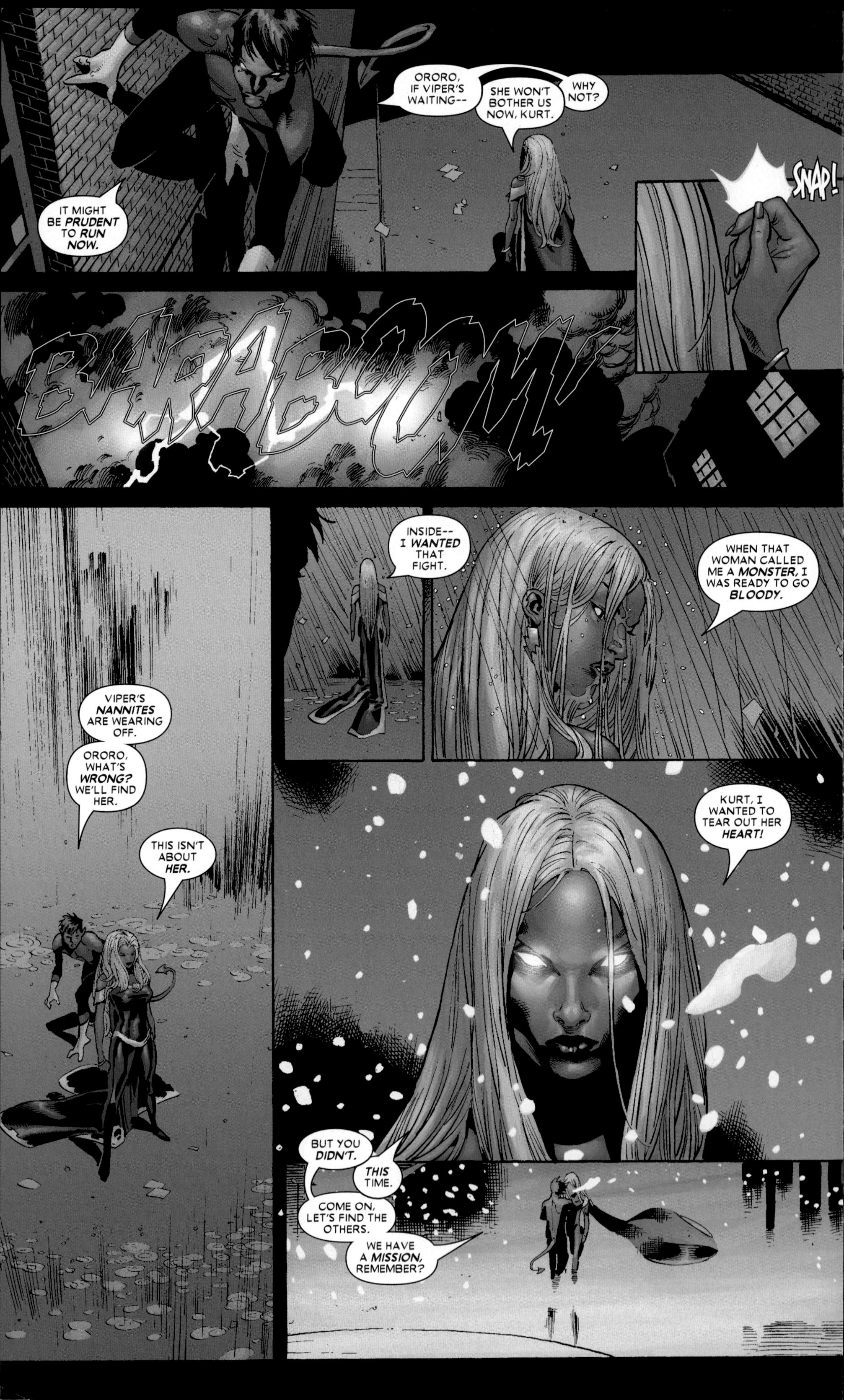

IT MIGHT BE PRUDENT TO RUN NOW.
ORORO, IF VIPER'S WAITING--
SHE WON'T BOTHER US NOW, KURT.
WHY NOT?
SNAP!
BARABOOM!
VIPER'S NANNITES ARE WEARING OFF.
ORORO, WHAT'S WRONG? WE'LL FIND HER.
THIS ISN'T ABOUT HER.
INSIDE-- I WANTED THAT FIGHT.
WHEN THAT WOMAN CALLED ME A MONSTER, I WAS READY TO GO BLOODY.
KURT, I WANTED TO TEAR OUT HER HEART!
BUT YOU DIDN'T.
THIS TIME.
COME ON, LET'S FIND THE OTHERS.
WE HAVE A MISSION, REMEMBER?

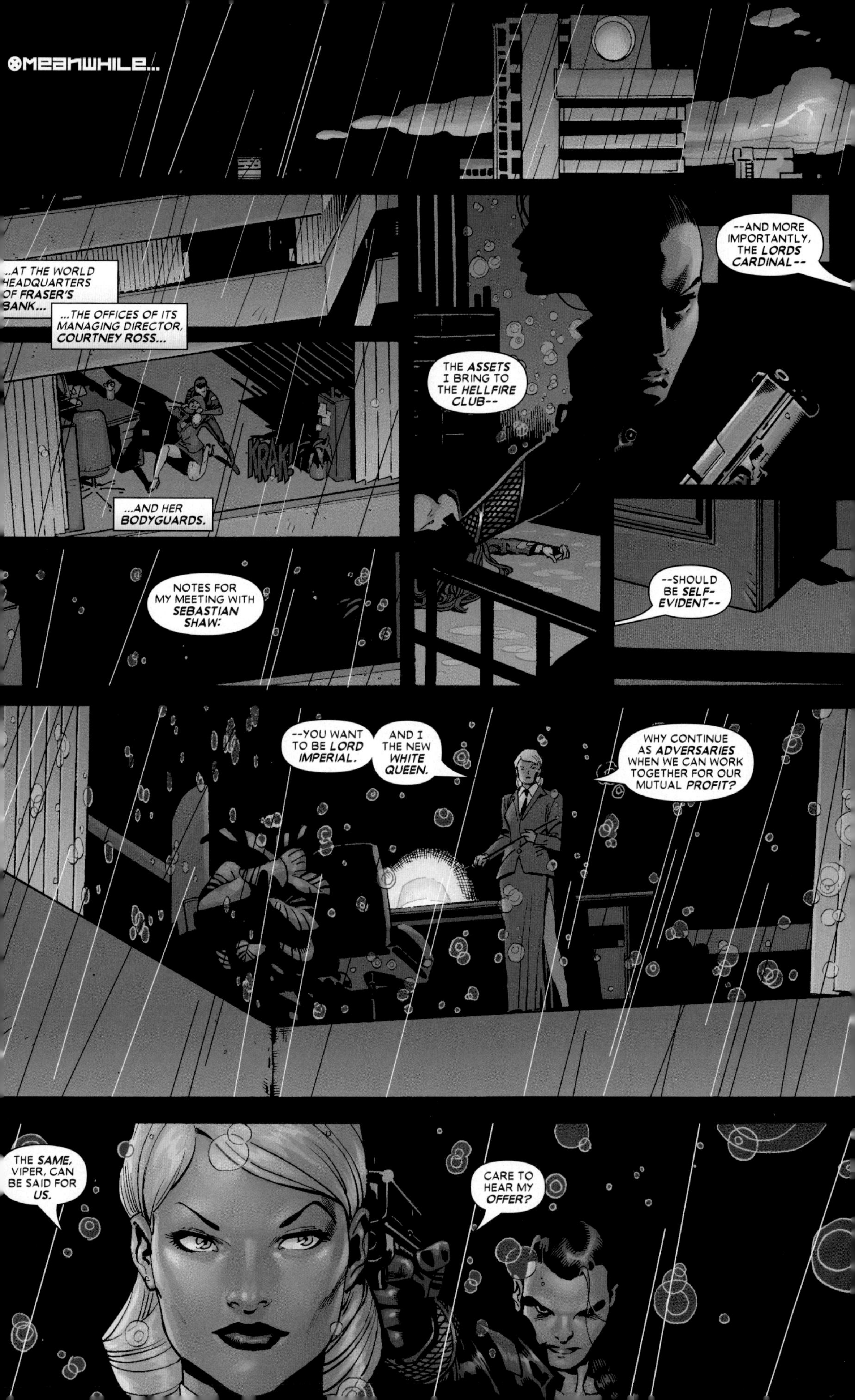
MEANWHILE...
...AT THE WORLD HEADQUARTERS OF FRASER'S BANK...
...THE OFFICES OF ITS MANAGING DIRECTOR, COURTNEY ROSS...
...AND HER BODYGUARDS.
KRAK!
THE ASSETS I BRING TO THE HELLFIRE CLUB--
--AND MORE IMPORTANTLY, THE LORDS CARDINAL--
NOTES FOR MY MEETING WITH SEBASTIAN SHAW:
--SHOULD BE SELF-EVIDENT--
--YOU WANT TO BE LORD IMPERIAL.
AND I THE NEW WHITE QUEEN.
WHY CONTINUE AS ADVERSARIES WHEN WE CAN WORK TOGETHER FOR OUR MUTUAL PROFIT?
THE SAME, VIPER, CAN BE SAID FOR US.
CARE TO HEAR MY OFFER?

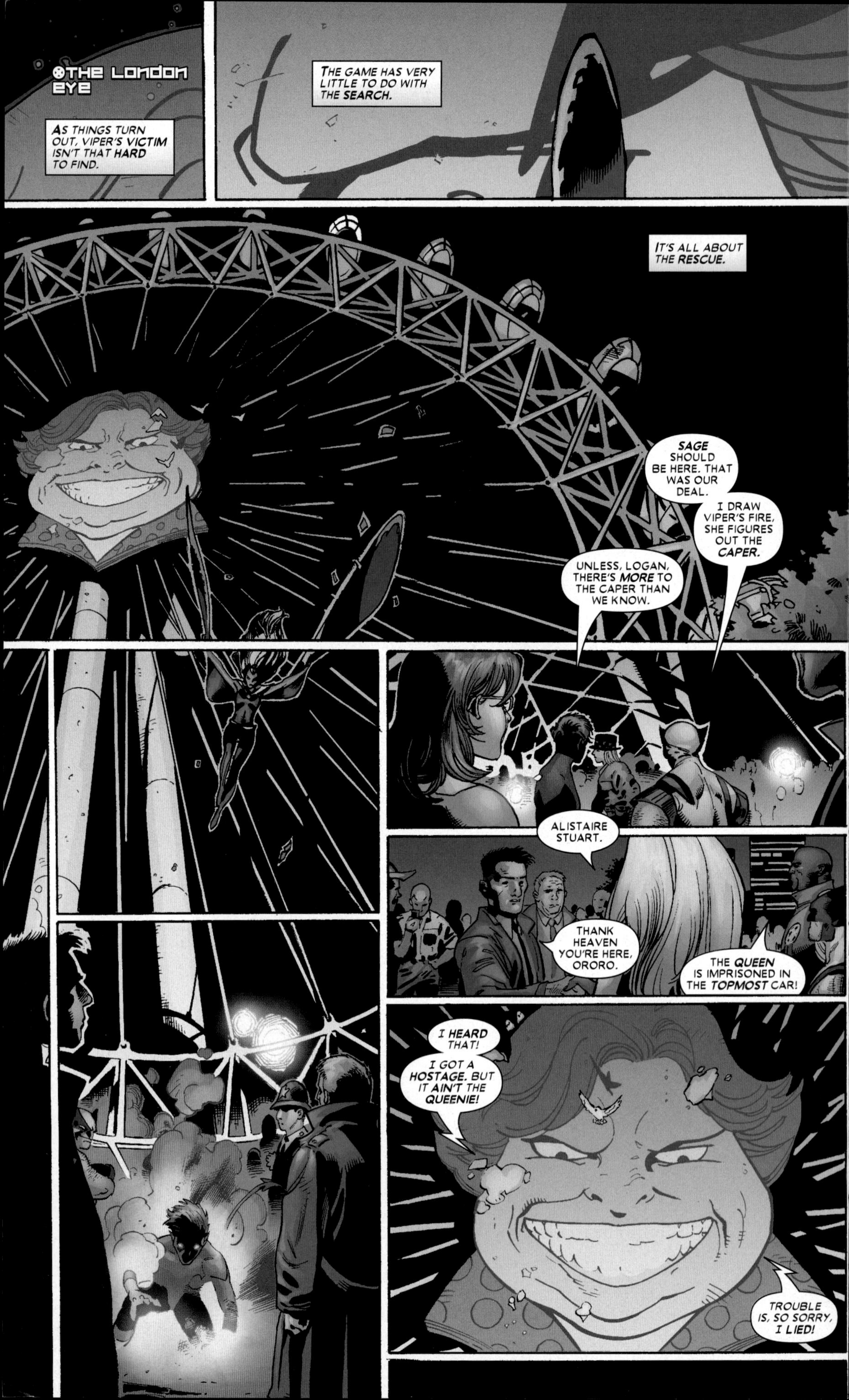
THE LONDON EYE
AS THINGS TURN OUT, VIPER'S VICTIM ISN'T THAT HARD TO FIND.
THE GAME HAS VERY LITTLE TO DO WITH THE SEARCH.
IT'S ALL ABOUT THE RESCUE.
SAGE SHOULD BE HERE. THAT WAS OUR DEAL.
I DRAW VIPER'S FIRE, SHE FIGURES OUT THE CAPER.
UNLESS, LOGAN, THERE'S MORE TO THE CAPER THAN WE KNOW.
ALISTAIRE STUART.
THANK HEAVEN YOU'RE HERE, ORORO.
THE QUEEN IS IMPRISONED IN THE TOPMOST CAR!
I HEARD THAT!
I GOT A HOSTAGE. BUT IT AIN'T THE QUEENIE!
TROUBLE IS, SO SORRY, I LIED!

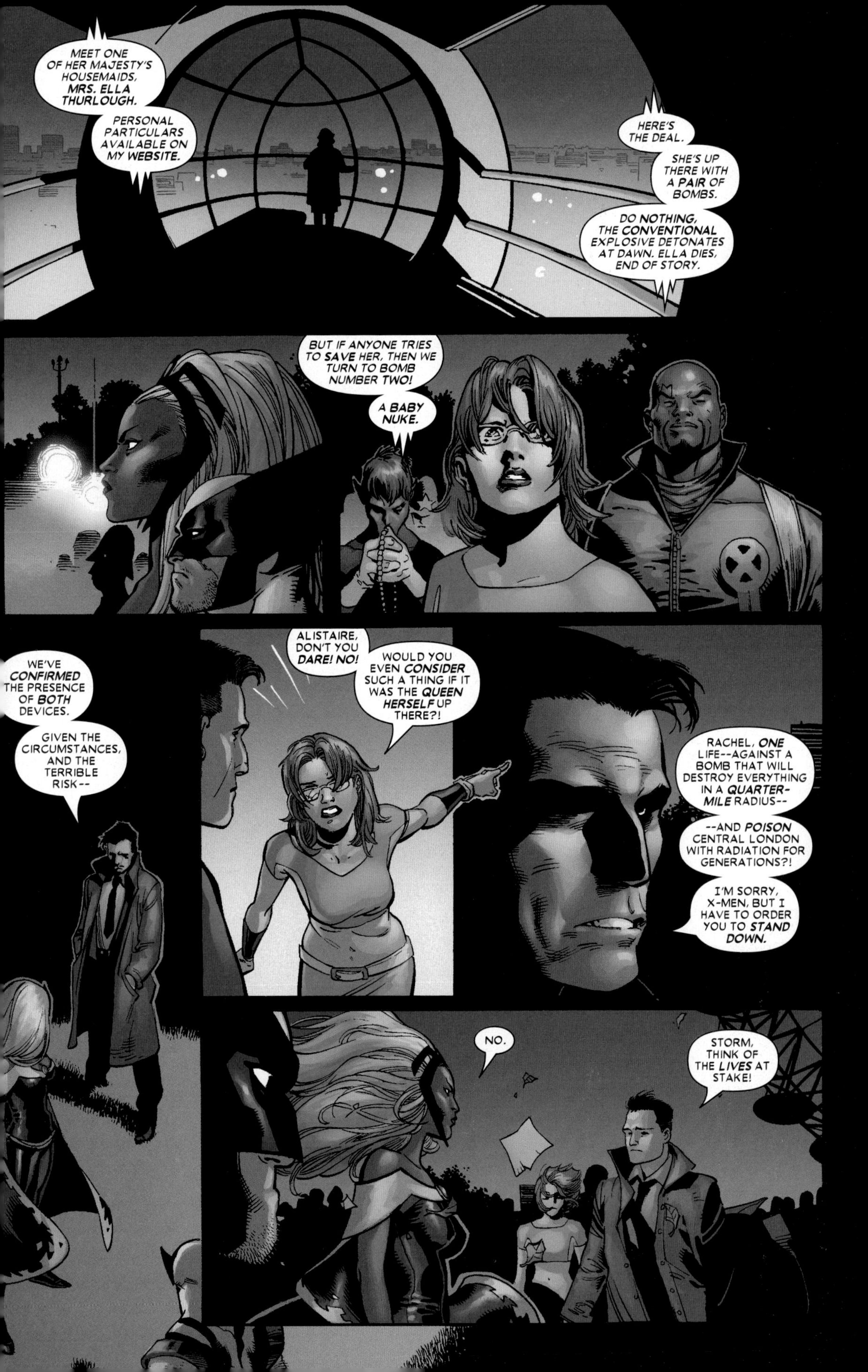
MEET ONE OF HER MAJESTY'S HOUSEMAIDS, MRS. ELLA THURLOUGH.
PERSONAL PARTICULARS AVAILABLE ON MY WEBSITE.
HERE'S THE DEAL.
SHE'S UP THERE WITH A PAIR OF BOMBS.
DO NOTHING, THE CONVENTIONAL EXPLOSIVE DETONATES AT DAWN. ELLA DIES, END OF STORY.
BUT IF ANYONE TRIES TO SAVE HER, THEN WE TURN TO BOMB NUMBER TWO!
A BABY NUKE.
WE'VE CONFIRMED THE PRESENCE OF BOTH DEVICES.
GIVEN THE CIRCUMSTANCES, AND THE TERRIBLE RISK--
ALISTAIRE, DON'T YOU DARE! NO!
WOULD YOU EVEN CONSIDER SUCH A THING IF IT WAS THE QUEEN HERSELF UP THERE?!
RACHEL, ONE LIFE--AGAINST A BOMB THAT WILL DESTROY EVERYTHING IN A QUARTER-MILE RADIUS--
--AND POISON CENTRAL LONDON WITH RADIATION FOR GENERATIONS?!
I'M SORRY, X-MEN, BUT I HAVE TO ORDER YOU TO STAND DOWN.
NO.
STORM, THINK OF THE LIVES AT STAKE!

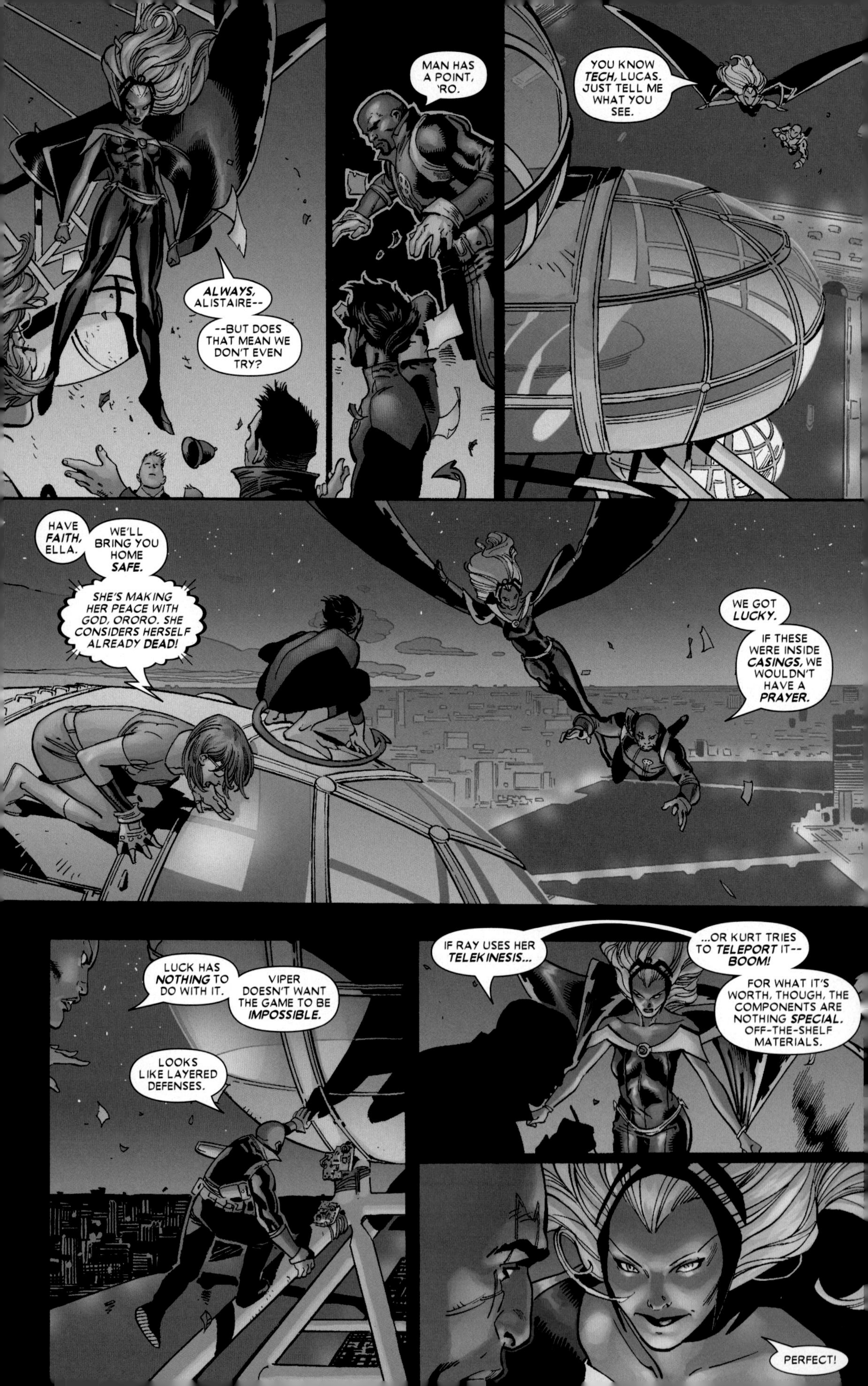
ALWAYS, ALISTAIRE--
--BUT DOES THAT MEAN WE DON'T EVEN TRY?
MAN HAS A POINT, 'RO.
YOU KNOW TECH, LUCAS. JUST TELL ME WHAT YOU SEE.
HAVE FAITH, ELLA.
WE'LL BRING YOU HOME SAFE.
SHE'S MAKING HER PEACE WITH GOD, ORORO. SHE CONSIDERS HERSELF ALREADY DEAD!
WE GOT LUCKY.
IF THESE WERE INSIDE CASINGS, WE WOULDN'T HAVE A PRAYER.
LUCK HAS NOTHING TO DO WITH IT.
VIPER DOESN'T WANT THE GAME TO BE IMPOSSIBLE.
LOOKS LIKE LAYERED DEFENSES.
IF RAY USES HER TELEKINESIS...
...OR KURT TRIES TO TELEPORT IT-- BOOM!
FOR WHAT IT'S WORTH, THOUGH, THE COMPONENTS ARE NOTHING SPECIAL. OFF-THE-SHELF MATERIALS.
PERFECT!

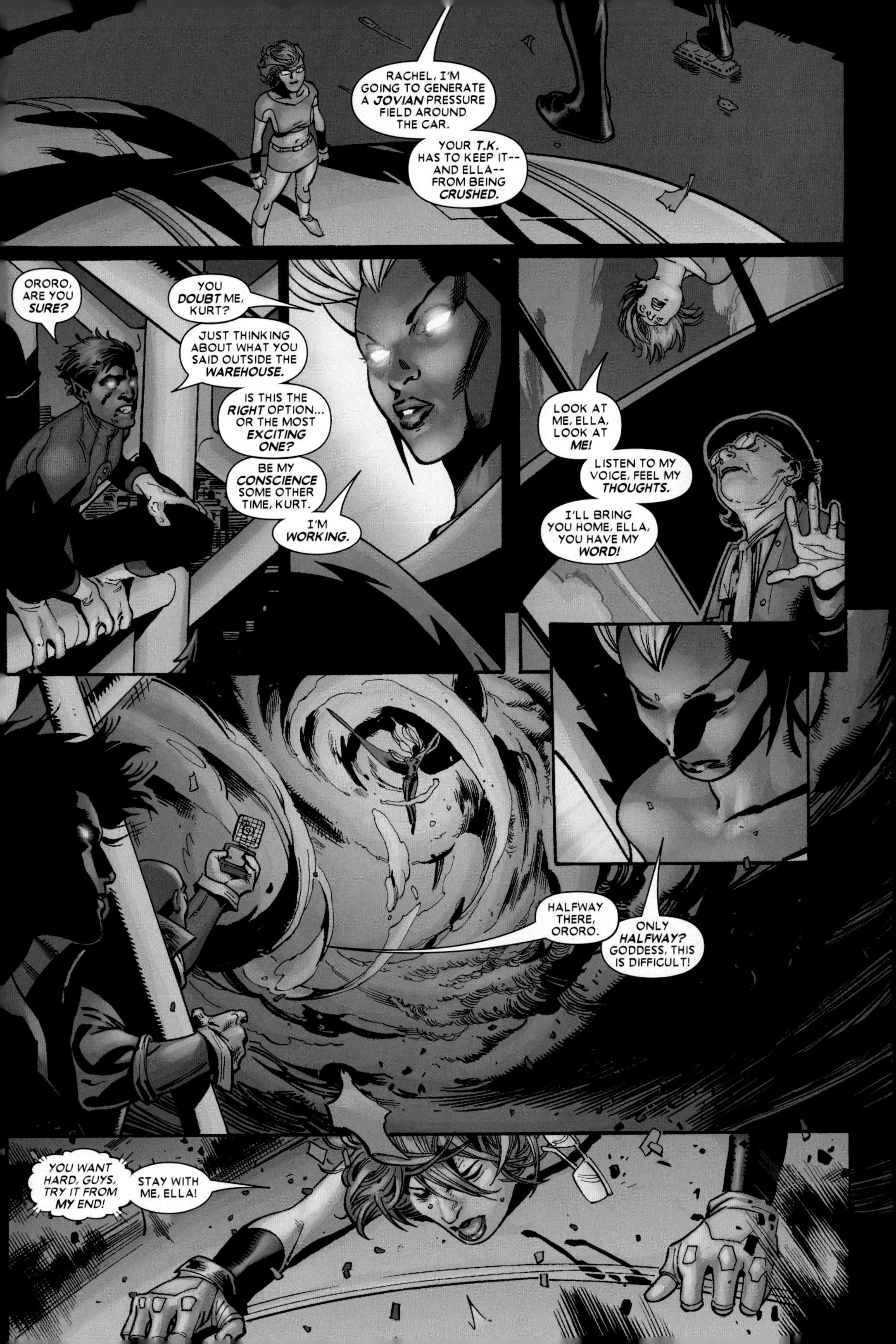
RACHEL, I'M GOING TO GENERATE A JOVIAN PRESSURE FIELD AROUND THE CAR.
YOUR T.K. HAS TO KEEP IT-- AND ELLA-- FROM BEING CRUSHED.
ORORO, ARE YOU SURE?
YOU DOUBT ME, KURT?
JUST THINKING ABOUT WHAT YOU SAID OUTSIDE THE WAREHOUSE.
IS THIS THE RIGHT OPTION... OR THE MOST EXCITING ONE?
BE MY CONSCIENCE SOME OTHER TIME, KURT.
I'M WORKING.
LOOK AT ME, ELLA, LOOK AT ME!
LISTEN TO MY VOICE, FEEL MY THOUGHTS.
I'LL BRING YOU HOME, ELLA, YOU HAVE MY WORD!
HALFWAY THERE, ORORO.
ONLY HALFWAY? GODDESS, THIS IS DIFFICULT!
YOU WANT HARD, GUYS, TRY IT FROM MY END!
STAY WITH ME, ELLA!

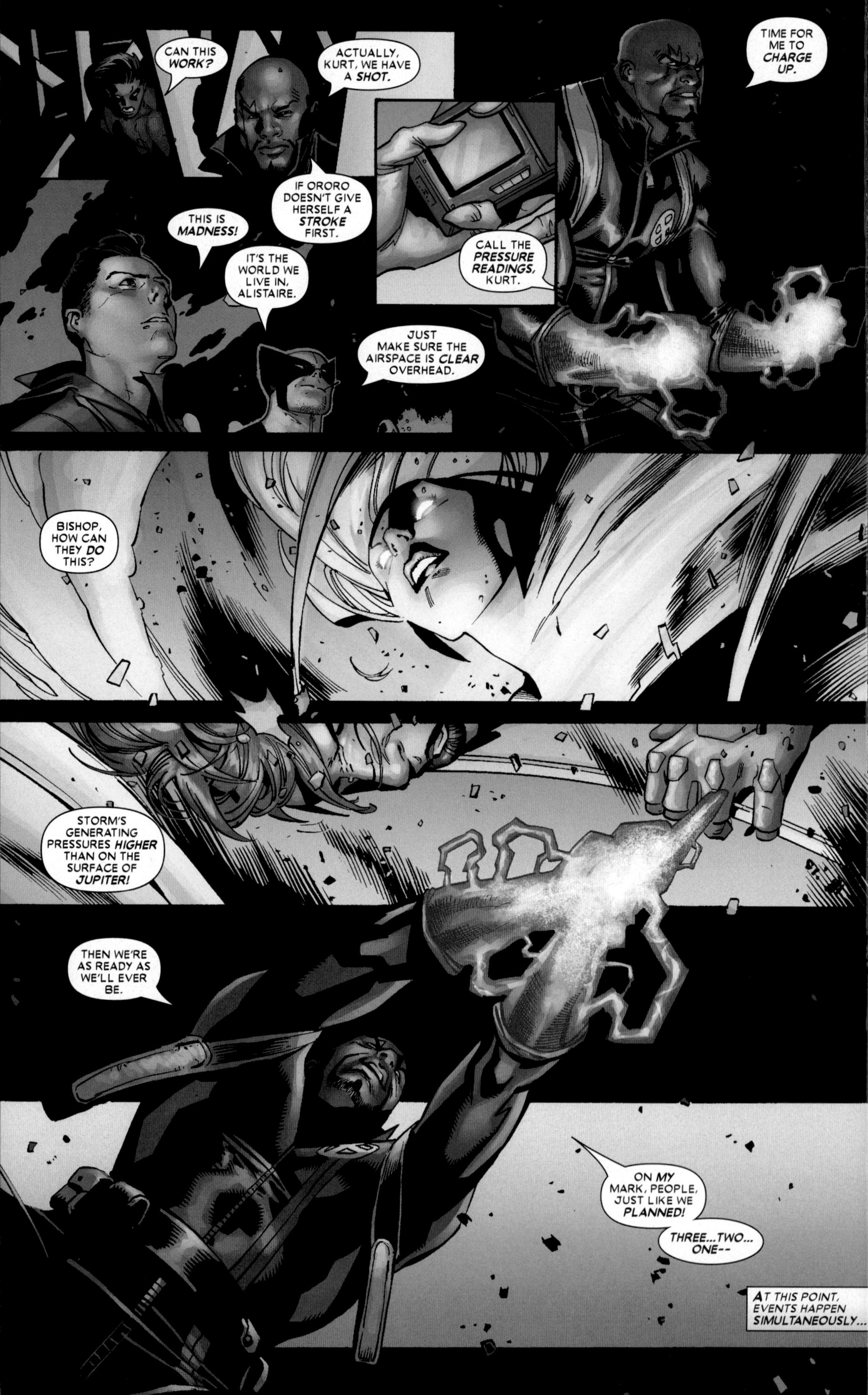
CAN THIS WORK?
ACTUALLY, KURT, WE HAVE A SHOT.
TIME FOR ME TO CHARGE UP.
IF ORORO DOESN'T GIVE HERSELF A STROKE FIRST.
THIS IS MADNESS!
IT'S THE WORLD WE LIVE IN, ALISTAIRE.
CALL THE PRESSURE READINGS, KURT.
JUST MAKE SURE THE AIRSPACE IS CLEAR OVERHEAD.
BISHOP, HOW CAN THEY DO THIS?
STORM'S GENERATING PRESSURES HIGHER THAN ON THE SURFACE OF JUPITER!
THEN WE'RE AS READY AS WE'LL EVER BE.
ON MY MARK, PEOPLE, JUST LIKE WE PLANNED!
THREE...TWO... ONE--
AT THIS POINT, EVENTS HAPPEN SIMULTANEOUSLY...

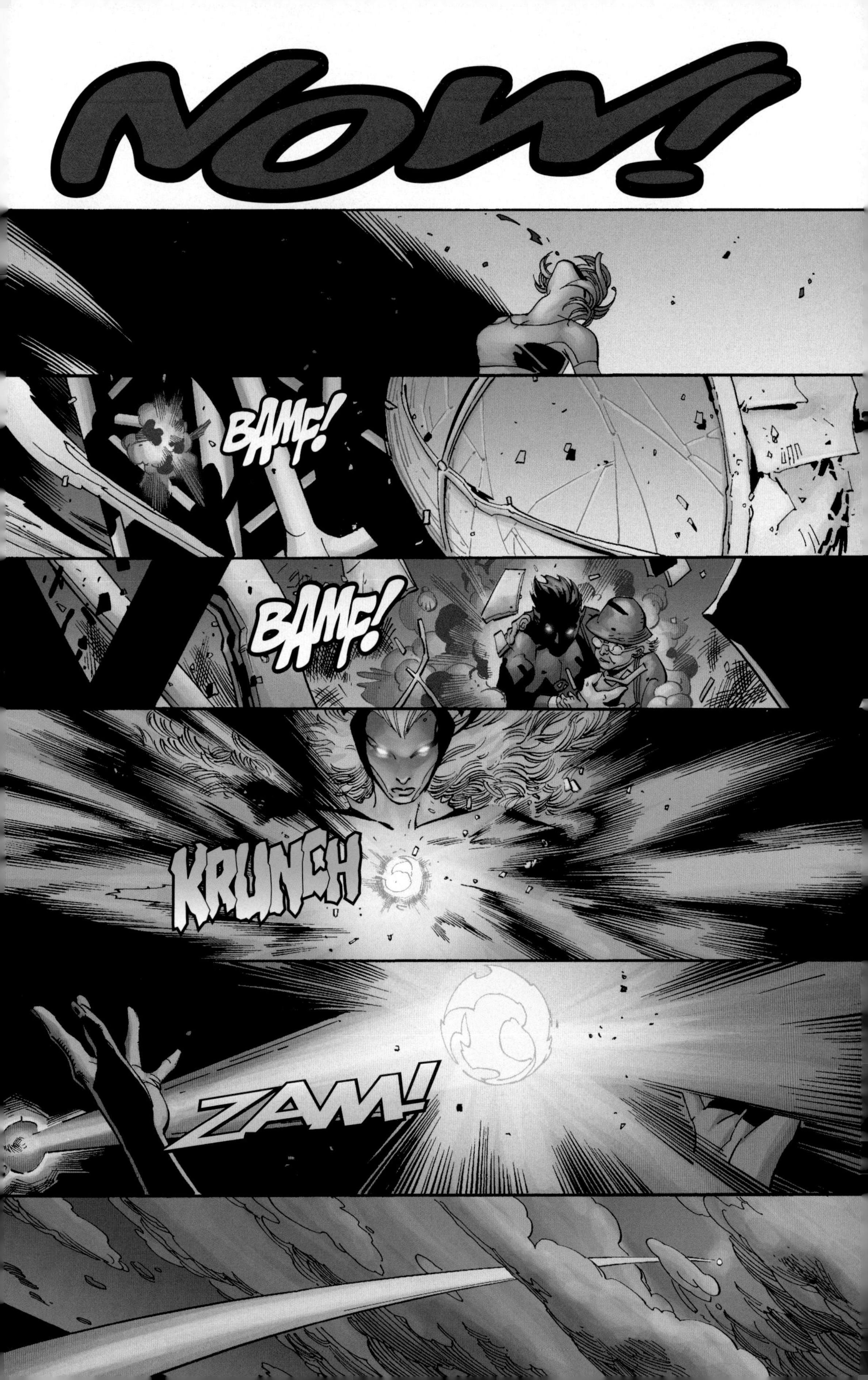
NOW!
BAMF!
BAMF!
KRUNCH
ZAM!

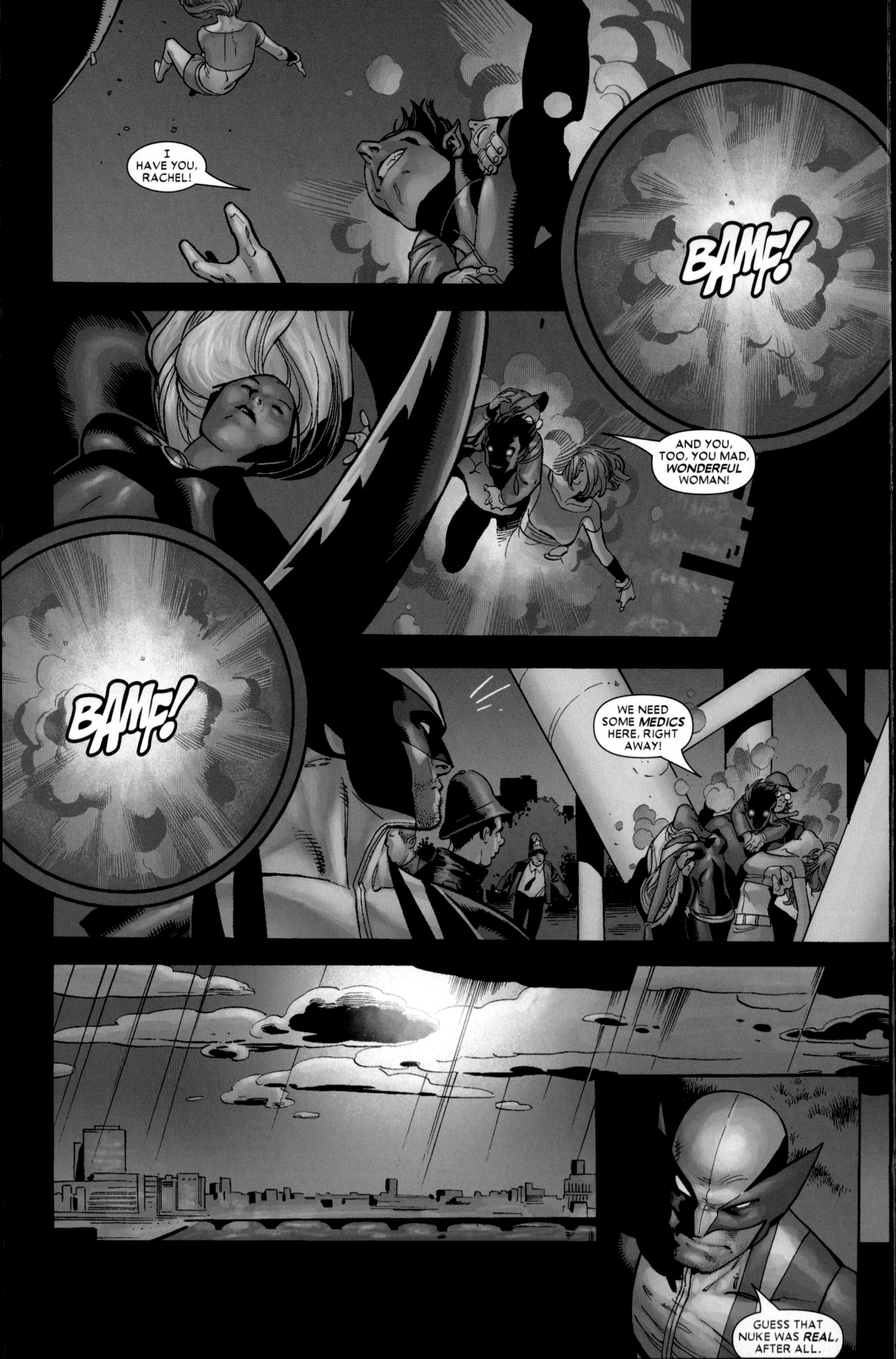
I HAVE YOU, RACHEL!
BAMF!
AND YOU, TOO, YOU MAD, *WONDERFUL* WOMAN!
BAMF!
WE NEED SOME *MEDICS* HERE, RIGHT AWAY!
GUESS THAT NUKE WAS *REAL*, AFTER ALL.

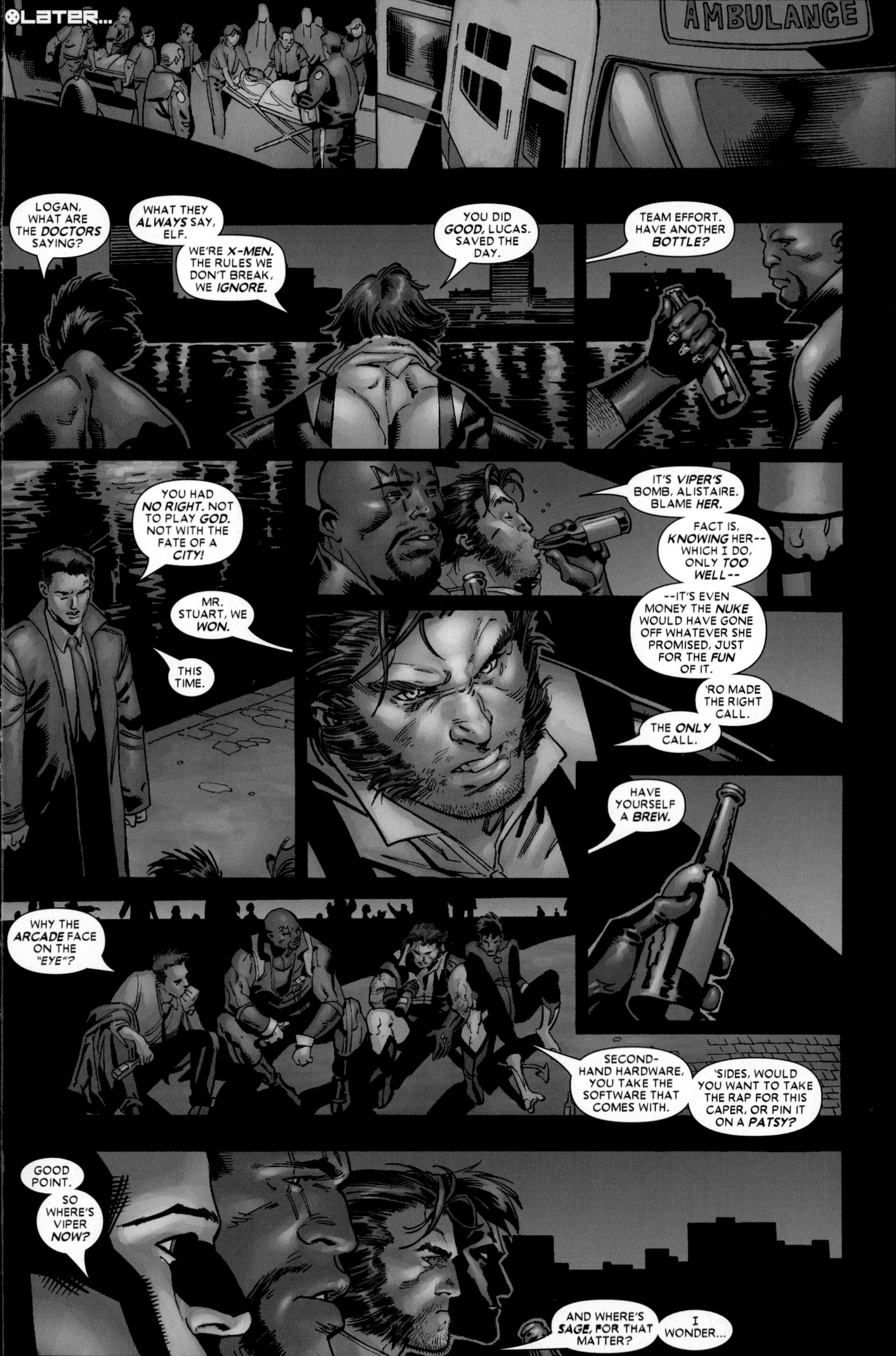

LATER...
AMBULANCE
LOGAN, WHAT ARE THE DOCTORS SAYING?
WHAT THEY ALWAYS SAY, ELF.
WE'RE X-MEN. THE RULES WE DON'T BREAK, WE IGNORE.
YOU DID GOOD, LUCAS. SAVED THE DAY.
TEAM EFFORT. HAVE ANOTHER BOTTLE?
YOU HAD NO RIGHT. NOT TO PLAY GOD. NOT WITH THE FATE OF A CITY!
IT'S VIPER'S BOMB, ALISTAIRE. BLAME HER.
FACT IS, KNOWING HER-- WHICH I DO, ONLY TOO WELL--
--IT'S EVEN MONEY THE NUKE WOULD HAVE GONE OFF WHATEVER SHE PROMISED, JUST FOR THE FUN OF IT.
MR. STUART, WE WON.
THIS TIME.
'RO MADE THE RIGHT CALL.
THE ONLY CALL.
HAVE YOURSELF A BREW.
WHY THE ARCADE FACE ON THE "EYE"?
SECOND-HAND HARDWARE, YOU TAKE THE SOFTWARE THAT COMES WITH.
'SIDES, WOULD YOU WANT TO TAKE THE RAP FOR THIS CAPER, OR PIN IT ON A PATSY?
GOOD POINT.
SO WHERE'S VIPER NOW?
AND WHERE'S SAGE, FOR THAT MATTER?
I WONDER...

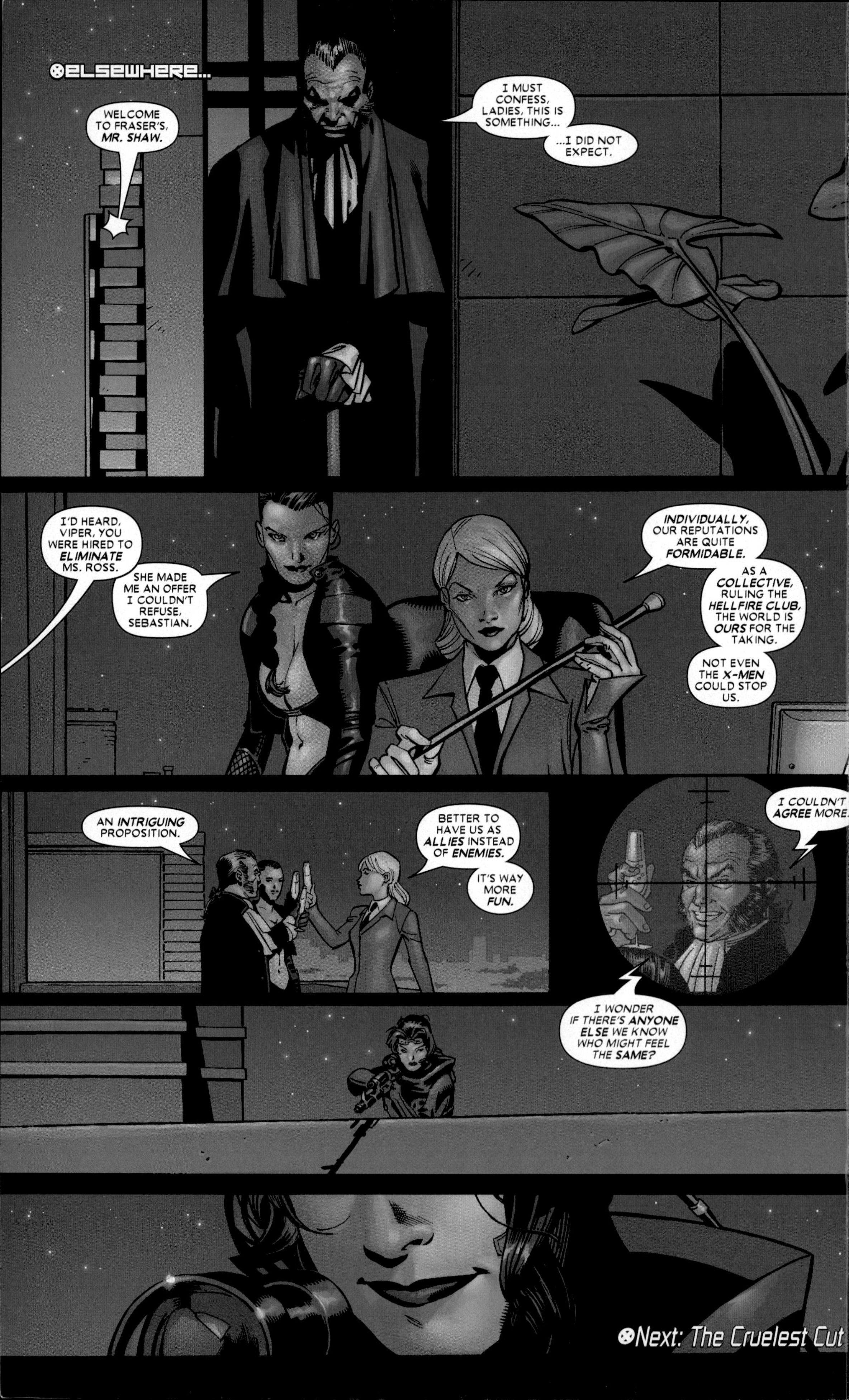
ELSEWHERE...
WELCOME TO FRASER'S, MR. SHAW.
I MUST CONFESS, LADIES, THIS IS SOMETHING...
...I DID NOT EXPECT.
I'D HEARD, VIPER, YOU WERE HIRED TO ELIMINATE MS. ROSS.
SHE MADE ME AN OFFER I COULDN'T REFUSE, SEBASTIAN.
INDIVIDUALLY, OUR REPUTATIONS ARE QUITE FORMIDABLE.
AS A COLLECTIVE, RULING THE HELLFIRE CLUB, THE WORLD IS OURS FOR THE TAKING.
NOT EVEN THE X-MEN COULD STOP US.
AN INTRIGUING PROPOSITION.
BETTER TO HAVE US AS ALLIES INSTEAD OF ENEMIES.
IT'S WAY MORE FUN.
I COULDN'T AGREE MORE.
I WONDER IF THERE'S ANYONE ELSE WE KNOW WHO MIGHT FEEL THE SAME?
Next: The Cruelest Cut

MARVELS

10TH ANNIVERSARY EDITION

MARVEL®

CELEBRATE 10 YEARS OF MARVELS!

KURT BUSIEK • ALEX ROSS

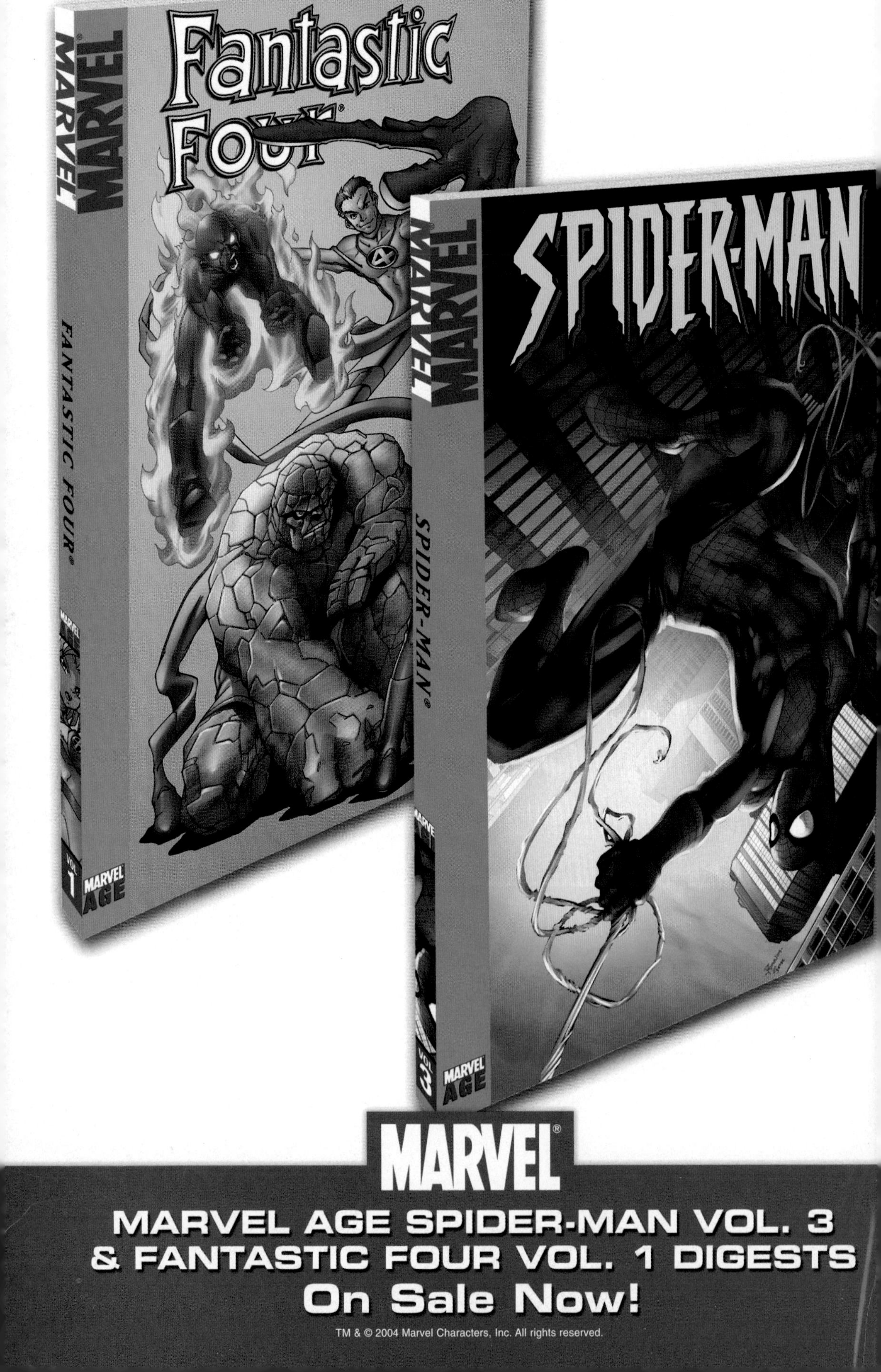
MARVEL
Fantastic Four
FANTASTIC FOUR
VOL 1
MARVEL AGE
MARVEL
SPIDER-MAN
SPIDER-MAN
VOL 3
MARVEL AGE